D1524072

WEIMAR CINEMA

FILM AND CULTURE SERIES

EDITED BY NOAH ISENBERG

AN ESSENTIAL GUIDE TO CLASSIC FILMS OF THE ERA

WEIMAR CINEMA

COLUMBIA UNIVERSITY PRESS   NEW YORK

COLUMBIA UNIVERSITY PRESS
Publishers Since 1893
New York   Chichester, West Sussex

Library of Congress Cataloging-in-Publication Data

Weimar cinema : an essential guide to classic films of the era /
edited by Noah Isenberg
p.   cm. — (Film and culture)
Includes bibliographical references and index.
ISBN 978-0-231-13054-7 (cloth : alk. paper) — ISBN 978-0-231-13055-4
(pbk. : alk. paper) — ISBN 978-0-231-50385-3 (ebook)
1. Motion pictures—Germany—History. 2. Silent films—Germany—
History and criticism.   I. Isenberg, Noah William.

PN1993.5.G4W357   2008
791.430943 ′09042—DC22
2008029682

References to Internet Web sites (URLs) were accurate at the time of writing. Neither the author nor
Columbia University Press is responsible for URLs that may have expired or changed since
the manuscript was prepared.

DESIGN BY VIN DANG

CONTENTS

ACKNOWLEDGMENTS

A book of this kind, truly collaborative and fundamentally dependent on the critical input of others, has arguably racked up more debts of gratitude than any other project with which I have been affiliated—more, in fact, than can be fully accounted for in this space. At the outset, a hearty thank you should be extended to the early pioneers of the field, especially to Tony Kaes, whose Weimar cinema courses (one of which I was fortunate to attend and for which I also served as a teaching assistant) have left a lasting imprint on the discipline at large and on this study in particular. The book began, several years ago, as a conversation over lunch with Film and Culture series editor John Belton and Columbia University Press editorial director Jennifer Crewe, both of whom expressed immediate support and who have maintained that support, and shown enormous patience, throughout the process. At Columbia University Press I have had the good fortune of working with Juree Sondker, who coached me through a few snags and offered astute advice at several junctures, and more recently with Afua Adusei, who has helped steer things through the thickets of production. Joe Abbott, the copy editor of the book, deserves much praise for his meticulous inspection of the entire manuscript and for his incisive queries and recommendations. I would also like to thank the three anonymous readers for their useful reports, which gave detailed and perceptive advice for revision, and the contributors themselves for their willingness to incorporate the suggestions. At the New School I would like to thank several colleagues who have offered support and encouragement at various stages of the project: Neil Gordon, Ann-Louise Shapiro and Jonathan Veitch. My student Cullen Gallagher, who helped compile the preliminary information for the volume's filmography, deserves thanks. And Melanie Rehak, who has lived with this project, and with Weimar cinema more generally, for more years than she may have bargained for—and who has lent a generous hand in the volume's editorial revisions—has earned the most gratitude of all.

WEIMAR CINEMA

INTRODUCTION

NOAH ISENBERG

FALLING IN LOVE AGAIN

There is a pivotal scene almost halfway into Josef von Sternberg's *Der blaue Engel* (*The Blue Angel*, 1930) in which the still upstanding Professor Immanuel Rath (Emil Jannings), a man who epitomizes imperial Prussian rigidity teetering on the brink of collapse, finds himself drawn back to the same seedy nightclub where he first encountered the enchanting songstress Lola Lola (Marlene Dietrich). There, as the stodgy old teacher makes his way to the balcony, he finds Lola onstage, swaying her hips nonchalantly while she belts out one of her signature ballads—pronouncing her inability to do anything but love and finally declaring her innocence vis-à-vis the men who swarm around her "like moths around a flame" and get burned in the process. Punctuating the scene, the "honorary guest" Professor Rath receives a hearty welcome and a call for applause from a gruff, surly magician called Kiepert (Kurt Gerron). From his perch above the main floor, Rath—and, of course, we together with him—can take in everything: the raucous, mixed crowd; the tawdry stage arrangement cluttered with scantily-clad female performers, Lola at its center; a melancholy clown, gazing up at him in ominous anticipation of an inevitable role reversal; and an oversized nude mermaid statue, whose voluptuous form catches him off guard and finally leads his attention back to the stage. As Lola strikes her seductive, by now iconic, pose atop a wooden keg (Fig. I.1), with legs in sharp focus in a tightly framed shot and a look of complete self-assurance on her face, Rath cannot contain his delight. In the end, he is positively smitten.

The scene is significant not only for its role in the basic plot development, as it prepares Rath for his ultimate descent into shame and humiliation, but also in

FIGURE I.1 Lola Lola (Marlene Dietrich) serenading Dr. Rath (Emil Jannings) in Josef von Sternberg's *The Blue Angel* (1930).

terms of its broader commentary on Weimar cinema as a whole. Quite self-conscious in its approach, the scene highlights the boldness of the New Woman, a stock character in Weimar cinema, at least since the so-called street films of the early 1920s, introduced here in the figure of the international star. It captures, moreover, the spirit of Weimar, or what has come to be seen as that spirit, "a dance on the edge of a volcano," in the words of Peter Gay (1968, xiv), or the "historical imaginary," as Thomas Elsaesser (2000) has since conceived it: the pulsating, decadent nightlife, where such slogans as "Everything that pleases is allowed" appear entirely credible; the powerful undercurrent of eroticism and unbridled sexuality that reached poignant expression in the visual arts, culture, and literature throughout the interwar years, threatening to subvert bourgeois morality; the paradox of love, often unrequited, in an otherwise seemingly cold, loveless society in which desire handily trumps emotion; and finally, the recurrent clashes between rival generations, classes, and political and social orientations, as well as between a heady force of internationalism and an unyielding German provincialism.[1] Even the film's music (Friedrich Hollaender's "Ich bin von Kopf bis Fuß auf Liebe eingestellt," or "Falling in Love Again" in the English rendition), coupled with rather racy narrative lyrics, strikes a resonant chord in many other films of the era, as it, too, underscores the sense of helplessness that overwhelmed those who fell into the trap that was the false promise of Weimar. It evokes the misplaced hope in the new—in democracy, a cosmopolitan urban culture, and a progressive ethos—that would ultimately prove impossible to sustain beyond the confines of a short-lived experiment.

On another level, von Sternberg arranges the nightclub interlude in such a way as to elevate Marlene Dietrich's status as a new film sensation, conveying beyond a doubt the "sex appeal"—a phrase that was often used in the original English—that is almost organically ascribed to such figures. Thus he places her in a venerated line of international stars that radiated from the Weimar screen, from the Danish-born Asta Nielsen and the Swedish Greta Garbo through the American dancer Louise Brooks, picking up on a notable strain of media-generated *Girlkultur* that first took root in the 1920s. As Patrice Petro has observed, referring specifically to Dietrich and Brooks, these women became "convenient figures upon which to project a reading of male subjectivity in crisis; as figures of female eroticism, they were typically featured in films where male characters are brought to their doom as a result of their uncompromising devotion to a feminine ideal" (Petro 1989, 159; see also von Ankum 1997). The most famous roles brought to life on the big screen during the Weimar years—perhaps foremost among them Brooks's Lulu and Dietrich's Lola Lola—demonstrate how indelible these images were in their day and how fundamental they have become to our understanding of Weimar culture. In a slight (more Americanized) variation on the same theme, there is a counterpart in what Detlev Peukert calls "the male-generated fantasy of the 'vamp': the glamour girl, a bit too independent to be true, armed with bobbed hair and made-up face, fashionable clothes and cigarette, working by day in a typing pool or behind the sales counter in some dreamland of consumerism, frittering away the night dancing the Charleston or watching UFA and Hollywood films" (Peukert 1993, 99).

Indeed, for Anglo-American viewers the visual conception of Weimar may be linked less to *The Blue Angel* than to Bob Fosse's *Cabaret* (1972), a film that appeared a good four decades later and yet managed to suggest a sensibility that, despite its tendency toward mythologizing, is taken for authentic (Jelavich 1993, 154–86). The "divine decadence" of which American showgirl Sally Bowles (Liza Minnelli) speaks oozes from Fosse's Kit Kat Club, as it does from the eponymous nightclub of von Sternberg's film, which boasts a similar kind of magnetic attraction. Yet ultimately it is not Bowles—that charming starlet extracted from Christopher Isherwood's imagination and his *Berlin Stories*, so reminiscent of the Kansas-born Brooks—who best represents the face of Weimar Berlin. Rather, as Ian Buruma has suggested in his trenchant analysis, it is the master of ceremonies and "androgynous host" (Joel Grey) (Fig. I.2):

> Grey managed to personify everything we now associate with the end of that giddy, sinister, brilliant decade between the two world wars, when Berlin was

FIGURE I.2   Joel Grey as the charismatic, androgynous Kit Kat Club emcee in Bob Fosse's *Cabaret* (1972).

the capital of sex, art, and violence. The sunken cheeks, the curled blood-red lips, the rouge and death-white powder, the lacquered black hair, the little dark eyes, darting about like malevolent black insects, and all this combined with that unforgettable voice—whining, lisping, sneering. He is the sum of everything we find repellent and yet deeply intriguing about Berlin at the dawn of the Third Reich. (Buruma 2006, 13)

This highly potent combination of "repellent" and "intriguing" was what passed for love—desire and temptation—as it was articulated during the Weimar years, both in everyday life and in the cinematic imagination.

In his memoirs, *The World of Yesterday* (1943), Stefan Zweig describes what he terms a transformation of Berlin "into the Babylon of the World," a place, as he puts it in his extended musings on the subject, which is tinged with an air of caution:

Bars, amusement parks, honky-tonks sprang up like mushrooms. What we had seen in [turn-of-the-century] Austria proved to be just a mild and shy prologue to this witches' Sabbath; for the Germans introduced all their vehemence and methodical organization into the perversion. Along the entire Kurfürstendamm powdered and rouged men sauntered and they were not all professionals; every high school boy wanted to earn some money and in the dimly lit bars one might see government officials and men of the world of finance tenderly courting drunken sailors without any shame. Even the Rome of Suetonius had never known such orgies as the pervert balls of Berlin, where hundreds of men costumed as women and hundreds of women as men danced under the benevolent

eyes of the police. In the collapse of all values a kind of madness gained hold particularly in the bourgeois circles which until then had been unshakeable in their
probity. Young girls bragged proudly of their perversion, to be sixteen and still
under suspicion of virginity would have been a disgrace in any school of Berlin
at the time, every girl wanted to be able to tell of her adventures and the more
exotic, the better. (Zweig 1964, 313).

Though the rhetoric in Zweig's portrait of Weimar Berlin may be overblown, he
gets at the heart of the tension between the development of an advanced erotic culture within a society that, at that same moment, was showing signs of wanting to
smother expression, sexual and otherwise (Peukert 1993, 170–171; Gordon 2000;
Weitz 2007, 297–330).

A REPUBLIC OF IMPOSTORS

In his *Critique of Cynical Reason*, Peter Sloterdijk brands the Weimar Republic the
"German Republic of Impostors." For Sloterdijk the impostor embodies the political and psychological instability of Germany's fledgling democracy during that
period. "In such an 'insecure' world," he writes, "the impostor grew into a character type of the times par excellence. Cases of fraud, deception, misleading, breach
of promise, charlatanism, and so forth multiplied not only in the numerical sense:
The impostor also became an indispensable figure in the sense of collective reas-
surance, a model of the times and a mythical template.... [T]he impostor became
the existentially most important and most understandable symbol for the chronic
crisis of complexity of modern consciousness" (Sloterdijk 1987, 484). As has been
amply documented by historians of Weimar, crime was, to a great extent, untram-
meled.[2] Indeed, the "insecure world" of which Sloterdijk speaks was precisely
the ideal milieu within which crime and deception could flourish. The face of the
impostor, as Weimar cinema would quickly attest, bore many guises: hypnotists,
wizards, street gangsters, mad scientists, fakes in uniform, female cyborgs, cross-
dressers, con artists, swindlers and more (Fig. I.3). In *The Haunted Screen*, Lotte
Eisner cites a passage from the nineteenth-century German romantic poet Ludwig
Tieck that serves to illustrate one of the many functions of cinema during the Weimar years: "We create fairy tales," writes Tieck, "because we prefer to populate the
monstrous emptiness and horrid chaos" (Eisner 1969, 97). German cinema, which
in its early days adhered more or less to the principles of a "cinema of attractions,"
shaped around the spectacle itself and less oriented toward visual storytelling,
quickly built on the more firmly established arts, drawing on folktales, legends,
romantic lore, and material that was extracted from literature, theater, and mass
culture. The cinema assumed the role that fairy tales had traditionally performed,
feeding into the curiosity and imagination of the viewing public.

FIGURE 1.3   Fanning the cards in search of an appropriate disguise in Fritz Lang's *Dr. Mabuse, the Gambler* (1922).

That need for fantasy only increased with the heightened sense of insecurity, the feeling of having been duped, which accompanied Germany's shaky transition to the Weimar Republic. Its inauspicious beginnings, borne out of the traumatic defeat of the First World War, were followed by years of extreme tumult—from the failed revolutions of its first years to the massive war debt and territorial losses incurred by the Treaty of Versailles, along with bloody political assassinations, runaway inflation and burgeoning opposition to the very idea of democracy. "The hyperinflationary excesses of 1922–3 have left a profound imprint on the German psyche," remarks Peukert (1993, 64). Among other factors, the economic instability heightened the sense of volatility and the notion that Germany's well-being was beyond its own control—or, perhaps, simply out of control. All who were associated with the republic's inception—and with the "unjust" deal that was cut with the victors of the war—were very quickly branded impostors, inauthentic Germans, and thus targets of violent attack (Peukert 1993, 73; Weitz 2007, 7–39). As Sloterdijk puts it, "If we wanted to write a social history of mistrust in Germany, then above all the Weimar Republic would draw attention to itself. Fraud and expectations of being defrauded became epidemic in it. In those years, it proved to be an omnipresent risk of existence that from behind all solid illusions, the untenable and chaotic emerged" (Sloterdijk 1987, 483).

In this paranoid world, built precariously atop the power vacuum that was left after the war, a need for projecting society's innermost anxieties, fantasies, and dreams onto the big screen arose almost as quickly as the republic itself was collapsing. The general atmosphere of political and social make-believe found its logical expression in the cinema. Perhaps there was no other, more effective, way to parlay the curious character of Weimar into aesthetic form (think, for instance, of the cold, cynical portraits of representative figures—the caricatures of types extracted from the political and social arena—in the portraits by Georg Grosz, Otto Dix, and others). In an oft-cited essay from the *Frankfurter Zeitung*, "The Cult of Distraction: On Berlin's Picture Palaces" (1926), Siegfried Kracauer, who spent much of the 1920s as the paper's cultural editor and a frequent contributor, gives us a contemporary take on cinema and the reality of the urban world: "In the streets of Berlin, one is often struck by the momentary insight that someday all this will suddenly burst apart. The entertainment to which the general public throngs ought to produce the same effect" (Kracauer 1995, 327). It is not surprising, then, that so much of Weimar cinema contained an explosive element, whether in the early adventure films, horror pictures, the so-called street films, melodramas, or futurist fantasies. Kracauer notes, in the same essay, the "bourgeois reproach" that Berliners were allegedly "addicted to distraction" (Kracauer 1995, 327). With all their new stimuli, in particular those that were awakened in the cinema, Berliners were thought to harbor a greater reliance on forms of mass entertainment than were people living elsewhere in Weimar Germany. Much of the cinema came back to a very specific idea of the city, often as a stand-in for Berlin, and found its proper milieu in the street. As Anton Kaes has argued, "The street became a staging ground for sex and crime, a setting where the individual encountered anonymous others, unsheltered and vulnerable" (Kaes 2004, 66; see also Tatar 1995). Or, as Gay has noted of Berlin, "It was a city of crooks and cripples, a city of hit songs and endless talk; with a press that was 'cruel, pitiless, aggressive, filled with bloody irony, yet not discouraging,' and with criticism that was, in the same way, harsh, nonconformist, but fair, in search of quality, delighted with excellence. [In the words of Carl Zuckmayer:] 'Berlin tasted of the future, and that is why we gladly took the crap and the coldness'" (Gay 1968, 132).

These developments were not met without a challenge, and a considerable segment of Weimar Germany's population harbored an antipathy toward the big city that is not altogether unlike the enmity occasionally directed at contemporary New York City. In this countermovement, one in which a return to a kind of imperial glory, or unified strength and stability, was often imagined, the figures who represented Weimar—those "outsiders" who had managed to make their way, temporarily, to the center—were the subject of scorn. "The hunger for wholeness," asserts Gay, "was awash with hate; the political, and sometimes private, world of its

chief spokesmen was a paranoid world, filled with enemies: the dehumanizing machines, capitalist materialism, godless rationalism, rootless society, cosmopolitan
Jews, and that all-devouring monster, the city" (Gay 1968, 96). It was precisely this
fractured nature that Weimar's best films took on as their subject and revealed,
knowingly or not, to the world at large.

With its so-called prestige films aimed at the export market—often with greater
pretensions to artistic quality than basic mass entertainment—Weimar cinema
made its way across Europe and to the other side of the Atlantic. Movies like *The
Blue Angel* had a purported mission "to synthesize art and commercial success" and
showed an acute awareness of the interplay (not to mention fierce competition)
between America and Germany—between the relatively new talkies and silent
cinema, between Universum Film Aktiengesellschaft, or Ufa, as Weimar Germany's biggest, most powerful film company was commonly known, and Hollywood
(Kreimeier 1999, 189).[3] From the very beginning, the Anglo-American reception
was slightly suspicious, if not altogether contemptuous. As in Germany, the debate
concerning cinema was more often than not carried out by writers and intellectuals rather than by the masses (Hake 1993). Virginia Woolf remarks in a 1926 essay
on film, commenting on *The Cabinet of Dr. Caligari*, that Cesare seems "to embody
some monstrous, diseased imagination of the lunatic's brain" (Woolf 1994, 39). A
New York Times article, published just a few years earlier, showed little patience for
the industry-imposed designation of "highbrow" motion pictures—Wiene's *Cabinet of Dr. Caligari*, Wegener's *The Golem*, and Lubitsch's *Gypsy Blood* listed among
them—used to distinguish intellectually ambitious (often German) films from
their Hollywood counterparts, the logic being that "the public doesn't want that
kind of stuff" (Anon. 1922, 69). Or, as another critic in New York's newspaper of
record wrote: "In Germany many of the important films are too gruesome for the
American public. . . . German filmmakers are producing many cubist effects. Some
of these films are skillfully done, but the themes are generally gloomy and not of
a character which Americans demand" (Kaes 1993, 71). Little did the critic know
that the demand for those same films, as well as many that followed, would only
increase with time.

THE LONG FAREWELL

For more than half a century the study of Weimar cinema has been dominated—
and, in large measure, continues to be dominated—by the work of two German
émigrés, Siegfried Kracauer's *From Caligari to Hitler* (1947) and Lotte Eisner's *The
Haunted Screen* (1969; first published in France in 1952). Both authors established
themselves as critics during the Weimar years and, having managed to flee Nazi
Germany, continued their careers in American and French exile. In their respective

studies the two critics sought to recall and reassess the profound developments made in German film of the 1920s and early 1930s, while also rendering the cultural and political intricacies of the period comprehensible to their respective non-German audiences. In spite of certain, by now well-established, shortcomings—an excessive emphasis on the collective German psyche in the case of Kracauer, on German aesthetic ingenuity in the case of Eisner—each of these works still has its share of merits, and both remain in print and serve as required reading for students of film.

What *Weimar Cinema: An Essential Guide to Classic Films of the Era* seeks to offer is not so much a replacement for, but a much-needed supplement to, Kracauer's and Eisner's work. It is a wide-ranging collaborative project that brings together an array of different authors and different approaches. It aims to revise and update earlier research, while presenting new insights to today's scholars, teachers, and students of Weimar cinema and to the general reader interested in this vital period in film history. The volume focuses on the most significant, most widely taught, and most widely available films of the period. Each of the film chapters attends to such fundamental concerns as technical advancements made in a given film; the film's production history and its place within the larger history of the German studio and of Weimar cinema in general; the signature style of the film's director and the mark that the film has left on the career trajectory of a given director; the acting talent and the rise of German (and non-German) stars in Weimar cinema; and the film's contemporary and subsequent critical reception and the debates unleashed both during and after a film's release.

Taken together, the films chosen for inclusion in this volume represent the extraordinary richness of Weimar's cinematic output in terms of style, genre, and innovation. There are horror films and melodramas, early gangster pictures and science fiction, avant-garde and fantasy films, sexual intrigues and love stories, classics of silent cinema and Germany's first talkies. Readers can follow the early careers of major directors, including F. W. Murnau, Fritz Lang, and G. W. Pabst, and examine the debuts of such international stars as Greta Garbo, Louise Brooks, and Marlene Dietrich; they can also chart the impact of such visionary producers as Erich Pommer, such influential cinematographers as Karl Freund, and pioneering art directors like Erich Kettelhut. There are 16-mm (and, in some cases, 35-mm) prints of all sixteen films in circulation, and all have been released either on DVD—the case for the vast majority of films represented in the volume, many of them transfers from high-quality, restored prints—or, in the few cases where DVDs have not yet been produced, on VHS (see the complete filmography).

Returning briefly to Kracauer's and Eisner's works, Dietrich Scheunemann has recently noted that "there is a growing awareness that the two books, although still recognized as the authoritative sources on the subject, do not tell the whole story of Weimar cinema" (Scheunemann 2003, ix). Over the past several decades, scholars and critics have pointed to the gaps, omissions, oversights, and methodological flaws in their respective approaches.[4] Although it is not the aim of the present study to tell the "whole story" of this legendary epoch, these individual contributions will undoubtedly help widen the scope of analysis; they offer new lines of inquiry and suggest additional possible entry points in the larger project of examining the films. There is no unified, monolithic approach. The diverse nature of the subject defies such a conception. As Elsaesser remarks in *Weimar Cinema and After*, "It seems that, starting with *The Cabinet of Dr. Caligari*, the films usually indexed as Weimar cinema have one thing in common: they are invariably constructed as picture puzzles. Consistently if not systematically, they refuse to be 'tied down' to a single meaning" (Elsaesser 2000, 4).

Near the close of his *Goodbye to Berlin* (1939), Christopher Isherwood writes, "Berlin is a city with two centres—the cluster of expensive hotels, bars, cinemas, shops round the Memorial Church, a sparkling nucleus of light, like a sham diamond, in the shabby twilight of the town; and the self-conscious civic centre of buildings round the Unter den Linden, carefully arranged. In grand international styles, they assert our dignity as a capital city—a parliament, a couple of museums, a State bank, a cathedral, an opera, a dozen embassies, a triumphal arch; nothing has been forgotten" (Isherwood 1945, 186). These two centers, the new and the old, the provisional and the official, represented just a few cracks in the already highly fissured Weimar Republic. By the time Germany's first democracy had run its short course, Kracauer's sense that at any moment Berlin could suddenly burst apart would seem more prescient than ever before. The era would come to an apocalyptic close, and with its destruction would come the end of an aesthetic movement—or, really, a series of movements, some of them related, others entirely independent—that often made a point of recognizing its artificial, ephemeral, contingent, quintessentially modern nature. Rather than bidding a final farewell to that epoch, it appears that we have instead spent some seventy-five years trying to make sense of what actually occurred, wrestling with the legacy of Weimar (Petro 2006). It is my hope that this volume will offer some additional assistance in that larger undertaking.

NOTES

1. In Gay's shorthand gloss, "Weimar culture was the creation of outsiders, propelled by history into the inside, for a short, dizzying, fragile moment" (Gay 1968, xiv).
2. In addition to the standard histories of Weimar, see the related collection of contemporary source documents, translated into English, in Kaes, Jay, and Dimendberg (1994, 718–41). See also Eric Weitz's new approach to the subject in his highly compelling chronicle of the period (Weitz 2007, 129–68).

3.   Thomas Elsaesser has remarked that

     many of Weimar cinema's classics are films about film making itself, that is, self-ref-
     erential. Such "reflexivity" is, however, in this case due less to the directors belong-
     ing to a specific aesthetic avant-garde and pursing a modernist agenda. Instead, I see
     it as evidence of a historical conjuncture in which a prominent segment of the Wei-
     mar film community (counting next to producers, directors and screenwriters also
     set designers and cameramen) found itself in an intense dialogue or even struggle on
     at least two fronts: domestically, they had to compete with other, more established
     arts and their social institutions, and internationally, with the permanent threat of
     Hollywood hegemony, both on the German market and in the rest of Europe. (El-
     saesser 2000, 5)

4.   According to Elsaesser, both books "have helped to popularize and at the same time de-
     monize this cinema, making it, under a double conjuncture, in one case representative
     of broader tendencies within society (Kracauer's collective soul of the recipients), and
     in another, more art-historical turn, of the German 'genius' (Eisner's individual soul of
     the creators) in art, reflected, expressed and embodied in German cinema" (Elsaesser
     2000, 34). On Kracauer's approach, in particular, see the extensive new introduction
     to the 2004 edition, "Rereading Kracauer," by the Italian scholar Leonardo Quaresima
     (Kracauer 2004, xv–xlix).

REFERENCES

Anon. 1922. "Screen: The Year in Pictures." *New York Times*, January 1.

Buruma, Ian. 2006. "Faces of the Weimar Republic." In *Glitter and Doom: German Portraits from the 1920s*, ed. Sabine Rewald, 13–20. New York: Metropolitan Museum of Art.

Eisner, Lotte. 1969. *The Haunted Screen: Expressionism in the German Cinema and the Influence of Max Reinhardt*. Trans. Roger Greaves. Berkeley: University of California Press. (Orig. pub. 1952.)

Elsaesser, Thomas. 2000. *Weimar Cinema and After: Germany's Historical Imaginary*. New York: Routledge.

Gay, Peter. 1968. *Weimar Culture: The Outsider as Insider*. New York: Harper & Row.

Gordon, Mel. 2000. *Voluptuous Panic: The Erotic World of Weimar Berlin*. Los Angeles: Feral House.

Hake, Sabine. 1993. *The Cinema's Third Machine: Writing on Film in Germany, 1907–1933*. Lincoln: University of Nebraska Press.

Isherwood, Christopher. 1945. *The Berlin Stories*. New York: New Directions.

Jelavich, Peter. 1993. *Berlin Cabaret*. Cambridge, MA: Harvard University Press.

Kaes, Anton. 1993. "Film in der Weimarer Republik: Motor der Moderne." In *Geschichte des deutschen Films*, ed. Wolfgang Jacobsen, Anton Kaes, and Hans-Helmut Prinzler, 39–100. Stuttgart: Metzler.

———. 2004. "Weimar Cinema: The Predicament of Modernity." In *European Cinema*, ed. Elizabeth Ezra, 59–77. New York: Oxford University Press.

Kaes, Anton, Martin Jay, and Edward Dimendberg, eds. 1994. *The Weimar Republic Sourcebook*. Berkeley: University of California Press.

Kracauer, Siegfried. 1995. *The Mass Ornament: Weimar Essays*. Ed. Thomas Y. Levin. Cambridge, MA: Harvard University Press.

———. 2004. *From Caligari to Hitler: A Psychological History of the German Film*. Rev. ed. Princeton, NJ: Princeton University Press. (Orig. pub. 1947.)

Kreimeier, Klaus. 1999. *The Ufa Story: A History of Germany's Greatest Film Company, 1918–1945*. Trans. Roger and Rita Kimber. Berkeley: University of California Press.

Murray, Bruce. 1990. *Film and the German Left in the Weimar Republic: From* Caligari *to* Kuhle Wampe. Austin: University of Texas Press.

Petro, Patrice. 1989. *Joyless Streets: Women and Melodramatic Representation in Weimar Germany*. Princeton, NJ: Princeton University Press.

———. 2006. "Legacies of Weimar Cinema." In *Cinema and Modernity*, ed. Murray Pomerance, 235–52. New Brunswick, NJ: Rutgers University Press.

Peukert, Detlev J. K. 1993. *The Weimar Republic: The Crisis of Classical Modernity*. Trans. Richard Deveson. New York: Hill and Wang.

Rentschler, Eric. 1990. "Mountains of Modernity: Relocating the *Bergfilm*." *New German Critique* 51 (autumn): 137–51.

Scheunemann, Dietrich, ed. 2003. *Expressionist Film: New Perspectives*. Rochester, NY: Camden House.

Sloterdijk, Peter. 1987. *Critique of Cynical Reason*. Trans Michael Eldred. Minneapolis: University of Minnesota Press.

Tatar, Maria. 1995. *Lustmord: Sexual Murder in Weimar Germany*. Princeton, NJ: Princeton University Press.

von Ankum, Katharina, ed. 1997. *Women in the Metropolis: Gender and Modernity in Weimar Culture*. Berkeley: University of California Press.

Weitz, Eric D. 2007. *Weimar Germany: Promise and Tragedy*. Princeton, NJ: Princeton University Press.

Woolf, Virginia. 1994. "The Movies and Reality." 1926. In *The New Republic Reader: Eighty Years of Opinion and Debate*, ed. Dorothy Wickenden, 37–40. New York: Basic Books.

Zweig, Stefan. 1964. *The World of Yesterday*. Trans. Harry Zohn. Lincoln: University of Nebraska Press. (Orig. pub. 1943.)

SUGGESTION, HYPNOSIS, AND CRIME

ROBERT WIENE'S *THE CABINET OF DR. CALIGARI* (1920)

STEFAN ANDRIOPOULOS

In February 1920 posters appeared throughout Berlin, addressing city dwellers with the forceful exhortation: "You must become Caligari" [Du musst Caligari werden]. The enigmatic slogan, also printed in several newspapers, was soon revealed to be part of an innovative advertising campaign for a new film. The movie, directed by Robert Wiene, was just completing the last stages of production at the Decla company. Immediately after its release, *The Cabinet of Dr. Caligari* was acclaimed a masterpiece of German expressionist cinema; its plot, unknown to the public, centered on a showman and hypnotist who forces a somnambulist under his will, compelling the docile medium to commit several murders.

Yet on the posters and in the newspaper ads no mention was made of the film's title, plot, or even the fact that the campaign was meant to advertise a film. Instead, only a hypnotic, vortical spiral and a note with the date and place of the opening night accompanied the mysterious command that called for each passerby to transform him- or herself into Caligari. The almost coercive imperative "You must" foregrounded and simultaneously enacted the "suggestive" or "hypnotic" power of advertising, which was still a fairly new mode of shaping social behavior. Just a few years earlier, the American psychologist Walter D. Scott had described the "*influencing* of human minds" as "the one function of advertising" (Scott 1917, 2).[1] According to Scott, a successful promotional campaign relied less on conveying information than on "suggestion"—a process that he contrasted to a mere proposal. For instead of appealing to rational faculties, "suggestion" was based on surreptitiously implanting an idea in a susceptible mind, without raising contrary or inhibiting thoughts. Scott asserted that "the most perfect working of suggestion is to be seen under hypnosis. . . . There is no possible criticism or deliberation and so we have the extreme case of susceptibility to suggestion" (Scott 1917, 82).

In this conceptualization of advertising, Scott invoked the medical theories of hypnotism and suggestion as they had been developed in the late nineteenth century by the French physician Hippolyte Bernheim. Around 1900, however, hypnosis was not merely linked to advertising; indeed, structural affinities also connected hypnotism with the newly emerging medium of cinema. Accordingly, numerous films such as George Méliès's *Le magnétiseur* (1897), Maurice Tourneur's *Trilby* (1915), Louis Feuillade's *Les yeux qui fascinent* (1916), Robert Wiene's *The Cabinet of Dr. Caligari* (1919), Fritz Lang's *Dr. Mabuse, the Gambler* (1922), Arthur Robison's *Shadows: A Nocturnal Hallucination* (1922), or Rex Ingram's *The Magician* (1926) enacted the ostensibly unlimited power of the hypnotist on the movie screen. At the same time, early theories of film described the new medium itself as exerting an irresistible, hypnotic influence on its spellbound audiences. In tandem with Robert Wiene's *The Cabinet of Dr. Caligari* and Walter D. Scott's *Psychology of Advertising*, many early-twentieth-century representations of cinema thus appropriated Bernheim's scientific notions of suggestion and hypnosis, notions that had been introduced to a German readership by medical researchers such as Sigmund Freud, Albert Moll, and August Forel.

Bernheim, who was the leading figure of the so-called Nancy School, had affirmed that not only hysterics but potentially everybody was subject to hypnosis. Whereas the neurologists Jean-Martin Charcot and Georges Gilles de la Tourette regarded hypnosis as a pathological disease of the nervous system, Bernheim conceived of it as a natural state akin to sleep. In a circular equation of hypnosis and suggestion, he wrote: "I define hypnotism as inducing a specific psychic condition of *increased suggestibility*. . . . It is suggestion that generates hypnosis" (Bernheim 1888/1964, 22/15*).[2] The emerging "rapport" between the hypnotist and the hypnotized subject was alleged to constitute a relationship of unlimited power on the hypnotist's part. As Bernheim and numerous other physicians affirmed, the hypnotized subject functioned as a sort of medium who could even be compelled to commit crimes against his or her own will. Similar to the plot of Robert Wiene's *The Cabinet of Dr. Caligari*, the medical theories of the *École de Nancy* raised the "terrifying specter of hypnotic crime" (Schrenck-Notzing 1900, 12).

Since there were no unequivocally verified cases of crimes committed under hypnosis, many medical researchers staged simulated hypnotic crimes in order to prove their possibility. August Forel, who taught in Switzerland, described one such experiment:

> To an older man of good suggestibility, whom I had just hypnotized, I gave a revolver that Mr. Höfelt himself had previously loaded with blanks only. Pointing to H., I explained to the hypnotized that the latter was a thoroughly evil person

and that he should shoot him dead. With utter determination he took the revolver and fired a shot directly at Mr. H. Mr. H., *simulating an injured person,* fell to the floor. Then I explained to the hypnotized man that the fellow was not quite dead yet and that he should shoot him again, which he did without hesitation. (Forel 1895, 198–99)

In addition to Forel, the physicians Bernheim, Bérillon, Beaunis, Crocq, Schrenck-Notzing, and the young Arthur Schnitzler staged similar "performances" (Vorstellungen) (Schnitzler 1920, 313)—all of this for the ostensibly scientific purpose of proving to their largely judicial audiences that hypnotic crimes were indeed feasible.

One particular fear concerned the possibility of implanting in a hypnotized person the order to commit a criminal action, long after waking from the hypnotic trance. Forel accordingly warned of "posthypnotic suggestions" in which, in addition to a crime and the time set for its execution, the idea of "free volition" was implanted in the hypnotized subject, causing the medium committing the crime to believe in his or her own free will. As Forel put it: "One of the most insidious ruses of suggestion, however, lies in the use of timing [Termineingebung] along with implanting amnesia and the idea of free volition in order to prompt a person . . . to perform a criminal act. That person then finds himself in a situation that is bound to create in him every illusion of spontaneity while in reality he is only following the command of someone else" (Forel 1889, 184). The belief in perfectly camouflaged suggestions thus produced the powerful paranoia that there might be an unlimited number of unknown hypnotic crimes that could not be recognized as such.

After the turn of the century, scientific interest in hypnosis was initially superseded by the emergence of psychoanalysis and a renewed concentration on physiology within medical research. But in the treatment of war neuroses and shell shock during World War I, hypnosis and suggestion had an unexpected resurgence. August Forel's and Albert Moll's medical treatises about hypnotism, first published in the 1880s, thus went through numerous new editions between 1918 and 1924.[3] Simultaneously, the extraordinarily successful late-nineteenth-century literary tales of hypnotic crime found an equally popular sequel within the postwar literature of the fantastic, in texts such as Gustav Meyrink's *The White Dominican* (1921), Cätty Bachem-Tonger's *Under the Spell of Hypnosis* (1922), Otto Soyka's *The Smith of Souls* (1921), or Hans Dominik's *The Power of the Three* (1922).

Although neglected by most historiographies of Weimar cinema, the intense medical debate about the possibility of hypnotic crimes was also constitutive for Wiene's *The Cabinet of Dr. Caligari,* which opened on February 26, 1920, at the Marmorhaus in Berlin. The first frame of the film shows, in a medium shot, two men with parched white faces, sitting on a bench. As if referring to his own status as a ghostly phantom on the cinematic screen, the older man says to the younger (Francis): "There are ghosts [Geister]—They are all around us." A woman dressed in white appears, gliding past the two men in a somnambulist trance. Referring to the almost spectral apparition, Francis calls her his "bride," continuing: "What I have experienced with her is much stranger still than what you have experienced—Let me tell you about it." And the camera cuts to a film set built of papier-mâché, representing a small town with narrow, winding streets.

From the very beginning the film emphasizes that the moving images on the cinematic screen are a simulation akin to a "phantom" or a "vision" (Mann 1924, 336, 335). Furthermore, the internal plot is marked as the (unreliable) narration of Francis, who is at the same time one of the protagonists of his own story. The pronounced artificiality of the set, in which both frame and internal story unfold, undercuts realist conventions. Painted shadows, dagger-shaped windows, a pale sky against which bare trees stand out in bizarre shapes—these visual markers of instability create a cinematic space of paranoia and distrust. In critical responses to the film, Robert Wiene's *The Cabinet of Dr. Caligari* was therefore instantly hailed as a powerful cinematic instantiation of expressionism (Anon. 1920; Flüggen 1920). "Le caligarisme," as the visual style of the film was called in France, thus left an imprint on film history, above all in its representation of magnified shadows, which reappeared in Murnau's *Nosferatu* and American film noir (especially powerful in *The Cabinet of Dr. Caligari* is the silhouette of a murderer who stabs his panicking victim with a dagger). But while the film certainly undertakes borrowings from expressionist art, recent scholarship has shown that the designers of the film set, Hermann Warm, Walter Reimann, and Walter Röhrig, had no direct relation to the avant-garde journal *Der Sturm*, as Siegfried Kracauer had claimed in his influential interpretation of the film (Kasten 1990, 43–44; Kracauer 1947, 68). Instead, the eclectic mise-en-scène of *The Cabinet of Dr. Caligari* amalgamated high art and mass culture, thereby appealing to a broad audience and ensuring the commercial success of the movie (Elsaesser 2000, 36–51). In addition, the strangely distorted spaces of the film set appear as a materialization of the visual hallucinations that Bernheim generated by means of verbal suggestion in his hypnotized patients, "populating" their "imagination" with "phantoms and chimeras" (Bernheim 1891/1980, 50/37*).

In a further reference to its own status as a spectacle, the film introduces the showman, Caligari, who exhibits a clairvoyant somnambulist at the fairground in the small town of Holstenwall. Aside from freak shows and cabinets displaying somnambulists, the fairground was also the site of the early "cinema of attractions" (Gunning 1990), which often toured in a tent from town to town. According to Hugo Münsterberg's *The Photoplay: A Psychological Study* (1916), one of the earliest texts on cinema that was written by a German-born psychologist who then taught at Harvard University, these circuslike performances centered on the "perfection" of the cinematic "apparatus," thus capturing the "attention" of the "spell-bound" audience (Münsterberg 1916, 57, 152).

The film shows Caligari at the fairground, advertising the exhibition of his somnambulist medium by assuring the crowd before his little tent: "Before your eyes, Cesare will rise from the *rigor of death*." Displaying the somnambulist inside his "cabinet" to the audience, Caligari transposes Cesare from the state of "lethargy," in which hypnotized persons present "the appearance of a corpse before the onset of rigor mortis" (Tourette 1887, 91), into the state of somnambulism. As if quoting from Tourette's description of this third stage of "grand hypnotism," the sleeper is represented as "a true *automaton* . . . , obeying all expressions of his magnetizer's will" (Tourette 1887, 96). In a close-up, the camera shows the somnambulist's face as he slowly opens his eyes, which are heavily accentuated by makeup (Figs. 1.1 and 1.2). The representation of Cesare's awakening thereby corresponds to Charcot's medical nosography of "grand hypnotism," which emphasizes the sleepwalker's open eyes, in artificial as well as in spontaneous somnambulism.

The film cuts to a medium shot, showing Cesare's complete body as he begins to move his arms and legs. The androgynous medium slowly steps forward, like a puppet that is held by invisible strings. His peculiar motions recall Haller's "automatonlike" (Lindau 1893, 58) walk in Max Mack's *The Other* (1913), the first film adaptation of a drama by Paul Lindau, which represented a district attorney who, in a state of somnambulism, commits crimes that he would abhor while awake. The original screenplay for Wiene's *Caligari* describes Cesare's movements: "Caesare [*sic*] stands motionless for several more seconds. Under the piercing gaze of Calligaris [*sic*], who stands next to him, something like a shudder quite subtly and remotely shows on his face! . . . His arms, pressed to his body, rise forward, *as if automatically*, in small, distinct intervals, as though they wanted to catch hold of something" (Mayer and Janowitz 1919, 65). Under Caligari's suggestive influence, Francis's friend Alan, who "concentrates, as if spellbound, on Caesare's [*sic*] awakening" (Mayer and Janowitz 1919, 65), poses the question of how much longer he has to live. "Till dawn," pronounces the clairvoyant medium.

A chain of mysterious crimes ensues, perpetrated not by the original suspect but by Caligari's somnambulist medium, Cesare. Francis pursues the fleeing showman to an insane asylum, discovering with dismay that Caligari and the director of the institution are one and the same. While Dr. Caligari sleeps (his repose shown from a strangely disorienting high-angle shot), Francis and three physicians from the mental asylum search the director's office. In a cabinet they find a book on his "special field of study." The title page is shown on the screen: "Somnambulism: A Compendium Edited by the University of Uppsala. Published A.D. 1726." Francis skims through the volume and comes across the following story, which is displayed on title cards:

FIGURES 1.1 AND 1.2 Transition from lethargy to somnambulism: Cesare's widely opened eyes correspond to Charcot's medical nosography of "grand hypnotism." (Robert Wiene's *The Cabinet of Dr. Caligari*, 1920)

The Cabinet of Dr. Caligari.

In the year 1703, a mystic by the name of Dr. Caligari along with a somnambulist called Cesare appeared at various country fairs in the small towns of Northern Italy. For months, he wreaked panic in one town after the other, by means of murders that were always perpetrated under the same circumstances—for he compelled a somnambulist, whom he had completely forced under his will, to carry out his monstrous designs. By means of a puppet figure, modeled in the exact likeness of Cesare, which he laid in the chest when Cesare was away, Dr. Caligari was able to disperse any suspicion which fell on the somnambulist.

As in Max Mack's film *The Other*, medical evidence supporting the possibility of hypnotic crimes is introduced in *The Cabinet of Dr. Caligari* by means of a scientific book, which is read by one of the protagonists. The story within the story, which seems to provide an explanation for the previous plot turns, appropriates the "fantastical tale[s]" (Tourette 1887, 183) in which late-nineteenth-century medicine conjured the unlimited power of suggestion. Next to the scientific treatise on somnambulism, Francis and the three doctors find a diary in the director's office. In interspersed flashbacks we are shown how the director of the insane asylum develops the "compulsive idea" (Zwangsvorstellung) to transform himself into the historical figure of Caligari: "You must become Caligari"—an autosuggestion that is repeatedly superimposed in writing on the actual filmic image (Fig. 1.3).

While writing in silent film is commonly restricted to the intertitles, it here intrudes on the cinematic image, a visual demonstration of the power of the director's compulsive idea to produce sensory hallucinations and to determine his actions. The episode in which the doctor succumbs to the idea of having to become Caligari thus contained the nucleus for the advertising campaign that exhorted inhabitants of Berlin, in the weeks before the film's release, "Du musst Caligari werden." At the same time, the obsession to which the director falls victim can also be linked to a literary text from which the film's script may have been adapted: the protagonist of Wilhelm Walloth's novel *Under the Spell of Hypnosis* (1897) has surprising parallels to Dr. Caligari. Walloth's text centers on the figure of Dr. von Haffner, who cannot stop pondering the question of whether "a skilled hypnotist could force even the most virtuous person to commit the biggest crime" (Walloth 1897, 155). After the idea of resolving the uncertainty by means of an actual murder enters Haffner's mind, his "constant dwelling on this sinister plan" turns into an "autosuggestion," which—like Caligari's compulsive idea—seizes control of his actions with "compelling force" [mit triebartiger Gewalt] (Walloth 1897, 240), turning him into a criminal.

In addition to these late-nineteenth-century tales about the unlimited power of suggestion, Wiene's *The Cabinet of Dr. Caligari* also adapts the "strange spectacle"

FIGURE 1.3   The director of the insane asylum succumbs to the compulsive idea: "You must become Caligari" (*Du musst Caligari werden*).

(Salten 1932, 55) of artificial hypnotic crimes, staged by numerous physicians with blank cartridges and wooden daggers. Bernheim and Forel regarded these simulations as authentic proof of criminal suggestion. Charcot's disciple Gilles de la Tourette, in contrast, denounced such enactments as devoid of any scientific value (Tourette 1887, 370, 378, 382). In an essay entitled "Hypnotism and Crime" (1908), Hugo Münsterberg was equally doubtful, stressing the difference between real life and playacting: "It is true, I have seen men . . . shooting with empty revolvers . . . in laboratory rooms with doctors sitting by and watching the *performance*. But I have never become convinced that there did not remain a background idea of *artificiality* in the mind of the hypnotized and that this idea overcame the resistance, which would be prohibitive in real life. To bring an absolute proof of this conviction is hardly possible, as we cannot really kill for experiment's sake" (Münsterberg 1908, 223).

The impossibility of enacting real murders allowed the opponents of the *École de Nancy* to discredit the science of such "fake crimes" (Scheinverbrechen)—as Sigmund Freud called them (Freud 1889, 138)—by equating their theatricality with the cultural institution of the theater. The German psychiatrist Binswanger, for instance, insisted that such "observations" only demonstrated "the success of puerile show pieces [kindliche Schaustücke]" (Binswanger 1892, 9). But, in

Binswanger's view, these experiments did not at all demonstrate the plausibility of hypnotic crimes:

> A wooden letter opener is put in the hand of a hypnotized woman and she is or-dered to stab her alleged enemy; powdered sugar is used to poison beloved fam-ily members. ... The patients ... perform ... these actions with greater or lesser reluctance, both in actual hypnosis and, under the influence of such criminal suggestions, for a shorter or longer period after the hypnotic state has ended. These actions are *invented* crimes of whose *purely theatrical significance* [rein schauspielerische Bedeutung] ... the hypnotized patients are fully aware. No conclusions must be drawn from these experiments in regard to the possibility of *real* criminal suggestions. (Binswanger 1892, 9–10)

The critique that hypnotized mediums clearly distinguished between "real" and "invented" crimes was also advanced by Gilles de la Tourette, Münsterberg, and Delboeuf, who described "these arranged dramas" as "devoid of truth, unable to deceive the actor, the spectators, or the inventor" (Delboeuf 1893/1894, 192).

Bernheim therefore conceded the theatricality of the staged hypnotic crime for "certain somnambulists." But he contrasted those cases in which the somnambu-list "knows that he is *performing* a *play*" to others where the somnambulists "have no power to resist and identify with their role. In these latter cases, the subcon-scious being overcomes the conscious being; the real conscience no longer exists, and these persons do become criminals" (Bernheim 1891/1980, 139/103–4*). In highlighting the issue of simulation, Bernheim succeeded in giving his opponents' argument an unexpected twist. He admitted that medical experiments could not transcend the status of artificial enactments, since it was impossible to commit real murders, which would be the only authentic proof of criminal suggestion. Yet instead of concluding that the staged hypnotic crime lacked scientific valid-ity, Bernheim pointed to a complex mode of simulation that actually confirmed his supposition of real hypnotic crimes. In these second-order simulations as they were described by Bernheim, the hypnotized persons conceived of themselves as performing the suggested actions only for the purpose of pleasing the hypnotist. But despite this belief in their own freedom, they were actually incapable of resist-ing the hypnotic commands. In Bernheim's words: "There are many persons who imagine that they were under nobody's influence, because they remember hearing everything; they truly believe that they were simulating, and it is sometimes diffi-cult to convince them that they did not possess the freedom *not* to simulate."[4]

This perfect immunization enables Bernheim to reveal the deceptive semblance of "freedom" as a simulation of simulation. The status of simulation thereby be-comes all-encompassing. The hypnotized mediums do "not possess the freedom not to *simulate*." It therefore becomes impossible to decide whether the staged hypnotic crime is only a drama devoid of any scientific value or, on the contrary, authentic proof of the possibility of real criminal suggestions—a proof that paradoxically consists of a second-order simulation. This undecidability becomes a constitutive structural feature of Wiene's *The Cabinet of Dr. Caligari*, for the film's closing scenes reveal the narrator and protagonist, Francis, to be an inmate of the insane asylum run by the Caligari figure. Francis's story may thus be the paranoid hallucination of a madman. In the film's last shot the director of the insane asylum assures the spectator, directly addressing the camera: "At last I understand his delusion; he thinks that I am that mystical Caligari!—And now I also know the way to his cure."

This unresolvable conflict between frame and Francis's narration is by no means an affirmation of totalitarian power, transforming an originally subversive or "revolutionary" screenplay into a "conformist" glorification of authority, as Siegfried Kracauer asserted in his influential study *From Caligari to Hitler* (Kracauer 1947, 67). Instead, the tension between frame and internal story functions as a metacommentary on the medical "fake crimes" (Freud 1889, 138), whose status as either authentic evidence for the possibility of criminal suggestions or as scientifically worthless "show piece" remains equally undecidable. But before further exploring the ways in which the narrative structure of *Caligari* replicates the ambiguous status of the medical experiments with criminal suggestion, I want to address Kracauer's arguments, which have shaped the interpretation of the film for several decades (see, e.g., Eisner 1969, 18; Murray 1990, 26–27).

Kracauer, who researched his "psychological history" of Weimar cinema during World War II, developed a political reading of the film that resonated with contemporary readers of his book, since it conceptualized the figure of Dr. Caligari as an allegorical "premonition" (Kracauer 1947, 72) of Hitler. Yet, while such a claim may have been compelling under the pressures of fighting and reeducating Nazi Germany, it ultimately presupposes a teleological perspective that negates historical contingency by implying that already in 1919 the rise of National Socialism was inevitable. To be sure, twenty years later Thomas Mann's narrative *Mario and the Magician* (1930) and Fritz Lang's film *The Testament of Dr. Mabuse* (1933) did allude to totalitarian fascism in their representation of hypnotic omnipotence. But in contrast to *The Cabinet of Dr. Caligari* these works were produced not in 1919 but in the 1930s.

To strengthen his teleological reading of the film, Kracauer therefore ascribed a prophetic "vision" (Kracauer 1947, 73) to the authors of the screenplay, Hans Janowitz and Carl Mayer. Kracauer justified this by relying all too heavily on a manuscript "Caligari: The Story of a Famous Story." This account of the film's production history was written around 1939 by the exiled Janowitz, who then, in hindsight, presented his script as a critique of totalitarian tyranny.[5] But the recovery of the original screenplay in 1976 has disproved a number of claims made by Janowitz. It still holds true that the frame, which makes Francis an inmate of the insane asylum, was not part of the original screenplay but added later by the film's director, Robert Wiene. The screenplay, however, did not only contain a framing device from the very beginning (see Mayer and Janowitz 1919, 51; Robinson 1997, 60); at one point, the script even hints at the possibility that Francis, the narrator, may be insane, when Francis himself questions his sanity on realizing that the showman Caligari and the director of the asylum are one and the same: "I felt as if I myself had lost my mind" (Mayer and Janowitz 1919, 98). Wiene's editorial intervention merely emphasized an ambiguity already inherent in the original screenplay. Simultaneously, the film's paradoxical structure appropriates contemporary concerns about the danger of criminal suggestion, thereby transforming the peculiar status that marked the medical spectacle of staged hypnotic crimes into a conflict between internal story and frame.

Within the internal story, Caligari realizes Delboeuf's dream of the *real*, truly scientific experiment "that end[s] with dead bodies" (Delboeuf 1893, 198) and must be regarded as unquestionable proof of the limitless power of hypnosis. In the diary that Francis finds next to the scientific study on somnambulism in Dr. Caligari's office, the director of the asylum jubilantly describes the long-awaited "admission of a somnambulist" as allowing him to finally execute a real-life experiment: "Now I shall solve the psychiatric riddle of that Caligari!! Now I shall fathom whether it is true that a somnambulist may be forced to commit acts that he would never commit in a waking state, that indeed he would loathe. . . . Whether it is true that the sleeper can be driven to the very act of murder . . ." (intertitles).

Medical experts from the late nineteenth century were not able to determine with any certainty whether hypnotic crimes were possible, because their scientific experiments could not transcend the status of simulation. As Hippolyte Bernheim put it in his lectures: "You see how divided opinions are at present on this fundamental question, which for all too obvious reasons has not been resolved yet by a *decisive* experiment" (Bernheim 1891/1980, 139/102*). The director of the asylum, in contrast, conducts a truly "decisive experiment" by compelling Cesare to commit actual murders, thereby resolving the all-important question of whether "it is true that the sleeper can be driven to the very act of murder" (intertitles). In this manner Dr. Caligari implements the kind of real-life experiment that had long existed as a paranoid fantasy of the neurologists and even underpinned the strange interpretation of an accident at the Parisian hospital of the Salpêtrière: When Gilles de la Tourette was attacked and seriously injured by a female patient in 1892, a rumor immediately circulated, denied by both the *Revue de l'hypnotisme* and the *Zeitschrift für Hypnotismus*, that the incident constituted a real hypnotic crime, designed to finally prove to the skeptic Gilles de la Tourette that criminal suggestions were in-

deed possible: "The assassination attempt committed against Mr. Gilles de la Tourette has given rise to a great variety of commentaries. It has been said that our
esteemed colleague was the victim of a 'criminal suggestion' intended to convince
him of the possibility of the realization of similar suggestions" (Anon. 1893/94,
173).

But the "absolute proof . . . [of] really kill[ing] for experiment's sake" (Münsterberg 1908, 223), enacted by Caligari in having the municipal secretary and
Alan murdered by his somnambulist medium Cesare, is called into question again,
since frame and narration denounce each other as paranoid hallucination. While
the medical performance of the staged hypnotic crime oscillates between a simple
and a second-order simulation, *The Cabinet of Dr. Caligari* leaves open the question
whether Francis or Caligari is insane. Francis's assertion—"All of you think—I am
mad—! That is not true. It is the director who is mad!"—is no less credible than
the director's assurance that he will cure his patient. The conflict between frame
and narrative, which mutually contradict each other, can therefore not be resolved
in favor of a coherent interpretation that would efface this structural uncertainty.
Contrary to the implications of Kracauer's reading of the film, there are no visual
indications that would lend more credibility to the world of the frame than to the
internal story. Instead, the tension between frame and narrative reduplicates the
ambiguous status of the medical "fake crimes" from which the film emerges.

At the same time, the paradoxical narrative structure of Wiene's film can also
be read as a self-reference to the "peculiar oscillation" in which, according to
Münsterberg, the spectators of early cinema alternated between the insight into
the mediality of the filmic projections and an intermittent suspension of disbelief
(Münsterberg 1916, 110). Münsterberg wrote in regard to the cinematic simulation
of depth and motion, describing a "conflict" between the viewer's perception and
knowledge: "We certainly see the depth, and yet we cannot accept it" (Münsterberg 1916, 70). In formalist film theory this "peculiar complex state" (Münsterberg 1916, 70), in which the viewer, despite better knowledge, concedes a certain
reality to the moving images on the cinematic screen, has often been compared to
Freud's conception of "disavowal," by which the fetishist allows two mutually exclusive assumptions to coexist side by side (Freud 1927, 316; Metz 1982, 72–74). But
instead of psychoanalytic theory, Bernheim's representation of suggestion, especially his description of visual, filmlike hallucinations produced by hypnotic suggestion, seems to offer a more pertinent parallel: just as the audience of Wiene's
Caligari alternates between believing in Francis's or Caligari's normalcy, and just
as the status of the filmic image oscillates between illusion and reality in the mind
of the viewers, so Bernheim's patients surrender to the vividness of the suggested
hallucinations while simultaneously understanding their illusory character: "The
hallucinations generated by suggestion can be as clear as reality; the hypnotized

person, *even though he knows* that it is a hallucination, cannot escape it" (Bernheim 1888/1964, 57/40*).

The complex narrative structure of *The Cabinet of Dr. Caligari* stages this tension between knowledge and perception. Conversely, Bernheim experimented with the hypnotic production of "passive hallucinations" (Bernheim 1891/1980, 117/86), which his patients experienced like the spectators of a movie. Although no material substrate corresponded to the suggested mental pictures, they were "as clear as reality" (Bernheim 1888/1964, 57/40*). Bernheim even claimed that the hypnotized persons "saw the images with their own eyes" (Bernheim 1888, 249/176*). The hallucinations engendered by suggestion took shape "as a passive dream" (Bernheim 1891/1980, 117/86*). The hypnotized subject lived through the "scene conjured up by his imagination . . . without any bodily participation." As "a second ego" he saw the suggested scenes while sitting "motionless in his chair" (ibid.*). Later films such as Fritz Lang's *Dr. Mabuse, the Gambler* (1922) represented such a hypnotic production of visual, filmlike hallucinations; and medical theories of hypnotism, formulated contemporaneous to the emergence of cinema, lend themselves to a reading as an implicit conceptualization of film.

In 1916 Hugo Münsterberg explicitly compared the workings of the human psyche and cinematic modes of representation when he defined the cinematic flashback as "an objectivation of our memory function" (Münsterberg 1916, 90). Yet Bernheim actually seems to anticipate this parallel between the cinematic medium and psychological accounts of memory. For already in 1886—nine years before the brothers Lumière presented for the first time the projection of moving photographs to an astounded audience—Bernheim described the functioning of memory as the "seeing . . . of *images that become alive before our eyes*, often as clear as reality" (Bernheim 1888/1964, 210/149*). Thus it is not surprising that the medical textbooks about hypnotism from the 1920s expressly emphasized the equivalence between watching a film and the hypnotic recall of a past event.

The film historian Anton Kaes, who has brilliantly linked Wiene's *Caligari* to the medical treatment of war neurosis and shell shock by means of hypnosis, has compared Francis's narration to the hypnotic therapy of trauma by recovering memory that has been repressed or forgotten: "The film's memory work is Francis' film" (Kaes 2000, 124; Kaes 2009)—an analogy that is corroborated by the psychoanalytic theorist Ernst Simmel, who in 1918 compared the hypnotic recovery of memory to the watching of a film: "the experience can be repeated. The 'film' is made to roll once again; the patient dreams the whole thing one more time" (Simmel, quoted in Kaes 2000, 124).

Similar to Simmel's *War Neurosis and "Psychic Trauma"* (1918), Ernst Kretschmer's treatise *Medical Psychology* (1922) likened the reliving of past events under hypnosis to the viewing of a film: "What the hypnotized otherwise only thinks, he now experiences pictorially [bildhaft], episodes from his past are actually lived through in orderly, comprehensible scenes that correspond to memory. The mental experience unrolls like a picture strip, 'film-like' [filmartig], before him. The experience is passive, like in the dream; he maintains the sensations of a spectator" (Kretschmer 1922, 71).[6] As if alluding to Francis's story about the showman and doctor Caligari, Kretschmer even invokes the expressionist acting style that marks the performance of the actor Friedrich Feher, who played the part of Francis: for in describing the "twilight state" (Dämmerzustand), in which a traumatic event is relived in a flashback, Kretschmer writes: "Thus the twilight state is often nothing else but the living photograph, a dramatic scene in which the original events are reenacted, so to speak cinematographically, with extremely *caricatured expression of affect*" (Kretschmer 1922, 72).

Wiene's expressionist film *The Cabinet of Dr. Caligari* thus stands at the very center of a lively intermedial exchange that links medical theories of suggestion and filmic representations of hypnosis. The structural affinities of hypnotism and cinema even gave rise to conceptualizations of film as exerting a suggestive influence on its spellbound audiences. Around 1900, a hypnotic power was thus ascribed not only to advertising campaigns that addressed susceptible minds with commands such as "You must become Caligari" but to cinema itself. Literary authors such as Jean Cocteau or Walter Hasenclever accordingly invoked the "collective hypnosis into which the cinema audience is plunged by light and shade" (Cocteau 1946, 25; Hasenclever 1913, 220). And numerous physicians and psychologists emphasized the "photoplay's tremendous suggestive power" (Hellwig 1920, 7). Hugo Münsterberg, for instance, explicitly employed the analogy of the "hypnotizer [*sic*] whose word awakens in the mind of the hypnotized person ideas which he cannot resist" (Münsterberg 1916, 97) in order to claim cinema's superiority over the theater. In addition, Münsterberg described how susceptible viewers developed sensory hallucinations of touch and smell when exposed to the suggestive influence of film:

> The *intensity* with which the plays *take hold* of the audience cannot remain without strong social effects. It has even been reported that sensory hallucinations and illusions have crept in; neurasthenic persons are especially inclined to experience touch or smell or sound impressions from what they see on the screen. The associations become as vivid as realities, because the mind is so completely given up to the moving pictures. The applause into which the audiences . . . break out at a happy turn of the melodramatic pictures is another symptom of the *strange fascination*. (Münsterberg 1916, 154)

In Germany Robert Gaupp's essay "The Cinematograph from a Medical and Psychological Perspective" (1912) conceived of the powerful impact of the new medium as "profoundly unsettling" the spectator's "nervous system" (Gaupp

1912, 9). According to Gaupp, cinema presented "everything to the eye as if it were real"—"under the psychologically most favorable conditions for a deep and often sustained *suggestive influence*": "The darkened room, the monotonous sound, the compelling nature of the exciting scenes that rapidly follow each other beat by beat—all of this *puts to sleep* any critical judgment in the receptive soul. … We know that all *suggestions* are more deeply imprinted when critical judgment *sleeps*" (ibid.). This comparison of cinema and hypnotic suggestion was also formulated by Konrad Lange, Albert Hellwig, and Georg Cohn, as well as by Hans Buchner, whose treatise *Under the Spell of Film* (1927) described "cinema man" as succumbing to "the hypnosis of the cinema" (41). And Max Prels's book *Cinema* (1926) similarly warned of "cinema's mass hypnosis" (67).

One particular fear expressed in these texts concerned the visuality of the medium. In comparing film to other established media such as theater and literature, the forensic psychologist Albert Hellwig conceived of the motion picture as "immediately" (unmittelbar) addressing and interpellating the human mind (Hellwig 1916, 116). Hellwig condemned the demoralizing effect of "trash fiction" (Schundliteratur), but he considered the moving image even more pernicious: "pictures generally exert a more strongly inciting influence than mere descriptions of the same object by means of language" (Hellwig 1916, 116). Hellwig, Gaupp, and other proponents of the so-called cinema reform movement thereby ignored the mediality of filmic representation, while simultaneously ascribing their own uncritical equation of image and reality to the ostensibly uneducated spectators (women, children, the working classes, and the "lower races"), who were allegedly unable to distinguish between visual representation and reality.

The texts of the German cinema reform movement therefore characterized the spellbound spectator of cinema as exclusively passive. Münsterberg's psychological study *The Photoplay* developed a complex theory, according to which the viewer's autosuggestion and the external, cinematic suggestion co-constituted the perception of depth and motion. Yet authors like Hellwig or Gaupp described the cinematic images as simply overwhelming the audience. According to them, the source of suggestive power resided only in the visual images of motion photography, not in the mind of the spectator. It is true that Münsterberg also replicated Bernheim's definition of hypnosis as a "psychic condition of increased suggestibility" (Bernheim 1888/1964, 22/15*) when he invoked the "high degree of suggestibility" (Münsterberg 1916, 155) of film spectators; but in accordance with the skeptical position of his essay "Hypnotism and Crime" (1908), he limited a direct connection between the suggestive power of "unwholesome photoplays" and "grave crimes" to "exceptional cases" (Münsterberg 1916, 154). In 1920—the very same year that Robert Wiene's *The Cabinet of Dr. Caligari* was released—Konrad Lange, in contrast, found it "incomprehensible how in an earlier period one could assert that nobody had ever been able to give a certain proof for such cases of a direct incitement to crime" (Lange 1920, 39). As Lange asserted, "given the powerful effect of motion photography, ... the young journeyman and apprentice" had "to succumb without a will of his own" to the filmic representations of crimes or suicides (Lange 1920, 39).

While replicating the medical tales of hypnotic crime, the accounts of cinema's suggestive power thus introduced a metacinematic dimension into filmic representations of criminal suggestion. For, similar to the plot of *The Cabinet of Dr. Caligari*, numerous medical researchers described the film spectator as the victim of a posthypnotic suggestion that controlled the spectator's thoughts and actions after he or she had left the movie theater. This anxiety seemed corroborated by a sensational child murder, frequently invoked as exemplary evidence for the pernicious influence of film. Albert Hellwig gave the first detailed account of the case in "The Harmful Suggestive Power of Cinematographic Displays" (1914), an essay that was published in the *Medical Expert Journal*.

According to Hellwig's article, the sixteen-year-old field hand of a farmer in Borbeck, a small village in western Germany, had murdered the four-year-old son of his employer in the fall of 1913, without any apparent motive. The perpetrator had always been kind to the child who later became his victim. Suspicions of any sadistic tendencies proved to be unfounded. The culprit was furthermore "very moderate in his drinking" and "equally restrained in his sexual practices" (Hellwig 1914, 119). He did, however, frequent the local movie theater "once a week, and occasionally even several times a week" (ibid.). On the days preceding the crime, the delinquent had thus seen a western and a cinematic adaptation of the fairy tale *Tom Thumb (Der kleine Däumling)*—films that "in certain telling details showed a striking resemblance to the circumstances of the crime" (ibid.). The investigating judge consequently reached the astonishing conclusion that these two films had "exerted such a *suggestive influence* on the accused that, unwittingly subject to their influence and without any other motive, he had killed . . . his employer's small son, on whom he ordinarily looked with fondness, when on the afternoon in question he found himself alone with his victim in the hayloft" (Hellwig 1914, 120–21).

The case history seems to anticipate current anxieties about adolescents and the incitement to violence ostensibly emanating from new media such as video games or the Internet. But the medical notion of hypnotic suggestion, central to this account of the "Borbeck child murder," has lost its relevance today and has been replaced by a vague condemnation of the "corrupting" or "desensitizing" influence of modern media. To be sure, the forensic conceptualization of the Borbeck case certainly contained a moralizing subtext. But the representation of film's hypnotic power invoked above all a then scientifically established notion of suggestion and hypnosis. For the judicial opinion that described the cinematic suggestion as controlling susceptible viewers even after they had left the theater, forcing them to commit criminal acts that they would abhor while awake, replicated August Forel's warning against crimes committed after awakening from hypnosis. According to Forel, the particularly "insidious ruse" (Forel 1889, 184) of such a criminal "posthypnotic suggestion" consisted in the perpetrator's belief to be acting freely, of his or her own volition, while in reality under the control of a foreign hypnotic command.

The sensationalist case history of the Borbeck child murder, which was often repeated in texts that warned against the danger of "trash movies" (Schundfilme), thus shows with unusual clarity why "crime and suggestion" became the "most popular subject" of Weimar cinema, as the avid moviegoer Victor Klemperer put it in his diary on April 18, 1921 (Klemperer 1921, 432). For filmic representations of hypnotic crimes appropriated not only a lively scientific, medical, and legal debate about the unlimited power of hypnotism. In addition, contemporary representations of the new medium itself were predicated on a structural analogy between cinema and hypnotism, thereby giving rise to the fear that the spellbound audience might succumb to the irresistible hypnotic influence emanating from the cinematic apparatus—just like Caligari's somnambulist medium Cesare.

NOTES

Portions of this text have been previously published in Andriopoulos 2000 and Andriopoulos 2008.

1. Throughout this essay all emphases in quotations are added unless noted otherwise.
2. Throughout this essay, page references that are divided by a slash (/) indicate first the page number in the original version of the quoted text (22) and then the corresponding number in the published English translation (15). An asterisk after the second number indicates that the translation has been modified.
3. For a detailed bibliography that lists the different editions of these medical texts and for a more comprehensive analysis of late-nineteenth-century medical theories of hypnotism see Andriopoulos 2000/2008.
4. "Qu'ils n'étaient pas libre de ne pas simuler" (Bernheim 1886, 268/190*). The published English translation of this passage unfortunately effaces Bernheim's double negation.
5. The text was published in excerpts in 1990 in Mike Budd's useful anthology *The Cabinet of Dr. Caligari: Texts, Contexts, Histories* (see Janowitz 1939).
6. I owe this reference to Haddock (2004).

REFERENCES

Andriopoulos, Stefan. 2000. *Besessene Körper: Hypnose, Körperschaften und die Erfindung des Kinos.* Munich: Fink.

——. 2008. *Possessed: Hypnotic Crimes, Corporate Fiction, and the Invention of Cinema.* Trans. Peter Jansen and Stefan Andriopoulos. Chicago: University of Chicago Press.

Anon. 1893/1894. "Mittheilung vermischten Inhalts." *Zeitschrift für Hypnotismus* 2:176.

Anon. 1920. "Robert Wiene's 'Das Cabinet des Dr. Caligari.'" *Lichtbild-Bühne*, February 28. Repr. in *Das Cabinet des Dr. Caligari: Drehbuch von Carl Mayer und Hans Janowitz mit einem einführenden Essay und Materialien zum Film*, ed. Uli Jung and Walter Schatzberg, 140–41. Munich: Edition text + kritik, 1995.

Bernheim, Hippolyte. 1888. *De la suggestion et ses applications à la thérapeutique. Deuxième édition*. Paris: O. Doin. (Orig. pub. 1886)

———. 1964. *Hypnosis and Suggestion*. Trans. Christian A. Herter. New York: University Books.

———. 1891. *Hypnotisme, suggestion, psychothérapie: Etudes nouvelles*. Paris: O. Doin.

———. 1980. *New Studies in Hypnotism*. Trans. Richard S. Sandor. New York: International Universities Press.

Binswanger, Otto. 1892. "Gutachten über Hypnose und Suggestion." In *Die Suggestion und die Dichtung: Gutachten über Hypnose und Suggestion von Otto Binswanger, Emil du Boys-Reymond et al.*, ed. Karl Emil Franzos, 3–11. Berlin: F. Fontane.

Buchner, Hans. 1927. *Im Banne des Films: Die Weltherrschaft des Kinos*. Munich: Deutscher Volksverlag E. Boepple.

Cocteau, Jean. 1946. "Speech at the Institut des hautes études cinématographiques." Repr. in *The Art of Cinema*, trans. Robin Buss, 25. New York: Marion Boyars, 1992.

Delboeuf, Joseph. 1893/1894. "Die verbrecherischen Suggestionen." *Zeitschrift für Hypnotismus* 2:177–98, 221–40, 247–68.

Eisner, Lotte H. 1969. *The Haunted Screen: Expressionism in the German Cinema and the Influence of Max Reinhardt*. Trans. Roger Greaves. Berkeley: University of California Press. (Orig. pub. 1952.)

Elsaesser, Thomas. 2000. *Weimar Cinema and After: Germany's Historical Imaginary*. New York: Routledge.

Forel, August. 1889. "Der Hypnotismus und seine strafrechtliche Bedeutung." *Zeitschrift für die gesamte Strafrechtswissenschaft* 9:131–93.

———. 1895. *Der Hypnotismus, seine psycho-physiologische, medicinische, strafrechtliche Bedeutung und seine Handhabung: Dritte Auflage mit Adnotationen von Oskar Vogt*. Stuttgart: Enke.

Flüggen, Christian. 1920. "Münchener Erstaufführungen." *Deutsche Lichtspielzeitung*, March 3. Reprinted in *Das Cabinet des Dr. Caligari: Drehbuch von Carl Mayer und Hans Janowitz mit einem einführenden Essay und Materialien zum Film*, ed. Uli Jung and Walter Schatzberg, 147. Munich: Edition text + kritik, 1995.

Freud, Sigmund. 1889. "Rezension von August Forel Der Hypnotismus." In *Gesammelte Werke: Nachtragsband: Texte aus den Jahren 1885 bis 1938*, 123–39. Frankfurt am Main: Fischer, 1987.

———. 1927. "Fetischismus." In *Gesammelte Werke*. Vol. 14, 309–17. London: Imago, 1948.

Gaupp, Robert. 1912. "Der Kinematograph vom medizinischen und psychologischen Standpunkt." In *Der Kinematograph als Volksunterhaltungsmittel: Vorträge gehalten am 21. Mai 1912 in Tübingen*, ed. Robert Gaupp and Konrad Lange, 1–12. Munich: Dürerbund.

Gunning, Tom. 1990. "The Cinema of Attractions: Early Film, Its Spectator, and the Avant-Garde." In *Early Cinema: Space, Frame, Narrative*, ed. Thomas Elsaesser, 56–62. London: BFI.

Haddock, Aaron D. 2004. "Cinematic Trance: Robert Musil's 'Toward a New Aesthetic.'" Master's thesis, Columbia University.

Hasenclever, Walter. 1913. "Der Kintopp als Erzieher: Eine Apologie." Repr. in *Prolog vor dem Film: Nachdenken über ein neues Medium, 1909–1914*, ed. Jörg Schweinitz, 219–22. Leipzig: Reclam, 1992).

Hellwig, Albert. 1914. "Über die schädliche Suggestivkraft kinematographischer Vorführungen." *Ärztliche Sachverständigen-Zeitung* 20, no. 6:119–24.

——. 1916. "Zur Psychologie kinematographischer Vorführungen." *Zeitschrift für Psychotherapie und medizinische Psychologie* 6:88–120.

——. 1920. *Die Reform des Lichtspielrechts*. Langensalza: Beyer & Mann.

Janowitz, Hans. 1939. "Caligari—The Story of a Famous Story (Excerpts)." Repr. in *The Cabinet of Dr. Caligari: Texts, Contexts, Histories*, ed. Mike Budd, 221–40. New Brunswick, NJ: Rutgers University Press, 1990.

Kaes, Anton. 2000. "War—Film—Trauma." In *Modernität und Trauma: Beiträge zum Zeitenbruch des Ersten Weltkrieges*, ed. Inka Mülder-Bach, 121–30. Vienna: WUV.

——. 2009. *Shell Shock Cinema: Weimar Germany and the Wounds of War*. Princeton, NJ: Princeton University Press.

Kasten, Jürgen. 1990. *Der expressionistische Film: Abgefilmtes Theater oder avantgardistisches Erzählkino? Eine stil-, produktions-, und rezeptionsgeschichtliche Untersuchung*. Münster: MAkS Publikationen.

Klemperer, Victor. 1921. *Leben sammeln, nicht fragen wozu und warum: Tagebücher, 1918–1924*. Ed. W. Nowojski. Berlin: Aufbau-Verlag, 1996.

Kracauer, Siegfried. 1947. *From Caligari to Hitler: A Psychological History of the German Film*. Princeton, NJ: Princeton University Press.

Kretschmer, Ernst. 1922. *Medizinische Psychologie: Ein Leitfaden für Studium und Praxis*. Zweite Auflage. Leipzig: Georg Thieme Verlag.

Lange, Konrad. 1920. *Das Kino in Gegenwart und Zukunft*. Stuttgart: Enke.

Lindau, Paul. 1893. *Der Andere: Schauspiel in vier Aufzügen*. Dresden: Teubner.

Mann, Thomas. 1924. *Der Zauberberg: Roman*. Frankfurt am Main: Fischer, 1989.

Mayer, Carl, and Hans Janowitz. 1919. "Das Cabinett des Dr. Calligaris [*sic*]: Phantastischer Filmroman in 6 Akten." In *Das Cabinet des Dr. Caligari: Drehbuch von Carl Mayer und Hans Janowitz zu Robert Wienes Film von 1919/20*, 47–111. Munich: Edition text + kritik, 1995.

Metz, Christian. 1982. *The Imaginary Signifier: Psychoanalysis and the Cinema*. Trans. Celia Britton, Annwyl Williams, Ben Brewster, and Alfred Guzzetti. Bloomington: Indiana University Press.

Münsterberg, Hugo. 1908. "Hypnotism and Crime." In *On the Witness Stand: Essays on Psychology and Crime*, 203–28. Garden City, NY: Doubleday.

———. 1916. *The Photoplay. A Psychological Study*. Repr. in *Hugo Münsterberg on Film*, ed. Allan Langdale, 45–162. New York: Routledge, 2002. Page citations refer to the reprint edition.

Murray, Bruce. 1990. *Film and the German Left in the Weimar Republic: From* Caligari *to* Kuhle Wampe. Austin: University of Texas Press.

Prels, Max. 1926. *Kino*. Zweite Auflage. Bielefeld-Leipzig: Velhagen & Klasing.

Robinson, David. 1997. *Das Cabinet des Dr. Caligari*. London: BFI.

Salten, Felix. 1932. "Über Schnitzlers hypnotische Versuche." Repr. in *Arthur Schnitzler: Aspekte und Akzente: Materialien zu Leben und Werk*, ed. Hans-Ulrich Lindken, 55. Frankfurt am Main–Bern: Peter Lang, 1984.

Schnitzler, Arthur. 1920. *Jugend in Wien: Eine Autobiographie*. Ed. Therese Nickl and Heinrich Schnitzler. Frankfurt am Main: Fischer, 1981.

Schrenck-Notzing, Albert von. 1900. "Die gerichtlich-medizinische Bedeutung der Suggestion." In *Archiv für Kriminalanthropologie und Kriminalistik* 5:1–36.

Scott, Walter D. 1917. *The Psychology of Advertising*. Boston: Small, Maynard. (Orig. pub. 1908.)

Tourette, Georges Gilles de la. 1887. *L'hypnotisme et les états analogues au point de vue médico-légale*. Paris: E. Plon.

Walloth, Wilhel. 1897. *Im Banne der Hypnose: Ein psychologischer Roman*. Jena: H. Costenoble.

OF MONSTERS AND MAGICIANS

PAUL WEGENER'S *THE GOLEM:*
HOW HE CAME INTO THE WORLD (1920)

NOAH ISENBERG

Always they treat it as a legend, till something happens and turns it into actuality again.   GUSTAV MEYRINK, *The Golem* (1915)

The gray soul of medieval Prague has been molded into these eccentric and errant crypts. They suggest a kind of Jewish Gothic—a blending of the flame-like letters of the Jewish alphabet with the leaf-like flame of Gothic tracery.
                    HERMAN G. SCHEFFAUER, "The Vivifying of Space" (1920)

Set against a lush, celestial backdrop and a flickering panorama of crooked gables and oblique rooftops, evocative of some sort of extraterrestrial urban sprawl, the opening sequence of Paul Wegener's *Der Golem: Wie er in die Welt kam* (*The Golem: How He Came into the World*) establishes a realm of limitless fantasy. It does so by introducing, in relatively rapid succession, the key elements that underpin the entire film and that lie at the core of the popular Jewish legend on which it is based: soothsaying, mysticism, violence, supernatural creation, mad science, sexuality, and the occult. Less than a minute of screen time elapses before, on the heels of the first foreboding intertitle ("The revered Rabbi Löw reads in the stars that the grave misfortune threatens the Jewish community"), we encounter the bearded magician and wonder rabbi (Albert Steinrück) at his telescope, scurrying about his observatory, peering into the galaxy and fitfully poring over his thick tomes (Fig. 2.1). Wegener then cuts to the rabbi's antechamber, where his assistant, Famulus (Ernst Deutsch), sits before a makeshift chemistry set—a powerful icon of modern science that stands in marked contrast to the strange, primordial set design of the sixteenth-century Prague ghetto—replete with glass beakers emitting billowy smoke. Wegener's choice of lighting, aided by cameraman Karl Freund, allows for only partial illumination of Famulus's shifty profile. The rabbi's daughter, Miriam

FIGURE 2.1 Rabbi Löw (Albert Steinrück) consulting one of his tomes in Paul Wegener's *The Golem: How He Came into the World* (1920).

(Lyda Salmonova), then enters the frame, her rapturous gaze highlighted by the candle she grips in one hand; the wild, unrestrained sexual energy she exudes, ultimately to a deadly effect, is made immediately palpable in the flirtatious interaction between her and Famulus. Rabbi Löw finally descends from his observatory and breaks the tension with his prophetic announcement of doom—a message that foretells the main story line and sets the remainder of the film in motion.

The golem legend, a kind of primal or *ur*-narrative of artificial creation, harks back to the Old Testament (Psalms 139:16), where the golem itself is conceived as "unformed substance," and is then taken up, somewhat later, in the rabbinic discourse of the Talmud concerning Adam. Owing to the enduring allure of the story of creation—or perhaps to its controversial nature and its malleability over time—the golem legend became a stock motif in religious and nonreligious writing from the Middle Ages through the rise of modernity. Commenting on the question of the unusually wide range of creative responses that the golem story has elicited since its entry into Western culture, the modern Yiddish writer Isaac Bashevis Singer noted: "It possesses the tension and the suspense of the supernatural. It is based on a faith almost as old as the human species—namely, that dead matter is not really dead but can be brought to life" (Bilski 1988, 6). As an artistic theme, the golem story gained currency in a variety of historical settings, not merely in the age of Hasidism in eighteenth-century eastern Europe but also in German romanticism at the start of the nineteenth century, with many renditions devised by non-Jewish authors (Achim von Arnim, E. T. A. Hoffmann, et al.) for a predominantly non-Jewish audience. The most famous, and certainly most influential, version of the golem story stems from the sixteenth century and centers on a charismatic Rabbi Judah Loew (i.e., Löw) ben Bezalel, the so-called Maharal of Prague, who conjured a golem to defend the Jews from persecution. In the words of Kabbalah scholar Gershom Scholem: "A famous scholar and mystic, he [the Maharal] is credited by Jewish popular tradition with the creation of a Golem—a creature produced by the magical power of man and taking on human shape. Rabbi Loew's robot was made of clay and given a sort of life by being infused with the concentrated power of the rabbi's mind. This great human power is, however, nothing but a reflection of God's own creative power" (Scholem 1971, 335). The affinity between this legend and the very act of filmmaking is both obvious and elemental, and the influence that this connection has exerted over artists, visual and otherwise, is inestimable. For it not only invites reflection on the act of aesthetic production—particularly on the art of cinema—but allows for exploration of the golem as a kind of artist's double, an analogous process to the Divine creation of human beings.

In terms of Wegener's personal attachment to the material, while working on location with the Danish director Stellan Rye on *The Student of Prague* (1913)—which would mark Wegener's screen debut as an actor and codirector—he is said to have become increasingly drawn to the legend of Löw and his golem (Goldsmith 1981, 143). In his collaboration with Rye, Wegener, who had up to that point been known mainly as a stage actor with Max Reinhardt's company, had the chance to explore the romantically inspired material—with the cornerstone idea of the *doppelgänger*, one's ghostly double—set in Prague's famous Jewish cemetery (where, to this day, Rabbi Löw's tombstone lies). Wegener's early preoccupation with various forms of fantasy, with precisely the kind of material that would pique the curiosity of a blossoming cinematic imagination, was not particularly unusual. With the outbreak of the Great War, the cultural climate seemed especially well disposed toward romantic and mystical currents. As Lotte Eisner observes near the outset of *The Haunted Screen*, "Mysticism and magic, the dark forces to which Germans have always been more than willing to commit themselves, had flourished in the face of death on the battlefields. The hecatombs of young men fallen in the flower of their youth seemed to nourish the grim nostalgia of the survivors. And the ghosts which had haunted the German Romantics revived, like the shades of Hades after draughts of blood" (Eisner 1973, 9).

Less than a year after *The Student of Prague* was released, when the war had already begun to rage, Wegener directed a modernist version of the golem legend, *Der Golem* (*The Golem*, 1915), using contemporary sets and adopting the theme to the world around him; not long after that, with some overlapping cast and crew (e.g., Salmonova, who played in *The Student of Prague*, as well as in Wegener's 1916 production of *Der Yoghi*, and would appear in all three Golem films), he shot an additional adaptation *Der Golem und die Tänzerin* (*The Golem and the Dancing Girl*, 1917), this time a bit more fanciful in nature (Bilski 1988, 50–51). Although we no longer have access to complete prints of these early pictures—only a smattering of frames, film stills, and publicity materials survived the war—we do have the original film criticism. For example, in his review of Wegener's first *Golem*, Arnold Zweig suggests a certain consistency in the entire three-film cycle: "What makes this film worthy of discussion is indeed above all the form (*Gestalt*) that Wegener gave to the Golem—the amazing figure of an artificial being who struggles to break free of his inanimate state and enter into a living, feeling existence with the world, to become a human being, to account for himself, to transform and purify his crude senses . . . into a redeeming feeling. Here, in the lyrical realm, the film gave Wegener the possibility that no theater ever could" (Greve 1976, 117). In this respect Wegener's golem trilogy seems to mirror not only the development of the director—who became known for his lyricism and for his aspiration "to enter the domain of the purely cinematic," as he called it in 1916 (Greve 1976, 119)—but also his auspicious transition from theater to film.

When the sold-out Berlin premiere of Wegener's third and final golem film opened at the majestic Ufa-Palast am Zoo on October 29, 1920, the German audience likely had at least some familiarity with the golem legend, having been exposed over the past decades to numerous popular renditions.[1] Aside from Wegener's first two golem films, there had been several successful early-twentieth-century literary treatments: Arthur Holitscher's renowned play *Der Golem: Ghettolegende in drei Aufzügen* (*The Golem: A Ghetto Legend in Three Acts*, 1908), offered to Max Reinhardt for theatrical adaptation; Gustav Meyrink's best-selling novel *Der Golem* (*The Golem*, 1915), first serialized in 1913–14 and often incorrectly thought to have helped form Wegener's connection to the legend; and Chayim Bloch's prose fiction treatment *Der Prager Golem: Von seiner "Geburt" bis zu seinem "Tod"* (*The Golem of Prague: From his "Birth" to his "Death,"* 1919). Yet in exploring the complexities of Wegener's film, what is most significant is not so much the familiarity with the past adaptations but how the legend fit into the Weimar-era understanding of horror and fantasy and into the wider discourse on German-Jewish culture at the time the film was produced.

Hinging as it does on the banishment of the Jews from the empire, Wegener's *The Golem* speaks immediately to the lingering Jewish Question—that is, what to do with the burgeoning number of Jews, many of them from central and eastern Europe, occupying German cities in the wake of the Great War. As the film's fictionalized documentary insert, the *Dekret wider die Juden* (*Decree Against the Jews*), reads: "The many serious charges against the Jews can no longer be disregarded, being that they crucified our Lord, wrongfully ignore the holy Christian holidays, thirst after the goods and lives of their fellow men, and practice the black arts. Hence we decree that all Jews must evacuate their quarter, known as the ghetto, before the new moon." Indeed, the sixteenth-century legend underlying Wegener's film serves as a modern allegory of invasion—one of horror's time-honored subjects and a subject that had enormous potential to resonate with the Weimar audience still reeling from the loss of the war and the division of its borders. In this light, Rabbi Löw's magical talents poignantly underscore his ability to transform the city—the Prague ghetto and, by extension, its modern offscreen counterpart—while his construction of a mechanical robot strikes a powerful chord in the 1920s discourse on industrial production. "The creation of the Golem," remarks Scholem, "is then in some way an affirmation of the productive and creative power of Man. It repeats, on however small of a scale, the work of creation" (Scholem 1971, 337). As Rabbi Löw toils in his study, creating his mystical and technological wonder—an archetypal scene that receives homage in such Weimar films as Murnau's *Faust* (1926) and Lang's *Metropolis* (1927) and then, in Hollywood, in James Whale's *Frankenstein* (1931)—the consummate modernist asserts his powers over nature. He operates on his own expressive terms, creating the mechanical object of horror and the ultimate symbol of modernity.

Wegener leads up to this scene by exposing the viewer to Rabbi Löw's deep immersion in the art of necromancy—as he consults his quasi-scientific, astrological, and religious treatises; examines obscure numerological charts; and works up various magical formulae and incantations—which will finally enable him to sculpt a golem out of clay and bring it to life. (The suspense surrounding Löw's attempt to create a robot that might save the Jews from expulsion is amplified by parallel editing in which the viewer simultaneously observes the formal *Decree Against the Jews* being delivered by the emperor's emissary, the handsome knight Florian [Lothar Müthel]; this adds to the already foreboding air, while it also brings a gentile "outsider" into the Jewish ghetto and into close contact with the rabbi's daughter, a crossing of cultural borders that invites later transgressions.) Working with his special-effects supervisor and codirector Carl Boese, together with Freund, Wegener pulls out all the stops to render a highly stylized enactment of supernatural creation, one that far transcends the original parameters of the Jewish legend (Fig. 2.2): donning a magician's hat (decorated with pseudo-kabbalistic symbols), waving a wand much like a sorcerer, and later brandishing a pentagram, Rabbi Löw casts a circle of flames around himself and his cowering assistant, Famulus; he demands that the spirit of Astharoth—a demonic figure whose origins lie in the occult, and who appears in Wegener's film as a crudely sculpted, free-floating white silhouette—reveal the magic word, which, when placed inside the amulet worn on the Golem's breast, will bring him to life; in coughs of sinewy smoke, the word

FIGURE 2.2 Triptych of the act of creation: Rabbi Löw waving his wand; Löw in poised anticipation with Famulus (Ernst Deutsch) at his side; Astharoth, revealing the magic word.

issues forth as "Aemaeth" (Hebrew for truth), and the rabbi, in a feat of triumph, collapses before a meteor shower of light that bursts from the spirit.[2] Thus, the golem is born.

Lumbering about the ghetto streets, exploring the world on his own and accompanying Famulus on his errands (in an incommensurately lighthearted scene that comes across as "Rabbi Löw's golem goes shopping"), the golem exudes the spirit of his original surroundings. Not unlike the rabbi himself, he serves as an embodiment of the ghetto city. "The city," writes Seth Wolitz, "the central figure of modernity for so much expressionist cinema, emerges in this film as the massive Golem itself, unnatural, unformed, incomplete, alone. The ghetto is the synecdoche of the city. Exotic, fascinating, it becomes modern urban life" (Wolitz 1983, 392). It is in the figure of the golem that the rabbi transforms the biblical Adam, himself referred to in Talmudic discourse as a "golem," into the modern Jewish robot (a human-made monster for the twentieth century). The blurred boundaries separating the ancient legend from the contemporary realm of political and cultural life around 1920 elicit a host of questions concerning Löw's Jewishness in his roles as producer and engineer, necromancer, strange magician, and mad scientist. How, for example, does the so-called *Wunderrabbi* and technological mastermind cultivate and wield his authority? Why, in a climate of great instability, do the Jews of the city pose a threat both to the empire within the film and to its contemporary counterpart, the Weimar Republic, at large? And how does a Judeo-Christian myth of creation resonate with the myth-based construction of Jewish identity?

Though Wegener's film is obviously set in the sixteenth-century ghetto, Rabbi Löw masters the economy of the city far more like a Weimar industrialist (à la Walther Rathenau) than a premodern alchemist. Considered in the wake of the Treaty of Versailles, and just months before Adolf Hitler's formal announcement of his twenty-five-point party program for the *Deutsche Arbeiter-Partei* (German Worker's Party), the precursor to the Nazi Party, Löw's negotiating power over the Jews in the German Empire appears to comment on the territorial struggles of the republic; indeed, as arbitrator between the German Empire and the ghetto world, Löw functions as foreign minister of the ghetto Jews. To be sure, the glimpse of the past in *The Golem*, evoked in the sixteenth-century ghetto, casts light onto the contemporary historical moment, circumscribing the Jew's presence in the modern German city, and in what was scornfully termed the "Jew-Republic" (Weitz 2007, 39). In a brief essay from 1915, "Schauspielerei und Film" ("Acting and Film"), written shortly before heading off to battle in the Great War, and published in the *Berliner Tageblatt*, Wegener points to the effect he had hoped to achieve in his *Golem* project: he saw himself as a "film arranger" (*Filmarrangeur*), as someone who was able to "translate, with the most subtle detail, such fantasy-laden ideas into film material" (Greve 1976, 116). Or, as he puts it more directly, "Here everything is rendered in the image, in a confluence of a fantasy-world of past centuries with everyday life" (Greve 1976, 116). In her extensive research on Wegener's film, on the intricacies of its production history as well as on its international release (and the different variations in circulation), Elfriede Ledig has commented on the original music, a symphonic score written by the composer Hans Landsberger, who at the beginning of the 1920s was composing for films. Although the score no longer exists—the current restored print of the film, released on DVD by KINO in 2002, includes an entirely new score composed by Alijoscha Zimmermann—Ledig points to an unsigned review from a Weimar-era trade publication: "Paul Wegener's 'Golem' has found in Hans Landsberger a composer, who wishes to be taken seriously. . . . He wants to do away with the medley of styles (with Potpourri) and supplement the mosaic through a logically linked sound image that has a symphonic life of its own. . . . Of course, Landsberger does not speak a folksy language; he created a grandly executed symphonic poetry which pairs together the assets of contemporary harmony with the instrumental arts of older lineage" (Ledig 1992, 200). This review may not provide a full sense of the original music. It does, however, provide an apt description of Wegener's film as a whole, blending as it does elements of the distant past with those of the present and thus aiming for a kind of screen poetry. The nature of the physical world is enmeshed with the fantasies of the cinematic world, revealing perhaps one of the film's greatest affective potentials.

THE POWER OVER THE SPECTACLE

As the historian Omer Bartov has argued in his recent study *The "Jew" in Cinema*, Wegener's *The Golem* reflects "a symbol of Jewish magical and destructive capacities; it also represents the Jews' ability to control the powers of nature, to subjugate everything that is beautiful and free, and to cast over the world the dark shadow of their morbid rites" (Bartov 2005, 3). One of *The Golem*'s central scenes, in which the rabbi visits the emperor's Rose Festival, illustrates the visual conflation of twentieth-century industrialism and ancient fantasy. Known to the court as the "strange illusionist," Rabbi Löw premieres his golem creation to the audience of the emperor's palace, boldly displaying his aesthetic power. Inside the lavishly decorated court, the wizardlike rabbi appears at once submissive, as he kisses the emperor's ring, and almighty, as he orchestrates the spectacle. While the camera focuses on Löw's position among the audience members at the emperor's court, the dimly lit "illusionist" takes on increasingly amplified dimensions. Not terribly different from Robert Wiene's *Das Kabinett des Dr. Caligari* (*The Cabinet of Dr. Caligari*, 1920)—which premiered only months before Wegener's *The Golem*—in which the mad scientist and sideshow performer Caligari exhibits his somnambulist, Cesare, before an eager crowd of spectators, Löw stands prominently framed alongside his golem "show" as the guests of the court curiously observe (in a string of terrified and, at least from today's vantage point, comically exaggerated reaction shots) (Fig. 2.3). In the same way that Caligari maintains control over his monster on display, Löw manipulates the movements of his robot-figure, withholding the secrets of his act. As the rabbi asserts via intertitle, "He is my servant and my creation called Golem. More I cannot say."

In Rabbi Löw, Wegener characterizes the Jew as master of the power over the spectacle—over the aesthetic medium—a power that is repeatedly emphasized throughout the film. Indeed, the subsequent series of scenes at the Rose Festival further affirms this trait. The emperor asks Löw, "What manner of marvel is this you display for us today, you strange illusionist? Let us see more of your art." The rabbi then proceeds, in a dazzling metacinematic gesture, to conjure up a film-within-a-film sequence of the biblical Exodus story through which his individual technological mastery and the status of the Jews forced to flee their homeland are simultaneously invoked. As Frances Guerin has recently observed, Löw "is the ersatz director of Wegener's film" (Guerin 2005, 126). Masses of Jews walk across the screen, ancient doubles of Löw's fellow ghetto inhabitants. Amid the Jewish procession a lone figure reaches the center of the screen, abruptly turning toward the

FIGURE 2.3 Debuting the golem (Paul Wegener) at the Rose Festival.

court spectators (Fig. 2.4). Although at first glance one might be tempted to regard this figure as Moses (Manvell 1973, 41), in the novelistic rendition of the screenplay published by the filmmaker in 1921, Wegener addresses him not as Moses but as "Ahasverus, the eternal Jew" (Wegener 1921, 50). In the role of "eternal Jew," the bearded mythical figure embodies a portrait of the exiled condition of the Jews in the emperor's city who likewise face expulsion from their non-Jewish domain. By invoking the figure of Ahasverus, not only does Wegener return the Jewish Question to the foreground, but he expands the mythical foundation of the film: the golem legend, the Exodus passage, and the citation of the "wandering Jew" render the film's narrative both culturally and historically familiar yet fantastically remote. The audience, already and often exposed to the stock motifs and metaphors of the golem, as well as the Faustian and biblical inflections, can identify the cinematic rendition in terms of its rootedness in German culture, while nonetheless distancing itself from the bizarre miracles on the screen. Or, put differently, like the audience members of the emperor's court, they too can enjoy the spectacle in terms of its uncanny, exotic qualities.

Analogous to the interaction of the golem narrative with the present, the skewed Exodus citation embodied in "Ahasverus" resonates with the story that Wegener's film tells. Both the figures from Löw's "show" and the figures in Wegener's narrative must flee their homes—the biblical Jews from the ancient homeland and the

FIGURE 2.4 Ahasverus, the wandering Jew.

ghetto-Jews from the German city. Both groups face persecution in their respective host countries and therefore must seek freedom elsewhere. The blurred configuration of genres, periods, and images conveys a jumbled composite of history, fiction, aesthetics, and myth. By introducing the biblical passage in the film, Wegener reconstitutes the past in the form of narrativized myth, freighted with the historical immediacy of the modern Jewish Question. As witnessed in Hans-Karl Breslauer's film of 1924 *Die Stadt ohne Juden* (*The City Without Jews*)—a utopian, futuristic fantasy that ultimately, in a very clever twist, turns the anti-Semitic impetus of the fantasy on its head—the question of expelling the unwanted inhabitants of the city provoked a wide range of responses in the years following Wegener's *The Golem*.

The artful production of the biblical scene and the creation of the golem also implicate the theological problem of profanely imitating the Divine, that is, the disavowal of the paramount Jewish biblical commandment against the creation of images resembling God or anything in the heavens or on the earth (Ex. 20:4; Deut. 5:8). In the intertitle announcing the rabbi's intentions, Löw instructively states, "Let me show you our patriarchs, mighty Emperor, so that you may better know our people." Löw's "show" offers precisely the mimetic photo-quality representation of the Jews that is proscribed. As Adorno remarks in *Aesthetic Theory*, "the Old Testament prohibition of graven images can be said to have an aesthetic aspect besides the overt theological one. The interdiction against forming an image—of something—in effect implies the proposition that such an image is impossible to form" (Adorno 1984, 100; see also Koch 1992, 16–29). Adorno's statement underscores the destructive nature of the film aesthetic; he insists on film's lack of autonomy and fetishistic nature. When considered in light of Wegener's *The Golem*, Adorno's thoughts point to a double fetish, as the Jew on the screen adds a second layer of false representation. The masses of Jews projected onto the screen in *The Golem* cannot possibly reflect the individuality of the living Jew. Rather, as Adorno would argue, they merely represent one-dimensional replicas of the absent object that can never be fully reproduced.

Interestingly, in a 1920 lecture on the future of film delivered at the *Filmliga* in Berlin, Paul Wegener spoke of an innate danger in film that he called the "Lebenslüge," the misrepresentation of life and nature. He observed how filmic images, in their unmediated affective capacity, "schematize," "stereotype," and graft characteristics onto an individual or a people [*Volk*] (Wegener 1920). As contradictory as his statement may appear against the backdrop of his film, Wegener reveals an explicit awareness of the problems of cinematic representation. For as seen in the film's depiction of the Rose Festival and the film-within-a-film projection, the nature of the filmic enterprise is called into question. Although Rabbi Löw tells the viewers of the court to show respect for his creation ("No one may speak or laugh, lest some terrible disaster occur"), they do not know how to behave at the movies—a scene reminiscent of the confusion in Edwin Porter's early short, *Uncle Josh at the Moving Picture Show* (1902)—mocking the fictional images before them as if they were real.[3] The court audience, led by the jester, ridicules the figures onscreen, affirming their odd appearance and the stark difference between Rabbi Löw's wandering Jews and the gentile viewers. As the Nazi myth-machine would later propagate, the Jews here become mere caricatures, types devoid of any human individuality.

THE ARCHITECTURE OF THE JEW

To understand the implications of Wegener's version of the Golem legend for the identity formation of Jews both on and off the screen, it is important to note the film's predilection for myth-based, caricatured constructions of Jewishness. Shown variously at work, at prayer, in the streets, and in acts of intrigue and conspiracy, the Jews of the ghetto city exude a patently undesirable air (bearing out affinities with the monster himself). Among Wegener's repertoire of Jewish figures, the viewer encounters a series of menacing characters: Rabbi Jehuda (Hans Stürm), the elder of the community, who must be consulted in the decision to act with power against the emperor's banishment; Famulus, the rabbi's scheming, vengeful assistant, who turns the golem loose only to run amok after the rabbi has already thwarted the plan for Jewish expulsion; the rabbi's unruly daughter, Miriam, whose oversexed gaze lures the gentile court messenger, Florian, back into the ghetto after he delivers the emperor's *Decree*, resulting in his death and the near destruction of the city.[4] As in the caricatured portraits of Jews widely appropriated for German and Austrian political campaigns in the years surrounding the film's production, and as in the 1920 publication of the German edition of *Protocols of the Elders of Zion*, the film's depiction of Jewishness reveals a strong bent toward a feared invasion.

Just as the film's *Decree Against the Jews* suggests that Jews "practice black arts" and endanger the lives of Christians, *The Golem*'s depiction of the main Jewish characters, and the world that they occupy, confirms these claims. "Magic and mystery dominate the lives of the film's alien Jews who scuttle about Wegener's expressionistic ghetto," writes Lester Friedman. "Wegener's use of Reinhardt's striking lighting effects and Poelzig's angled sets combine to give the ghetto's mise-en-scène a dark and dangerous look, emphasizing the superstition and sorcery that rule the lives of its bizarre inhabitants. The endlessly twisting staircases, narrow crowded streets, dimly illuminated rooms, and sinister bellow-lit figures encourage us to believe the Emperor is correct: these people do practice black magic and are a threat" (Friedman 1984, 52–53). Such ominous affinities attributed to the "Jew"—which is to say, the screen personae projected in the film—foster a clear division between the dark mysterious ghetto and the enlightened empire, between Jewish sorcery and German culture, between the perceived threat of Jewish power and the vulnerable German state. The film's final scene, in which the Golem encounters a group of small children playing outside the ghetto walls, where one especially innocent, blonde little girl, holding an apple in her hand, unsuspectingly renders him inanimate—pulling the amulet from his breast, while being held in his hulking arms—further accentuates the formidable gulf between the ghetto Jews and the outside world (Fig. 2.5). In this regard Wegener's film presents an iconography of Jewishness that far exceeds the mythical foundation of the Golem story, thus highlighting the contemporary issues beyond the legend.

One of the most salient issues underlying Wegener's golem story is the problem of Jewish masses in the city. As was well known at the time, since the German defeat in World War I, waves of migration of East European Jews had increased in unprecedented numbers, heightening the already acute awareness of Jewish presence. The approximately ninety thousand East European Jews who lived within German borders prior to the war nearly doubled, as another seventy thousand new immigrants made their way west. *The Golem*'s focus on the crowds that occupy the ghetto city serves, perhaps unwittingly, to foreground this new consciousness of Jews. A 1920 review of Wegener's film appearing in *Der Kinematograph* notes

FIGURE 2.5 The golem carrying an innocent young girl, outside the Ghetto gates.

this imperceptible line separating the cinematic world from the real world: "The crooked buildings, the twisty alleys of the ghetto which appear in near inexhaustible fullness, indeed even the people who live in them are without any distortion of a non-reality that moves far beyond everyday life" (Greve 1976, 120). The Jewish setting, the *Kinematograph* critic suggests, along with the Jews portrayed on the screen, correspond to the common images of Jews in Weimar society. Indeed, as representatives of Weimar mass society, the Jews paradoxically evoke at once capitalistic dominance, political prowess, and scientific insight on the one hand and stifling swarthiness, exotic practices, and ghetto sensibilities on the other.

Whereas the eastern Jewish Question had been commonly conflated with the general Jewish Question, throughout the years of the Weimar Republic, the stereotype of the *Ostjude* (East European Jew) became a master icon of identification for Jews at large (Aschheim 1982). In the cinema, then, signs of Jewishness had to rely on cultural references to overt differences such as eastern Jewish physiognomy, religious and ritualistic symbols, and ghetto markings, while also relying on the latent anxieties surrounding ostensibly Jewish trades and professions (e.g., urban industrialists, free-market capitalists, revolutionary intellectuals, and scientists). One of the great fears concerning assimilated German Jews was precisely their lack of overt characteristics, their mastery of blending in with the gentile majority. Hence, a considerable enigma of Weimar cinema was how to represent the Jew if not by invoking stereotypical physiognomic traits of the East European Jews (i.e., those whose religious garb or general comportment would make their Jewish identity plain). Although the films of the Weimar era dealing with Jewish subjects did not necessarily aim at propagating anti-Semitism, nor at inciting violence against Jews, the filmic portrayal of Jews during this time widely partook of various historical, sociopolitical, and cultural discourses inflected with notable anti-Jewish strains. What is most remarkable, however, is not so much that the filmic discourse of Weimar Germany incorporated anti-Jewish currents but how these currents were employed to convey the dominant notions of Jewishness.

Signifying a meeting ground for the Jewish city-dwellers, the streets in Wegener's film fuse with the masses, becoming a unified symbolic expression of the stylized setting (Fig. 2.6). The amorphous crowds of Jews, swarming through the various passages of the ghetto city, resemble the arteries of an urban body.[5] In an article from the *Neue Berliner Zeitung*, published just days before the debut of Wegener's film, Joseph Roth took notice of the stilted social perception of an overwhelming presence of *Ostjuden* (East European Jews) in Berlin: "On the whole, 50,000 human beings [i.e., Jews] have come to Germany after the war. It appears, of course, as if it were millions" (Roth 1920/1996, 78). It is precisely this sense that is so dramatically depicted in *The Golem*. Like much of the late-nineteenth- and early-twentieth-century reactionary discourse on Jewish identity, the Jews in *The Golem* are perceived as quintessentially urban. By combining the Jewish and urban metaphors, Wegener obscures the differentiation of the Jewish masses immersed in the animated quality of the city. "It is not Prague," he explains in a *Film-Kurier* interview introducing the film, "that my friend, the architect [Hans] Poelzig, has erected. Rather, it is a poem of a city [*Stadt-Dichtung*], a dream, an architectural paraphrase of the golem theme. These alleys and squares should not call to mind anything real; they should create the atmosphere in which the golem breathes" (Andrej 1920, 2). The art historian John Clarke suggests that the collaboration between Wegener and Poelzig, who at the time was most widely recognized for his design of the grand *Deutsches Schauspielhaus* in Berlin, was built on their "shared interests in the mysterious and the fantastic." As Clarke puts it, "Poelzig understood that Wegener did not want a re-creation of an actual medieval village, but rather buildings, streets, and interiors which were a formal equivalent of the ideas of mystery and the supernatural which underlie the film" (Clarke 1974–75, 115; cf. Schönemann 2003, 82–90). Given the remarkable visibility of the *Ostjuden* occupying the postwar German city (most prominently in the so-called *Scheunenviertel*, the Jewish district, of Berlin) and the eastern Jewish swarms occupying Poelzig's fantasy city, the critique of the historical problem, whether willful or inadvertent, cannot be overlooked. That Poelzig himself expressed the desire to make the ghetto buildings evoke a kind of Yiddish vernacular—his biographer, Theodor Heuss, asserts that Poelzig once claimed,

FIGURE 2.6 Production
still of the Golem superim-
posed over the ghetto masses.
Courtesy of the Filmmuseum
Berlin, Stiftung Deutsche
Kinemathek.

"wenigstens sollten die Häuser mauscheln" ("at least the buildings should speak
[Jewish] jargon")—only affirms the artfully constructed bond of Jew and city, a
bond that runs from nineteenth-century discourse through that of the postwar period (Heuss 1948, 69–70).[6]

Because in silent cinema nothing can speak in audible terms, everything must
speak in an alternative visual language. In the same 1920 *Film-Kurier* interview
with Wegener, the director proclaimed, "Film is not narrative; film is also not
drama; film is, above all, moving image" (Andrej 1920, 2). Just as Poelzig had hoped,
the buildings that were to communicate in Yiddish do conjure an air of *Yiddishkeit*.
The distorted shapes, dark cavities, and hunchbacked structures all serve to invoke
the visual characteristics of the figures who occupy their expressive space (this is
equally true in the publicity materials—posters and lobby cards—that Poelzig designed for the film). In her history of Weimar cinema Eisner underscores the fantastic atmosphere of the Jewish ghetto city in Wegener's *The Golem* and the integral relationship that the setting has to its inhabitants: "[T]he houses in the Prague
ghetto, which have sprouted like weeds, seem to have an insidious life of their own
'when the autumn evening mists stagnate in the streets and veil their imperceptible grimace.' In some mysterious way these streets contrive to abjure their life

and feelings during the daytime, and lend them instead to their inhabitants, those enigmatic creatures who wander aimlessly around feebly animated by an invisible magnetic current" (Eisner 1973, 23). The ghetto city, so Eisner argues, draws a portrait of the Jewish body defined in graphically urban terms. Poelzig's buildings convey the Jewishness of the ghetto as the organic space from which an imagined physiognomy emerges.

Small wonder, then, that the film's earliest critics both in Germany and abroad turned with such great frequency to the dynamic architectural mystique of Poelzig's ghetto city. Paul Westheim's review in the *Kunstblatt* recalled the atmospheric tension projected between the ghetto walls and the synagogue, conveying what he pronounces a "strongly expressive unity of scenery" (quoted in Greve 1976, 120), and *New York Times* correspondent Hermann Scheffauer observes, in his reflections on film space, an "eerie and grotesque suggestiveness" of the houses and streets in the Golem's city. "The will of this master architect," he continues, "animating façades into faces, insists that these houses are to speak in jargon—and gesticulate" (Scheffauer 1920, 84). More than a half century later, John Gross's reconsideration of the film declares the true costar of the film not Rabbi Löw but "the Prague ghetto, or rather the imaginary Prague ghetto dreamed up by Wegener's art director, Hans Poelzing [*sic*]—a fantastic world of crooked alleys, lopsided gables, pointed roofs, writhing architectural forms" (Gross 1988). The physiognomy of the Jew—a subject that at the time of the film's debut was being widely explored in literary, popular, and political writings—emerges in Wegener's film in the architectural construction of Jewishness. As attested to by the creators of the film and their critics alike, the contemporary face of the Jew emanates from the historical surface of the ghetto buildings.[7]

THE AFTERLIFE OF THE GOLEM

According to the advertisements published in the *Film-Kurier*, *The Golem* played in Berlin's Ufa theaters continuously for two straight months, attracting the crowds that would warrant such a robust run, before making its way across the rest of Germany and, ultimately, across the Atlantic. Wegener himself pronounced it a "powerful film, perhaps my most powerful" (Andrej 1920, 2). After the advent of sound in the early 1930s, he reportedly expressed hopes of reviving it as a talkie, at a time when the political climate would have no longer been so receptive to such ideas.[8] But Wegener's association with mysticism and magic, alchemy and mad science, exoticism and the esoteric, was forever sealed with *The Golem*. During the 1920s, a result in large part of the precedent he set in *The Golem*—and the extraordinary quality of his face, a "Mongolian face," in the words of Siegfried Kracauer, that "told of the strange visions that haunted him" (Kracauer 1947, 28)—he would play the title roles in Rex Ingram's MGM production *The Magician* (1926) and Gennaro Righelli's *Svengali* (1927), as well as the mad scientist in Henrik Galeen's *Alraune* (*Unholy Love*, 1928), while also directing and cowriting *Lebende Buddhas* (*Living Buddhas*, 1925), this last film another in a string of personal engagements with an exotic, non-German culture. Unlike many members of *The Golem*'s extended cast and crew (Ernst Deutsch, Karl Freund, Henrik Galeen, et al.), Wegener never migrated to Hollywood after the Nazi takeover but instead continued to work, mainly as an actor, in Germany throughout the late 1930s and 1940s (he died in Berlin in 1948). This has prompted some critics, such as Kracauer, himself an émigré from Hitler's Germany, to take a rather dismissive position vis-à-vis Wegener's career. To do so, however, denies the extraordinary formal influence of a film like *The Golem*, not only on subsequent Weimar-era productions but also on the horror genre as it was conceived in Hollywood from *Frankenstein* to *King Kong* and beyond.

Revisiting the film in 1934, a critic for the *New York Times* hailed it as "one of the outstanding events in the silent screen world back in 1921 [the year of its American release]" (Anon. 1934), and another critic, writing in 1937, drew the line between Wegener's production and the Frankenstein films that followed it, branding Wegener's film, in Hollywood shorthand, the tale of a "Karloffian clay image brought to life by an old rabbi in the Middle Ages" (Anon. 1937). *The Golem* would ultimately find a place in the pantheon of great German films of the Weimar era. But beyond that, the idea would be recast on American shores. In 1943 Henrik Galeen, the original scriptwriter of Wegener's *The Golem*, teamed together with fellow Weimar émigré Paul Falkenberg, who had worked as editor for Fritz Lang's *M*, to produce a new golem screenplay, one that would lend itself to the anti-Nazi war effort. The opening lines of their text read: "Did Hitler know what he was doing when he deported a helpless crowd of Jews, of all walks of life, from European nations to Chelm in the district of Lublin? Did he know at this very spot 350 years ago the Holy Rabbi Baalschem had brought to life an image of clay, called the GOLEM, in order to save his people from ruthless persecution? Did Hitler know that the now lifeless clay figure of his Golem was underneath the narrow streets where modern Jews were thronging this new Ghetto?" (Galeen and Falkenberg 1943, 97). Fritz Lang signed on as director, but the film was never made.

After the war, however, the golem story would ingratiate itself further into American popular culture. In the early 1970s, in the guise of the "Galactic Golem," it would make a cameo in the *Superman* comics series (Goldsmith 1981, 151–52), and by the late 1990s it formed the basis of an entire episode of the popular television show *The X-Files* (and, still later, made a memorable, unusually witty appearance in *The Simpsons*). Finally, in his novel *The Amazing Adventures of Kavalier & Clay* (2000), Michael Chabon blends several of the American precedents, including a subtle variation of the Galeen-Falkenberg collaboration, introducing a comic-book superhero—a savior of the Jews and Superman in one—known as the "Escapist," a name that has a powerful ring in the wartime setting. Perhaps Isaac Bashevis Singer was not wrong when, in the 1980s, he claimed, "I am not exaggerating when I say that the golem story appears less obsolete today than it seemed one hundred years ago" (Bilski 1988, 6).

NOTES

1. As Seth Wolitz has argued, "The German film audience in 1920 vaguely knew the contours of this motif and expected a *nouveau frisson* when the lights went out" (Wolitz 1983, 385).

2. Various versions of the golem legend have the word *aemaeth* written in Hebrew across the head of the monster. When the "alef" (the first vowel in the word) is removed, what is left is the word *maeth* (Hebrew for death). The dialectical tension between "truth," i.e., what the miracle-working rabbi may ostensibly be seeking, and "death," i.e., what the monster is capable of inflicting should he be unleashed by his master, undergirds the story in a number of significant ways (see Bilski 1988).

3. For further discussion of this problem regarding the "cinematic illusion" see Levin 1998, 122–23. I am indebted to Levin for calling my attention to this aspect in Wegener's film.

4. In Wegener's melodramatic subplot—the affair between the rabbi's daughter and the gentile messenger—the symbolic interaction is by no means as insignificant as critics like Eisner and Kracauer have suggested. To dismiss the subplot as merely a secondary parallel story line is to overlook the highly charged issue of miscegenation and the threat of the Jewess. As we might recall, it is Miriam's enticing gaze that lures Florian into her web. Next to Rabbi Löw, Miriam thus appears to be the most dangerous of the Jews occupying the ghetto. Moreover, as a type of modern Sulamith figure, her body imagery exudes a haunting dark eroticism specific not only to the film's story but also to the writings on Jewish sexuality and interracial relations around the year 1920 (for a further discussion see Gelbin 2003). In his recent analysis of the film, S. S. Prawer categorically refutes such a line of inquiry—what he calls a "newly fashionable reading" (40) of the film—downplaying the role of ethnic stereotyping and anti-Jewish sentiment altogether (Prawer 2005, 33–41).

5. In his essay on Poelzig's film sets for *The Golem*, Wolfgang Pehnt asserts that the ghetto buildings not only invoke a certain corporality but also "appeal to the spectator's own bodily senses, as if the drama of Rabbi Löw and his creation, the collapse of the royal palace and the burning of the ghetto take place not in some external location, but in the labyrinth of the human body itself" (Pehnt 1987, 85).

6. As Klaus Kreimeier has noted in his study of the Ufa film company, "Poelzig had constructed a medieval Prague of the imagination on a hermetically closed set consisting of fifty-four buildings, some of them life-sized, others in miniature. Tied in as they were

with the city walls and the synagogue and woven together with steps, fountains, and arches, they seemed parts of an organic whole" (Kreimeier 1996, 105).

7. According to the unpublished memoirs by Carl Boese, the architectural composition of the film was to produce "an entirely new face," one that reflects the mystique of the material. See his fragmentary manuscript on the *Golem* project, "Erinnerungen an die Entstehung" (Memories of the Genesis), contained in the Archiv der Stiftung Deutsche Kinemathek, currently housed in the Filmmuseum, Berlin.

8. According to a close friend of Wegener's, Kai Möller, "the golem topic was not popular on the eve of the Nazi regime" (Bilski 1988, 124).

REFERENCES

Adorno, Theodor W. 1984. *Aesthetic Theory*. Trans. C. Lenhardt. London: Routledge and Kegan Paul.

Andrej, 1920. "Ein Gespräch mit Paul Wegener" (A Conversation with Paul Wegener). *Film-Kurier*, October 29.

Anon. 1934. "A German Drama." *New York Times*, April 13, 25.

———. 1937. "Early German Films to Be Shown Tonight." *New York Times*, January 10, 42.

Aschheim, Steven E. 1982. *Brothers and Strangers: The East European Jew in German and German Jewish Consciousness, 1800–1922*. Madison: University of Wisconsin Press.

Bartov, Omer. 2005. *The "Jew" in Cinema: From* The Golem *to* Don't Touch My Holocaust. Bloomington: Indiana University Press.

Bilski, Emily, ed. 1988. *Golem! Danger, Deliverance, and Art*. New York: Jewish Museum.

Clarke, John R. 1974–75. "Expressionism in Film and Architecture: Hans Poelzig's Sets for Paul Wegener's *The Golem*." *Art Journal* 34, no. 2 (winter): 115–24.

Eisner, Lotte H. 1973. *The Haunted Screen: Expressionism in the German Cinema and the Influence of Max Reinhardt*. Trans. Roger Greaves. Berkeley: University of California Press.

Friedman, Lester D. 1984. "The Edge of Knowledge: Jews as Monsters/Jews as Victim." *MELUS* 11, no. 3 (autumn): 49–62.

Galeen, Henrik, and Paul Falkenberg. 1943. "The Golem." Repr. in *Sequenz: Film und Pädagogik* 7 (1994): 97–100. Special issue on *Der Golem*. Nancy, France: Goethe Institute.

Gelbin, Cathy. 2003. "Narratives of Transgression, from Jewish Folktales to German Cinema." *Kinoeye* 3, no. 11 (October): www.kinoeye.org/03/11/gelbin11.php (accessed November 6, 2006).

Goldsmith, Arnold L. 1981. *The Golem Remembered, 1909–1980: Variations of a Jewish Legend*. Detroit: Wayne State University Press.

Greve, Ludwig, ed. 1976. *Hätte ich das Kino! Die Schriftsteller und der Stummfilm*. Stuttgart: Ernst Klett.

Gross, John. 1988. "The Golem—As Medieval Hero, Frankenstein Monster, and Proto Computer." *New York Times*, December 4, H41.

Guerin, Frances. 2005. *A Culture of Light: Cinema and Technology in 1920s Germany*. Minneapolis: University of Minnesota Press.

Heuss, Theodor. 1948. *Hans Poelzig: Das Lebensbild eines deutschen Baumeisters* (*Hans Poelzig: The Portrait of a German Master Architect*). Tübingen: Ernst Wasmuth.

Koch, Gertrud. 1992. *Die Einstellung ist die Einstellung: Visuelle Konstruktionen des Judentums*. Frankfurt am Main: Suhrkamp.

Kreimeier, Klaus. 1996. *The Ufa Story: A History of Germany's Greatest Film Company, 1918–1945*. Trans. Robert Kimber and Rita Kimber. New York: Hill and Wang.

Ledig, Elfriede. 1992. "'Wer kann sagen, dass er über den Golem etas wisse . . . ?' Aspekte der Rekonstruktion des Paul-Wegner-Films *Der Golem: Wie er in die Welt kam* (1920)" ("Who Can Say That He Might Know Something About the Golem . . . ?" Aspects of the Reconstruction of Paul Wegener's film *The Golem: How He Came into the World*.) In *Sequenz: Film und Pädagogik* 7 (1994): 193–201. Special issue on *Der Golem*. Nancy, France: Goethe Institute.

Levin, David J. 1998. *Richard Wagner, Fritz Lang, and the Nibelungen: The Dramaturgy of Disavowal*. Princeton, NJ: Princeton University Press.

Manvell, Roger. 1973. *Masterworks of the German Cinema*. New York: Harper & Row.

Meyrink, Gustav. 1995. *The Golem*. Trans. Mike Mitchell. London: Dedalus Books. (Orig. pub. 1915.)

Pehnt, Wolfgang. 1987. "La porta sul prodigioso: Le architetture di Hans Poelzig per il film *Der Golem*" (A Window into the Inexplicable: The Architecture by Hans Poelzig for the Film *The Golem*). *Domus* 21 (November): 83–85.

Prawer, S. S. 2005. *Between Two Worlds: The Jewish Presence in German and Austrian Film, 1910–1933*. New York: Berghahn Books.

Roth, Joseph. 1920/1996. "Flüchtlinge aus dem Osten" (Refugees from the East). *Neue Berliner Zeitung*, October 20, 1920. Repr. in Michael Bienert, *Joseph Roth in Berlin*. Cologne: Kiepenheuer & Witsch, 1996.

Scheffauer, Hermann. 1920. "The Vivifying of Space." Repr. in *Introduction to the Art of the Movies*, ed. Lewis Jacobs, 76–85. New York: Noonday, 1960.

Scholem, Gershom. 1971. "The Golem of Prague and the Golem of Rehovot." In *The Messianic Idea in Judaism*, 335–40. New York: Schocken.

Schönemann, Heide. 2003. *Paul Wegener: Frühe Moderne im Film*. Stuttgart: Edition Axel Menges.

Wegener, Paul. 1920. "Die Zukunft des Films" (The Future of Film). In *Stimmen eines Jahrhunderts 1888–1990: Deutsche Autobiographien, Tagebücher, Bilder und Briefe*, ed. Andreas Lixl-Purcell, 118–21. Fort Worth, TX: Holt, Rinehart and Winston, 1990.

——. 1921. *Der Golem: Wie er in die Welt kam: Eine Geschichte in fünf Kapiteln*. Berlin: August Scherl.

Weitz, Eric D. 2007. *Weimar Germany: Promise and Tragedy*. Princeton, NJ: Princeton University Press.

Wolitz, Seth L. 1983. "*The Golem* (1920): An Expressionist Treatment." In *Passion and Rebellion: The Expressionist Heritage*, ed. Stephen Eric Bronner and Douglas Kellner, 384–97. New York: Universe.

MOVIES, MONEY, AND MYSTIQUE

JOE MAY'S EARLY WEIMAR BLOCKBUSTER,
THE INDIAN TOMB (1921)

CHRISTIAN ROGOWSKI

August 25, 1921, was no ordinary day.[1] German newspapers reported riots in India, where Muslims clashed with Hindus in Malabar. On a happier note, representatives of the American and German governments were to meet in Berlin that day to sign a peace treaty.[2] Although the fighting had ended with the armistice of November 11, 1918, the United States and Germany were, up to that point, technically still at war. Despite his busy schedule on such an auspicious day, Friedrich Ebert, the president of the fledgling Weimar Republic, found time in the morning to visit a different kind of India, where troubles of a different sort were brewing. Accompanied by his wife and a host of officials, Ebert paid a visit to the gigantic film lot at Woltersdorf, near Berlin, where director and producer Joe May was busy working on what was modestly called, "the world's greatest film," a two-part feature entitled *Das indische Grabmal* (*The Indian Tomb*) (Anon. 1921a; Anon. 1921b). May proudly presented to Ebert and his entourage of dignitaries the fabulous sets that sought to recreate the immeasurable splendor of India; the "cast of thousands" of extras whom he controlled with military precision; an illustrious group of top-notch movie stars like May's wife, Mia, Conrad Veidt, and Paul Richter; and an impressive array of animals—alongside countless horses, there were tigers, alligators, elephants, and peacocks, hired out from the Hamburg company of Hagenbeck, the Berlin zoo, and circus Sarrasani of Dresden (Ramm 1997, 53–54). Ebert had visited a movie set only once before during his presidency: in the fall of 1920 he paid a widely publicized visit to Berlin Tempelhof, where Ernst Lubitsch was filming *Anna Boleyn*, a lavish historical costume drama featuring two superstars of early Weimar cinema: Henny Porten (in the title role) and Emil Jannings (as Henry VIII). Was Ebert seeking another photo opportunity to benefit from the glamour derived from an association with movie stars? Or was he throwing his weight behind the impressive efforts of the German film industry? Why would a political leader of Ebert's stature be interested in the production of mass cultural myths, be they set in Tudor England or in a mythically remote India? What was it that turned ambitious projects such as those of Lubitsch and May into matters of national importance?

While Lubitsch continues to be recognized as one of the master filmmakers of early Weimar German cinema, primarily on account of his masterful comedies, for a long time Joe May's name, and his filmic work, had been all but forgotten. It was not until the early 1990s, when well-preserved copies of some of his major films were restored and rereleased, first at festivals devoted to film history and later to a general audience, that the importance of his contribution to the nascent Weimar film culture could be reassessed. The tremendous early success of May's big-budget spectacles attests to his business savvy and his knack for knowing what audiences wanted, later earning him the moniker "the Steven Spielberg of the Weimar Republic" (Cornelius 1990). The years 1918 to 1923 are characterized by an explosion of creative talent, not only in the well-known art films by acknowledged masters such as F. W. Murnau, Fritz Lang, and G. W. Pabst but also in genre films explicitly and unabashedly directed at a broad general audience by lesser-known directors and producers like Joe May. Today we are fortunate that his two-part epic fantasy adventure *The Indian Tomb* is available on DVD in a beautifully restored version that gives us some idea of the extraordinary visual quality and technical sophistication of a noncanonical silent film from the early Weimar period.

In what follows I would like to place May's exotic adventure film in the overall context of the history of silent film in Germany before and up to the early 1920s. Developments in the interrelated spheres of film production, distribution, and exhibition provide the backdrop for May's career as a filmmaker (comprising the roles of scriptwriter, producer, and director). I will also address the potential appeal of films like *The Indian Tomb* to a contemporary mass audience by highlighting how May's adventure drama is embedded in a variety of cultural and historical contexts. To do this, I will approach the film primarily as a commodity manufactured for an audience of consumers (rather than as a work of art that seeks to convey a particular message encoded in its story line, its thematic motifs, and its formal composition). A historically and aesthetically informed approach addresses genre films as products of modern mass culture. I hope to show that Weimar cinema consisted not only of the widely recognized canonical masterpieces—art films in the narrow sense—but also of an extraordinarily rich and varied culture of mainstream spectacles—populist and popular "movies" that deserve to be remembered and appreciated on their own terms.

The history of Joe May and his various business ventures provides a vivid illustration of the opportunities and challenges that presented themselves to the German and Austrian film industry in the imperial years, as well as into the early years of the Weimar Republic. Born Julius Otto Mandl in 1880 in Vienna into one of the wealthiest families of the Habsburg Empire, May led a playboy's existence, squandering the family inheritance. He studied at trade schools in Leipzig and Berlin and tried his hand at a number of odd jobs (such as running a racehorse stable and working as a car salesman). In 1902 he married operetta singer and actress Hermine Pfleger (1884–1980), who bore him a daughter, Eva, some seven weeks after the wedding. Adopting his wife's stage name—she called herself "Mia May"—he followed her to an engagement to Hamburg. There, in 1911, May made his directorial debut, with a two-reel introductory film, *Die Fahrt nach Hamburg* (*The Trip to Hamburg*), for a revue entitled *Rund um die Alster* (*Around the River Alster*) that featured his wife. In 1912 the Mays moved to Berlin, where Joe May found a job with a small company called Continental Filmkunst, writing scripts and beginning to direct films, including melodramas starring his wife. In 1913 he launched an interesting marketing experiment with "May's Preisrätsel im Film"—short feature films that contained riddles for which the audience could win prizes if they solved them before the next episode came out (six such two- to three-reel films were released) (Bock and Lenssen 1991).

Until the outbreak of World War I, the German film industry held a market share of only some 10 to 15 percent against foreign imports, primarily from France, followed by America, as well as films from Italy and Scandinavia (Müller 1990). The market was primarily driven by the exhibition sector, with most cinema chains owned by foreign suppliers. Exhibitors demanded vast numbers of films to satisfy the craving for novelty among their audiences, turning films into cheap commodities with a very short shelf-life. In this situation German production companies found it difficult to compete with foreign imports that could be offered cheaply on the German market since they had already recouped their production costs at home. Until about 1911, films in Germany were sold to exhibitors directly, who naturally had an inclination to keep prices down, favoring foreign products. The following years saw a fundamental structural shift that put the German film on a sounder economic footing: cinema programs evolved from motley assortments of disparate short novelty items to the presentation of full-length narrative feature films; new, purpose-built, large and lavishly decorated picture palaces appealed to a wider cross-section of the public. In the wake of the *Monopolfilm* booking system (which forced exhibitors to purchase blocks of films in return for a "monopoly," i.e., guaranteed exclusive rights to certain major films in a given region), a star system emerged that helped the German film industry grow and consolidate its domestic market share. The result was a "first flourishing of a narrative star-and-genre-cinema" in Germany between 1911 and 1913 (Elsaesser 1996, 25).

During the war, films from "enemy countries" were banned in Germany. Encouraged by the vacuum created in the absence of French and British, later also

Italian and American, imports in a market hungry for new product, dozens of new production companies popped up. The easiest and most efficient manner of production was the use of established, often foreign, formulas, based either on a filmic genre (such as the detective thriller or crude comedies derived from operettas) or on a star persona. Joe May was among the most successful pioneers in the arena of such *Serienfilme*. From 1914 onward he directed and produced a popular series of crime thrillers set in Anglo-American milieus, featuring Ernst Reicher as the savvy detective Stuart Webbs. May served a short stint in the Austrian army during World War I, after which disagreements with Continental and Reicher prompted him in 1915 to set up his own production company, May Film GmbH, where he launched two different types of serials: the "Joe Deebs Adventures" of crime thrillers and a "Mia May Series" of melodramas and comedies that consolidated his wife's status as one of the prime movie stars of the Wilhelmine period. May produced both serials but shared directorial duties with others, including Harry Piel and Paul Leni.

Throughout the war, the German-speaking market was flooded with such low-budget, formulaic *Serienfilme*, churned out by a multitude of companies at a breathtaking pace. For instance, at the peak of Henny Porten's popularity a new film starring the matronly German diva was released roughly every four to six weeks into an apparently insatiable market (Müller 1990, 104). The serials based on a fictional persona anticipated certain aspects of the franchise films of today, such as James Bond movies: the role of Joe Deebs, for instance, was shared in successive seasons by Max Landa, Harry Liedtke, and Heinrich Schroth. The serials centering on famous actors also indicate that, even before the outbreak of the war, the German film industry had clearly adopted an American-style star system (complete with fan press, clubs, collectable picture postcards, and other publicity accoutrements). Reicher, who after Joe May's departure continued the Stuart Webbs franchise, was one of the top male stars, alongside Landa, Liedtke, and Piel. More important, a significant number of female movie stars emerged during this period: besides Danish actress Asta Nielsen, Henny Porten, and Mia May, there were lesser-known and now largely forgotten stars such as Ellen Richter, Lu Synd, Wanda Treumann, all of whom spearheaded their own serials.

If the final years before the war had seen the German film industry become a profitable industry, the war itself helped consolidate and protect the domestic market for German products and even to expand it through extension into occupied territories. The German government also recognized the propagandistic potential of film, not only through the control of journalistic coverage of the war through weekly newsreels but also through ostensibly apolitical quality feature films that would project a benevolent image of Germans both at home and abroad. The military leadership believed that this propagandistic purpose could be best accomplished by pooling resources into a large-scale corporation under the covert control of the government. In the fall of 1917, as the result of secret deals between

the military and the film industry, three major German production companies—
Nordisk-Film, Messter-Film, and Paul Davidson's PAGU—were merged into the
Universum-Film Aktiengesellschaft (Ufa), a stock company of unrivaled size and
resources. Although the deal was kept secret and the constituent companies continued to exist as semi-independent brand names, the resulting large film company
created an imbalance in the German market: Ufa began to dominate the German
market not so much through film production but through control of the distribution and exhibition sectors. Ufa emerged as the one large-scale studio system in
the world that could potentially rival the major Hollywood studios. In February
1918 May was compelled to sell parts of his company May-Film to Ufa, exchanging
part of his independence as a producer for access to the cinema chains controlled
by Ufa. The roster of projects for Ufa's inaugural 1918–19 season gives an interesting picture of the output in audience-oriented films in Germany during the transition from the *Kaiserreich* to the Weimar Republic: PAGU was to contribute four
melodramas with Pola Negri, six comedies with Ossi Oswalda, two comedies with
Ernst Lubitsch, and two fantasy films with Paul Wegener; there were to be eight
comedies with Henny Porten from Messter Film; Joe May's company was to supply
two adventure films and four to six romantic Mia May films; the program was to be
rounded off with six detective films with Lotte Neumann and six comedies with
Fern Andra (Bock and Töteberg 1992, 35).

The end of the war, with the collapse of the German and the Austro-Hungarian
empires, left the film industry in German-speaking Europe in a peculiar situation;
with the artificial protection removed, the disparity between disproportionately
large production facilities and a drastically shrunken domestic market became
evident: with the Treaty of Versailles Germany lost around a quarter of its territories, primarily Alsace-Lorraine and areas in the East that were ceded to Poland; the
foreign market was largely blocked off by way of import embargoes now imposed
on German products. Moreover, the German film industry was structurally weak-
ened by the odd juxtaposition of dozens of small, often underfunded, production
companies against one major player, Ufa. Midsize companies like Erich Pommer's
Decla and Joe May's May-Film found themselves faced with multiple challenges:
domestically they had to fight the potentially overpowering competition of Ufa;
internationally they had to overcome either direct embargoes or lingering anti-
German resentment. The American film industry, in turn, had used the war to
consolidate its influence abroad, primarily in Europe. To survive, midsize German
film companies had to create films that would appeal both to a domestic audience
(against Ufa and a host of smaller competitors) and to an international audience
(one primarily attracted by the increasing predominance of Hollywood).

Joe May confronted the challenge by shifting the focus of his energies from the
cheap serial films that had little if any chance of success in the international arena
to ambitious large-scale productions that sought to dazzle domestic and interna-

tional audiences alike: with the lavish historical costume extravaganza entitled
Veritas vincit (*Truth Prevails*, 1919), May skillfully emulated foreign models such as
the Italian monumental historical epic *Cabiria* (Giovanni Pastrone, 1914), as well as
the episodic structure of the American costume drama *Intolerance* (D. W. Griffith,
1916). Clocking in at around three and a half hours, May's colossal film featured Mia
May in three historically distinct episodes (set in ancient Rome, Renaissance Italy,
and the present) and presented a story of redemption and revenge. May spent unheard of amounts of money on the production of the film and experimented with
innovative advertising strategies: before the film premiered, on April 4, 1919, in Berlin, at four first-run movie theaters simultaneously, thousands of advertising leaflets were dropped on the city from airplanes, and billboards all over the city were
plastered with the film's triumphant title. May's gamble paid off: the film became
a blockbuster success and enabled him to buy back parts of his company from Ufa,
yet Ufa retained a claim on the profits for his films in exchange for an arrangement
with Ufa's distribution and exhibition facilities (Kreimeier 1991).

May's next project was, if anything, even more ambitious: combining the *Se-
rienfilm* format with the monumental blockbuster genre, he launched *Die Herrin der Welt* (*Mistress of the World*), a series of eight full-length films that could be
viewed independently but that were also held together by an overriding narrative
surrounding a young woman's quest for rehabilitation. Even before the series was
released, critics proclaimed that the large-scale project would enable the German
film industry to succeed in the "battle on the world market" ("Kampf auf dem
Weltmarkt" 1919). Indeed, after the first part premiered in Berlin on December 5,
1919, the series broke all box-office records and was hailed by critics and audiences
as a major breakthrough.[3]

Joe May was not the only one to opt for big-budget spectacles in hopes of appealing to domestic and international audiences alike. Ernst Lubitsch, who during
the war had emerged as the undisputed master of German film comedy, turned to
historical costume dramas and achieved international success. His *Madame Dubarry*, released in the United States in December 1919 under the title *Passion*, was the
film that broke the American embargo against German film. Set in prerevolution-
ary eighteenth-century France, the film chronicles the story of a pretty milliner
(Pola Negri) who becomes the mistress of King Louis XV (Emil Jannings). It was
not without irony that the first postwar German film to become an undisputed
commercial and critical success abroad would be one set in Versailles, the very
place in which the harsh sanctions imposed on Germany after its defeat in the war
had been negotiated. The international success of the film was perceived by many
German critics as a kind of symbolic rehabilitation of the German nation after the
humiliating defeat. The Germans had, in a sense, successfully appropriated French
history to their own advantage. One critic, for instance, noted that Lubitsch's film

amounted to "a German victory" that would compel the French to concede "that a defeated, impoverished, exploited, and insulted Germany has passionately thrown herself into film production, thereby creating a means through which to conquer the world market."[4] To many Germans it seemed that Germany was redeeming herself, at least in one arena, by outdoing the French and by beating the Americans at their own game—making quality movies.

Alongside the patriotic fervor of the hopes that were pinned on big-budget film production, there were some very practical business considerations that prompted German filmmakers to pursue the strategy of making large-scale genre films aimed at both a domestic and an international audience. To recuperate production costs, German films needed to make money abroad, even though during the first few years after the war, film production in Germany was relatively cheap: with the return of discharged soldiers from the front, unemployment was high, resulting in masses of people that could be hired at minimum cost as extras in lavish spectacles. Moreover, the lingering inflation—partly a result of irresponsible governmental wartime spending—rendered the German mark cheap, even before the onset of hyperinflation in 1923, but also put at an advantage those filmmakers who had access to convertible foreign currency as a more stable source of revenue. For a while it seemed to make sense that those filmmakers who were willing to invest large sums of money into big spectacles were most likely to earn the francs, U.S. dollars, and British pounds that could be reinvested into new projects. Yet conditions were anything but stable: in 1920, German film production peaked with an output of 510 full-length features, a phenomenal number that could not be sustained in a shrinking and bitterly contested market. The number plummeted to 370 films in 1921, the decline continuing—with ups and downs—to 114 films in 1933 (Prinzler 1995, 53).

As Thomas J. Saunders (1994, 89) has noted, the main question confronting the German film industry in the immediate postwar period was "whether to pursue a national or international motion picture identity." Self-consciously experimental and artistic films such as Robert Wiene's *Das Cabinet des Dr. Caligari* (*The Cabinet of Dr. Caligari*, 1920), produced by Erich Pommer's Decla, sought to overcome anti-German resentment abroad by appealing to traditions of German culture that had a largely positive connotation, including the somber mysticism of early-nineteenth-century romantics and the rebellious energy of the expressionist movement that had flourished in the visual arts, in poetry, and in the theater from about 1905 into World War I. A contemporary trade magazine, *Film-Kurier*, succinctly highlights the choice available to German filmmakers of the time, with the formulaic question, "*Caligari* oder *Herrin der Welt*?" ("*Caligari* or *Mistress of the World*?") (R. P. 1920). The unnamed critic argues that the two near simultaneous releases represent two different options for the German film industry in its effort to succeed in the international arena: one could produce either low-budget but artistically ambitious expressionist films that banked on the prestige of highbrow avant-garde traditions, or one could produce *Prunkfilme*, lavish big-budget spectacles in various guises (as historical costume drama, exotic adventure film, crime thriller, or fairy-tale fantasy) that appealed to a more general audience across different nations on account of superb production values.

The majority of German filmmakers opted for such genre films based on international formulas. Economic and political considerations led Lubitsch, May, and countless others to downplay the national origins of their products. With the exception of some melodramas and comedies, most early Weimar genre films go to great lengths to camouflage their German origins: an Anglo-American milieu predominates in crime thrillers and Teutonic westerns; exotic adventure films were set in Africa or various Asian countries, including China and Japan; fantasy films were set in the Oriental world of the Middle East; historical costume dramas took spectators to the aristocratic world of nineteenth-century Europe, medieval or Renaissance Italy, sixteenth-century England, or even into the biblical past.[5]

Even in most genre films with a contemporary setting, the characters were not identified as German but rather as British, American, or Scandinavian. Foreign audiences could thus easily be led to believe that the films they were seeing did not come from Germany. Domestic audiences, in turn, had the pleasure of identifying either with representatives of neutral countries (such as Mia May's Danish Maud Gregaards in *Mistress of the World*) or those of victorious Western nations (such as the British architect Herbert Rowland in Joe May's *The Indian Tomb*). By unabashedly identifying with the "good guys," German audiences could feel compensated for the shameful humiliation of Versailles. At a time of extreme economic deprivation, with crippling reparations payments, food shortages due to trade embargoes, increasing unemployment and mounting inflation, the lavish sets and extravagant costumes, together with exotic locales and exciting adventures, appealed to the desire to indulge in visions of plenty, at times even of excess. In a situation of profound disorientation after the collapse of old power structures and the ensuing chaos, when street battles raged, attempted coups d'état from the extreme left and the extreme right hampered Germany's first effort at democracy, and political assassinations shook the nation, these films offered a reassuring vision of moral and political order restored. It is perhaps no wonder, then, that German audiences, faced with the pressures of an increasingly urbanized and industrialized modernity, welcomed the opportunity to escape into fantasy worlds of easy erotic, economic, and moral fulfillment.

For a while the strategy seemed to pay off, as German films could be produced at a relatively low cost for a rapidly declining mark and sold cheaply against hard currency on the international market. From 1920 onward the commercial success and artistic quality of German films caused a considerable degree of nervousness among the American film industry. One company in particular, Famous Play-ers–Lasky (Paramount), in response to the influx of German films into the United States in the wake of Lubitsch's *Madame Dubarry* and Wiene's *Caligari*, bought up the rights to a substantial number of German films. These German films were often reedited and shortened to make them conform to American tastes.[6] Sometimes American film companies sought control over German films to prevent them from competing with their own products by taking them out of circulation and shelv-ing them: both Joe May's *Mistress of the World* and *The Indian Tomb* were shown in truncated versions on limited runs in New York City, to scathing reviews, only to disappear from American screens altogether.[7]

Another strategy American companies employed was to seek contact with Ger-man filmmakers and actors who were dissatisfied with their situation at Ufa and to lure them away into collaborative German-American deals. In April 1921 Famous Players set up a company based in Berlin to rival Ufa on the German market and bypass German import restrictions on foreign films: the *Europäische Film Allianz* (EFA or European Film Alliance), which included renegade Ufa greats such as pro-ducer Paul Davidson and director-producers Ernst Lubitsch and Joe May. May, who had started preproduction on *The Indian Tomb* in the spring of 1920, right after the phenomenal success of *Mistress of the World*, eagerly sought financial support from his American partners in his effort to escape the stranglehold of the Ufa com-pany. It was with money from its German-American rival, EFA, that May was able to embark on his most ambitious project yet, *The Indian Tomb*.

May's monumental epic is thus both a German and an American film: it is a large-scale blockbuster that seeks to efface its German origins and aims at domes-tic and international audiences alike; it does so with the help of American financial backing and by emulating some of the narrative formulas developed by Hollywood. Like the second film financed by EFA, Ernst Lubitsch's *Das Weib des Pharao* (trans-lated as *The Loves of Pharaoh*, 1922), it is typical of German commercial genre films of the early Weimar period—paradoxically—by trying to be as American as possi-ble. Yet while Lubitsch would go on to master the American formulas (and be lured to Hollywood in 1922), May's *The Indian Tomb*, in its mixture of grand ambitions and often embarrassing clichés, in many ways represents a not entirely successful, uneasy compromise.

With the money from his American backers, as well as credits supplied by the German government, May set out to create an unparalleled vision of India in his company's studios in the Berlin suburb of Weißensee, as well as on a gigantic out-door lot on the shores of a lake at Woltersdorf, a popular small weekend resort a few miles southeast of Berlin. The site, which May's company had purchased for the shooting of *Mistress of the World*, contained a former lime quarry that, at least to German audiences, looked sufficiently exotic to stand in for all sorts of foreign locales. The choice of India as the setting for May's next large-scale project appears as a logical step: in his previous eight-part blockbuster May had sent his "mistress of the world" all over the globe, from Europe to China, then to Africa, America, and back to Europe, and it stands to reason that May would turn his attention to India as an unexplored exotic locale. Yet there are other, more culturally significant, reasons that moved May to set his next ambitious adventure extravaganza in India.

From the eighteenth century onward, when information on India first became readily available to a German reading public, Germans laid claim to a special affinity with the mysterious country in the East. It was philosopher Johann Gottfried Herder who, in his critique of Enlightenment rationalism, held up India's mystical spirituality as a counterexample to the dry rationality of the West. The romantics picked up on this anti-Enlightenment stance, at the same time intensifying serious scholarly engagement with Indian culture, language, and traditions: the poet Novalis explored Indian mysticism; philologists like the brothers Jacob and Wilhelm Grimm pioneered the study of Sanskrit, finding commonalities between Eastern and Western languages, now known as Indo-European languages; and literary critic and philosopher August Wilhelm Schlegel established the first chair in Indology at a European university, in Bonn, Germany, in 1818.

German interest in India and its spiritual and philosophical traditions continued throughout the nineteenth century, culminating in the appropriation of Eastern thought by the various *Lebensreform* (life reform) initiatives around 1900. In a quest for alternatives to alienating, industrialized mass society, increasing numbers of disenchanted city dwellers turned to Indian culture for reorientation and spiritual renewal. Many, like novelist Hermann Hesse (1877–1962), actually traveled to India (in 1911), anticipating the quests of hippies in the 1960s, who were likewise to flock to ashrams and bhagwans to seek spiritual enlightenment at the feet of Indian gurus. India, with its alleged spirituality, it seems, helped Germans articulate their misgivings about a modernity that they experienced as oppressive and soulless.

In film, representations of India had begun with documentaries and newsreel footage, followed by fictional narratives such as L. A. Winkler's *Lotus, die Tempeltänzerin* (*Lotus, the Temple Dancer*, 1913) and Paul Wegener's *Der Yoghi* (*The Yogi*, 1916) that reinforced the image of India as a land of spirituality and exotic allure. As early as 1917, film critics noted a veritable boom of German films set in India (Schultze 1997). That same year, Thea von Harbou's novel *Das indische Grabmal*, which would later provide the basis of May's ambitious film project, was serialized in a Berlin magazine. May was quick to respond to this interest in things Indian, when in the summer of 1918 he embarked on his first monumental film, *Veritas vincit*: the film's three episodes are held together by the character of an Indian mystic, who enables the contemporary heroine, countess Helen (Mia May), to experience the power of truth over lies in a journey into the past: in the mystic's palace she confronts a mirror that allows her to experience her earlier incarnations, as Helena in ancient Rome and as Ellinor in Renaissance Italy. The Indian mystic was played by Bernhard Goetzke, who would later play Yogi Ramigani in *The Indian Tomb*. Likewise, Conrad Veidt, May's immeasurably rich Rajah Ayan, had in 1917 appeared—alongside Goetzke—as an Indian priest in Robert Wiene's *Furcht* (*Fear*) and in 1918 as Dinja, the mysterious Indian in a fantasy adventure film entitled *Das Rätsel von Bangalor* (*The Mystery of Bangalore*, Alexander von Altaffy and Paul Leni). Both Goetzke and Veidt also appeared in *Das Geheimnis von Bombay* (*The Secret of Bombay*, Artur Holz, 1920), which featured Lil Dagover (who had shared the screen with Veidt in *The Cabinet of Dr. Caligari*) in the double role of an Italian singer and Indian dancer. More recently, there had been an Indian episode in *Das Brillantenschiff* (*The Diamond Ship*), the second part of Fritz Lang's two-part crime thriller, *Die Spinnen* (*The Spiders*, 1920), which featured a mysterious yogi named All habmah (Kabatek 2003).

In the summer of 1921, as May was shooting his film in and around Berlin, German enthusiasm for Indian culture reached fever pitch when Rabindranath Tagore (1861–1941), the Bengali poet who had been awarded the Nobel Prize in Literature in 1913, visited Germany. His lecture at the University of Berlin on June 2, 1921, turned into a triumph, followed by a much-publicized invitation to the School of Wisdom at Darmstadt, where Hermann Count Keyserling (1880–1946), a German aristocrat turned advocate of Eastern spirituality, had organized a "Tagore Week" (from June 9 through 14, 1921) in honor of Tagore and the spiritual legacy he represented. By the early 1920s, India, it seems, was on everybody's minds in Germany, ranging from clichéd pulp fiction to serious intellectual engagement with a complex cultural tradition. Joe May, with his keen instincts for popular tastes, could count on a great deal of interest in things Indian and things mystical among a German audience.

The Indian Tomb brought together a team that would later write German film history: it marked the first collaboration between Fritz Lang, then Joe May's assistant, and novelist Thea von Harbou. Since von Harbou was as yet inexperienced in the writing of film scripts, Lang was assigned to help her turn her serialized novel of 1917 into a movie scenario. The two would later marry and go on to create some of the most remarkable films of the era, including *Dr. Mabuse* (1922), *Die Nibelungen* (*The Nibelungs*, 1924), *Metropolis* (1927), and *M* (1931). Originally, Lang was supposed to direct the two-part epic, yet Joe May himself decided to take over, presumably because he felt the project was too precious to be entrusted to his assistant.

As was his wont, May exploited the interest in India to the full in generating a great deal of publicity before the release of the film and in running a skillful advertising campaign. Von Harbou's novel was republished in 1921 to coincide with the release of the film. Trade publications and popular press alike featured news of unheard of superlatives: the upcoming film, it was noted, featured some two thousand extras in addition to a cast of well-known popular actors; for five months, a staff and crew of three hundred was busy building the sets (at a cost of 3.5 million marks) and sewing thousands of costumes (for half a million marks); hiring and maintaining a veritable menagerie of animals from the zoo and circus cost a reported 1.5 million marks. May had a reputation as a notorious perfectionist, accepting nothing less than the best and sparing no expense or effort until the scenes he shot were exactly as he had intended them. There were reports of boats being destroyed by renegade alligators; dozens of chickens lost their lives during rehearsals for the scene in which British officer MacAllen is thrown to the tigers—since May was not satisfied with the manner in which the tigers, lured by offscreen chickens, pounced toward the camera.[8]

For months Joe May ruled like a military despot over a gigantic makeshift tent city that housed his cast and crew at Woltersdorf. Day in and day out he could be seen on horseback charging across the terrain, dispatching messengers here and there, directing outdoor scenes by shouting into his megaphone or gesticulating wildly to get the cast and the extras into action. May's self-professed aim was to combine American largesse with German thoroughness in his approach to directing (Dahlke and Karl 1993, 61). His ambition, bordering on megalomania, and his relentless pursuit of perfection down to the smallest conceivable detail put a tremendous pressure on finances: each day of shooting was rumored to cost 230,000 marks. Three years earlier, May's first monumental film, *Veritas vincit*, in its entirety had been budgeted at 500,000 marks but ended up costing nearly twice as much (930,000 marks). With *The Indian Tomb* the budget had been generously projected at 15 million marks, yet in the summer of 1921 May had already exceeded that projection by 3 million, and there was no end in sight. The two-part film would ultimately cost an estimated 24 million marks, an unheard of sum at the time, even taking the gradual devaluation of the German mark into account. Compared to such expenses, the eight-part series *Mistress of the World*, at a cost of around 5.8 million marks, had been a veritable bargain.

In this context it becomes clear that when President Ebert visited May's set in August 1921, it was not only a question of the figurehead of the Weimar Republic showing an interest in the prowess of a well-known filmmaker or of Ebert showing his support for the efforts of the German film industry to conquer the export market. Ebert and his entourage of government officials clearly also wanted to see where the credits that the German government had issued to May were going and to put pressure on May to display greater fiscal responsibility. May managed to impress his visitors, proudly displaying the sumptuous sets and skillfully stirring patriotic sentiments. Ebert and his officials left with the sense that their money had, after all, been prudently invested.

Things were not quite so harmonious with May's American business partners. Escalating production costs, the political and economic instability of Germany, and the increasing devaluation of the German mark during the early stages of inflation put a damper on the EFA arrangement. The optimism with which EFA had entered the German film market in the spring of 1921 waned quickly. May, ever the shrewd businessman, reacted without pause: even before *The Indian Tomb* was released in the fall of that year, he pulled out of the deal, although this forced him back into an uneasy arrangement with his former partners at Ufa. EFA, the international alliance initiated by Americans eager to cash in on the phenomenal success of Lubitsch's *Madame Dubarry* by co-opting major German filmmakers, folded a little more than a year later, in the fall of 1922, leading a German critic to quip sardonically that it had been the ill-fated progeny of a "liaison between Madame Dubarry and the exchange rate" (Schwarzschild 1922, 1612).

Die Sendung des Yoghi (*The Mission of the Yogi*), part 1 of *The Indian Tomb*, opened on October 22, 1921, at the Ufa-Palast am Zoo, Berlin's largest and most prestigious picture palace. Part 2, entitled *Der Tiger von Eschnapur* (translated as *The Tiger of Bengal*), followed a month later, on November 19. The premiere of a major motion picture in those days was a glamorous social occasion, a glittering red-carpet event. The invited audience of dignitaries, celebrities, and representatives of the press were expected to appear in tuxedos and evening gowns. Outside, the movie theater would be adorned with displays associated with the respective film's setting, sometimes the entire facade would be turned into a replica of the movie set (see Ward 2001). Inside, foyers and hallways would be decorated to reflect the world of the film, often incorporating actual props or pieces of the sets from the film, together with flowers and exotic plants. Costumed ushers would welcome the guests and hand out special program booklets, containing lists of credits, plot synopses, and other information, as well as pictures from the film. Sometimes the stars of the film would present a short introduction or perform a song or dance before the start of the feature. After the screening, of course, all those who bore major responsibility for the film would take their bows in front of the audience.

First-run picture palaces usually employed a full-scale orchestra that would perform a live score specifically composed for any major release. In other cinemas there would be a small band, usually composed of a violinist, pianist, and small rhythm section, that would perform an adapted version of the original score. In smaller houses and in the provinces, however, musical accompaniment sometimes consisted of little more than a piano player improvising with a number of musical set pieces (such as snippets from operas and classical compositions) to match each particular mood or situation on the screen. A composer named Wilhelm Löwitt wrote an ambitious orchestral score for *The Indian Tomb* that was much praised in the critical press. Unfortunately, the score is lost, and the music we now have on the DVD release, while not without its own merit, is at best a pale reflection of the impact of the original music to May's epic double feature.

Another tradition worth noting is the practice of tinting particular scenes in films, either by dipping the film stock in paint or by coloring the film strip by hand. This was done to enhance the atmosphere or to indicate time and location. Contemporary audiences understood that, for instance, a golden tint indicated an indoor scene set at night (imitating artificial gas lights) or that a blue tint showed that a night scene took place outdoors (mimicking natural moonlight). The DVD version of May's film retains some remnants of such tinting, although probably not to the original extent. This may explain why some night scenes that may appear too unrealistically bright to our eyes, would have looked perfectly convincing to contemporary audiences. The scene in which rebellious natives burn down the hut of British officer MacAllen would most certainly have been tinted red, the color connoting fire.[9] Even the most painstakingly restored DVD thus presents only an approximation of the actual moviegoing experience afforded a contemporary audience. At the very least it is important to remember that as much as silent films never actually were totally silent, black-and-white films were often not merely black and white.

Part 1 of *The Indian Tomb* opens with a prologue, preceded by titles that remind the viewer of the long-standing image of India as the country of mysticism and mystique. The reminder that "laws of nature do not apply to the Yogi in the ecstasy of willpower" serves a dual function: it makes a claim to veracity while also claiming absolute poetic license for what is to follow. A frame is set for the film's main plot: if a yogi, who had himself been buried alive "to deaden his senses," we read, "is revived from this sleep of death, he must fulfill his awakener's deepest wish." Ramigani (Bernhard Goetzke) is thus beholden to Rajah Ayan (Conrad Veidt), who in the opening shots of the film is seen standing next to the hole where the yogi is buried, ordering his men to revive the yogi. Ayan gives his mysterious command: "You are omniscient, Ramigani. . . . Go to Europe! You know my plans . . ."

Viewers are invited fully to suspend their disbelief; by the end of the prologue, it is obvious that in the magical world we are encountering, the laws of everyday logic do not apply. The film proceeds to make good on its promise by cleverly exploiting filmic special effects to illustrate the miraculous powers of Yogi Ramigani. At Ayan's behest Ramigani uses his willpower to teleport himself to Europe to deliver Ayan's message to architect Herbert Rowland (Olaf Fönns) and invite him to construct a magnificent mausoleum. He magically appears in Rowland's study and manages to transform his penitent's garb into a dignified Indian outfit. A kind of mental connection between Ayan and Rowland is suggested visually: even before

FIGURE 3.1 Using his telepathic powers, Yogi Ramigani (Bernhard Goetzke) causes an accident with Irene's car as she tries to reach her fiancé, Herbert, in Joe May's *The Indian Tomb* (1922).

Ramigani arrives, Rowland is shown wistfully contemplating an image of the Taj Mahal, expressing his desire to construct something equally magnificent. The double-exposure film trick is used to show the power of Ramigani's will: a vision of a splendid dome appears next to Rowland as he considers Ramigani's offer; the yogi lures Rowland's fiancée, Irene (Mia May), away by making the phone ring with a fake call from her father; he uses the power of his gaze to sever the telephone chord to disrupt communication between Irene and Rowland; he halts her effort to get back to Rowland by causing a tire on her car to come loose (Fig. 3.1). When Rowland wants to call Ramigani back, it is clear that the yogi is indeed omniscient; he has waited outside and now comes back to tell the British architect, "No one can ignore the unborn children of his soul, Sahib!"

Such lofty rhetoric and visual design create a world that fully confirms whatever preconceptions the audience may have held about mystical and mysterious India, a country that inspires fascination and fear, in opposition to the bland Europe that Raja Ayan denounces as "un-mysterious, fearless, serene" (Fig. 3.2). It turns out that a colonial romance between Ayan's wife, Savitri (Erna Morena), and the dashing British officer MacAllen (Ernst Richter) fuels the background of the plot. Rajah Ayan shows himself to be a typical oriental despot, in charge of countless servants

FIGURE 3.2 Indian Prince Ayan's troops and entourage welcome architect Herbert Rowland to the prince's splendid palace.

and soldiers but unable to control his vindictive emotions. A contrast is established between European moral principles and a malicious conniving associated with India, when Rowland is outraged to learn that the mausoleum he is supposed to build will house a living woman. The land of allure turns into a land of menace when Rowland is cursed by a leprous penitent he inadvertently injured. Servants are either loyal and self-sacrificing, like Mirrjha (Lya de Putti) or secretly scheming to overthrow their masters, like MacAllen's black servant, who betrays him to the Indian natives. There is the requisite number of thrills and chills: Irene finds herself in the tigers' yard (Fig. 3.3); there is a dungeon with mysterious self-chastising penitents; MacAllen survives a shootout with the natives. Part 1 ends with a veritable cliffhanger as Rowland confirms his willingness to build the mausoleum, despite being stricken with leprosy.

As cliché is heaped on cliché, suspense is carefully manipulated, allowing the audience to overlook some gaping holes in the logic of the plot. If Ramigani is indeed omniscient, how is it that he did not foresee the trouble caused by the arrival of Europeans? And, if he is omnipotent, he could presumably have fulfilled Ayan's wish by making a magnificent mausoleum appear through the power of his will. Given that Indian ingenuity was capable, as early as the seventeenth century, to design and build the Taj Mahal—the very mausoleum Rowland is shown to admire at

FIGURE 3.3 Yogi Ramigani uses his magic powers to protect Irene from Prince Ayan's tigers.

the beginning of the film—why would the Indians have to appeal to a European for help? Such gaps in the motivational logic of the film seem to reinforce the notion of Western "natural" cultural and technological superiority: the Indians may be able to manipulate people and individual gadgets (like telephones and cars), but they seem incapable of the sustained feats of engineering that only men like Rowland can ostensibly accomplish.

Part 2, *The Tiger of Bengal*, owing to a number of skillfully inserted flashbacks that explain the plot situation, can be viewed independently from part 1. It spins the clichés further as it attempts to unravel the various strands of the plot: Ayan falls in love with Irene, who heroically resists his advances in a lavish temple scene; Ramigani's powers are put to the test in a ritual to heal Rowland's leprosy; Ayan's appalling lack of humanity is evidenced in his brutal treatment of the captured Mac-Allen, when he forces Savitri to watch as her lover is thrown to the tigers; to everybody's horror, Irene is chased by a flock of lepers; we finally get the requisite temple dancer—without whom no "Indian" film would be complete—when Mirrjha dances at Ayan's party in front of the European guests; tigers, snakes, and alligators all do their duty, killing those who are unfortunate enough to come too close; in order to save Rowland, Irene agrees to become a priestess for Ayan's cult—giving the two an opportunity to sport the film's most outlandish costumes (Fig. 3.4); suspense

FIGURE 3.4 Irene Amundsen (Mia May) tries to stab herself rather than yielding to the amorous advances of Prince Ayan (Conrad Veidt).

reaches fever pitch as Irene, Rowland, and Savitri flee from Ayan and his henchmen across a perilous mountain ridge; a grand gesture of self-sacrifice on Savitri's part unties all the knots and brings the whole thing to a close; in an epilogue we get the briefest glimpse of the "Indian Tomb" that Rowland was able to build, and a final surprise documenting a profound change in Ayan. All of this should keep us on the edge of our seats. Or does it?

When May's two-part film came out in the fall of 1921, Germany was in political turmoil and on the brink of its most disastrous economic crisis ever: on August 26, 1921, the very day after President Ebert's visit to May's film set, the country was shaken by one of the most significant political assassinations of the Weimar era: conservative politician Matthias Erzberger, minister of finance under Chancellor Gustav Bauer and one of the signatories of the ill-fated Treaty of Versailles, was shot by right-wing extremists. Less than a year later, on June 24, 1922, just as *The Indian Tomb* was ready to test the waters on New York's Broadway, Walther Rathenau, then foreign minister and the architect of the Franco-German postwar rapprochement, was likewise assassinated by members of the right-wing Free Corps. In between, when the two parts of *The Indian Tomb* premiered in Berlin, Chancellor Joseph Wirth was desperately trying to keep his government together, as the city was in the grips of a strike by the gastronomic industry; workers demanding subsistence wages were protesting in the streets, and there were incidents of looting and street violence. Publicity for May's film was hampered by a strike of newspaper workers, during the week just before the premiere of part 1. That fall, the exchange rate for the mark dropped to 262.96 marks to the U.S. dollar in November, down from 150.20 in October and nearly sixty times the rate from the end of World War I (4.5 marks to the dollar) (Widdig 2001, 37). Compared to the astronomical devaluation in currency and the complete collapse of the German monetary system in 1923, this may not appear very dramatic, but it was cause for considerable hardship among Germans, as wages did not keep up with increasing prices.

Under such circumstances May's costly epic stood little chance of recouping its production costs. To make matters worse, critical reaction was mixed. On the political right, the film's release was hailed as a "Großkampftag" (major battle day) that scored an important victory for German film (Wittner 1921). Yet the same critic who voiced such jingoistic rhetoric in praise of the film as a logistical accomplishment could not refrain from expressing certain reservations concerning the contrived plot. Other critics found fault not only with the preponderance of unlikely "dramatic" incidents but also with the overall pacing of the film. The slow pace of the opening, some critics conceded, might work well in establishing a trancelike effect appropriate to the hypnotic allure of the Indian setting, evoking a sense of "Indian stoicism" with its "Adagio tempo." The film seems to invite its audience to marvel at its visual splendor, the camera often lingering on a shot beyond what is required to move the plot along. It could be argued that the film's slow pace helps flaunt the extraordinary production values, as the camera seems reluctant to leave a given setting before having drawn the attention of viewers to each minute detail. In many ways, then, May's film seems a throwback to the "cinema of attractions" of the early silent film period, when visual appeal was more important than the unfolding of a narrative (Gunning 1990). We thus often find ourselves admiring the splendid sets and the equally magnificent costumes instead of focusing on character motivation and plot development. Yet for the main part of the film, it seemed even to contemporary audiences that May was asking for too much patience. It was felt that he had failed to create an accelerating curve of dramatic tension. Instead, the film was criticized for plodding along from episode to episode, neglecting the key requirement of a "sensational film": "Tempo, Tempo, Tempo." The film thus betrays its origins in a serialized novel, where a sequence of suspenseful episodes can make up for a lack of overall momentum of the plot toward a climactic resolution. It is clear that Fritz Lang and Thea von Harbou, in their first collaboration, had not solved these problems.[10]

Critics were almost unanimous, though, in their praise for the film's lavish sets, noting that Martin Jacoby-Boy, together with his team—which included Otto Hunte, Erich Kettelhut, and Karl Vollbrecht (all of whom would later design the spectacular sets of Lang's *Metropolis*)—had excelled in creating a perfect illusion of India.[11] Given the emphasis on the perceived "authenticity" of the settings, it is surprising that critics on the whole did not object more to the problematic depiction of ethnic difference in the film. To today's audiences the film abounds not only in racial stereotypes but also in blatant disregard for ethnic credibility: the film, with its cast of thousands, features some extras who could, from the brief glimpses we get of them, be assumed to be Indian, yet none of the bit players that get significant screen time, primarily as servants, priests, and soldiers, looks altogether convincing. Add to that the odd fact that both Ayan and MacAllen are shown to have black (i.e., African) servants (one unquestionably loyal, the other deceitful and conniving). Joe May had already employed the same actor, Louis Brody, from Cameroon, who plays Ayan's servant, as a "Malayan" servant in the Chinese episode of *Mistress of the World*, suggesting that blacks, no matter where, are destined to serve "superior" civilizations. In its naive disregard for ethnic difference and in its racial stereotyping the film steers perilously close to racist caricature. Early Weimar audiences clearly had few qualms about the racial stereotypes that were foisted on them in contemporary films such as the John Hagenbeck *Abenteuer- und Raubtierfilme* (films featuring adventures and beasts of prey) or Hans Schomburgk's colonial African fantasies. Compared to the fare of these lesser filmmakers, whose cheaply made films abound in blood-thirsty savages and ferocious cannibals, May's two-part epic may indeed appear as a lesson in subtlety.[12]

Despite such objections, some of them already voiced by contemporary critics,[13] *The Indian Tomb* retains a great deal of interest today as a film historical document: it is one of the few well-preserved specimens of what constituted the mainstream of early Weimar genre film, the monumental spectacle. In many ways the manner in which it handles genre conventions is surprising: gender expectations are to a certain extent reversed, with an extraordinary degree of assertiveness granted to the female lead, Irene, in her quest to find and save her fiancé, Herbert. The emphasis on a strong woman harks back to Wilhelmine serials featuring female stars. The film also features a patchwork of different acting styles: Mia May, Olaf Fönns, and Erna Morena (all stars of their own serials during the 1910s) represent a traditional style of dignified, often stereotypical, poses. Conrad Veidt, Bernhard Goetzke, and Paul Richter represent on occasion an understated approach that anticipates more modern, subtler, modes of character acting.

In all its outlandish splendor and improbability the film speaks to the cravings of a German mass audience in a situation of profound disorientation, from the motif of being buried alive (a reality for many soldiers in the trench warfare) to the necessity of overcoming vengefulness (the widespread resentment toward what was seen as an unfair and cruel national humiliation in the wake of Germany's defeat). The visual pleasures and the fantasies that the film provided, although dated, to a certain extent continue to live on in the desires and dreams we all project onto the screen when we sit down today with popcorn and a drink, hoping to be swept away by the magic of a movie. Joe May's not-so-cheap thrills endure to exert a strange fascination. In this context it is of interest to note that the film was rereleased in 1929 (with a new music score by Paul Dessau) and that it was remade twice: in 1937–38, by Richard Eichberg, one of the most accomplished directors of mainstream genre films, and in 1958–59, by Fritz Lang, who finally got the opportunity to work on the project May had wrested away from him nearly forty years earlier.[14] If one of the acknowledged masters of world cinema saw fit to indulge in the guilty pleasure of pulp fiction, why shouldn't we?

NOTES

1. This research was supported, in part, by a grant from the Amherst College Faculty Research Award Program, as funded by the H. Axel Schupf '57 Fund for Intellectual Life.

2. The headlines, "Der Friede mit Amerika" and "Unruhen in Indien," appear on the title page of *Berliner Tageblatt*, August 25, 1921, Abendausgabe.

3. For a detailed discussion of the film see Rogowski 2003.

4. K. K., "*Madame Dubarry*—ein deutscher Sieg." *Lichtbild-Bühne*, April 10, 1920, 27 (quoted in Hake 1992, 121).

5. The titles of such popular genre films—in their clichéd cosmopolitanism—speak for themselves: *Mr. Wu* (Lupu Pick, 1918); *Harakiri* (Fritz Lang, 1919); *Opium* (Robert Reinert, 1919); *Darwin, oder unter Afrikas Tropensonne* (*Darwin, or Underneath Africa's Tropical Sun*, Fritz Bernhardt, 1919); *Die Pest in Florenz* (*The Pestilence in Florence*, Otto Rippert, 1919); *Sumurun* (*An Arabian Night*, Ernst Lubitsch, 1920); *Anna Boleyn* (Ernst Lubitsch, 1920); *Julot, der Apache* (*Julot, the Apache*, Joseph Delmont, 1921); *Die Geisha und der Samurai* (*The Geisha and the Samurai*, Carl Boese, 1921); *Lady Hamilton* (Reinhold Schünzel, 1921); *Lucrezia Borgia* (Richard Oswald, 1922); *Paganini* (Conrad Veidt, 1922); *Sodom und Gomorrha* (*Sodom and Gomorrha*, Michael Kertész, 1922, an Austrian production); *I.N.R.I.*, (Robert Wiene, 1923).

6. It is a bitter historical irony that many of the films from Weimar cinema survived only in these cut—some would say, mutilated—American versions. Such versions, now circulating on videos of questionable visual quality and often with appallingly inappropriate music tracks, make it difficult, if not impossible, to reconstruct the shape these films had on their original release.

7. See the reviews of March 10, 17, and 24, 1922 (for three parts of *Mistress of the World*), and of July 28, 1922 (for the condensation of May's two-part epic into a single film, *Mysteries of India*), in *Variety Film Reviews, 1907–1980*, vol. 2, *1921–1925*. New York: Garland, 1983, no pagination.

8. A lively account of the filming of *The Indian* Tomb can be found in Ramm 1997, 51–57.

9. On the practice of color-coding certain settings or situations see Stiftung Deutsche Kinemathek (Berlin) and Goethe-Institut (Munich) 1995.

10. On "overall pacing of the film" see "Das indische Grabmal im Ufa-Palast," *Berliner Tageblatt*, October 26, 1921; on "Adagio tempo" see Ramm 1997, 64 (quoting *B. Z. am Mittag*, October 5, 1921); on "Tempo, Tempo, Tempo" see *"Das indische Grabmal*: Erste Abteilung," *Lichtbild-Bühne*, October 29, 1921, 24.

11. "Die Illusion von Indien, die glaubwürdig Exotik, überzeugt die meisten" [It is the illusion of India, a credible exoticism, that most found convincing] (*Deutsche Lichtspielzeitung*, October 29, 1921; quoted in Ramm 1997, 63).

12. John Hagenbeck, the Hamburg animal trader, produced films with titles such as *Die Rache der Afrikanerin* (*The Revenge of the African Woman*, Erich Wendt, 1922); Hans Schomburgk is responsible for racist concoctions such as *Eine Weiße unter Kannibalen* (*A White Woman Among Cannibals*, Hans Schomburgk, 1921), which was filmed in Germany but incorporated "documentary" footage shot on location in Africa before 1914. For more on Schomburgk see Waz 1997.

13. See, e.g., the polemic by Willy Haas, written after a visit to the set during the shooting of the film: "Reflexionen vor einem indischen Grabmal," *Film-Kurier*, May 18, 1921; see also Dr. Sievers, "Das indische Grabmal und die Echtheitsfrage," *Film-Kurier*, November 7, 1921.

14. On the remakes see Ramm 1997, 84–89.

REFERENCES

Anon. 1921a. "Der Welt gröfster Film *Das indische Grabmal*: Nach dem gleichnamigen Roman von Thea von Harbou." *Der Film* 33:52.

——. 1921b. "Reichspräsident Ebert in der Filmstadt Woltersdorf." *Berliner Tageblatt*, August 26, Abendausgabe.

Bock, Hans-Michael, and Claudia Lenssen, eds. 1991. *Joe May: Regisseur und Produzent*. Munich: Edition text + kritik.

Bock, Hans-Michael, and Michael Töteberg, eds. 1992. *Das Ufa-Buch: Kunst und Krisen, Stars und Regisseure, Wirtschaft und Politik*. Frankfurt am Main: Zweitausendeins.

Cornelius, Hans-Peter. 1990. "Der Steven Spielberg der Weimarer Republik: Hamburger Kongrefs mit *Die Herrin der Welt* von Joe May." *Der Neue Weg*, November 23.

Dahlke, Günther, and Günter Karl, eds. 1993. *Deutsche Spielfilme von den Anfängen bis 1933*. Berlin: Henschel.

"Das indische Grabmal im Ufa-Palast." 1921. *Berliner Tageblatt*, October 26.

Elsaesser, Thomas. 1996. "General Introduction. Early German Cinema: A Second Life?" In *A Second Life: German Cinema's First Decades*, ed. Thomas Elsaesser and Michael Wedel, 9–37. Amsterdam: Amsterdam University Press.

Gunning, Tom. 1990. "The Cinema of Attractions: Early Film, Its Spectator, and the Avant-Garde." In *Early Cinema: Space, Frame, Narrative*, ed. Thomas Elsaesser and Adam Barker, 56–62. London: BFI.

Hake, Sabine. 1992. *Passions and Deceptions: The Early Films of Ernst Lubitsch*. Princeton, NJ: Princeton University Press.

Kabatek, Wolfgang. 2003. "Imagerie des Anderen im Weimarer Kino." Bielefeld: transcript.

"Kampf auf dem Weltmarkt." 1919. *Lichtbild-Bühne*, October 15, 23.

Kreimeier, Klaus. 1991. "David und Goliath: Joe May und die Ufa." In Bock and Lenssen 1991, 103–14.

Müller, Corinna. 1990. "The Emergence of the Feature Film in Germany Between 1910 and 1911." In *Before Caligari: German Cinema, 1895–1920*, ed. Paolo Cherchi Usai and Lorenzo Codelli, 94–113. Pordenone: Edizioni Biblioteca dell'Immagine.

Prinzler, Hans-Helmut. 1995. *Chronik des deutschen Films, 1895–1994*. Stuttgart: Metzler.

Ramm, Gerald. 1997. *Das märkische Grabmal: Vergessene Filmlegenden zweier Drehorte*. Woltersdorf: Verlag Gerald Ramm.

Rogowski, Christian. 2003. "From Ernst Lubitsch to Joe May: Challenging Kracauer's Demonology with Weimar Popular Film." In *Light Motives: German Popular Cinema in Perspective*, ed. Randall Halle and Margaret McCarthy, 1–23. Detroit: Wayne State University Press.

R. P. 1920. "Caligari oder Herrin der Welt?" *Film-Kurier*, March 9.

Saunders, Thomas J. 1994. *Hollywood in Berlin: American Cinema and Weimar Germany*. Berkeley: University of California Press.

Schultze, Brigitte. 1997. "Land des Grauens und der Wunder: Indien im deutschen Kino." In *Triviale Tropen: Exotische Reise- und Abenteuerfilme aus Deutschland, 1919–1939*, ed. Jörg Schöning, 72–83. Munich: Edition text + kritik.

Schwarzschild, Leopold. 1922. "Die Vertreibung der EFA aus dem Paradies." *Das Tage-Buch*, November 18, 1612–17.

Stiftung Deutsche Kinemathek (Berlin) and Goethe-Institut (Munich), eds. 1995. *Rot für Gefahr, Feuer, und Liebe: Frühe deutsche Stummfilme = Red for Danger, Fire, and Love: Early German Silent Films*. Berlin: Henschel.

Ward, Janet. 2001. "Into the Mouth of the Moloch: Weimar Surface Culture Goes to the Movies." Chapter 3 in *Weimar Surfaces: Urban Visual Culture in 1920s Germany*. Berkeley: University of California Press.

Waz, Gerlinde. 1997. "Auf der Suche nach dem letzten Paradies: Der Afrikaforscher und Regisseur Hans Schomburgk." In *Triviale Tropen: Exotische Reise- und Abenteuerfilme aus Deutschland, 1919–1939*, ed. Jörg Schöning, 95–110. Munich: Edition text + kritik.

Widdig, Bernd. 2001. *Culture and Inflation in Weimar Germany*. Berkeley: University of California Press.

Wittner, Doris. 1921. "Das indische Grabmal." *Roland* 19, Nr. 43, October 27.

NO END TO *NOSFERATU* (1922)

THOMAS ELSAESSER

APPOINTMENTS IN CARPATHIA

"Where do you think you're going?" Professor van Helsing calls after Harker in F. W. Murnau's *Nosferatu, eine Symphonie des Grauens* (1922). "You cannot escape your destiny by running away." Both the film and Bram Stoker's original novel, *Dracula*, bear a family resemblance to "Appointment in Samarra," the W. Somerset Maugham story of a merchant who came across Death at noon in Baghdad and, panic-stricken, fled to Samarra, unaware that his real appointment with Death was not until the evening—in Samarra. Harker travels to Transylvania, thinking he is selling the mysterious count a piece of real estate, but what the two also trade when they exchange contracts is the portrait of Harker's fiancée, Mina, giving Nosferatu access to and possession of her person—the main reason, at least in Murnau's film, why the count acquires real estate in the first place. And when Harker manages to escape from the count's castle, making his way home on horseback, little does he know that in the meantime the count is already sailing ahead to await him in the becalmed port of Harker's native city, ready to land his deadly cargo of plague-carrying rats. Murnau, too, was involved in appointments in Samarra: for instance, he seems to have undertaken what would prove his last journey from Los Angeles to Monterey in order to evade the very fate that lay in store for him. He died on March 11, 1931, in a freak automobile accident near Santa Barbara on his way to arrange a steamship passage to New York after having been warned by his astrologer that he should avoid traveling on land.

The making of Murnau's last film, *Tabu, a Story of the South Seas* (1931), which opened nine days after his death, was similarly ill-fated. Not only did the production—its auspicious beginning was as a collaboration between Robert Flaherty and Murnau—break up in disarray, and have to be rearranged around Murnau alone by Bill Bambridge and Flaherty's cameraman Floyd Crosby, but it seems that Murnau himself was proceeding at cross-purposes. According to his correspondence, he actually undertook his South Sea journey to visit not Tahiti, where the film was shot, but Bali, where a longtime friend and former associate had made his home. *Tabu* has often been regarded as Murnau's intimate film diary, the ultimate home-movie: beautiful bodies diving into the deep for pearls, darting canoes, languid and yearning limbs stretched out or embracing. But in its somber, ominous, and uncanny mood in the midst of the noontime heat, its empty landscapes and restrained framing, *Tabu* is actually a companion film to *Nosferatu*. The old Hindu priest, who impartially but implacably pursues the young couple, fulfills at plot level a function similar to that of the vampire, namely to split the couple, and in the name of the father (or the feudal law of the first night) to reclaim the virgin bride. And as in *Nosferatu*, doom in *Tabu* comes in the form of a ship, pushing its way gently into the perfectly framed shot of a peaceful port. In Murnau's cinema, it seems, few boats can hope to come home to a safe harbor—but they are expected, nonetheless.

Nosferatu's cast, crew, and backstories are reminiscent, besides the appointment in Samarra, also of the proverbial "Spanish inns" so beloved by Luis Buñuel (e.g., *La voie lactée* [*The Milky Way*], 1969), where fates cross and chance encounters give rise to unexpected chain reactions. Despite the detailed research of Michel Bouvier and Jean-Louis Leutrat, the question of how *Nosferatu* came to be made is still something of a mystery. It was virtually the only film made by this particular production company, called Prana—Sanskrit for "breath of life"—which seems to have been from the start a sinking ship, whose financial woes were further aggravated when the owners were subsequently taken to court by Bram Stoker's widow, Florence, and the British Society of Authors for copyright violations. The project owed much to the enigmatic figure of Albin Grau, the managing director of Prana, who signed for the decor and costumes but was also the driving force behind the production, both financially and artistically (Bouvier and Leutrat 1981, 230–33). Very little is known about Grau, though an article by Enno Patalas depicts him variously as a student of Eastern philosophy, a freemason and master of the "pansophic lodge of the light-seekers" in Berlin, a fan of Aleister Crowley, a friend of novelist-painter Alfred Kubin, and the author of a pamphlet about the use of color in decor and lighting in black-and-white films (Patalas 1999). About another mysterious figure—the actor playing Nosferatu—I offer more below, but barely less mysterious figures include Greta Schroeder, the actress playing Ellen/Mina, who may have been married to Ernst Matray, a well-known actor used by Max Reinhardt, before she was briefly the wife of Paul Wegener (director of *Der Golem, wie er in die Welt kam* [*The Golem: How He Came into the World*], 1920), as well as Ruth/Lucy, played by a schoolgirl Murnau had observed outside his house in Berlin-Grunewald and whom he recruited for the role.

More straightforward collaborators were consummate film-industry professionals: screenwriter Henrik Galeen (who also wrote *Der Golem, wie er in die Welt kam*) and director of photography Fritz Arno Wagner, one of the three top cameramen at Ufa. Also well-documented is the actor playing Knock/Renfield, Alexander Granach, who was to have a distinguished career in the United States, both as a theater actor in New York and a film actor in Hollywood. His most impressive part was undoubtedly that of the Nazi police inspector Gruber, in Fritz Lang's *Hangmen Also Die!* (1943), a bitter historical irony that Granach, a Jew from Galicia and refugee from Nazi Germany, had sufficient wit to relish (Granach 1945). Gustav von Wangenheim, who played Jonathan Hutter/Harker, had to emigrate in 1933 as well, but given his political sympathies for the socialists, he went east rather than west and spent his exile in the Soviet Union, returning in 1945 to East Berlin, where he became the long-serving director of the Deutsches Schauspielhaus.

BALKAN WARS

Germany in 1921 and 1922 was recovering from the bloodletting of World War I. The specters that haunted the new republic included the Spartakist uprisings in Berlin and Munich, based on the Soviet model and bloodily suppressed; a bout of raging inflation that bled the economy like an internal hemorrhage; and an army of horribly disfigured war cripples. But it was another memorable event that left its echo in *Nosferatu*: in the winter of 1918–19 a Spanish flu epidemic and famine hit Germany, ravaging the country and reportedly killing more civilians than the Great War itself. So the cholera of which *Nosferatu* is supposed to record the origins is itself doubled by several successive disasters befalling a defeated Germany, during which public opinion only too readily blamed the victors of Versailles for not coming to the country's aid. Instead, the French, adding insult and humiliation to injury and penury, insisted on the prompt payment of war reparations and annexed the Rhineland, setting off a chain of events that gave the nationalist right its first electoral successes among the working class.

The war itself had perhaps also left less visible scars in the shape of traumas, especially on the veterans. In the run-up to the opening of *Nosferatu*, Grau published an essay in *Bühne und Film* explaining how he had come by the story and why he had wanted to turn it into a film. It has, perhaps unsurprisingly, to do with the war in Serbia and his experiences as a soldier of the infantry. Dispatched to a remote village as part of what Grau called "a vermin-extermination commando" (Grau 1921), he is billeted with an old peasant who tells him the story of his father, who, killed in a blood feud, was buried without sacraments and haunted the village as a vampire.

FIGURE 4.1 Nosferatu (Max Schreck), in a two-shot with Harker (Gustav von Wangenheim), cast as exotic Other, in F. W. Murnau's *Nosferatu, a Symphony of Horror* (1922).

The peasant even shows Grau an official paper about his father's disinterment in 1884, where the body is discovered fully preserved, except for two front teeth now protruding over the lower lip. The prefect ordered a stake to be driven through the heart of this "nosferatu" (Romanian for undead), who expires with a sigh.

What comes into view in Bram Stoker's original *Dracula* as much as in Grau's tale and Galeen's unauthorized adaptation for Murnau is Britain and western Europe's relationship with "Mitteleuropa" and its eastern flank: the Slav peoples in general and those of the Balkans in particular, a world the Germanic West had for centuries studied with fascinated antipathy. And "Mitteleuropa" also encompassed "the Pale"—the home territories of the eastern Jews whom the collapse of the Austro-Hungarian Empire in 1918 had forced to move westward. Conjoined in the figure of Nosferatu are several contradictory and conflicting ethnic or racial "others," making him at once an "in-between worlds" creature and a babushka doll of "worlds-within-worlds" (Fig. 4.1). Put differently, the story prefigures in some sense even the imperial colonizers' bad dreams of a reverse colonization of the mother country through the colonized subjects. The earth he brings in his coffins, as well as the name of his ship (*Demeter*, i.e., "Mother Earth"), gives a clear hint of this return. That such an influx of the subjugated and exploited should be seen in terms of rats, contagion, and contamination speaks volumes: about the unselfconscious racism of the educated classes during the last but one turn of the century but also about "us" hyper-self-conscious readers of literary texts and filmic discourses. Among the citizens of "Fortress Europe" today, some harbor their own, or similar, nightmare visions of history's undead heading west from the "land beyond the trees" (Transylvania) and farther east.

SIX DEGREES OF MURNAU

Nosferatu is a film about networks of contagion and contamination that are also networks of secret and subversive communication. The lines of attraction and repulsion that link Nosferatu with Harker and Nosferatu with Mina weave a subtle web of interaction and dependency, of transfer and substitution. These different levels of making contact charge the film with the kind of energy that alone gives vampirism its extended metaphoric significance, reverberating, for instance, in the film-within-the-film (a spoof on Ufa's recently inaugurated *Kulturfilm* documentaries, also spoofed by French filmmaker Jean Painlevé, who pays homage to *Nosferatu* in *Le vampire* [*The Vampire*], 1945, a film about nature's own vampires and predators). A mutually sustaining symbiosis mingles passion and revulsion with petrified fascination and drifting abandonment: it takes over the ship, the unfortunate crew, and then the burgers of Wisborg. But it is also the subject of Professor van Helsing's natural-history lesson, when he traces a malevolent genealogy from plant life to animal existence, from carnivorous orchids, polyps, spiders, flies, and rats (which Murnau's parallel editing links back to hyenas and horses) all the way to the beginning and Mina's playfulness with the cat and her kitten. But a similarly fatal chain of eating or being eaten goes from Mina's anxious possessiveness as Harker sets off, to the servility of the Transylvanian peasants, the dangerous hospitality of Nosferatu, the craven submission of Renfield, and the sadistic exploitation of the ship's crew by its master, until it returns full circle with Mina's sacrifice when she offers herself to Nosferatu during his terrible visitation (Fig. 4.2).

The idea of unpredictable patterns of propagation is perhaps not so dissimilar from what in more recent times has been studied by mathematicians and statisticians under the name of small-worlds syndrome. Small-worlds scientists are trying to understand the dynamics of groups and open systems and the patterns of their interaction, which tend to oscillate between total randomness and total organization. Small-worlds syndrome is a key issue for biologists (how do thousands of crickets manage to chirp in unison within seconds of starting up, or how do glow-worms synchronize their light emissions?), and its mathematics are used by economists when predicting global stock exchange movements or the effects of a particular market's collapse. Small-worlds syndrome is of interest to preventive medicine when looking at the spread of viruses and devising methods of disease control, and it helps designers of mobile communications networks trying to

FIGURE 4.2   The sacrifice of Mina (Greta Schröder).

determine the shortest route between two long-distance parties, connecting them by piggybacking on local data traffic. To the rest of us, the small-worlds syndrome is better known as "six degrees of separation," according to which everyone knows someone famous across the overlap between one's own circle of friends, acquaintances, and associates and the circles of friends of these friends. If we use *Nosferatu* as a template, then the six degrees of Murnau open up intriguing connections.

Born in Bielefeld in 1888, the son of a textile manufacturer, Friedrich Wilhelm Plumpe adopted the name Murnau as a young adult. The fact that he did so to disguise an unflattering surname and in homage to an artists' colony south of Munich already leads to Wassily Kandinsky, Franz Marc, and other members of the expressionist group *Der blaue Reiter* who used to spend time in Murnau. Murnau the place joins Murnau the man up with the circle around expressionist poet Hans Ehrenbaum-Degele and connects him to other important avant-garde artists in 1920s Berlin, including the charismatic poetess Else Lasker-Schüler and the sculptress Renée Sintenis, both outstanding women in a world of men.

Grau may have connected Murnau to Alfred Kubin and such Prague Gothic writers as Gustav Meyrink, Gustav Janouch, and Franz Kafka, but he was an outsider to the film industry, while Galeen and Wagner belonged to several of the production units that existed at Ufa under Erich Pommer. What is today called expressionist film mainly reflected common tastes and preferences among this remarkably tightly knit community of professionals—no more than two dozen names—operating as teams and skills networks, many of them first brought together by Pommer and subsequently dominating the creative input (and output) at Ufa. With the exception of Lang, Murnau, and a few others, the directors were no more than first among equals, with their set designers probably leaving the most lasting impression on the look of the films. By the mid-1920s, male stars, above all Emil Jannings, had considerable power, and it was as Jannings's preferred director that Murnau was put in charge of some of Ufa's most market-oriented, "international" projects, such as *Der Letzte Mann* (*The Last Laugh*, 1924), *Herr Tartüff* (*Tartuffe*, 1926), and *Faust* (1926), aimed at establishing the Ufa brand name worldwide and maintaining the studio's reputation for special effects and other technical innovations. Jannings also opened doors, when it came to Murnau's post-*Nosferatu* Hollywood career.

Murnau's reputation is that of the German cinema's most exquisite romantic poet, in contrast to the technophile Lang, who had astounded the film world with trick effects since *Die Spinnen* (*The Spiders*, 1919) and *Der müde Tod* (*Destiny*, 1921). In 1915 Murnau was called up and served in the infantry in East Prussia—he hated it and was bored to distraction. The following year he managed to get transferred to the Luftwaffe, the German air force, where he flew combat missions over France until after an emergency landing during fog he came to spend the remainder of the war as an internee in neutral Switzerland. Murnau's time as a pilot suggests that the tender soul had nonetheless shown a remarkable appetite for the storms of steel, blending his high-romantic sensibility with a taste for "top-gun" technology typical of the aristocratic German dandy in the von Richthofen mold. Murnau's obsession with gliding camera movements and intricate spatial setups associated with the unfettered camera of *The Last Laugh* and with Karl Freund's ingenious photographic contraptions suggest analogies with the perception of pliable space and horizonless, unbounded vistas as experienced by a fighter pilot.

NOSFERATU IN LOVE

Most cultural-studies approaches to *Nosferatu* (or indeed to Bram Stoker's *Dracula*) have little trouble relating the myth of the vampire to a historically new and politically troubling awareness of female sexuality. The Lucy figure in the novel and the somnambulist Ellen/Mina in the film have been compared to the hysterical females treated by Jean-Martin Charcot in Paris at the Salpêtrière, where they were photographed by Albert Londe, thanks to his newly developed chronophotographic camera, while two young doctors from Germany and Austria, Josef Breuer and Sigmund Freud, looked on.

Stoker is in fact quite explicit when he introduces Dr. Seward and Dr. van Helsing. These two suggest different treatments for Lucy's symptoms, with the Dutchman van Helsing supporting his diagnosis by a pointed reference to having studied in Paris under Charcot. But *Nosferatu* is open to another reading of its sexual

FIGURE 4.3   Nosferatu's animal-like features.

pathology. Vampires in the movies are usually bisexual, often letting ambiguity hover over the question of whether, say, Dracula's brides are for the count's ends in themselves or merely means to an end (as Venus-traps, to attract young men to their rescue who then become the juicier victims). But Murnau's Nosferatu would seem to be the prototype of another gender, not least because of the vampire's many animal features, from his pointed ears and birdlike claws to his rodent teeth (Fig. 4.3), rather than the more usual fangs suddenly bared on an otherwise impeccably gentleman-dandy face and physique (Bela Lugosi or Christopher Lee).

The French surrealists admired *Nosferatu* mainly for its eroticism, contrasting the anodyne puppy love of Mina and Harker with Nosferatu's necrophiliac lust, musty and potent at once, exuding the aroma of dank crypts and leathery flesh. According to Robin Wood, however, sexuality is branded in Murnau's films as *the* source of evil. Nosferatu stands for raw carnal desire, which must be kept in check, if not altogether suppressed, in the interest of higher, spiritual values; so Mina, expressing that mixture of desire, curiosity, and horror typical of patriarchal culture when depicting female sexuality, must die along with Nosferatu (Fig. 4.4). But the love triangles in the film also lend themselves to an interpretation that brings out a more layered structure of sexual attraction and ambivalence. For instance, underlying the secret heterosexual bond between Nosferatu and Mina is the Renfield-Jonathan-Nosferatu relation. It is similar to depictions of homosexuality in

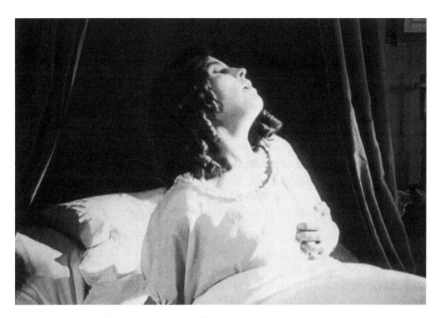

FIGURE 4.4 Mina's dramatic expression of desire.

German films from the immediate postwar period, of which the best-known example is Richard Oswald's *Anders als die Anderen* (*Different from the Others*, 1919),
in which a young Conrad Veidt is seduced by an older man, played by Reinhold
Schünzel, after being introduced to him by a fellow student. The initial situation in
Nosferatu suggests that the film weaves two plotlines, one heterosexual, the other
developed around the homosexual relationship between Nosferatu and Renfield,
doubled by the homosocial story of Harker's being befriended by Renfield, where-
upon the older man introduces his younger friend to a very experienced "queen."
Likewise, the protagonists of Murnau's *Faust*—Mephisto and the rejuvenated
Faust—could be called a queer couple, especially on their extravagant travel adventures to that celebrated destination of homoerotic desire, the Mediterranean,
their romance thinly disguised by the excessively heterosexual story of Faust and
Gretchen.

   Siegfried Kracauer argued that Weimar cinema tended to stage anxieties about
male self-images and male sexuality: his *From Caligari to Hitler* even ties the theme
of damaged masculinity to the vanishing of paternal authority after a lost war (Kracauer 1947, 86–87). Certainly the preferred stories of expressionist cinema focus
on male identity crises, often signaled by the appearance of a double, and they toy
with bisexuality by featuring love triangles in which the two males are usually "best
friends" or business associates who show an obvious, sometimes fatal, but rarely

openly acknowledged attraction to each other. In this respect Murnau's films are neither an exception nor unusually explicit. Doubles abound in Murnau as they do in the works of other directors, whether by way of disguise (*Tartuffe*) or across a split male character (the eponymous protagonist of *Faust* both old and young; the porter of *The Last Laugh* at the hotel and at home; the hero of *Phantom* [1922], timid by day, a criminal at night). Likewise there are several crucial films where a pure, almost asexual, love is threatened or destroyed by the intrusion of another male's predatory attentions—to the man (Nosferatu/Harker, Wigottschinski/Lubota in *Phantom*, Mephisto/Faust, Tartuffe/Orgon, Hitu/Matahi in *Tabu*). These depictions, in turn, can be ranged side by side with the troubled male-male relations to be found in, for instance, Dimitri Buchowetzki's *Danton* (1921), E. A. Dupont's *Varieté* (*Variety*, 1925), and Fritz Lang's *Metropolis* (1927), all the way to G. W. Pabst's *Die 3 Groschenoper* (*The 3 Penny Opera*, 1931) and Piel Jutzi's *Berlin Alexanderplatz* (1931).

For the novelist Jim Shepard, though, Murnau's homosexuality is crucial to both his films and his life; sorrow and secrecy become the wellsprings of his creative drive, the motives behind a tale of love, longing, guilt, and self-abjection. In his fictionalized biography of Murnau, *Nosferatu in Love*, Shepard makes the twin poles of self-deprecating humor and self-lacerating grief the protective armor behind which the director feeds on lascivious thoughts furtively indulged. For Shepard, the deepest wound the war inflicted on Murnau was the death on the eastern front of his intimate friend Hans Ehrenbaum-Degele, on whom he once recklessly cheated. Baffled and hurt, Hans voluntarily enlists and soon gets himself killed, to the undying shame and mortification of Murnau, at least according to Shepard.

It is true that Hans Ehrenbaum-Degele (1889–1915) was an expressionist poet who with Else Lasker-Schüler, Robert Meidner, and Paul Zech edited the magazine *Das neue Pathos*. He was the son of a Jewish banker and art collector, whose mother, Mary, a concert singer, virtually adopted Murnau after his return from Zurich at the end of the war. It is also true that the Ehrenbaum-Degele villa in Berlin-Grunewald remained Murnau's home from 1919 until he left for America in June 1926. But Shepard's fictional diary spins its tale around a number of characters, situations, and incidents for which there is no evidence in the historical records.

There are two other "degrees of separation"—one that might underpin and the other undermine Shepard's speculations. The first is a suggestion, already made obliquely in the press reports after the opening night, that *Nosferatu* is something of a spoof, the camp interpretation and insider's tale of characters and antics at home in another castle from that of Count Orlok—the private retreat (a castle in Austria) and very public court (the Deutsche Schauspielhaus in Berlin) presided over by the reigning monarch of Berlin's artistic circles and theater worlds, Max Reinhardt. (From 1911 to 1914 Murnau was a pupil of Reinhardt's in Berlin, working as an actor and assistant director.) In his brief study of Murnau published in 1977, Stan Brakhage first reads *Nosferatu* as a primal-scene fantasy of Murnau himself, linking it to a homosexual childhood fantasy and the wish to do away with his parents and at the same time play father to his mother. But he, too, links the film to Reinhardt ("Max Schreck," the enigmatic actor playing Nosferatu, would thus be an insider joke about Reinhardt, i.e., "Max the terror") and to his circle, where homosexual eccentricity and extravagance was tolerated, if not encouraged (Brakhage 1977). Although hetero himself, Reinhardt offered homosexuals with talent, flair, and panache a safe haven and congenial company amid the strict antihomosexual legislation of the otherwise broad-minded Weimar Republic.

Shepard describes these excesses with some gusto by introducing a character called Spiess, who plays the role of seducer, Mephisto and evil genius to the hesitant Murnau-Faust. Both the orgy and the careless betrayal of Hans that follow appear as the work of Spiess, and in the end Shepard's novelized biography stands or falls by the credibility one is prepared to give to this figure and his influence on Murnau's life. As it happens, a Walter Spies did in fact exist, and he was present— another "degree of separation"—during the shooting of *Nosferatu*, though he never appeared on any list of credits. But he was not the figure depicted by Shepard, and his subsequent life is too important, both in Murnau's life and in many other histories of dance, music, movies, and photography, to leave Shepard's account unchallenged.

Although definitely an intimate of Murnau's in the early 1920s—Murnau invited Spies to live with him and asked him to decorate his villa—Spies left Germany soon after the making of *Nosferatu*, disenchanted by the empty frivolity of the film world and its hangers-on. Spies was a painter and musician, born in Moscow in 1895— another Slav—whose family fled west to Berlin in 1909 and who sent their son to study in Dresden with Oskar Kokoschka and Otto Dix. In the ethnological museums of Berlin and Amsterdam he discovered the visual and musical culture of what was then the Dutch East Indies. In 1923 he boarded a ship for Java and settled in Jogyakarta, where he stayed for four years before moving on to Bali. His letters to his mother, as well as the few to Murnau, make it clear that Murnau remained his sponsor (he bought several of Spies's paintings) and close friend (Rhodius 1964). A visit to Spies in Bali was on Murnau's mind when, disappointed with his work in Hollywood, he bought a yacht, called it *Bali*, and set off on a voyage on the high seas in the direction of the South Sea Islands and East Indies. If he was indeed haunted, and if the prematurely ruptured, unfulfilled relationship with Hans Ehrenbaum-Degele made Murnau into something of an undead, a "Nosferatu in love," then it certainly was not because of Walter Spies. On the contrary, Spies's invisible presence during the shooting of *Nosferatu* makes him a more likely candidate for the haunter, giving another twist to the mystery surrounding the real identity of the central figure.

THE VAMPIRE AS METHOD ACTOR

The suggestion (found also in E. Elias Merhige's *Shadow of the Vampire* [2000]) that Nosferatu is not played by an actor but by a real vampire was first made by Ado Kyrou in *Le surréalisme au cinéma*: "In the role of the vampire the credits name the music-hall actor Max Schreck, but it is well known that this attribution is a deliberate cover-up. . . . No one has ever been willing to reveal the identity of the extraordinary actor whom brilliant make-up renders absolutely unrecognizable. There have been several guesses, some even mentioning Murnau. . . . Who hides behind the character of *Nosferatu*? Maybe Nosferatu himself?" (Kyrou 1985, 35).

The actor-as-star-as-vampire, needing fresh blood and being paid in unsuspecting victims, is in the film business not such a far-fetched metaphor. Many a great star has been known to terrorize the cast with his caprice or turn the set into a bloody battlefield of violated egos and raped reputations. But an even more archetypal movie situation is that of the scientist harnessing the dangerous powers of nature or the unconscious in order to realize his vision at whatever cost to himself and others: every Dr. Jekyll trying the serum on himself is a stand-in for the artist-director as sorcerer, no longer in control of the apprentices he has summoned. It is Faust calling on Mephisto, selling his shadow or his soul (elaborated in *Shadow of the Vampire* where the director's ruthlessness in sacrificing his leading lady to his vampire-actor for heightened artistic effect is depicted as equal to the vampire's thirst for blood). But the conflation of actor and vampire only appropriates what lies ready-made in the filmographies not only of Murnau but of German expressionist cinema in general, with their ubiquitous ventriloquists' dummies, waxworks coming to life, warning shadows, golems—all caught in the confusion between art and life, or rather of art as more truthful, more youthful, and more authentic than life. Why is—with Francis Ford Coppola's *Bram Stoker's Dracula* (1992) or *Shadow of a Vampire*—this standard trope of movie lore making a comeback? Perhaps it is the old problem of realism, mimesis, and art that needs to be revived in the digital age, where the fake looks more real than the real thing but where we have also become deeply suspicious of authenticity. Have the image worlds we inhabit taken on such universal duplicity that it is axiomatic for us only to have faith in fakes?

Some of the most intriguing questions at the heart of many of the Weimar films we still value today—and this includes *Nosferatu*, as well as Robert Wiene's *Das Cabinet des Dr. Caligari* (*The Cabinet of Dr. Caligari*, 1920)—are philosophical and thus perennially relevant: the epistemological problem of "other minds," for instance, and the ontological problem of "other worlds." In the first case, what would it mean to "know" what goes on in someone else's mind, and what proof do I have that others actually exist? And in the second, if the world I live in is merely someone else's fiction, where would the "outside" be, from which I could ever see that

I am trapped "inside"—if not inside someone else's inside? These are problems to which the answers are versions of Pascal's wager: the leap into faith (which may be the void) remains the sole cure for such radical skepticism.

The vampire movies, as suggested, are more in the line of a Faustian pact than a Pascalian wager, whether entered into out of world-weary longing for youth, love, and eternal life or out of a quest for truth, beauty, and the perfection of artifice by ambitious artists or mad scientists. Chances are that in either case they get more than they bargained for, either dying in horrible agony like Dorian Gray or suffering the apparently inverse but in truth complementary fate, namely becoming one of the undead and wishing for mortality: in both cases ending up as monsters, excluded from the community of ordinary humans, and carrying with them an unredeemed or irredeemable surplus.

ETERNAL REPETITION OF MECHANICAL INSCRIPTION

What is this surplus energy or meaning that brings forth these figures of excessive but also inextinguishable desire? Excess there is, yet is it actually a matter of desire? "We bring them the plague, and they don't even know it," Freud is supposed to have said to Jung the day the two of them disembarked in New York harbor in 1908. Whether Freud's alleged remark was spoken in jest or not, some would surely agree, given the strange history of psychoanalysis in the United States, and in the present context, the anecdote shows another "degree of separation" at work. Indeed, it was Carl G. Jung who related Freud's remark to Jacques Lacan, who was fond of quoting it to his students (Mannoni, 1971, 168).

The theories of female sexuality woven around Dracula/Nosferatu all suggest that these attractive/repulsive monsters embody the vagaries of desire. But psychoanalysts, especially Lacanians, might well argue that vampires are drive creatures, not desire creatures, meaning that it is the death drive, the repetition compulsion, the entropic principle of life that animates them, not desire, based on (and sustained by) lack, renewing itself around the perception and disavowal of difference. Yet there may be another way to describe both the elements of excess, surplus, and residue in these figures, confirming the sense that they are creatures driven not by (human) desire but by some other force and energy—that of our technical revolution, as it has impacted the domains of information and communication. Dracula may be the only original myth that the age of mechanical reproduction has produced. This, at any rate, is the notion Friedrich Kittler harbors about the figure's attraction. For him Dracula stands for the eternal repetition of mechanical inscription, which entered the Western world with the typewriter, the gramophone/phonograph, and the cinema (Kittler 1993, 12; 1989, 146). But what the myth tells us about these new media is still a moot point.

Kittler, for instance, argues that *Dracula* is the story of how women themselves become media, how their susceptibility and sensitivity is discovered in the middle of the nineteenth century as a resource and raw material. Charcot, Breuer, Freud— for Kittler, they all line up as men who "harvest" the mediatic powers of women, and it is Bram Stoker who calls their bluff, who both exposes the patriarchal mechanisms and offers—like every good myth—the imaginary solution that allows Victorian society to live with this shocking realization and its real contradictions. In the contrasting and complementary figures of Mina and Lucy, and in the descriptions of their symptoms, Stoker makes hysteria and somnambulism appear as the human equivalents of wireless transmission (invented by Guglielmo Marconi in 1886). On their journey in pursuit of Dracula back to Transylvania, Mina serves the men as both medium and messenger—thanks to her vampiric contact with Dracula, she is able to track his global position through the transmissions emanating from him, but also, being familiar with the technically advanced, instant and universal transcription device of the typewriter, she records and fixes the "messages" he unwittingly still sends across the ether, while the posse of pursuers travel toward *their* appointment in Samarra/Carpathia. As Kittler dryly remarks, women around 1890 had only two choices: to become hysterics or typists (Kittler 1993, 17). Mina, after the demise of Lucy, is both.

Freud, by contrast, was a notorious technophobe, who, according to his son, hated both the radio and the telephone. The only piece of technology he ever pronounced on—and that Jacques Derrida (1978), among others, has critically reinterpreted—is the mystic writing pad, basically a child's toy and more akin to the wax tablets of the Romans or the palimpsests of the medieval monks than to Edison's, the Lumières', or Marconi's inventions (although as RAM or ROM on a CD or chip, the mystic writing pad has had something of a comeback). Freud's obdurate refusal to have anything to do with cinema, notably his utter lack of cooperation in the making of G. W. Pabst's *Geheimnisse einer Seele* (*Secrets of a Soul*, 1926), is also well documented (Chodorkoff and Baxter 1974; Sklarew 1999).

Psychoanalysis and the cinema—they were born together but have been on a collision course ever since. Freud was right: they are antagonists, but they came together when realizing they had a common enemy, which it now seems it was their historical mission to kill: literature and the literary author (Kittler 1993, 96; Heath 1999, 46). For the first one hundred years, the technological media and psychoanalysis competed around literature's prime task and near-monopoly: "representing"—that is, recording, storing, repeating—individual human experience. Cinema and psychoanalysis translated experience into images and sounds, text and traces, embodied or imagined, manifest as physical symptoms or as phantom sensations. Where the cinema does it mechanically, using a synthetic support, psychoanalysis retained the (female) body and the (human) voice as material support. It, too, however, tried to automate the recording process as much as possible through free association as "automatic writing" and through the analyst as passive recording device. In the process both media produced that famous "excess" that in various generic formulas (from musical and melodrama to special effects and body-horror) feminism and film studies have been trying during the last thirty years to come to grips with.

In the new century it is psychoanalysis that is in full retreat, a mere ghost haunting the hermeneutic mills of the humanities. Yet *Nosferatu* is still with us: the excess energy of the undead is now readable as belonging to the cinema and its viral patterns of propagation and proliferation across the culture at large. Not only in the way films have deposited their coffins in galleries, museums, schools, and libraries but also, thanks to the Renfields—cinephiles turned necrophiles—at home in archives, lovingly restoring formerly perished prints and reviving the "originals" at Sunday matinees or special retrospectives. Less fancifully perhaps, remakes of the cinema's own classics and restorations of the cinematic patrimony are also part of the many efforts to banish and "contain" the mysterious forces or life-forms that the sound-image media have brought into (human) existence: not the least of the reasons for wishing that there be no end to Nosferatu.

REFERENCES

Bouvier, Michel, and Jean-Louis Leutrat. 1981. *Nosferatu*. Paris: Gallimard.

Brakhage, Stan. 1977. "F. W. Murnau." In *Film Biographies*, 245–70. Philadelphia: Turtle Island Press.

Chodorkoff, Bernard, and Seymour Baxter. "Secrets of a Soul: An Early Psychoanalytic Film Venture." *American Imago* 31, no. 4 (winter 1974): 319–34.

Derrida, Jacques. 1978. "Freud and the Scene of Writing." In *Writing and Difference*. Trans. Alan Bass, 196–231. London: Routledge.

Granach, Alexander. 1945. *There Goes an Actor*. Trans. Willard Trask. Garden City, NY: Doubleday.

Grau, Albin. 1921. "Vampire." In *Bühne und Film*, no. 21.

Heath, Stephen. 1999. "Cinema and Psychoanalysis: Parallel Histories." In *Endless Night: Cinema and Psychoanalysis, Parallel Histories*, ed. Janet Bergstrom, 25–56. Berkeley: University of California Press.

Kittler, Friedrich A. 1989. "Dracula's Legacy." Trans. William Stephen Davis. *Stanford Humanities Review* 1, no. 1:143–73.

——. 1993. "Die endlose Wiederholung durch automatische Aufzeichnung." In *Draculas Vermächtnis: Technische Schriften*, 11–53. Leipzig: Reclam Verlag.

Kracauer, Siegfried. 1947. *From Caligari to Hitler: A Psychological History of the German Film*. Princeton, NJ: Princeton University Press.

Kyrou, Ado. 1985. *Le surréalisme au cinéma*. Paris: Ramsay. (Orig. pub. 1963.)

Mannoni, Octave. 1971. *Freud*. Trans. R. Belice. New York: Pantheon.

Patalas, Enno. 1999. "Arthur Robison—Albin Grau—Ernst Moritz Engert: Drei Schattenfiguren." *FilmGeschichte* 13 (June): 49–53.

Rhodius, Hans, ed. 1964. *Schönheit und Reichtum des Lebens: Walter Spies, Maler und Musiker auf Bali, 1895–1942: Eine Autobiographie in Briefen mit ergänzenden Erinnerungen*. The Hague: Boucher.

Shepard, Jim. 1998. *Nosferatu in Love*. London: Faber and Faber.

Sklarew, Bruce. 1999. "Freud and Film: Encounters in the Weltgeist." *Journal of the American Psychoanalytic Association* 47, no. 4:1238–47.

FIVE

FRITZ LANG'S
DR. MABUSE, THE GAMBLER (1922)

GRAND ENUNCIATOR OF THE WEIMAR ERA

TOM GUNNING

THE TERRAIN OF MODERNITY:
SPACE, TIME, AND THE MASTERY OF COMMUNICATION

Decla Bioskop's publicity for *Dr. Mabuse, der Spieler* proclaimed, "Mabuse doesn't just want to amass a fortune, he wants to be Master—Master of the city in which he lives, Master of the land in which he dwells, Master over all men."[1] With Mabuse, Lang created not only his ultimate figure of urban crime but his most complex Enunciator figure, the author of crimes who aspires to be a demiurge in control of his own creation, Lang's own *doppelgänger* as director and author who haunted him for nearly the full extent of his career (from 1922 to his last film in 1960). In the first scene of *Dr. Mabuse, the Gambler* Lang places Mabuse in the center of a network of events and messages against a background of the rationalized space and time of the contemporary environment. Lang tackles the way one form of technology interacts with another to create the abstract and fully coordinated grid of space and time that forms the terrain of modernity, producing a unique playing field for the Master Criminal. In this sequence (and throughout the film as a whole) Lang creates an image of the new empty and standardized modernity, based on uniform measurement and systematic interrelation. The dominant mechanisms employed are the pocket watch, the railway, and the telephone, all interacting with the cinematic device of parallel editing.

Mabuse sits at his desk apparently passive, his pocket watch engaging his full attention. A close-up of the watch follows, its circular form filling the screen (Fig. 5.1). This form is immediately echoed by a circular iris that opens on a high-angle

FIGURE 5.1 Close-up of Mabuse's pocket watch in Fritz Lang's *Dr. Mabuse, the Gambler.*

shot of a train moving toward and past the camera. We cut to inside a compart-ment of this train, where two men are seated across from each other, the one on the right apparently dozing, the one on the left checking a briefcase next to him, which we see in close-up. After cutting over to the apparently dozing man (who seems to glance surreptitiously at the briefcase as well), Lang returns to the briefcase in close-up; only this time he provides an overlap-dissolve that reveals the business contract inside. It is the theft of this document that will be Mabuse's first move in his plot to destabilize the stock market.

After this dissolve we return to the supposedly sleeping man, actually Mabuse's henchman, as he surreptitiously removes something from his pocket. The close-up shows it to be another pocket watch: the time is 8:18. The close-up of a watch trig-gers a cut to another location, where we see a man waiting beside a car. He, too, fish-es something from his pocket, and the succeeding close-up reveals another pocket watch: the time is now 8:19. In the following shot the man seems galvanized by this sight and begins cranking his car, then gets in. We return to Mabuse at his desk, framed a bit more closely as his manservant, Spoerri, begins to arrange his hair. His eyes remain riveted on the watch as if it enables him to see the scenes we have just witnessed. Without taking his eyes from the watch, his other hand moves to the left of the frame toward the telephone on his desk. We cut back to the train com-partment, where Mabuse's henchman still surreptitiously regards his watch. Another close-up follows, showing the watch: it is 8:20. We cut back to long shot as the henchman rises, stretches, and then abruptly throttles the commercial courier. We cut to a long shot of the road as the car approaches the camera, framed by an arching underpass. In the next shot we see the train traveling over an embankment.

Then, viewed from outside the train from a slightly low angle, the henchman appears at the compartment window and tosses out the briefcase. Lang cuts to a slightly high angle of the car's driver as he looks up. The following shot of the backseat of this open car shows the briefcase landing perfectly on the upholstery. The two lines of action, train and car, brought together and the exchange made, we now cut in another element: a man shot from a low angle perched on a telephone pole like a repairman, framed within a circular iris. Watching something from his perch, he waves his cap in a broad signaling gesture, then connects some wires. We return to Mabuse at his desk, watch still in one hand but the other arm fully stretched out to the telephone. With a sharp, almost mechanical jerk, he pulls the receiver to him and swivels his head away from the watch, looking up expectantly. We cut to the man on the telephone pole as he picks up a receiver and speaks into it. A title gives the coded message of success: "Va Banque." Mabuse, receiver to ear, stares toward the camera exultantly, almost demonically. He slowly puts the receiver down. The title gives his reaction: "Bravo Georges!" The film cuts back to a medium long shot as Mabuse hangs up the receiver and leans back in his chair, relaxed for the first time (Fig. 5.2).

This justly famous sequence exemplifies Lang's mastery of the coordination of space and time through parallel editing. The various elements of the heist—Mabuse at his desk; the henchman on the telephone pole watching and conveying the action to Mabuse; the train compartment in which the robbery occurs; and the car that passes beneath the train overpass at the precise moment the contract is thrown from the window are cut together in a manner that not only narrates the events but portrays them as interlocking parts of a grand plan, the mobile mechanism of Mabuse's criminal design. Lang coordinates separate points in space in terms of a rigorous and unswerving temporality. These events literally unwind like clockwork, capturing, as Ravi S. Vasudevan has observed, the uniquely modern culture of space and time: "rather than our being given an awareness of different events taking place, it is one event, divided into specific functions, that unfolds before our eyes" (Vasudevan 1995, 2811). Mabuse appears as the evil genius of modernity, able to extend his power through space through his careful control of time, like a spider sitting in the center of a technological web.

But if Mabuse sits at the center of a network that conveys his power to its furthest reaches, what constitutes the stuff of that web? Clearly there are several elements that form the tangle of modernity as Lang conveys it. Mabuse's watch, held in his hand and consulted, provides the reference point by which the separate

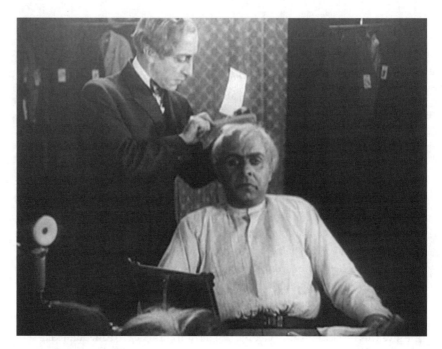

FIGURE 5.2 A relaxed Mabuse (Rudolf Klein-Rogge) with his assistant Spoerri (Robert Forster-Larringa).

actions become one event. The watch, which immediately finds its *doppelgängers* in the hands of the train murderer and the chauffeur (as well as visual echoes in the circular irises and the arching underpass), conveys the synchronized nature of the action, a plan devised by Mabuse with a scenario timed to the second. As Mabuse and his henchmen stare at their watches, Lang shows us the precisely determined events unfolding at their allotted moments. This sort of temporal precision depends on a third emblem of the modern culture of space and time, the railway. The theft of the commercial contract and the murder of its courier is timed to take place at a precise moment, a unique position within the system of time-space, shortly before the train reaches the overpass, so that the contract can then be tossed to the automobile passing below. Mabuse's plans depend, then, on a system already obsessed with precise timing and schedules. Sociologist Anthony Giddens, in his discussion of the space and time of modernity, has pointed out the terrain of coordination a railway timetable implies: "A timetable, such as the schedule of times at which trains run, might seem at first sight to be merely a temporal chart. But actually it is a time-space ordering device, indicating both when and where trains arrive. As such it permits the complex coordination of trains and their passengers and freight across large tracts of time-space" (Giddens 1990, 19–20). As in the railway, Mabuse's precise timetable does not simply express an obsessive concern with punctuality but forms the linchpin of a scenario based on transfers and exchanges. Mabuse's criminal conspiracy is less an anarchistic threat to order than a parasite dependent on the systematic nature of modernity.

The telephone's ability to cross space instantly and the precision of railway schedules rely on a geography of interlocking technologies (the railway, the pocket watch, the telephone system) that creates a system in which action can be coordinated and regulated without, as Giddens says, direct face-to-face interaction. Power and command, as well as obedience and subordination, are technologically mediated. Lang's sequence makes us experience this interlocking technological landscape as a lived and dramatic event, conveyed through the relatively new technology of film, especially through one of its specific means of representation, editing. Lang's editing models itself on the telephone's ability to carry instantaneous messages across space and on a new temporality founded on instants and synchronization. It images modernity as a carefully gridded playing field of calculation and power. Mabuse's body as he sits apparently immobile at his desk stretches between these two devices, the watch and the telephone and his nearly mechanical interaction with them—marked immobility giving way to sudden jolting motion—make him seem a part of the mechanism, the relay between two devices.

THE MECHANICAL PRODUCTION OF COUNTERFEIT IDENTITY

Before Mabuse takes his phone call, Lang presents an emblematic shot of the film's main character. The film opens with a close-up of a series of cards spread out for the camera, held in Mabuse's hand. Mabuse draws several from a pile to the right, adds them to his hand, and fans them so that they are all visible. This opening close-up, as Noel Burch (1991, 6–7, 207–8) has pointed out, dynamically starts the film with a view of a detail rather than an establishing shot, the image evoking the title of the film, *Mabuse, the Gambler*. These cards, however, are not playing cards; they are palm-sized photographs, such as an actor or movie star might autograph or hand out to fans. Mabuse's hand holds a series of character poses, like a succession of images of a famous actor in his most characteristic roles. The stack of cards blends two realms of reference: gambling and role-playing. Lang's title, *Dr. Mabuse, der Spieler*, has at least a double meaning. A *Spieler* is a player, a gambler, but also an actor, and this sequence unites both in its imagery (Fig. 5.3).

The image of a hand "holding all the cards" is, of course, an image of control and power. The images on the cards, the series of character poses, portray Dr. Mabuse's various character disguises; we see (along with a couple I don't recognize from the film) Mabuse as the stockbroker; as the elderly business man; as Dr. Mabuse, the

FIGURE 5.3 Mabuse shuffles his cards.

psychoanalyst; as the Dutch gambler; as the conjurer Sandor Weltmann; and as the drunken sailor. What Mabuse controls is his own multifaceted identity, which is to say, the way other people see him; he is a master of appearances, an illusionist, an actor. With a brief overlap-dissolve Lang cuts to the reverse angle, a medium shot of the man who holds the cards, Mabuse, as he collapses the cards and deftly shuffles them, then places them on the table. The gestures not only return us to his role as professional gambler but to his skill and control.

For the moment Lang lets Mabuse hold all the cards. As we will see, Mabuse's character as master of appearances and role-playing, as controller of other people's destiny, becomes an analogy to the film director or author. Mabuse stands as the archetypal Angina enunciator figure who attempts to maintain control of the film's narrative action and the processes of the systematic arrangement of entrapment in Lang's films, which I have termed "the Destiny-machine," by becoming the master criminal organizer, the energy at the center of the technological web. But in *Dr. Mabuse, the Gambler* Lang also explores the subject of the film's subtitle, *An Image of Our Times*. Lang constructs Mabuse's power through the various aspects of modernity. In the opening robbery he establishes Mabuse's relation to technology and the overlapping of space and time it allows. In the sequences that follow immediately, Lang uses Mabuse to explore the disembedded nature of modern identity, of a money economy, and of the fascination inherent in gambling.

Placing the shuffled pack of cards before him, Mabuse draws one, which he hands to his underling, Spoerri, to use as a model for his transformation. In spite of his imperious air in both speech ("Spoerri, have you taken cocaine again?") and gesture, Mabuse remains in a sense a tabula rasa, awaiting the imprint of his chosen face. But it is precisely in Mabuse's ability to assume different identities that his power lies, his extraordinary control over appearances that allow his nefarious activities to occur under the appearance of everyday, simple, or even negligent actions. In the scenes that follow he conveys information written on a banknote carelessly dropped into a false beggar's hand and has a rendezvous with a member of his gang under the cover of a traffic "accident." When he visits his counterfeiting den, he arrives as an apparently drunken sailor and receives the key to the door hidden in a ball of yarn a woman throws at him as if in disgust at his lurching, intoxicated gait. It is when he seems most inactive that Mabuse becomes most fiendishly effective.

Mabuse must both understand and adapt to the modern world. He molds his identity to contexts: the stockbroker at the Bourse, the psychoanalyst at the society party, the elderly capitalist in his limousine, even the political radical at the working-class café or the drunken sailor in the slum alleyway. In modernity individual identity becomes largely determined by its role within a profession, institution, or social event, and Mabuse never appears in any of his roles out of place. Instead, as in the opening sequence, his power comes from the ease with which he situates himself within a preexistent web of interlocking pieces.

This is nowhere clearer than in Mabuse's manipulation of the stock market. As with all of Mabuse's disguises, his role as stockbroker reflects not only the structures of modernity but immediate Weimar current events as well. The sudden drop in the value of the mark in the late summer of 1921 led to what historian of the inflation era Gerald D. Feldman (1997, 390) has called "an orgy of stock market speculation." Stock market investment took the form of frenzy, so that by November of 1921, when *Mabuse* began shooting, the Berlin exchange was so overloaded with business that it opened for only one day a week. Mabuse acts as behind-the-scenes author in this sequence, as well as costumed lead player. The theft of the commercial contract on the train (itself so carefully coordinating different elements) now fits into the larger scheme of Mabuse's manipulation of the stock market. The intricacy of his plot seems designed to demonstrate Mabuse's symbiosis with the arbitrary nature of the rise and fall of stock prices. It is not that Mabuse has stolen information that will allow him to make a killing in the market. Rather, the theft gives him *control* of information. Like a skilled author or dramatist, Mabuse asserts his authority by managing information, first withholding it, then releasing it at precisely the most effective moment. Mabuse counts on the news of the theft of the commercial contract to cause prices in the stock involved to plummet. Buying those shares once they have reached rock bottom, he then arranges for the discovery of the contract, apparently unopened, to be revealed. In reaction, the stock prices rise again. Mabuse does not need the information contained in the contract; he simply uses its appearance and disappearance as a lever to manipulate the mood on the floor. His power may still rely on moments of violence, such as the assault in the train compartment, but it is his mastery of the abstraction of the stock market system that provides his most powerful weapon.

Lang fashions the stock market sequence, as he did the opening heist, through the coordinated rhythmic interaction of several elements functioning like a machine and regulated by the huge clock that dominates the set of the Bourse. Although contained within a single space, the drama again stretches between two apparatuses, the clock and, on the left, the board listing stock prices, which is continually serviced by minions who erase one price and inscribe another. In between the two is a tumultuous sea of speculators whose top hats rock back and forth with each new price. After the newspapers report the theft of the contract, Lang shows a bearded speculator (ostensibly coded as Jewish) taking off his glove and conveying a secret signal to his underling.[2] Amid this chaos an iris isolates an immobile figure whom we recognize as one of the faces from Mabuse's cards: Mabuse himself with top hat and trimmed mustache, calmly observing all as he puffs on his cigar. Lang cuts rhythmically from broad long shots to details of the frenzied price changes and the anguished looks on the brokers' faces. Mabuse climbs up on a desk and mechanically raises his arm to announce he is buying.

Lang cuts away to frenzied activity in the offices where an exhausted messenger delivers the news of the discovery of the intact commercial contract. We cut back to the floor where Mabuse towers above the rest, still immobile, no longer buying. In medium shot he glances offscreen, and Lang cuts for the first time to a shot centering only on the clock (another unusual clock face, this one showing twenty-four hours) as it marks five minutes to the closing bell. Mabuse remains standing still above the frenzied crowd. The office boys throw out leaflets announcing the discovery of the contract from a balcony just below the clock face. They rain on the crowd below, and the prices on the board begin to mount. Mabuse continues standing on his desktop, hands in pockets, barely shaking his head as he refuses to sell to the hands raised beseechingly toward him. Then, after a glance at the changing price board, his arm goes up again and he announces, "I am selling." A cut to the clock and the attendants ringing bells announce the closing of the market. A shot of the price board shows the figure 1,300, up from the price of 178 at which Mabuse had begun to buy. Lang ends the sequence with the figure on the board and then a shot of the now empty exchange room, littered with detritus of the battle—leaflets and papers, stockbrokers' abandoned hats. Over this empty, devastated space Lang superimposes a close-up of Mabuse as the stockbroker. Then the stockbroker's face fades away, and it is Mabuse's face without disguise that stares at us from the stock exchange floor (Fig. 5.4).

FIGURE 5.4 Close-up of Mabuse's face superimposed over the floor of the stock exchange.

Lang here visualizes the abstraction and mechanical rhythm of a money economy typified by the stock exchange. For Giddens money is one of the major means of the "disembedding" of modernity. Like the technologies of communication and transportation Mabuse employs in the opening robbery, money is, as Giddens puts it, "a means of time-space distanciation. Money provides for the enactment of transactions between agents widely separated in time and space" (Giddens 1990, 24). The whole institution of the stock exchange expresses this disembedding of space and time as shares are exchanged, and their relation to complex industries or services becomes reduced to the column of numbers rising and falling on the blackboard.

Human beings in this sequence are shaken like marbles in a tin pan by the collision of information, the clock, and the rise and fall of prices. If Mabuse seems unmoved by this tumult, it is precisely because he identifies with it so thoroughly. His control of the system takes the form of melding with it, becoming part of it. The sudden gestures of his arm and his surreptitious glance at board and clock show his almost mechanical alignment with them. The shots that end the sequence summarize his influence with a firmly written round number on the board and an image of emptiness, a space now bereft of human presence. The superimposition of Mabuse's face as the ultimate shot of the sequence announces his dominance and clearly displays his manipulation of disguise and identity as a major tool. The shot proclaims him the motive force beyond this scene, the author appearing before the now empty stage. But it also puts a face to the system, marking Mabuse as the demon of abstraction, disguise, and control—of modernity.

Mabuse's comfortable fit within the systems of modernity does not undermine the obvious fact that he manipulates these systems with force and violence. Rather than undermining them, he relies on their smoothly functioning calculability. Mabuse operates by pushing the "empty" abstraction of time and money ever further. His multiple manufactured identities reflect the abstraction inherent in his major criminal enterprises: stock market manipulations, the manufacture of counterfeit bills (in subterranean factories staffed by the blind), and gambling. All of these processes undermine any notion of the unique and genuine, subverting in particular any connection between money and intrinsic value. Money works in Mabuse's schemes precisely because it has no value other than that with which it is momentarily endowed by panicked (and misled) buyers or sellers, ignorant dupes passing forged notes, or concupiscent gamblers hoping to find in their wager a way to compel fortune to smile on them.

In this sequence Mabuse also embodies more immediate events in the Weimar economy. For filmgoers in the Weimar Republic the simultaneously arbitrary and dire nature of money and prices was not a theoretical concept but a matter of survival in everyday life. Besides chronicling the stock market speculation of late 1921, Mabuse and his manipulative relation to money and prices—both the stock market scheme and his printing of counterfeit money—make him the image of galloping inflation of the period. As Gerald Feldman says, the Mabuse character "was a genuine and conscious product of the inflation" (Feldman 1997, 513).[3] Inflation had been a very real problem in Germany since the end of World War I, a problem that the fledgling republic avoided facing head-on and that was complicated (and perhaps obscured) by the controversy over the payment of war reparations to the Allies. By 1922 the price index compared to the prewar period was nearly 350 percent. Early 1921 had seen a brief stabilization, but by November 1921, when *Dr. Mabuse, the Gambler* began shooting, the value of the mark had dropped to one-quarter of what it had been at the beginning of the year. The film was released (part 1 in April of 1922, part 2 in May) as the inflationary spiral was increasing once again. But by August, spurred partly by the chaos following Walter Rathenau's assassination, it had moved from galloping inflation (a yearly rate of 50 percent or more) to hyperinflation (*monthly* increases of 50 percent or more). Of course, by the end of 1923 this index had reached billions.[4] Whether reflecting the already serious inflation of prices at the time it was released or the truly surreal demonstration of the arbitrary relation between goods and money that the film shortly anticipated, the image of Mabuse's sinister manipulations of stock prices became emblematic for the experience of hyperinflation. Feldman's history of the inflation period, *The Great Disorder*, actually calls 1922 "the year of Dr. Mabuse," and Lang himself, in the film's sequel, *The Testament of Dr. Mabuse* (1932), has his detective Lohmann recall Mabuse as a personality from the inflation era. In retrospect, Mabuse's role as the prophet of a degree of chaos that had not yet transpired reveals the strength of von Harbou's and Lang's "image of our time" as an exaggeration of forces already in motion, unaware that the times themselves would exaggerate them beyond their imaginations.

Mabuse's symbiosis with the inflation era derives from more than the stock market sequence and permeates the film. The frenzied pursuit of pleasure in the nightclubs and gambling halls of *Dr. Mabuse, the Gambler* captures the culture and attitudes of those who were either profiting from inflation (the *Schieber*, those dealing in black-market or illegal goods—such as Schramm, the owner of the grill-cum-nightclub, whose career from peddler to wealthy inflation profiteer Lang chronicles in a four-shot, beautifully elliptical, minimovie) or who, seeing the value of their savings or wages evaporate, were, as Feldman puts it, "willing to live for the day and to spend their money as quickly as they got it" (Feldman 1997, 535). Mabuse's role as a printer of counterfeit currency also offers a commentary on the Weimar Republic's tendency to respond to its economic problems by simply printing more money. Thus when hyperinflation arrived in August, Adolf Hitler could revile "this weak republic [which] throws its pieces of worthless paper about wildly," as if he were describing the final scenes of Mabuse with his clandestine printing press, wallowing in his now worthless currency.

If the forged banknote, a piece of paper with a spurious claim to legal tender based on a (manufactured) resemblance, circulates throughout this film as the emblematic sign of Mabuse's simultaneous faith in, and manipulation of, the money economy, gambling takes us into the true center of Lang's exposition of his times. Walter Benjamin, in his discussion of the image of the gambler in Baudelaire, realizes the profound connection between the modern world of empty abstraction and the gambler's passion. Winning cannot be calculated because no game depends on a previous one; therefore, no experience accumulates as a basis for future action. Like the factory worker on the assembly line, Benjamin claims, the gambler deals with a time that is emptied out, inaccessible to experience, sharing with the worker "the futility, the emptiness [and] the inability to complete something" (Benjamin 1985, 134–35). The repetitive rhythm of gambling, always awaiting the "ivory ball that falls into the *next* compartment, the *next* card that lies on top" (ibid., 136), captures the hellish time of modernity as a succession of autonomous empty instants. The gambler in effect "kills time" as he or she plays, an experience that Lang visualizes by cutting from his romantic hero/victim Edgar Hull as he begins to gamble under Mabuse's hypnotic suggestion to a clock whose hands turn rapidly from two o'clock to nearly five o'clock. Time passes relentlessly but unnoticed.

It is the mingling of apparent passion and boredom that makes the gambling hall such a dramatic setting for Mabuse's plots. Each gambler awaits not only the *next* chance to win but also the *next sensation*. As in the stock market, the gamblers whose identity Mabuse assumes—Hugo Balling or the Dutch professor—fit in perfectly with the other eccentric characters at the gaming tables. The gambling halls are themselves disguised: from the dive Andalusia (which detective von Wenk penetrates with the password *pineapple* and gets the response, "Cocaine or cards?") to the elegant Petite Casino, which has devised a cabaret stage that can descend from above and conceal the gaming tables in the event of a police raid. But Mabuse lacks the gambler's surrender to pure chance and empty time; he, in fact, plays another game while appearing to gamble (Carozza, Mabuse's mistress, calls it "gambling with human beings"). Mabuse's hypnotic control over his gambling victims sets him outside the game, as both observer and manipulator. Once again the cards he holds are not the true pieces of the game but the human beings he manipulates.

THE GRAND ENUNCIATOR AND THE POWER OF THE GAZE

We first encounter the true power of Mabuse's gaze as he himself watches a theatrical spectacle, Cara Carozza's dance. Mabuse's point of view comes into focus, masked to indicate a view through opera glasses. The camera pans slightly and rests on Hull, an iris closing in to frame him in a circular vignette. Hull watches the erotic spectacle on the stage, but Mabuse's gaze remains fixed on the young millionaire. While Carozza's spectacle is given tumultuous applause from the audience, including Hull, Lang cuts to a close-up of Mabuse staring directly at the camera (Fig. 5.5). Although Mabuse's look at his underlings earlier in the film has often been withering, this is the first portrayal of the occult powers of his vision, his ability to hypnotize victims at a distance, bend them to his will through a focused stare. Lang uses the device of the look at the camera, partly to indicate the intensity of this look, its terrifying force, but also as an extradiegetic claim to power. By his direct gaze, Mabuse stakes a claim over the visual apparatus of the film and its narrative destiny.

Mabuse's gaze operates in two ways. The first method creeps up on its unaware victim from the back, as here on Hull and, later, at the Tolds' soiree to force the count to cheat. The gaze operates as a ray of power coming from Mabuse's eye and hitting its victim in the back of his head (both Hull and Told reach back and hold the back of their necks when they feel its influence). The second mode calls on all of Lang's visual flair and involves the shot/reverse shot, as Mabuse looks directly into the eyes of his victim and the victim receives his gaze. This exchange first occurs when Mabuse, disguised as Hugo Balling, plays cards with Hull in the Incognito club. Lang shows Hull's viewpoint: his own hand of cards in the foreground, Balling staring toward him from the background. Lang then reverses the angle and shows Hull holding his cards from Balling's viewpoint. Cut back to Balling, now framed more closely, still staring. Reverse angle to Hull as he slowly puts down his cards, declares he has lost (although we saw he had the winning cards), and stares blankly into the camera.

FIGURE 5.5   The intense gaze of Mabuse, the hypnotist.

The real visual pyrotechnics come when Mabuse, disguised as the Dutch professor, encounters von Wenk (also in disguise) at the Club Andalusia. Mabuse's gaze is again associated with an optical device, a pair of antique spectacles, which he unfolds and flashes in von Wenk's direction, attracting his attention. Lang cuts between von Wenk and close-ups of the glittering spectacles as Mabuse plays with them, the closer framings and a masking around the glasses endowing them with a sense of power. Von Wenk's eyes flutter, as if he were fighting off sleep, and he swallows hard, his eyes becoming fixed on the camera. In reverse angle Mabuse holds the spectacles and likewise looks at the camera. In response to von Wenk's question, Mabuse answers that these are Chinese spectacles from Tsi-Nan-Fu.

The state's attorney seems to shake off Mabuse's influence, and the game begins. In the wide shot of von Wenk arranging his money, however, black masking closes in around him, and Lang cuts to an extreme close-up of Mabuse's eyes, also surrounded by darkness and dramatically lit from one side. The mysterious words *Tsi-Nan-Fu* are repeated in an intertitle. Von Wenk takes his cards with a labored movement, as if going into a trance. A point-of-view shot shows his cards, but a dissolve makes the same mysterious words appear on them: *Tsi-Nan-Fu*. An extraordinary shot follows. We see Mabuse across the table, apparently from von Wenk's point-of-view, but the space of the table seems to have changed. Mabuse and his cohorts seem far away, a product both of a wide-angle lens and most likely an actual distance greater than in previous shots, allowing for the trick camera movement that follows. A combination of a lighting change and dark masking wreathes everything in the frame in obscurity—except Mabuse's head, which sharpens in illumination and seems to float uncannily in a black void. This disembodied head, abstracted from all space, seems to move toward the camera, or to enlarge, its eyes fixed on the lens (Lang tracks in toward Mabuse here, although the elimination of surrounding space makes the motion ambiguous: are we moving forward, or is the head rushing toward us, or even simply enlarging?). Finally the face with its unswerving, baleful eye fills the entire screen, as its mouth grimaces, demanding, via an intertitle, that von Wenk take the next card. This trick shot expresses all the power Lang places in Mabuse's gaze. It lunges toward the character and toward the audience, its thrust and size bearing down on us with a hypnotic willpower, expressing a command. The camera's movement follows the trajectory of the gaze, giving it an almost ejaculatory power.

Rather than simply returning to a reverse angle of von Wenk fighting off this mystical influence, Lang uses another optical trick. Shot from above, von Wenk reaches to turn his cards over, but beneath them the magical words *Tsi-Nan-Fu* sparkle. He vainly tries to cover them with the cards. The battle of wills continues in shot/reverse shot, Mabuse continuing to stare at the camera in close-up, widening his eyes demonically as he demands again that von Wenk take a card. Von Wenk, however, refuses, and in reverse angle we see that Mabuse nearly collapses from this failure. As his head falls forward, the black iris around him opens, expressing his loss of concentration, and cementing the link between Mabuse's powers and the devices of the cinema, so many of which—lighting, framing, masking, editing, camera movement—have been associated with his will to power.

For the most part Lang emphasizes the power of Mabuse's gaze rather than the visual fascination of his victims. But Lang draws strong connections between Mabuse's gaze and the role of spectatorship. The most powerful demonstration of the relation between spectatorship and hypnosis comes with one of Mabuse's final avatars, the psychic performer Sandor Weltmann. The performance takes place in a conventional theater, with Weltmann performing within a proscenium stage. He announces as his first demonstration an experiment in mass suggestion. Weltmann moves to the side, closes his eyes, and concentrates. Through an overlap-dissolve, a desert landscape appears on the stage's back curtain. From the depths of the landscape an Arabian caravan emerges, crossing over the stage and descending into the audience, parading down the central aisle, to the astonishment of the spectators. Then, Sandor makes a sudden sweep of his arm, and the caravan vanishes, greeted by enthusiastic applause.

In this sequence Lang presents Mabuse as an embodied visual illusion apparatus. The spectacle he conjures appears as a sort of supercinema, appearing first on the curtain and then expanding into three-dimensional space. The mise-en-abyme of the audience perceiving and applauding Weltmann's minimovie and the audience we constitute as we watch Lang's film become an emblem for the issues Lang raises about enunciation in this film. Sandor controls the gaze, both his own and that of his victims. Can he claim, in some sense, to control the movie we are watching? It seems to me that rather than simply embracing the identification of Mabuse with the cinematic apparatus, Lang engages it dialectically. Weltmann's performance is a high point of Mabuse's power, his identification with the actual powers of the film he exists within. He presents himself as the creator and master of his world. But Lang questions this complete control, and the remainder of the film enacts its dialectical reversal.

PLAYING WITH TIME

Fittingly, the last day at Mabuse's hideout includes a close-up of an alarm clock awakening his henchmen. But as they head outdoors they find the street filled with police. Alerted, Mabuse looks out the second-story window and from a high angle (that allows Lang again to stress the topographical geometry), he sees a semicircular arc of police. As the alarm clock at the beginning of this last sequence announces that Mabuse's time is up, in symmetry with the opening sequence, a phone call now shows that his space has become utterly circumscribed. As Mabuse orders the barricading of the windows and begins to burn incriminating documents, a middle-aged woman leads von Wenk to a telephone in a shop on Mabuse's block. Lang cuts to a switchboard operator making the connection. Mabuse looks over at the telephone and answers it. In medium close-up we see von Wenk speaking on the phone; then we cut to Mabuse, seemingly aghast at this technological invasion of his domain. Von Wenk demands Mabuse's surrender, and Mabuse laughs in scorn, declaring the autonomy on which his power rests: "I feel here like a state within a state with which I have been in a state of war for a long time!" When Mabuse hangs up on his caller, we see von Wenk jiggling the receiver and we return to the switchboard operator, who tries vainly to restore the connection. But if Mabuse asserts his independence over the phone by severing the connection, this action also announces his downfall. The technological web no longer responds to his desires but carries messages he doesn't want to answer.

Mabuse's claim to be a state within a state not only expresses his megalomania but also acknowledges the fragmentation of power, especially the control of force and violence in Germany after the Great War. The images of warfare in the city streets, especially when the police force gives way to the military armed with grenades, certainly recall the battles between Freikorps and revolutionaries in various German cities. These, among the most realistic images in a film often classified as "expressionist," strongly support Anton Kaes's claim that for the Weimar cinema, as for Germany generally, the image of the war was a traumatically repeated and never resolved theme (Kaes 1993; see also Kaes 2009).

His henchmen dying, his stronghold invaded by troops, Mabuse escapes through subterranean passageways, one of his secret networks through the city. The image of Mabuse, his head bandaged, slogging through a tunnel filled with sewer water does not express mastery but desperation; his surface empire crumbling, Mabuse has become a sewer rat, escaping as best he can. His escape route leads to the most hidden part of his domain, the secret counterfeiting operation operated by blind workers. As Mabuse emerges from a trapdoor, Lang cuts to a reaction shot of the blind, alarmed by this unaccustomed noise, rising from their work and casting their sightless eyes toward Mabuse. Mabuse himself seems startled by their presence and drops the trapdoor. A close-up of the reverse side of this door shows its self-locking mechanism shoot its bolt into place. Mabuse's henchmen had explained earlier that, when locked, there is no way to open this door from above.

The locked door seals Mabuse's fate, entrapping him in this small dungeon, reducing the reach of his empire to a small underground space, the kingdom of the blind. The cutaway to the lock closing provides an emblematic image of the Destiny-machine, no longer at Mabuse's beck and call, following its own implacable rules. Why does Mabuse drop the door? Clearly this is a reverse of deus ex machina, the plot machinery now working to entrap and destroy its former master. But Mabuse's reaction to the blind, causing him to forget how his own mechanism works, spawns associations as well. Mabuse's power has been the power of the gaze, both his own occult visual powers to compel others by focusing his stare and the ability to attract the gaze of others, to fascinate them as performer. Here he confronts the image of lack, of the sightless, whose absence of sight he has previously exploited. Although the meek body language of the blind as they hesitatingly retreat from Mabuse into a corner shows that they pose no physical threat to him, they confront him with an image of absolute powerlessness, the inverse of his former glory. They cannot see, and he cannot fascinate them.

Mabuse scurries about the room trying the doors he himself has made impregnable, trying his pocketknife on the locked door. Then, fully aware of his impotence, Mabuse perceives the surrounding space in a new way. Whereas previously the whole world seemed to respond to his will, now his last domain becomes populated by specters of his own imagination, visions of those Mabuse himself has killed appear as black-habited, white-faced transparent phantoms looming before him in every corner of the room. First Edgar Hull appears, then vanishes; then in another spot (each figure given via Mabuse's point of view) Pesch, the henchman he had killed after his arrest; then Count Told, holding up a playing card. A phantom of Cara Carozza walks toward Mabuse, hands outstretched. Mabuse huddles in a corner more terrified than his blind workers who creep forward to look at him.

As Mabuse cowers before his blind employees, an overlap-dissolve transforms them into his black-clothed victims. Hull and Told beckon him toward a table for one last game of cards. Hull hands him the cards, and Mabuse shuffles and deals. When he shows his hand, Told points his finger and declares, "Cheat!" Mabuse rises in anger, and the wraiths vanish suddenly like the illusions in Weltmann's mental theater. We are at the high point of Mabuse's madness as he stares into the empty space that his vision had just filled with his own crimes. Gathering the counterfeit bills from the table, in a fit of manic joy he tosses them in the air, surrounding himself with a shower of worthless paper, the riches of his counterfeit kingdom. But then his face contorts in horror, and he looks over his shoulder. We see from his point of view a large wheel-like shape with spokes radiating from a center, presumably part of the printing press for the counterfeit bills. The wheels take on the face of a fiend with glowing eyes and then (through overlap-dissolve again) a gnashing maw with clawlike, snapping arms.

Mabuse backs away from this vision, as he falls prostrate in the foreground on the table covered with counterfeit bills. The machines flanking either side of the devouring sun-faced monster also transform into threatening entities. Each possesses glowing eyes, while the figure on the right takes on a human form with huge muscular arms and a scaled back and begins to rock back and forth. Mabuse collapses to the floor, and we see him burrowing into a heap of false money, hiding his face as he crumbles the paper around him. The police arrive, led by von Wenk. Before they enter the cellar an intertitle proclaims: "The Man who had been Mabuse." This abject figure sits on the floor, his mouth slack, folding his false currency and staring at the camera with dull sightless eyes. He grabs the bills without looking at them, as if blind (one more masquerade to avoid capture? or the ultimate loss of his visual power?). Von Wenk and another officer raise him to his feet as he gathers a heap of counterfeit money to his chest desperately. As they lead him out, the bills fall from his hands one by one. An iris closes over Mabuse being led up the stairs to end the film.

This last scene functions like an extended vision, revealing to Mabuse the true nature of his power. In contrast to most of the visionary scenes in the allegorical films, this one is coded as madness. But Mabuse's vision expresses more than his subjective state, unmasking forces actually operating in the films. Mabuse discovers several things in his madness. First, he recognizes that he has surrounded himself with the dead, as both foes and allies whom he has killed confront him. Second, he realizes his own impotence, his inability now to make anything work for him; his own mechanism entraps him, his money is valueless, and his crimes haunt, rather than exalt, him. The vision of the demonic machine poses another literal image of the Destiny-machine, threatening and devouring and subject to no master other than its own repetitive actions, titanic energy, and insatiable demand.

FIGURE 5.6   "The man who *was once* Mabuse."

This is the apparatus that Mabuse believed he had mastered in all its forms: the people whose destinies he played with, the false money he manipulated, the engines of destruction he devised—even the visual illusions he seemed to summon up for others. All these things now confront him and declare their independence from him. He is their subject now, no longer their enunciator. The power in his eyes is extinguished, and his final identity mimes that of his most abject laborers, the blind, with shaky hands, unfocused gaze, and repetitive motions. The man who could manipulate and transform his identity ends up without one—"the man who *was once* Mabuse" (Fig. 5.6). He is now restricted to the tabula rasa that underlay all his identities, the blank paper awaiting the counterfeit stamp. His power finished, the film ends precipitously. The iris that closes it no longer expresses Mabuse's focused gaze or power of enunciation. He is led haltingly out of the film.

NOTES

1.   Uco/Decla-Bioskop Program for *Dr. Mabuse Part I*, reprinted in Scholdt 1987, 173. I thank Emily Godeby for help with the translation.
2.   Is Mabuse also coded as Jewish, particularly in this scene, where he acts as stock speculator, a profession that Weimar associated with Jews (as they did, as Anton Kaes pointed

out to me, psychoanalysts!)? Certain reviewers saw the film this way. A reviewer for the *Munchener Gazette* from 1925, quoted by Gunter Scholdt (1987, 149), described Mabuse as a "typical picture of the criminalistic Jew." However, this review also attacks the film as a Jewish product from author Norbert Jacques and publisher Ullstein, and it refers to Thea von Harbou as "a teachable student of the Jewish master." I thank Emily Godeby for help with the translation.

3. I want to thank Anton Kaes for encouraging me to think about Mabuse in terms of the inflation.

4. Percentages in this paragraph pertaining to Germany's post–World War I inflation come from Peukert 1989, esp. 5, 7, and 62–65.

REFERENCES

Benjamin, Walter. 1985. *Charles Baudelaire: A Lyric Poet in the Era of High Capitalism*. Trans. Harry Zohn. London: Verso.

Burch, Noel. 1991. *In and Out of Synch: The Awakening of a Cine-Dreamer*. Trans. Ben Brewster. Aldershot: Scolar Press.

Feldman, Gerald D. 1997. *The Great Disorder: Politics, Economics, and Society in the German Inflation, 1914–1924*. Oxford: Oxford University Press.

Giddens, Anthony. 1990. *The Consequences of Modernity*. Stanford, CA: Stanford University Press.

Kaes, Anton. 1993. "The Cold Gaze: Notes on Mobilization and Modernity." *New German Critique*, no. 59 (spring/summer): 105–17.

——. 2009. *Shell Shock Cinema: Weimar Germany and the Wounds of War*. Princeton, NJ: Princeton University Press.

Peukert, Detlev J. K. 1989. *The Weimar Republic: The Crisis of Classical Modernity*. Trans. Richard Deveson. New York: Hill and Wang.

Scholdt, Gunter, ed. 1987. *Norbert Jacques Fritz Lang Dr. Mabuse: Roman/Film/Dokumente*. Ingebert: W. J. Rohrig Verlag.

Vasudevan, Ravi S. 1995. "Film Studies, New Cultural History, and Experience of Modernity." *Economic and Political Weekly*, November 4.

WHO GETS THE LAST LAUGH?

OLD AGE AND GENERATIONAL CHANGE IN
F.W. MURNAU'S *THE LAST LAUGH* (1924)

SABINE HAKE

Der letzte Mann (*The Last Laugh*, 1924), the most famous collaborative effort by director Friedrich Wilhelm Murnau, screenwriter Carl Mayer, and cinematographer Karl Freund, has been overshadowed by its critical reputation and canonical status. In fact, its most fascinating qualities today are not necessarily those highlighted by the numerous contemporary reviews or examined in the surprisingly few scholarly articles on the film. Like the creative individuals involved in the production, most critics from the 1920s concentrated on the film's innovative cinematography and dynamic conception of narrative space. Very few mentioned the melodramatic elements, and if they did at all, they did so only to dismiss the tragic story of an elderly hotel porter's demotion to washroom attendant as exaggerated and overwrought. The film's many technical accomplishments, from the freely moving camera to the use of perspectivism in set design, were quickly incorporated into mainstream practices. By contrast, already in 1924, the film's emotional universe of degradation, despondency, and disavowal struck most non-German audiences as incomprehensible and utterly strange. Yet even for Germans who had lived through the trauma of World War I, the collapse of the monarchy, and the postwar years of continuing political instability and economic crises, the porter provided not only a figure of identification with their own suffering but also a figure of distanciation through which to move beyond the political legacies of the past.

In recognition of such contradictory responses and effects, my reading of *The Last Laugh* focuses on Emil Jannings's portrayal of the title figure to shed new light on the pervasiveness of generational conflict in Weimar society and to trace the overdetermined function of this conflict in the film's innovative visualization and narrativization of social change. In reading the story of the aging hotel porter in this self-reflexive fashion, however, we cannot reduce the traumatic loss of patriarchal power to our contemporary interest in questions of masculinity and ignore the historical dimensions of the fundamental rift between young and old. Similarly, we cannot dismiss the question of generational conflict as a mere displacement of the hopes and fears generated by increased social mobility and its resultant destabilization of class identities. Instead, we must approach the film's treatment of old age as an expression of the deep generational divide that, even when approached through father-son conflicts, affected all areas of Weimar culture and society and took particularly antagonistic forms in the workplace and in public life. Whether as social problem, literary motif, or critical metaphor, generational conflict dominated the period's own narrativization of historical change, including in the new medium of film. Yet understanding the mechanisms of embodiment that turned the title figure of this Weimar classic into both a signifier and a signified requires that we move beyond the standard auteurist readings focusing on director and screenwriter and pay equal attention to the film's one and only star, Emil Jannings.

His virtuoso performance of the hysterical or feminized male thematized the complicated relationship between masculinity and professional identity and, in so doing, provided the filmmakers with a tool for measuring the profound impact of modernization on social relations, psychological dispositions, sensory perceptions, and aesthetic sensibilities. Jannings had started his film career by playing mighty and lustful rulers in the costume dramas of Ernst Lubitsch, *Madame Dubarry* (*Passion*, 1919) and *Anna Boleyn* (*Deception*, 1920). After the success of his performance in *The Last Laugh*, Jannings began to specialize in stories of defeat and humiliation, including the kind of sexual humiliation portrayed in E. A. Dupont's *Varieté* (*Variety*, 1925) and Josef von Sternberg's *Der blaue Engel* (*The Blue Angel*, 1930). In all these films his reenactment of the undoing of the authoritarian subject, the Wilhelminian *Untertan*, not only expressed historical audiences' deep ambivalence about modernity and modernization but also translated the shock of the new into the gendered *and* generational terms that connected politics and erotics in highly suggestive and often problematic ways. Through his roles, Jannings came to personify the once powerful father figure who, since the heyday of the expressionist drama, had united young men and women in their ardent desire to change traditional gender roles and family structures and thereby to change the social institutions and economic conditions sustaining them. Yet through his screen persona, Jannings also articulated the humiliation and betrayal both of an entire generation of obedient *Untertanen* and of all those who, for various reasons, experienced a postwar loss of power and influence.

In narrativizing the older generation's sense of trauma, *The Last Laugh* takes full advantage of the heightened terms of nineteenth-century melodrama. The story of a hotel porter who, because of failing health, is demoted to the position of washroom attendant could be an episode from the popular novels of Eugenie Marlitt or Hedwig Courths-Mahler—if the main protagonist were a young woman. The difference in sex and age is significant for the contradictory emotional investments that distinguish this highly ambivalent treatment of male suffering from the more predictable identificatory effects found in most female melodramas. Working for a luxury hotel in a big city resembling Berlin, the porter derives his entire personal and professional identity from his splendid uniform and its symbolic meanings (Fig. 6.1). This uniform gives him a clearly defined role both in the economy of the hotel and in the social structure of his working-class neighborhood. When the young hotel manager notices the porter's difficulties in unloading a large steamer truck, he offers him the position of washroom attendant as a form of semiretirement. For the porter, the loss of his beloved uniform is tantamount to a complete loss of self. Unable to accept the fact of his demotion and unwilling to be shamed in front of his relatives and neighbors, the old man steals the uniform and starts a secret double life to keep up appearances at home. His desperate scheme falls apart, however, when the elderly woman living in his household (referred to in the credits as the fiancé's aunt) comes to the hotel to bring him his lunch and discovers his shameful secret.

Her shocked reaction, which repeats his initial trauma, and the *Schadenfreude*, the proverbial joy in someone else's misfortune, displayed by his neighbors, causes an unexpected break in the narrative. Thus when the porter returns the uniform to the hotel in one final act of defeat, the first and only intertitle appears: "Here the film was supposed to end. In real life the unhappy old man would hardly have something other to expect than death. But the screenwriter took pity on him and added a somewhat improbable epilogue." In this epilogue the porter becomes the sole heir of an American millionaire who, by sheer coincidence, died in the washroom in his arms. He celebrates his sensational inheritance with a sumptuous meal for himself and his best friend, the night watchman, before both, together with a street beggar, take off in a luxury car: a fairy-tale ending indeed.[1]

As a prestige production with a big budget, *The Last Laugh* brought together a highly qualified group of professionals: director Friedrich Wilhelm Murnau, scenarist Carl Mayer, cinematographer Karl Freund, set designers Walter Röhrig and Robert Herlth, and character actor Emil Jannings. The Ufa studio had originally purchased the script from Mayer for Lupu Pick, who was scheduled to direct the film as part of a trilogy alongside *Scherben* (*Shards*, 1921) and *Sylvester* (*New Year's Eve*, 1924). Shooting took place during the spring and summer of 1924 in the Ufa-Tempelhof studios and on the Babelsberg lot. The collaborative approach taken by producer Erich Pommer followed the *Bauhüttenprinzip*, the artisanal mode of production cultivated at the Ufa studios throughout the 1920s. Although the

FIGURE 6.1 The hotel porter (Emil Jannings) arrives home in F.W. Murnau's *The Last Laugh* (1922). Courtesy of the Filmmuseum Berlin, Stiftung Deutsche Kinemathek.

making of art films required the innovative work of scenarists, cameramen, and set designers, as well as directors, advertising campaigns and critical reviews had already begun during the 1920s to privilege the director as the unifying creative force. The *auteurist* approaches dominant during the initial rediscovery of Weimar cinema in the late 1960s have translated these promotional strategies into interpretative dogmas, with the result that *The Last Laugh* continues to be read primarily as a film by F. W. Murnau (Eisner 1973; Gehler and Kasten 1990; Prinzler 2003).

Expanding the definition of authorship requires not only closer attention to the screenwriter, however, a process that has already been initiated; it also means to take seriously the contribution of actors in creating filmic meanings and producing subject effects. In discussing questions of authorship in Murnau, Thomas Elsaesser refers to a peculiar division of labor between Murnau, the sadistic ironist, and Mayer, the masochistic expressionist (Elsaesser 2000, 232). Vacillating between submission and domination, Jannings's screen persona in *The Last Laugh* was organized around a similar sadomasochistic structure that duplicates the dynamics of the Murnau-Mayer collaboration. Working again with Murnau and Mayer on a modern adaptation of Moliere's *Tartüff* (*Tartuffe*, 1925), the actor remained closely identified with the underlying crisis of masculinity and, more specifically, of patriarchy. By embodying experiences of disorientation and disempowerment, he came to stand in for the affective dilemmas of an entire generation confronted with the inherent violence behind the process of modernization.

For such emotional investments to take place, Jannings had to remain a Wilhelminian character in appearance and attitudes: paternalistic, misogynistic, and authoritarian but also extremely status-conscious and hierarchy-oriented. Many critics (before and after 1933) saw him as a quintessential German film actor: larger than life in physique and personality, a figure compelled by raw emotionality and sheer physicality and therefore to be identified with deep essences and truths. With his long sideburns reminiscent of nineteenth-century burghers and patriarchs and with his massive body suggestive of even earlier notions of the king's two bodies (one of them as a version of the body politic), Jannings personified one of the hidden secrets of Weimar modernity: the continued existence of the authoritarian past. Through his association with a particular national physiognomy, social type, and historical consciousness, Jannings offered a uniquely German perspective on the profound changes in gender relations and definitions of masculinity. When the camera in *The Last Laugh* assumes his point of view, the actor appears initially as a figure of sympathetic identification; he may be vain, but his is a benign vanity tempered by his jovial disposition, as evidenced in his interactions with children. Yet with the gradual unraveling of his public persona, the psychological pathology of this typical product of Wilhelmine society comes into sharper focus. All of his character traits, from smugness and pretension to servility and self-pity, attest to the sadistic and masochistic tendencies that have been analyzed as central to the authoritarian personality by members of the Institute of Social Research in exile, including by Theodor W. Adorno in *The Authoritarian Personality* (1950). In his work with Murnau, Jannings plays down the sexual implications of this personality type, unless one wanted to think of the porter's uniform as, quite literally, a fetishistic love object. Yet in his later work with von Sternberg, the erotic obsessions of the authoritarian personality assume central significance, a point acknowledged by the director's remark about Jannings that "to be humiliated was for him ecstasy" (Coates 1991, 64).

The Last Laugh can be seen as Murnau's first attempt to explore the dynamics of identity and space in the modern metropolis, a project that culminated in his Hollywood masterpiece *Sunrise* (1927). Influenced by German romanticism and its thematization of transitional states and transgressive experiences, Murnau approached the drama of modern subjectivity from the perspective of fantasy and desire, including their visual and spatial dimensions. Liminal states such as hallucinations or dreams allowed him to experiment with the possibilities of the filmic apparatus and, in so doing, to move beyond conventional notions of realism and reality. From fantastic films like *Nosferatu* (1922) to literary adaptations like *Faust* (1926), the director explored the ambiguous relationship between domination and submission, between terror and attraction, and between violence and dread as constitutive of the modern condition. These oppositions gave rise to the sublimated eroticism that for Murnau distinguished spectatorship in the cinema, a point that is especially relevant to *The Last Laugh*. For by problematizing the relationship between vision and visuality, Murnau sheds light on the social, sexual, and generational divisions that structure both the porter's life and Weimar society as a whole.

Murnau shared his affinity for social outsiders and marginal perspectives with his frequent collaborator Carl Mayer (Kasten 1994; Weihsmann 1997). This true "film poet," to quote Joseph Roth (1976, 493), approached the film script as a genre in its own right by simulating filmic effects through his distinctive short phrases, incomplete sentences, and montagelike exclamations; he also included detailed instructions for camera positions and movements. Hailed by many contemporaries as the unifying force behind the expressionist film, Mayer for *The Last Laugh* wrote an entire screenplay without intertitles, that is, except the one announcing the unexpected happy ending. Apparently lost, the screenplay was considered so innovative at the time that several excerpts were reprinted, including once by Vsevolod Pudovkin in his famous *Film Direction and Screenwriting* (1928). The literary journal *Das Tagebuch* started the trend by publishing the fateful scene in which the porter mistakes his successor as a reflection of himself: "Now he steps in the revolving door. And! Now he moves with it: There, he stops. Because: In this very moment: Someone moves through. Indeed! This someone almost seems to be his double. Because: He, too, wears a uniform and hat. As he does. With all the braids. Only he seems somewhat younger. And very tall. But with an indifferent gait. That is how he now steps outside. Assuming the position. And there! Our porter! Bewildered he follows the other with his gaze" (1924, 1854; my translation).[2]

Speculations continue to this day about whether the film's surprise ending was forced on Mayer by Ufa executives. In either case, the addition of the intertitle can be read as an assertion of his own authorial voice and, more specifically, a critical comment on the sociopsychological function of entertainment cinema. The intertitle separates the trivial elements of the happy ending from the serious treatment of a human tragedy that may have been inspired by the many reports of suicides, suicide attempts, and other acts of desperation during the inflation years (Hempel 1968, 85–86). Moreover, the insertion of an author's voice prevents the elevation of the main character to a figure only of pity, empathy, and compassion and forces spectators to take a more distanced perspective on his traumatic experience and the melodramatic conventions used to present this exemplary story of downward mobility and male humiliation.

The film's innovative approach to narrative space would not have been possible without the contribution of two of Ufa's most famous set designers, Robert

FIGURE 6.2   Street scene in front of the Atlantic hotel. Courtesy of the Filmmuseum Berlin, Stiftung Deutsche Kinemathek.

Herlth and Walter Röhrig. Gone were the painted backdrops from *Das Kabinett des Dr Caligari* (*The Cabinet of Dr. Caligari*, 1920) that required a static camera and that, despite the fantastic qualities, remained indebted to a theatrical mise-en-scène. Four years later, Herlth and Röhrig took a uniquely filmic approach to the two main settings in *The Last Laugh*, the hotel and the tenement, and designed their interiors and exteriors specifically for a moving camera. Creating such an "optical vision" (Herlth) required elaborate planning and exact calculation. On Ufa's large outside lot in Babelsberg they used hundreds of extras and a large number of cars and buses to shoot the busy street life in front of the Atlantic Hotel (Fig. 6.2). Taking full advantage of the laws of perspective, the set designers even incorporated model cars and skyscrapers in the filmic mise-en-scène. According to *Film-Kurier*, the row of houses on the lot decreased from 8 meters to 4 meters. And the skyscrapers in the distance were no taller than 12 meters, reason enough for the reporter to conclude that "this will surpass everything because of its incredibly daring use of perspectivism in the film set, because of the astonishing lighting scheme, the exemplary sense of timing, and the spectacle of the teeming crowds surging past the hotel during a rainstorm" (Jacobsen 1992, 86).

Because of Herlth's and Röhrig's creative contribution, *The Last Laugh* has sometimes been described as an architectural film. Its tightly constructed spaces, however, become alive only through the innovative cinematography of Karl Freund. Already in his earlier work with Murnau, Freund had contributed greatly to the director's unique combination of psychological realism and object symbolism (Eisner 1973, 105–35). Together with his assistant Robert Baberske, the famous Weimar cinematographer used the creative challenges of *The Last Laugh* to animate filmic space through a new technique known as "unfettered" or "unchained" camera (*entfesselte Kamera*). Elaborate tracking shots had become possible through dramatic advances in camera technology such as the introduction of smaller and lighter cameras, more light-sensitive lenses, and a motor-driven cranking device. These features allowed Freund to experiment with an early version of a Steadicam, with the camera in one case tied to his body suspended in midair. Remarkable for its time, *The Last Laugh* contains several extended camera movements, beginning with the spectacular opening sequence, in which the camera assumes the position of an imaginary hotel guest as he is greeted by a page; walks across the bright, spacious lobby; and leaves through the revolving glass door. As the camera becomes, in the words of Murnau, a "recording apparatus freely movable in space" (Gehler and Kasten 1990, 141), it gives rise to an aesthetic of the camera eye that is both embodied (e.g., in the porter's later hallucinations) and disembodied (e.g., in the above-mentioned opening scene). And through the use of subjective camera, the title figure is not merely a sociopsychological type but a function of the competing perspectives of narrator and spectator. In achieving this destabilizing effect, Freund benefited greatly from the atmospheric score of composer Giuseppe Becce, whose Wagnerian approach to melos, together with the effective use of jazz and folklore motifs for different narrative settings, strengthens the implied link between motion and emotion and thus confirms the dynamization of filmic space as a hallmark of modern subjectivity and visual consciousness.

Last but not least, the 1924 production bore the signature of independent producer Erich Pommer, who had charged his creative team with the following task: "Please invent something new, even if it is crazy!" (Eisner 1979, 90). Pommer's approach was part of Ufa's expansionist strategy that, built around the notion of the quality film, aimed at a greater German presence in domestic and international markets. The stabilization of German currency in 1924 put an end to the favorable economic conditions that had given rise to the expressionist cinema as a cinema of inflation in the literal and figurative sense. From then on, German films strove to be both similar to, and different from, other Hollywood productions by meeting international standards of technical quality but emphasizing national characteristics in the approach to artistic quality. By transforming German film into a category of product differentiation, studio executives and producers achieved the difficult compromise between art and industry in the essentialist terms of national identity. In the words of influential Weimar theater critic Herbert Ihering, "*The Last Laugh* is international because it is a German prestige film (*Spitzenfilm*), in the same way that an American production is international because it is an American prestige film" (1961 2:487). It is this seeming paradox that also holds together the film's double ending. The introduction of an all-powerful narrator evokes the kind of self-reflexivity characteristic of art cinema. Meanwhile the expansion of the happy ending into a farcical second story line, which takes up almost twenty minutes in an approximately eighty-minute film, accommodates the generic conventions of melodrama and comedy. As a result, *The Last Laugh* ends up both emulating and mocking Hollywood—an ambiguous position that undoubtedly contributed to its remarkable success with film critics, studio bosses, and other filmmakers.

As Pommer had hoped, the film's critical reception surpassed all expectations. After an extensive advertising campaign and a spectacular opening night at the Ufa-Palast am Zoo on December 23, 1924, which included an orchestral performance of Becce's original score, German critics topped one another in their use of superlatives and bold pronouncements on the birth of film as art. Yet as was often the case with art films, great critical reviews did not necessarily produce the kind of box-office successes that could have helped Ufa in its growing financial difficulties. Many reviewers referred to *The Last Laugh* as a masterpiece and an instant classic. Not known for his love of modern mass diversions, Joseph Roth called it "the best film not just in Germany but in the entire world" (1976, 493). In the *Berliner Börsen-Courier*, Herbert Ihering praised the film as "a true light play (*Lichtspiel*), a true moving play (*Bewegungsspiel*)" (Ihering 1961, 488) that proved the new medium's potential as an art form. In *Film-Kurier* Willy Haas described it as a work of stylistic perfection, signaling a formal revolution, "the beginning of a new era in the history of cinematography" (Jacobsen, Prümm, and Wenz 1991, 108). While joining his colleagues in acknowledging the film's formal qualities, Kurt Pinthus, in *Das Tagebuch*, spoke more critically of the kind of mannerisms often found during transitional periods, concluding that "they [these filmic techniques] aim at a heightened reality but sometimes only look exaggerated" (Pinthus 1925, 27).

American reception of *The Last Laugh* was likewise split between critical acclaim and limited mass appeal. An advance press screening prompted a reporter from the trade journal *Variety* to conclude that "if it [the film] is to be accepted as a criterion of what the Ufa is going to offer in this country, then by all means throw open the screens of the country to pictures of this type" (December 10, 1924). After the 1925 New York premiere, the response in the *New York Times* was equally effusive, with Mordaunt Hall confessing that "there were tears to the left of us, tears to the right of us and tears in our own eyes as we looked at this production for a second time" (January 29, 1925). Even more than in Germany, the enthusiasm of the educated elites did not extend to mass audiences unable or unwilling to appreciate the uniquely German qualities of this somber tale of downward mobility. Despite early successes with expressionist art films and elaborate costume dramas, Ufa ultimately failed to gain a foothold in American markets, and its film imports remained limited to the small art-house circuit. Nonetheless, the studio's quality films left a strong impression on Hollywood moguls looking for new talent. Thus in 1926, when *Motion Picture Magazine* introduced the director of *The Last Laugh* as *the* German film genius, Murnau was already in contract negotiations with William Fox; similar deals with Mayer and Jannings soon followed.

How did historical audiences respond to the high degree of ambiguity in the film, especially as regards its melodramatic structure? Patrice Petro has suggested that the figure of the feminized man, far from being of interest only to male audiences experiencing a crisis of identity, offered a point of identification for a female audience searching for figures on which to project their own desire for freedom from patriarchal domination (Petro 1989, 23–25). Complicating such readings, does the main character in *The Last Laugh* announce the long-awaited demise of patriarchal authority or its replacement by more elusive structures of domination and control? Is the old man a figure only of compassion and pity, or does his emotional appeal depend on the degree to which historical audiences could both sympathize with his suffering and participate in his humiliation? Resisting the tendency to reduce such alternatives to essentialist gendered binaries, Richard McCormick reads "the blurring and confusion of traditional categories of identity" as an emancipatory process within Weimar culture (McCormick 2002, 6). Accordingly, the downfall of the porter can be interpreted as a reenactment of this long-overdue process of social change. Overdetermined in its social, political, and psychological references, Jannings's performance connects the crisis of masculinity to more fundamental questions about gender relations and family life.

The underlying discourse on generational change played a central part in the balancing of competing audience expectations and spectatorial investments that defined much of Weimar cinema between the difficulties of the early postwar years and the more hopeful scenarios that began to take hold of the filmic imagination after 1924. The year of the film's production marked the beginning of the so-called stabilization period that, with the introduction of the new currency, brought a few years of healthy economic growth and relative political stability before the world economic crisis of 1929. At first glance the figure of the porter personifies typical war and postwar experiences, from the trauma of political and military defeat and the pervasive sense of national humiliation to the shock of hyperinflation and the attendant devaluation of social traditions and conventions. As Karl Prümm argues, the explicit and implicit references to the breakdown of social and political hierarchies gave the film its heightened political significance (Prümm 2003, 44). The experience of profound loss, however, cannot be understood without recognition of the considerable gains and advances made after the collapse of the old system. As a temporal marker from which to view the past and imagine the future of the Weimar Republic, the year 1924 consequently provides the film historian with two very different vantage points for situating *The Last Laugh* in the larger context of Weimar culture. According to an optimistic version, 1924 stood for the promise of progress and democracy after years of political and economic crises. According to a more pessimistic version, the year marked the beginning of full-fledged modernization, including the worst excesses of Fordism, Taylorism, and Americanism. The adjustments and sacrifices made in the process have often been seen as a contributing factor to the rise of conservative, nationalist, and anti-Semitic ideologies. By offering a pessimistic and an optimistic ending, *The Last Laugh* not only acknowledged these deep contradictions within German modernity but also thematized its own precarious position within the metanarratives of Weimar cinema that continue to complicate our understanding of the period.

The film's year of production is often cited as a dividing line between the exploration of imaginary worlds attempted by the expressionist film and the rediscovery of physical reality by the writers, painters, and photographers associated with *Neue Sachlichkeit* (New Objectivity). The story of *The Last Laugh* represents this expressionist–New Objectivist divide along generational lines. Expressionist tendencies are subsequently identified with old age and New Objectivist tendencies with youth; in the mise-en-scène this is most evident in the juxtaposition of old dark tenement and new shiny hotel. Chiaroscuro lighting and object symbolism place the film within a recognizably expressionist tradition of abstraction and empathy, to evoke the terminology introduced by Weimar art historian Wilhelm Worringer. The dramatic use of screens and windows and the many high- and low-angle shots clearly follow expressionist conventions of establishing *Stimmung* (mood). At the same time, the influence of New Objectivity is apparent in the camera's almost fetishistic involvement with the surface splendor of modern consumer culture and the social and cultural physiognomy of Americanism, suggesting a growing interest in, and appreciation for, the materiality of everyday life. Commenting on these competing influences, Helmut Weihsmann sees the formal qualities of *The Last Laugh* as indicative of Weimar's culture of nonsynchronicity (Weihsmann 1994, 27). In a similar vein Thomas Elsaesser connects the dynamization of filmic space to a constitutive tension within Weimar cinema between ambiguous narratives and narratives of ambiguity (Elsaesser 2000, 86–90).

The same constitutive tension accounts for the many references to other film genres that make *The Last Laugh* also a film about film. Its thematic choices evoke the early social drama of the Wilhelmine period, which focuses on the problems of the poor and oppressed and relies on melodramatic conventions to invite identi-

fication with their suffering. In its approach to filmic space the film reveals obvious similarities with the chamber-play film (*Kammerspielfilm*), an intimate genre
modeled after the modern drama, both naturalist and symbolist, and distinguished
through its highly stylized use of interiors as extensions of the bourgeois self (Eisner 1977, 207–21). Finally, in its treatment of the modern metropolis the film betrays
the strong influence of the contemporaneous genre of the street film (*Straßenfilm*),
whose characters' movements between public and private sphere invariably reveal
the limits of individual freedom and social mobility (Vogt 2001, 114–24).

These generic references place *The Last Laugh* in a uniquely German tradition
of staging subjectivity, a tradition that extends from the bourgeois tragedy of the
Enlightenment to the social dramas of early cinema and that frequently includes a
direct confrontation with the problems of aging and generational strife. By refus-
ing to validate the central conflict through a tragic ending, Mayer and Murnau move
beyond the prewar melodrama's infatuation with fate and destiny. Similarly, their
ironic use of the happy ending can only be understood as an implicit critique of the
social drama's reformist ethos of moral uplift and its enduring belief in self-im-
provement. By separating the porter from the traditional family structures known
from the chamber play, the narrative avoids the confining effects of oedipalization
and instead focuses on the emotional complexities of a singular crisis experience.
And by ignoring the attractions of the street film, which usually revolve around the
spectacle of a simultaneously alluring and threatening sexuality associated with
the figure of the prostitute, the filmmakers are able to explore the metaphorical
function of masculinity in relation to professional identities and generational differences. Finally, by essentializing the workplace problems that are a specialty of
the critical social drama, *The Last Laugh* avoids any reductionist treatment of social
and professional milieus in favor of the emotional effects of job loss and demotion
and its allegorical function within the underlying narrative of disempowerment.
As a consequence, the main protagonist has little in common with the exploited
employee of the social drama, the authoritarian father of the chamber-play film,
or the straying husband of the street film. Precisely this resistance to the determinants of gender and class creates the conditions for a sustained reflection on the
psychological mechanisms of domination and submission underlying Weimar discourses of social mobility and generational change.

Like other classics of Weimar cinema, *The Last Laugh* reenacts the experience
of generational change in highly emotional terms, but it does so with great ambivalence and ambiguity. This unsettling quality can be observed on two levels:
through the main character as the embodiment of historical trauma and through
the filmic representation of modernity as an experience of that trauma. Within
the dual structure established by the dramatic/comical story line, the main char-
acter/actor functions as a conduit for two opposing forces and developments. His

attitudes and behaviors reflect the authoritarian, militaristic, and hierarchically structured society of the Wilhelmine Empire. Yet his dismissal also highlights the cold rationality of a modern society organized according to capitalist principles. The porter's inability to deal with the loss of social status and male authority shows the resilience of established psychological patterns. Yet it also makes the spectator painfully aware of the problematic connection between profession and identity. Similarly, the man's unwillingness to deal with the realities of old age draws attention to the pervasive cult of youth in Weimar culture, at the same time validating the younger generation's need to remove all obstacles to their ambitious projects of innovation and change.

With his enormous body suggesting strength as well as weakness, Emil Jannings proved ideally suited to perform the confrontation between young and old in relation to the changing definitions of work and profession. When he first appears on the scene, the porter seems like the personification of competence and confidence. All of his gestures attest to the unity of individual and role: when he salutes the guests, expands his chest, strokes his beard, and folds his hand as pedestrians walk past the hotel entrance. The spectacular uniform with the gold tresses and shiny buttons gives him a military bearing. It functions like an external armor that imposes a distinct form and structure on a malleable, amorphous body. Like a prosthesis—or an external crutch of sorts—the uniform holds him up and provides him with a sense of wholeness. To what degree the uniform *is* indeed his identity becomes painfully obvious when the old porter confronts his younger successor, for whom it is nothing more than professional attire that can be exchanged at any time. Paralyzed by the shock over his dismissal, the old man is unable to remove the uniform himself and has to be undressed like a little child. In the process a button is torn off, which prompts him to lose his posture entirely and slump forward, as if his back were broken. As he puts on the simple white frock of the washroom attendant, he assumes the status of a civilian and becomes what the ambiguous title, in one of its meanings, refers to as "the last man."

Jannings expertly uses his compelling physical appearance, facial expressions, and body movements to elicit a wide range of reactions in the spectator. As the proud man in uniform, he represents a figure of sympathy as well as mockery. Yet as the embodiment of victimhood, the man in the white frock invites equally strong feelings of compassion and contempt. Associated with the opposing forces of tradition and modernity, his performance structures the two-part narrative and its contradictory forms of identification in highly ambivalent terms. Significantly, the trauma of demotion cannot be resolved through the body but, instead, requires its containment within the field of vision. The blurring of vision when he reads the letter of dismissal or when he awakens from a drunken sleep represents the optical equivalent of his loss of authority. Yet these crisis situations also give rise to the extended hallucinations compensating for such traumatic loss. Using super-imposition, trick photography, distortion mirrors, and anamorphic lenses, both sequences openly reference the avant-garde film, with the initial trauma depicted through Caligaresque effects and the subsequent wish fulfillment shown in almost surrealist styles. The first hallucination occurs when the porter flees the hotel without his uniform, then looks back one more time and, with eyes wide open, sees the building collapsing and almost burying him. The moving camera in this scene performs the detachment that he himself, paralyzed by fear, fails to achieve. The second hallucination, whose function can be likened to secondary revision in the Freudian sense, takes place after the drunken revelries of the wedding party. In this dreamlike sequence, the porter returns to a fantasy hotel with grotesquely exaggerated dimensions to prove his supernatural physical strength by juggling enormous suitcases in front of admiring onlookers.

The uniform as the founding site of male identity reveals the porter as a product of prewar militarism and authoritarianism, and the close-up on the word *Alterss-chwäche* (fragility of age) in the dismissal letter clearly presents his demotion as a generational experience. Significantly, all of the main contributors to *The Last Laugh* were from the generation of former emperor Wilhelm II (born 1888): Jannings (born 1884), Murnau (born 1888), Freund (born 1890), and Mayer (born 1894). Historically, this was the generation that had welcomed the war and seen the largest number of fatalities and injuries. They had been most heavily invested in the survival of the monarchy and most passionately opposed to the principles of social and sexual equality. During the postwar period, they witnessed the transition from the old political and military elites of the empire to the new managerial and technocratic elites of the republic, a process the critical members of this generation registered with the mixture of expectation, trepidation, and resentment typical of the victims of progress and change.

The porter's inability to demonstrate the kind of New Objectivist "cool conduct" cultivated to perfection by the hotel manager makes him a perfect exemplar of what Helmut Lethen has described as the persona of the "poor creature" (*arme Kreatur*). Identified with "the other side of modern consciousness," this creature is perceived to be authentic; yet it is a mask like all others. Its function within the modern imaginary is to announce the disappearance of a particular set of masks (e.g., the type of the subordinate) and prepare for its subsequent identification with (pathetic) authenticity in the new rituals of public shaming. Under these conditions, the physiognomy of the creature "reflects a social situation, shields nakedness, overcomes shame, evidences a defensive reaction to mortal fear or an ambition to be demonic, striking a ferocious pose among the besiegers" (Lethen 2002, 195).

How does Jannings perform this physiognomy of the creature? By identifying victimization with old age. In accordance with old-fashioned views of maturity and old age, the forty-year-old actor looks and acts more like a man in his sixties. The aging porter is removed from the sphere of productive labor and marginalized within the social hierarchies that defined traditional masculinity at the time. As the older generation personified by the porter, the night watchman, and the governess is banned to the underground of the hotel economy, a younger generation of managers, porters, and pages takes control of its public spaces and vital functions. The dynamic manager in his office, the international travelers waiting in the lobby, and the elegant guests dining in the restaurant are all in their twenties—too young to have consciously experienced the monarchy but old enough to enjoy the promises of social mobility and the blessings of modern consumer culture. The differences between these two generations are made clearly visible through their physical appearance and choice of clothes and accessories. For the young men this means mustaches rather than beards, cigarettes rather than cigars or pipes; for the young women it means short hair and short dresses rather than the braids and long skirts with aprons worn by the perennially middle-aged women of the tenement.

Generational conflict not only creates two very different sets of characters but also establishes two very different narrative settings: the modern luxury hotel and the lower-class tenement. Divided by the street as the site of perpetual movement and an almost utopian mobility, both places appear as highly gendered spaces. The lobby and restaurant of the hotel, itself a symbol of wealth, luxury, and sophistication, provide the perfect stage for the performance of masculine strength and efficiency. During the daytime the tenement is ruled by housewives and children. After work the porter returns to this domestic sphere as a worldly visitor demanding admiration and respect. Lighting and set design contribute to this highly gendered division of hotel and tenement and determine its symbolic contribution to the generational divide in the narrative. The porter's apartment, the staircase, and the narrow inner courtyard are dark and confining spaces, reminiscent both of the oppressive familiarity explored by the chamber-play dramas and the unhealthy living conditions depicted in the so-called Zille films. By contrast, the luminous interiors of the modern luxury hotel—with its open spaces, shiny floors, smooth walls, and large window panes—give rise to the spectacle of movement and change captured so compellingly by the revolving door as a foremost symbol of cinema and modernity.

The porter not only moves between two worlds but, after his demotion, is also forced to alter his movements inside and between these worlds. Not surprisingly, many of these movements involve spatial hierarchies and divisions. Before his demotion the porter climbs the staircase in the tenement and bathes in the admiration of his neighbors. After his demotion he descends the stairs leading to the washroom as the embodiment of debasement. This downward movement is repeated later when he returns to the tenement, now a figure of public ridicule. In accordance with expressionist conventions of mise-en-scène, the main character's movements inside this symbolically changed space can be read in sexual terms, with scenes of climbing equated with virile strength and of descending with impotence. The extreme close-up of the aunt's face offers a visual reenactment of the implied act of castration; likewise, the montage sequence of gaping mouths, with its multiple exposures an homage to the abstract film, alludes to the threat of *vagina dentata*. Accusing Murnau or Mayer of misogynistic tendencies, however, would miss the point. The women's laughter, while unmistakably gendered, expresses above all the revenge of the powerless witnessing the fall of a once-powerful person; their vicious gossiping articulates what Kracauer, somewhat problematically, refers to as "the evil lower middle-class instincts" (Kracauer 1947, 100). For the same reason, the image of the porter scrubbing the restroom floor on his knees intentionally references a traditionally female activity to corroborate the defeat of the older generation and announce its replacement by a young, dynamic, and new middle class.

One of the blind spots in the portrayal of the porter is the question of sexual desire, a characteristic that makes *The Last Laugh* the uncanny double of *The Blue Angel* and brings us back to the central role of Jannings in organizing the various layers of social commentary, formal experimentation, and self-reflexive commentary in this film. The porter lives with an incomplete family consisting of a niece, her fiancé, and his aunt; after the young couple marry, the husband assumes the role of head of household. This domestic arrangement has caused some confusion among scholars, with some describing the fiancé's aunt as the porter's wife or others, rather improbably, referring to her as his own aunt. Such lack of clarity is not only typical for Murnau, who throughout his work remained indifferent to marital relations and familial structures, exploring instead the ambiguities of sexual desire. Very concretely, the expanded definition of family also reflects the improvised living arrangements endured by many inhabitants of the infamous tenement city. The fiancé's aunt, it seems, harbors some romantic feelings for the porter until she discovers his loss of the uniform—his castration, as it were. Estranged from his relatives, the sad old man finds true companionship only with the night watchman. It is he who joins the porter on his spending spree, first as his "female" date during a sumptuous meal and later on their journey to an unknown destination. Some scholars have read their relationship in homoerotic terms. For instance, Stephan Schindler argues that the film "constructs a world without women, a homosocial environment where 'social bonds' are negotiated exclusively between men" (Schindler 1996, 40). And Elsaesser describes the ending as "a homoerotic scenario, in which the doorman and the night watchman ride off as the perfect couple, with the young beggar boy they just picked up as their 'son' in tow" (Elsaesser 2000, 247; see also Elsaesser 2003). But can we really describe the two old men as two feminized men, as Schindler does, without taking into account the historically specific function of feminization and infantilization as a displacement of the on-going struggle between the generations? Renouncing all forms of adult sexuality (whether homosexual or heterosexual), both men regress to an infantile state of pure orality, a point underscored by the childish joy with which they devour the restaurant's delicacies while coyly playing husband and wife. For that reason their final exit from the stages of Weimar modernity must be read as a happy ending not only for these two victims of historical change but also for all those nameless sup-porting characters on the margins of the narrative who can now continue to realize the new promises of social mobility and equality.

As I hope to have shown, the dynamization of narrative space that so enthralled contemporary critics of *The Last Laugh* has a powerful equivalent in the contradic-tory identifications that link character, star, and spectator and that account for the film's continuous relevance as a highly self-conscious reflection of ambivalence as the very condition of modernity. For that reason I disagree with Kracauer's conclusion that "since the film implies that authority, and authority alone, fuses the disparate social sphere into a whole, the fall of the uniform representing au-thority is bound to provoke anarchy" (Kracauer 1947, 100). Greater attention to Jannings's screen persona and performance suggests something very different, namely that these authoritarian structures represent a disturbance in the struggle for more democratic structures and egalitarian principles. Unmasked as someone still caught within the old dynamics of domination and submission, the old porter must be expelled from the modern designs for living. All too evidently, this process is painful, with the happy ending offering only some compensation for the victims of modernization and the enemies of democratization. The film's German title, which translates literally as "the last man," recognizes this inevitability of social and cultural change, whereas the English title emphasizes the psychological re-lease promised by the proverbial "last laugh." Yet one question remains ultimately unanswered: Who in fact gets the last laugh? The old porter (and with him, Jan-nings) as a representative of the Wilhelmine Empire or the young men and women as the true representatives of the Weimar Republic?

NOTES

1. Rejecting such inflation-driven fantasies as too artificial, the film's 1955 remake with Ger-man screen hero Hans Albers in the title role opts for a more conventional happy ending in accordance with the can-do mentality of the Economic Miracle; thus the "last man" is promoted and becomes senior manager of the hotel. Whereas the Weimar original of-fers a critique of authoritarian structures that extends to its emotional foundations, the remake accommodates a deep sociopsychological need for patriarchal authority. Ironi-

cally, in 1955 the reaffirmation of authority was achieved by an aging male star, Albers, who could have played the young hotel manager in the 1924 original.

2. Unless otherwise indicated, all translations are my own.

REFERENCES

Arnheim, Rudolf. 1977. *Kritiken und Aufsätze zum Film*. Ed. Helmut H. Diederichs. Munich: Hanser.

Coates, Paul. 1991. *The Gorgon's Gaze: German Cinema, Expressionism, and the Image of Horror*. Cambridge, UK: Cambridge University Press.

Eisner, Lotte. 1973. *Murnau*. London: Seeker and Warburg.

——. 1977. *The Haunted Screen: Expressionism in the German Cinema and the Influence of Max Reinhardt*. Trans. Roger Greaves. Berkeley: University of California Press.

Elsaesser, Thomas. 2000. *Weimar Cinema and After: Germany's Historical Imaginary*. London: Routledge.

——. 2003. "Weimar Cinema, Mobile Selves, and Anxious Males: Kracauer and Eisner Revisited." In *Expressionist Film: New Perspectives*, ed. Dietrich Scheunemann, 33–71. Rochester, NY: Camden House.

Esser, Michael, ed. 1994. *Gleißende Schatten: Kamerapioniere der zwanziger Jahre*. Berlin: Henschel Verlag.

Frankfurter, Bernhard, ed. 1997. *Carl Mayer: Im Spiegelkabinett des Dr. Caligari. Der Kampf zwischen Licht und Dunkel*. Vienna: Promedia.

Gehler, Fred, and Jürgen Kasten. 1990. *Friedrich Wilhelm Murnau*. Berlin/GDR: Henschel.

Hempel, Rolf. 1968. *Carl Mayer: Ein Autor schreibt mit der Kamera*. Berlin/GDR: Henschel.

Ihering, Herbert. 1961. *Von Reinhardt bis Brecht: Vier Jahrzehnte Theater und Film*. Vol. 1. Berlin/GDR: Aufbau-Verlag.

Jacobsen, Wolfgang, ed. 1992. *Babelsberg: Ein Filmstudio, 1912–1992*. Berlin: Argon.

Jacobsen, Wolfgang, Karl Prümm, and Benno Wenz, eds. 1991. *Willy Haas, der Kritiker als Mitproduzent: Texte zum Film, 1920–1933*. Berlin: Edition Hentrich.

Jansen, Peter W., and Wolfram Schütte, eds. 1990. *Friedrich Wilhelm Murnau*. Munich: Hanser.

Kasten, Jürgen. 1994. *Carl Mayer: Filmpoet: Ein Drehbuchautor schreibt Filmgeschichte*. Berlin: Vistas.

Kracauer, Siegfried. 1947. *From Caligari to Hitler: A Psychological History of the German Film*. Princeton, NJ: Princeton University Press.

Leder, Dietrich. 1988. "Tragischer Abstieg: Zur Archäologie der Psyche in *Der letzte Mann*." In *Friedrich Wilhelm Murnau, 1888–1988*, ed. Klaus Kreimeier, 69–75. Bielefeld: Bielefelder Verlagsanstalt.

Lethen, Helmut. 2002. *Cool Conduct: The Culture of Distance in Weimar Germany*. Trans. Don Reneau. Berkeley: University of California Press.

Mayer, Carl. 1924. *Der letzte Mann. Das Tagebuch* 5:1854–56.

McCormick, Richard. 2002. *Emancipation and Crisis: Gender, Sexuality, and "New Objectivity" in Weimar Film and Literature.* New York: Palgrave and St. Martin's.

Omasta, Michael, Brigitte Mayr, and Christian Cargnelli. 2003. *Carl Mayer: Scenarist.* Vienna: Synema.

Petro, Patrice. 1989. *Joyless Streets: Women and Melodramatic Representation in Weimar Germany.* Princeton, NJ: Princeton University Press.

Pinthus, Kurt. 1925. "Zwei Jannings-Filme." *Das Tagebuch* 6:26–28.

Prinzler, Hans Helmut, ed. 2003. *Friedrich Wilhelm Murnau: Ein Melancholiker des Films.* Berlin: Bertz.

Prümm, Karl. 2003. "Die bewegliche Kamera im mobilen Raum: *Der letzte Mann* von Friedrich Wilhelm Murnau." In *Diesseits der "Dämonischen Leinwand": Neue Perspektiven auf das späte Weimarer Kino,* ed. Thomas Koebner, Norbert Grob, and Bernd Kiefer, 41–57. Munich: Edition text + kritik.

Roth, Joseph. 1976. Review of *Der letzte Mann.* In *Werke,* ed. Hermann Kesten, 4:493–96. Cologne: Kiepenheuer.

Schindler, Stephan. 1996. "What Makes a Man a Man: The Construction of Masculinity in F. W. Murnau's *The Last Laugh.*" *Screen* 37, no. 1:30–40.

Vogt, Guntram. 2001. *Die Stadt im Film: Deutsche Spielfilme, 1900–2000.* Marburg: Schüren.

Weihsmann, Helmut. 1994. "Virtuelle Räume: Die Formsprache der Neuen Sachlichkeit bei Friedrich Wilhelm Murnau." In *Die Metaphysik des Dekors: Raum, Architektur, und Licht im klassischen deutschen Stummfilm,* ed. Klaus Kreimeier, 22–48. Marburg: Schüren.

———. 1997. "Die Stadt im Helldunkel: Konzept der Großstadt im deutschen Filmexpressionismus in Bedacht auf Carl Mayers Filmskripten." In *Carl Mayer: Im Spiegelkabinett des Dr. Caligari: Der Kampf zwischen Licht und Dunkel,* ed. Bernhard Frankfurter, 64–86. Vienna: Promedia.

SEVEN

INFLATION AND DEVALUATION

GENDER, SPACE, AND ECONOMICS IN
G.W. PABST'S *THE JOYLESS STREET* (1925)

SARA F. HALL

In the mid-1920s a walk down the street of a European metropolis could be a stimulating experience. Photographs on the covers of illustrated magazines jumped out from the newsstands, and display cases outside businesses and department stores tempted window-shoppers into making spontaneous purchases. Arc lamps cast pools of light and contrasting shadows onto the asphalt, and cinema marquees and signs above dance halls flashed, competing for pedestrians' attention and, ultimately, for their leisure time. Throngs of people bumped and bustled by, with individuals registering to one another as barely more than blurry shapes and vague features. Streetcars, buses, and automobiles whisked by at speeds no one could have imagined just ten years earlier, while traffic cops tried to maintain order with the aid of newly invented signals and lights. When the times were good, wares were exchanged with unprecedented ease and rapidity, and people entered into spaces and relationships previously inaccessible to them. But when times were not so good, the troubled masses protested, calling attention to their dissatisfaction about the limitations set on their access to resources and opportunities.

The city street was where much of twentieth-century modernity, with all its inherent contradictions, came to life. As the stage for dramatically new ways of living, this public thoroughfare became an emblem for novel and sometimes disorienting dimensions of urban experience. In the early years of the Weimar Republic the word *Straße* (street) itself began to appear with notable frequency in the titles of books, paintings, poems, and films. While some of the meanings attributed to a jaunt down the avenue in the cultural discourse of the time were based on firsthand experience, others were the fantasies (and nightmares) of individuals for whom the cityscape served as a projection surface for otherwise inexpressible desires and fears, representing all of the promises and concomitant dangers of venturing outside the safe walls of home.

In the fall of 1923 the many readers of the popular Viennese newspaper *Der Tag* were enjoying a serialized novel that evoked all of the ambivalence and complexity surrounding this mythology of the street with its title alone, *Die freudlose Gasse* or *The Joyless Street*. Written by Hugo Bettauer, a prolific novelist, magazine publisher, and controversial advocate for the sexual liberation movement, this pulpy murder mystery appealed to readers with its glimpses of the flashy allure of urban high society and revelations of the harsh financial and social realities that could easily turn the bright city street into a deadly trap. Bettauer's work tells the stories of several men and women who live, work, and play on a single street in Vienna, the *Melchiorgasse*, the "joyless street" of the title. Although originating from vastly differing financial and social circumstances, the characters in the elaborately woven narrative find themselves inhabiting a common space of social, moral, and economic crisis as a result of the extreme inflation that arose in Austria after World War I.

After appearing in installments from October 18 to December 16, 1923, the much discussed serial was published as a complete book in 1924, selling three hundred thousand copies that year alone (Noveck 1995, 367). Within months of the novel's publication, steps were taken to adapt it for a film to be directed by G. W. Pabst, whose debut films *Der Schatz* (*The Treasure*) and *Gräfin Donelli* (*Countess Donelli*) had premiered in 1923 and 1924 respectively. Even in its earliest incarnation, the sensational story seemed destined for the big screen. Bettauer, who would have nine of his novels transformed into movies over the span of his short career (Hall 1999, 156), had consciously foregrounded the cinematic qualities of this melodramatic murder mystery at several points in the story, where either the narrator or an individual character points out how a specific event or action resembles something straight out of a movie.

The roles in the film were cast in such as way as to guarantee both public attention and box-office draw, featuring a range of well-established film actors, along with some intriguing newcomers. The thirty-five-year-old veteran actress Asta Nielsen was cast as the poor and desperate Marie Lechner; the active and wide-ranging Werner Krauss would play the local butcher, Geiringer; the expressionist dancer and stage performer Valeska Gert took on the role of the dress-shop owner and madam, Frau Greifer; and a fresh face recruited from Sweden, twenty-year-old Greta Garbo, was cast as the resolutely innocent Grete Rumfort.

Because *The Joyless Street* was made at a moment when small production companies were having trouble getting loans from German banks, casting that would capture both national and international attention was an important part of making the project seem financially viable. Ironically, the German film industry had flourished under rampant inflation, which allowed cheap productions to be distributed to foreign markets for payments based in more valuable currency, but it was hurt by the stabilization brought on with the Dawes Plan in 1924 (Cook 1981, 131). As it worked out, the money to make the film came from mostly foreign sources, marking what was, according to a report in the *Berlin Lokal-Anzeiger*, the first German-Russian-French coproduction in film history.

In December 1924 Pabst met with his initial funder, a Russian-Jewish sugar manufacturer based in Paris named Romain Pinès, who had originally agreed to support the director's plan to adapt a Yiddish play called "The Dybbuk" for the screen. When Pinès seemed to express some hesitancy about the financial risk involved in this production, Pabst put forth a suggestion to create instead a movie version of Bettauer's popular inflation drama, *The Joyless Street*. The terms of the contract were changed, and Pinès gave Pabst $40,000 to commence filming (Pabst 1997, 138).

The production was overseen by a company called Société des Films Artistiques, "Sofar Films" for short, which was headed up by a Russian attorney named Michael Salkin. As both names of the production house might suggest, this was an independent firm; working with Sofar allowed the team of Pabst, Marc Sorkin, and Willy Haas to make the film quickly and outside of a studio system increasingly controlled by American interests ("Interview with Marc Sorkin" 1995, 25–26). The cast and crew shot the film on a studio lot in Berlin in just thirty-four days, working sixteen hours a day (yet still exceeded the $40,000 budget). Production wrapped up in late March 1925, and the premiere took place at the Mozartsaal cinema in Berlin on May 18. Sofar Productions also controlled the film's distribution, reaping substantial profits from a film so popular that in June of 1925 it played in twenty-three cinemas in the greater Berlin area alone. According to ads that ran for the film in the trade papers, five of these venues were in Neukölln, a predominantly working-class neighborhood. *The Joyless Street* also went on to play in Paris's Les Ursulines cinema for almost two years running (Koll 1998, 75).

The projected success of the film seemed to ride not only on the cast but also on people's familiarity with Bettauer's book, so just as principal photography was beginning, the author's persona was mobilized in a clever ad published in the trade paper *Die Lichtbild-Bühne* in February of 1925. The notice took the form of a (presumably) fictional business letter to the author, printed on the letterhead of the Sofar Film Company, announcing that the entire cast of the film (whose names were listed in eye-catching capital letters) would be coming to Vienna to visit the places where the events of the fictional story were supposed to have taken place. In an effort to establish the film as an authentic portrayal of social hardship, the letter proposed the following: "Because the group ... desires to study the life and activity on the 'joyless street,' its members will do without any creature comforts when it comes to accommodations; they want to have nothing to do with Hotel Carlson and have asked us to bid you kindly that you please do your best to assure them a reservation at the Hotel Merkl in the Melchiorgasse" (*Die Lichtbild-Bühne*, February 1925; my translation).

Of course the Hotel Carlson (the location of the high-society indulgences in the story) and the Hotel Merkl (the dive frequented by clandestine lovers and prostitutes) did not really exist in Vienna, nor did the Melchiorgasse itself. Descriptions of the setting in the novel would indicate that it represented a fictional version of a street like the Neustiftgasse, which traverses a broad range of socioeconomic settings, starting at the heart of the city's cultural center near the Volkstheater and running west, bisecting the seventh district, an area known in the period as a setting for illegal activity (Eichner 1994, 119). With its allusion to the fictional spaces as though they were real, the advertisement reveals just how familiar readers of the journal would have been with the details of Bettauer's story and how hungry movie audiences were expected to be for a visual portrayal that corresponded to the version of Vienna created in it. The author also offered his endorsement of the production, though his intentions to visit the set were never realized—he was assassinated in his Vienna office by a right-wing extremist on March 12, 1925, the same month shooting concluded in Berlin.

Despite the fact that so much of the film's publicity emphasized its connection to the work of the vastly popular, and recently martyred, Bettauer, screenwriter and prominent literary editor Willy Haas took strides over the course of his own career to distinguish his craftsmanship from the original work. Looking back on the evolution of the adaptation project, Haas noted:

> I read the book. It was a miserable crime novel, a thriller from Vienna's inflation years. But I knew right away exactly what appealed to G. W. Pabst, with his unmistakable flair for all things contemporary: it was the harsh social portrayal of inflation, the bankruptcy of the old-established patrician circles of civil servants and academics, the corruption, the moral decay, which we also experienced in Berlin. We concurred at once that the film had to be geared toward the social, and that the criminal elements would fall aside. Almost all that would remain was the title, which Pabst found appealing. (Haas 1957, 88)

Although the resemblances are more striking than the scenarist might have wanted his readers to believe, he and Pabst did indeed alter the story in their adaptation. In addition to many plot changes, references to specific streets, neighborhoods, and popular operas and songs that made the serialized novel so vivid to contemporary audiences are absent from the film, seemingly because it was produced to appeal to broad audiences internationally. Overall, the sensationalist tone of Bettauer's novel is darkened by a mood of desperation and claustrophobia in Pabst's rendition. The resultant portrayal of poverty, along with the parallel scenes of exaggerated indulgence on the part of those in Vienna who still had access to money and the good times it could buy, earned the film its place in international cinema history and Pabst his early reputation as a politically progressive critic of his times.

The fact that *The Joyless Street* proved to be a theatrical success, as well as a turning point in the career of the director and some of his cast members, does not, however, mean that the film adaptation was met only with positive reviews when it premiered. Overt praise was especially hard to come by in comments from fans of Bettauer's novel, such as those in a review from the Vienna paper, the *Neue Freie Presse* on November 13, 1925, which evaluated the adaptation somewhat ambivalently:

> Throughout its entire development, this novel was born to be a film.... However, some of the alterations and rearrangements complicate, erase and mangle the clever and logically thought-out, albeit shallow, plot and the superficial, but accurate portrayal of the characters from the original work, which revolves around the harsh depiction of the post-war circumstances and with their partially lamentable, partially disreputable and even criminal life forms. Nonetheless, the direction achieves outstanding effects in some scenes: just to name an example, in the scene of standing in line, in which the true-to-nature characters awaken chilling memories.

Almost all reviewers—whether positively or negatively disposed or ambivalent, like the one cited here—were impressed by the film's divergence from more common visual styles of the day, in particular by its naturalistic rendition of poverty. *The Joyless Street* is neither a painterly, subjective expressionist drama nor a stagy melodrama nor a quick and light serial adventure, although for various reasons its cast and title would have appealed to the fans of any of those types of films. The mode of representation is strikingly realist, although the realism is couched in a melodramatic narrative form. Without discarding entirely the visual elements associated with other styles and genres, for example menacing shadows, uncanny spaces, and emotionally laden symbolism, in *The Joyless Street* Pabst manifested a new kind of "innate realism" in the words of Siegfried Kracauer, who praised the film: "nothing is stylized; rather it springs from the desire to watch the course events take of their own accord.... Instead of arranging significant pictorial compositions, Pabst arranges real life material with veracity as his sole object. He is the spirit of the photographer" (Kracauer 1947, 168).

This cool and critical view of social reality would come to be identified as *Neue Sachlichkeit*, or New Objectivity, a visual and narrative style that featured prominently in the artistic, literary, and journalistic culture of the stabilization period and onward in, for example, the art of Otto Dix and George Grosz, writing by Egon Erwin Kisch, and some of Pabst's later films. The qualities in *The Joyless Street* that we now identify as characteristic of New Objectivity are the result not just of the unique directorial vision of Pabst but also of a confluence of creative energies on the part of Haas, Sorkin (editor), and a highly skilled team of set designers, cinematographers, and lighting experts. In the winter of 1924–25 production designers Otto Erdmann and Hans Sohnle went to work creating the decrepit, confining environment of the Melchiorgasse by painting over indoor sets already standing on the lot at the Zoo Atelier in Berlin, darkening them to look more decayed. The gloomy, confining outdoor sets were built at the Staaken studio, a converted Zeppelin hangar west of the city, where German filmmakers were beginning to experiment with the use of elaborate artificial lighting on a scale comparable to that already in place in the major Hollywood studios. Kracauer and others have noted that in the subject matter, the setting, and some of the staging (especially the line outside the butcher shop), Pabst and his team borrowed from *Isn't Life Wonderful*, D. W. Griffith's 1924 film about a family of Polish refugees trying to survive in Germany during the postwar inflation, the exterior shots of which were actually recorded in Germany (Kracauer 1947, 169).

Pabst and his producers assembled a team of skilled cameramen including Robert Lach, Curt Oertel, and Guido Seeber to shoot the film. Their innovative play with high- and low-contrast light, camera movement, thematically motivated close framing, different film stocks, and variable recording speeds contributed not only to the *Stimmung*, or feeling and atmosphere, as has been noted by such critics as Lotte Eisner, but also to character development and to the value that individual cast members added to the story. For example, the female leads were shot in the manner believed to be most becoming to their faces and most in keeping with the star image they aspired to project. Guido Seeber had been working with Asta Nielsen since her early films in Denmark and had been instrumental in her rise as the iconic face of silent-film emotion and eroticism. He shot her as Marie in *The Joyless Street* in such a way as to create the image of a striking, but aging, femme fatale who was at the same time emotionally complex and sympathetic. And it is in large part due to the camera work that Greta Garbo's character, and her developing star persona, evolve in the film as they do. For example, the use of slow motion contributes an intense yet ethereal quality to her performance in dramatic moments such as when Grete Rumfort is pursued by her boss in the office or when Lieutenant Davy chases after her backstage at Frau Greifer's performance hall.

Allegedly, this mode of shooting Garbo's scenes was devised as a solution for the ingénue's apparent nervousness before the camera. According to those present on the set, her self-consciousness sometimes reduced her to quivering. After shooting a scene between Egon Stirner and Marie in which a briefcase falls to the floor between them, the crew observed that when shot at the normal recording speed, the fall of the briefcase barely registered on film. They repeated the take and this time sped up from the usual eighteen frames-per-second to twenty-five frames-per-second on the hand-cranked camera. As a result, the fall of the briefcase appeared slow and drawn out when projected, achieving a more dramatic effect. It occurred to Pabst that if he shot the shaky Garbo in this way, her performance would look more natural. Indeed, the slow-motion technique provided a softness and an emphasis on Garbo's eyes and hands that would have been passed over at a regular shooting speed. This technique was carried over into Garbo's earliest American movies as well (Pabst 1997, 148).

Greta Garbo was relatively new to the film industry, and her interests were protectively represented by the director Mauritz Stiller, with whom she had been working closely in Sweden. Stiller was so intimately involved in the young actress's work on this first film outside of her home country that he changed aspects of the script and tried to control the production conditions for her scenes. According to at least one Garbo biographer, Stiller was responsible for the addition of the purchase of the fur coat as a plot element, and he and Pabst together agreed on the type of film stock with which all of Garbo's close-ups were to be recorded (Payne 2002, 77–94). As a result, the shots in which she appears have a slightly brighter and softer quality. This minor detail wound up adding dramatically to the visual contrast that develops between the scenes portraying Marie's tale of desperation and murder and those relating Grete's tale of noble moral rectitude and salvation through a romantic relationship.

Pabst's subject matter seemed to necessitate this highly nuanced and critically realist visual style that was the result of such an innovative combination of set design, lighting, performance, cinematography, and careful editing. The narrative is set in the Austrian capital in the fall of 1921, a period of spiraling inflation following from the circumstances accompanying the culmination of World War I and the abdication of Austro-Hungarian emperor Karl I in November 1918. As in Germany, excessive wartime spending and import deficits had created a large national debt, and the end of the war meant the slowing and eventual end of the revenue from the tax on war profits that had been in place. In 1919 the Treaties of St.-Germain and Trianon, between Austria and the Allies, not only reduced foreign assistance and saddled the vanquished nation with reparation payments but also stripped the former Habsburg Empire of many of the resources that might have helped to balance the budget. Protests and riots erupted, and relief efforts in the form of soup kitchens and public-aid initiatives were undertaken. Where possible, Austria borrowed large amounts of money from domestic and international sources, which had the effect of depreciating the value of its currency, the crown. The national treasury began printing more money in 1920 to make up for the lessened cash flow, which set inflation into a violent spiral: prices multiplied by a factor of about eleven thousand times over the years between 1914 and 1922.

In early 1922 the British granted a large credit to Austria, which alleviated conditions for a short while, but prices still increased by 2,400 percent between the summers of 1921 and 1922 (Myers 1993, 50–51). At that point the Austrian government turned again to the Allies, who agreed to provide a loan under the auspices of the League of Nations but only on the condition that no further currency be issued. This arrangement stabilized the currency but also reduced purchasing power, which meant a slowdown in industrial production, so workers were laid off, and unemployment in Vienna increased by 400 percent from August 1922 to February 1923. At the end of 1924 a new currency unit, the shilling, was introduced to eliminate the spiraling deflation of the value of the crown, and in a euphoric response to the improved outlook, the stock market boomed in early 1924. But once reality set in, investors wavered, and the market index dropped, which resulted by mid-decade in the failure of many banks.

By tracing the effects of the Austrian financial crisis on the day-to-day lives of a cast of individuals from class backgrounds ranging from the homeless, to the working poor, to respected professionals, and to high-rolling financiers, *The Joyless Street* seems to have encouraged its original audiences to make direct associations between the economic events around them and the experiences and actions of specific characters. Following this train of association, audiences in 1925 would have seen Marie Lechner's father (Max Kohlhaase) as representative of the unemployed proletariat; Grete Rumfort's father (Jaro Fürth) as emblematic of the disenfranchised imperial civil servants previously employed by the royal Habsburg court; Cañez (Robert Garrison) as representative of foreign investors who dump overvalued foreign currency into the market at the cost of local stability; Egon Stirner (Henry Stuart) as the embodiment of self-indulgent and inexperienced speculators whose imprudence gives rise to social tragedy; and Lieutenant Davy of the American Red Cross as the beneficent Allied presence who comes in from outside and reestablishes order in the place of chaos, magnanimity in the place of greed (Fig. 7.1).

It is interesting, however, that while these male characters mark the tale in terms of economic history, their stories are not where the substantial narrative interest lies. They shape the social and material circumstances in this fictional version of postwar Vienna, but it is the women who must navigate the fallout. The challenges they face constitute the emotional, dramatic, and symbolic focus from the very beginning of the film, where, in the opening sequence the camera follows Grete as she meets up with her father and Marie as she tries to avoid hers. The first shots orient the viewer to the fact that these women's efforts at social and economic catch-up and self-protection will play out as the physical navigation of their "joyless street," whose labyrinthine spaces become a social and moral minefield for those women who seek a better life.

FIGURE 7.1 Grete Rumfort (Greta Garbo) and Lieutenant Davy (Einar Hanson) represent hope and romantic love in the face of tragedy in G. W. Pabst's *The Joyless Street* (1922).

Spatial relationships are thus central to the film's narrative. The arrangement of the domestic, entertainment, and business venues serves as a representational code that, when deciphered, reveals just how prominently geography and real estate figure in the formation of identity and morality in the society depicted. Cracking this code is made difficult, though, because of a complicated history of censorship and the vicissitudes of film preservation; not all versions of this film that are currently in circulation are edited in the same way. Regardless of the copy of the film at hand, however, certain observations hold true. For example, the spaces of *The Joyless Street* are conceptually (if not always visually) organized around vertical and horizontal axes. Along the vertical axis, the underground spaces are akin to one another; for example, the Lechners' apartment and Geiringer's butcher shop are both places where men violently exploit women and are sites of potential violent rebellion on the part of those women (Fig. 7.2). Second-story spaces are the sites of either romantic or sexual encounters. Along the horizontal axis, the seemingly upstanding places of business, such as Frau Greifer's dress shop, the office in which Grete works, and the butcher shop itself, possess back rooms (sometimes also on the second floor) where the true business of life in Vienna goes on: prostitution, sexual harassment, exploitation, and even murder (Koll 1998, 98) (Fig. 7.3).

FIGURE 7.2 A site of violent exploitation and potential rebellion: the shop of Geiringer, the Butcher of Melchiorgasse (Werner Krauss).

FIGURE 7.3 Frau Greifer (Valeska Gert) tempts Grete with a fur coat.

Despite this well-conceived code, there is something fundamentally disorienting about the representation of the spaces and the crossing points between them. The spectator's view of one space from another is often blocked or partially obscured by a curtain or door or etched glass, and access to adjacent spaces is usually mediated through a point-of-view shot on the part of an emotionally excited character or is reflected in a mirror. Together, space and vision factor into the major misunderstandings that complicate the plot, such as Lieutenant Davy's thinking that Grete has become a prostitute or the police suspecting Cañez and then Egon of murder. In reality, Grete, Cañez, and Egon have simply been seen in the wrong place at the wrong time.

Throughout most of Pabst's film, the viewer has the sense that something that should be clear, that is, the location of the apartments, shops, and rooms along the Melchiorgasse in relation to one another, is not in fact clear. This effect of disorientation within a very closed world speaks to the film's historical moment. Underlying the New Objectivity portrayal is an unspoken memory (perhaps a fantasy) of a time before the war and inflation, when spatial and social relations were much more transparent and where members of the various classes circulated safely among their own kind. Middle-class values reigned in middle-class spaces, and spaces of illicit and dangerous behavior were recognizable as such. In this earlier reality one knew what kind of person one was dealing with according to the part of town in which the meeting occurred (Koll 1998, 77–120). In the early and mid-1920s, however, everything was in a state of flux, which in the film is translated into spatial transformations that either happen prior to the unfolding of the story or over the course of the film's narrative. A dress shop, which in an earlier day would have been a privileged space of middle- and upper-class consumer indulgence, serves as a front for a brothel where the daughters of those formerly middle- and upper-class families are exploited. The Rumforts' home, previously a pillar of bourgeois security and proper values, is reduced to the status of a boardinghouse when the family must take in Lieutenant Davy as a tenant.

The negative impact of that incursion on the stability of patriarchal family life becomes apparent when Lieutenant Davy's friend alleges that little Marie has taken some of the canned food brought by the Americans out of the cabinet. The father's instinctive pride leads him to defend his daughter, despite all indications that the girl has indeed taken the food, which costs the household the sum of Davy's rent when Rumfort drives out the Americans. The economic reality no longer accommodates emotional responses based on old-fashioned values and assumptions.

Along with the loss of such social distinction comes a loss of spatial distinction. Therefore, although the spaces along *The Joyless Street* are carefully organized and distinguished from one another along the horizontal and vertical axes, they are also attached in an unsettling circularity, which allows characters to move about

FIGURE 7.4   The crowd of hungry citizens swells outside of Geiringer's butcher shop.

in seemingly socially inappropriate ways: middle-class girls end up in brothels, and upper-class women sneak off in the night to seedy hotels, and these two worlds are linked by back doors, dark hallways, and translucent panes of glass. The moments when the characters cross over between the socially marked spaces, such as when Marie enters the room in which Egon and Lia Leid share their tryst or when Grete is pushed out onto the stage with Frau Greifer's entourage of girls, constitute some of the most significant turning points in the film. Once-discreet borders are now cracks in the foundation of the social world.

Parallel editing draws connections between the various sections of the cityscape, lest the audience be inclined to see the upstanding bourgeois world and the seedy back rooms as distinct from one another and deny their imbrication. In a classic example of Pabst's and Sorkin's highly innovative use of the technique, the film moves back and forth between the decadent party at the Hotel Carlson and the line outside the butcher shop, going so far as to imply a cause-and-effect relationship between the social excesses of financial exploiters like Cañez and the suffering of Grete, Marie, and Else at the hands of the butcher Geiringer and the shopkeeper and madam Greifer (Fig. 7.4). The audience sees, and is asked to judge, that which the revelers and gamblers refuse to acknowledge.

With its thematic emphasis on vision and subjectivity, crime and sexuality, the relationship between private and public life in the city, and the decline of the middle class, *The Joyless Street* stands as one of the major representatives of the Weimar street film. Like *film noir*, the term *street film* was not a prescriptive generic designation per se but a set of characteristics that became useful over time, first in marketing and then, retrospectively, in categorizing certain Weimar films. Made between 1923 and 1930, these urban melodramas most often take place in a contemporary setting and feature a dissatisfied middle-class man who, burning to break out of home and routine, ventures into the city at nightfall, coming face-to-face with the criminal underworld and a dangerous seductress on his way. In many such films the urban avenue is portrayed as a threatening and anxious space, which the protagonist then attempts to escape by returning home to the safe structure of middle-class family life. In some scenarios that domestic space remains a place of refuge; but in Pabst's film and others something in the outside world has disrupted the tranquility and reliability of home, and the street and the living room are equally fraught with problems. In another stock street-film scenario, which also plays out in Pabst's 1925 film, a lower-class woman tries to escape poverty or the underworld but eventually perishes, a victim of her circumstances. This plot characterizes Bruno Rahn's *Dirnentragödie* (*Tragedy of the Street*, 1927), an example of a subset of the street films that have come to be identified as the *Dirnenfilme* (prostitute films).

The street film's cast of characters, the setting, and the style also carry over into the noir crime films made in the United States by German and Austrian émigrés such as Edgar G. Ulmer, Robert Siodmak, and Billy Wilder in the 1940s. Both film series involve the urban explorer, the femme fatale, and the grounded, maternal female in a psychologized melodrama where nocturnal studio sets are shot with evocative lighting and controlled framing in order to contrast the criminal underworld with the precarious stability of the bourgeois interior. One film in particular is regarded as a prototype of this genre: Karl Grune's 1923 *The Street*, which premiered in Berlin in exactly the same month that Bettauer's readers were enjoying the serialized version of *The Joyless Street* in *Der Tag*. Grune's film tells the story of a middle-class man who is drawn out of his staid home life and away from his plain wife when the flashing lights and whirling images of the city catch his eye through the window of his comfortably appointed living room. Despite signals that warn him against big-city dangers, such as the flashing eye of an optometrist's sign and a police officer working assiduously to maintain order in the midst of thundering traffic, the man, guided only by his desires, joins a young woman (presumably a prostitute) who invites him to accompany her to a dance hall where several characters indulge in a game of cards (Fig. 7.5). The man's curiosity gets the best of him, and he follows the woman and her other companions out of the dance hall and through a back alley to an apartment building, where he sees the woman's criminal associates rob and murder a naive country bumpkin who had won their money at cards. Although merely a witness to the crime, the protagonist is mistaken as the culprit when the police arrive on the scene. He desperately considers suicide in his

FIGURE 7.5 Middle-class stability is threatened by the lure of the urban underworld. A nocturnal encounter beneath the optometrist sign in Karl Grune's *Die Straße* (*The Street*, 1923).

jail cell but is stopped just in time when the real killers are identified by the prostitute's child, who lives in the apartment where the murder took place. Shaken by the experience, the protagonist meekly returns to the safety of his middle-class home and the familiar routine of life with his spouse.

The Street presents a series of diverse views of the urban thoroughfare that are very different from those offered in Pabst's 1925 film. In fact, with its wide range of female characters and critical exploration of the economic hardships that lie behind the facades of the shop windows, cafés, and dance halls, *The Joyless Street* provides speculative answers to a question never even raised, let alone addressed, in many other street films of the era: what is the prostitute's story?

Because it confronts that question head-on, Pabst's film met with resistance from critics and censors. Conditions in Austria had improved in the years between the time when *The Joyless Street* is set (1921) and when the book and movie came out (1924–25), and inflation there was never as severe as that which Germany experienced (Fig. 7.6). But when it came to the concomitant shifts in social relations, especially the commodification of sex, the devaluation of love, and the outbreak of violence in women's lives, a sense of discomfort still reigned. Not everyone at the time approved of such a vivid portrayal of disorder and malaise. The review published in the German social democratic newspaper *Vorwärts* put things this way:

FIGURE 7.6 Historical photo of women standing in a Berlin food line, overseen by police officers, 1923. Ullstein Bild / The Granger Collection, New York.

"We still stand too close to these events, and we experienced them all too much in our own bodies for us to be able to face them with the appropriate distance. We are still stirred into a frenzy by the film's contents, still moved to deep compassion for the victims of this pestilence that ate away at humanity's physical and moral health; we still shake our fists at those who shamelessly exploited this crisis and at the impudent users who captured their prey wherever they could" (Myers 1993, 44n3; my translation).

The vividness of the portrayal became a bone of contention for censors, both locally and abroad, and the varied actions they took to tone down or recast the impact and message of the film over the years led to a proliferation of significantly different versions of the film being distributed, seen, and reviewed. This situation makes the film difficult to examine in search of definitive interpretations based on highly specific formal elements such as editing, shot length, tinting, or narrative structure, but it also makes it a perfect case study in the history of film reconstruction efforts on the part of censors, exhibitors, and restoration specialists at archives and museums.

It is important that today's viewers of the film know at the outset that the Kino International version on VHS, which is the most complete version currently in commercial distribution with English intertitles, is based on a French version preserved at the Cinémathèque Française that is known to be missing more than four reels of the original footage (Horak 1998). The running time of the Kino International version is ninety-six minutes, whereas the original projection time was well over two hours. Those of us watching the film today are not alone in our attempts to appreciate and study the film on the basis of a recut facsimile, though—even the earliest "standard" interpretations by Siegfried Kracauer and Lotte Eisner written after World War II were formulated with no access to the film as it was originally conceived and cut by its creators.

The story of how such a truncated and radically altered version of the film ended up in movie houses, video stores, and classrooms is a long and complex one, which began when the film first came before the German censorship board on May 25, 1925, where the first four meters were removed. Cutting continued on the night before the film's premiere, when Sorkin and Pabst are said to have been asked to shorten the film by a theater owner who wanted a less lengthy program, and the alterations were compounded according to different agendas in the various export destination countries.

In Germany the film came before the national censors again in March 1926, when the authorities in the state of Baden hoped to have it banned on the basis of the 1920 "Reich Moving Picture Law" (*Reichslichtspielgesetz*), which forbade the exhibition of films that would endanger public order or safety, injure religious sensibilities, or have an immoral effect on audiences. The board of review did not find the film to be generally immoral or seditious; however, it did agree that seven specific scenes were problematic and decided that only with their removal could the film be rendered harmless. *The Joyless Street* was thereby reduced from 3,738 meters to 3,477 meters in an act of editing that was in no way motivated by narrative or formal considerations. As a result, crucial developments in the plot and character motivation were lost, and the film became harder to follow and less consistent dramatically. According to the documentation of the March 1926 censorship hearing, among the crucial sequences removed were a close-up of the butcher peering through his basement shop window at the bare lower legs of two women passing by, a man tearing the blouse from a woman's shoulders, an allusion to the butcher raping Else in the meat locker while Marie waits to get some food for her own family, a shot of Marie grabbing the neck of Cañez as she relives the moment that she strangled Lia, a couple of revealing shots of women who are half-dressed or wearing revealing clothing, and a close-up of the butcher's face streaming with blood after Else has struck him on the head during the uprising of the hungry populace at the film's end.

In an outraged article entitled "The Castrated Butcher" that Willy Haas himself published in the highbrow literary journal *Die literarische Welt* in June 1928, the scenarist rails against the latest cut of the film, which he had just seen screened. He describes the most recent excisions as follows:

The real hero of this film is a typical inflation-era butcher shop owner, who officially is "out of meat," but who behind closed doors distributes as much as anyone wants, especially to young women and girls who do favors for him. And so he prostitutes an entire street. The fact that this and much worse happened during the inflation is documented in hundreds of newspaper reports. The main scene has been eliminated, the one in which a young woman hears the price that her friend pays for her meat in the adjacent room. I did not show any of this overtly at the time, only the horrified face of the girl who hears what is happening, a pantomimed monologue scene played by the great Asta Nielsen. But now the censor has cut out this scene—now, after three years. The butcher now gives the girl meat for some inexplicable reason, probably out of magnanimity. The film is ruined.

It is undeniable that these and other excisions confused the plot and destroyed some of the transitions that had been carefully chosen by Pabst and his editor, Sorkin, who were already becoming masters of such continuity techniques as the eyeline match, the match-on-motion, and parallel editing. On almost every occasion of censoring and shortening, the film's pieces had to be rearranged to make the story intelligible again, and as a result the versions proliferated exponentially. Only by carefully comparing the various prints in circulation and stored in archives around the world were the members of a team at the Munich Filmmuseum able to put together a definitive version that closely resembles the original print—and even that is available from only a few very protective archives (Horak 1998).

Understanding this film thus means considering it with and without the various pieces that were rearranged, removed, and replaced along the way. In fact, the major cuts made in Germany in 1926 can themselves tell us a great deal about how the film was conceived and how its themes and story resonated with the times (Petro 1990). All seven sequences display one or more of the following qualities: they show a man taking violent sexual advantage of a woman with no financial resources; they show women's bodies in varying states of undress; they display female sexual appeal in an overt manner; or they represent a desperate act of violence on the part of a distraught and impoverished woman. The selection of such scenes reveals a deep anxiety toward and about women as sexual and financial agents in the tumultuous inflation years, displaying a conflicted sense of protectionism surrounding female virtue, which coexists uncomfortably with fear toward the potential excessive tendencies of a femme fatale. Grounding their response to the film in the 1920 Reich Motion Picture Law, which concerned itself mostly with films' effects rather than their contents, the 1926 censorship board focused its attention on the film's likely demoralizing influence on women in the audience, who censors assumed might conclude that prostitution and murder could be justified as the necessary consequences of misery and deprivation.

Moreover, although the censors did not comment explicitly on the distinctly different conclusions of each of the film's narrative threads, one can see how such a multifaceted ending would make the film hard to categorize and contain politically. Because each of the film's female protagonists chooses a unique path to overcome her hardship and to vent (or quiet) her frustrations, the film offers multiple, very distinct, points of emotional and political identification for the female viewer. Without privileging one over the other, the film threatens to radically destabilize the social status quo, which in a patriarchal society like the one prevailing in 1920s Austria and Germany would tend to favor the type of outcome achieved by Grete, who escapes the brothel to be united with an upstanding family-oriented man. Yet how is one to judge Marie, who is antagonized by a violent father and finally snaps when faced with the fact that she has sacrificed her integrity to raise money for a callous and self-interested boyfriend who only wants to use that money to woo a wealthier woman? The film implies that for every Grete, there are numerous other women who will never find a place in the patriarchal bourgeois moral order. In that regard Grete's little sister Mariandl (or Marie as she is named in the English intertitles of the film) serves, as do many children depicted in Weimar cinema, as a warning to look out for the interests of future generations.

On the one hand, Pabst's film foregrounds the experiences of women and appeals specifically to female viewers (Petro 1989) and working-class spectators (Murray 1990). It also holds a magnifying glass to the social ills that lead some of them into seemingly immoral behavior, implying that they ought not be judged blindly for their decisions and impulses without attention being paid to their personal circumstances. In a climate in which women's bodies are traded like meat, real estate, and stocks, modern women seem to have no truly free choices in the first place. The film thus gestures toward a radical social and legal critique carried over from Hugo Bettauer's own positions on the relationship between economics and marriage and sex reform as they were spelled out in his magazine *Er und Sie: Wochenzeitschrift für Lebenskultur und Erotik* (He and She: Lifestyles and Eroticism Weekly), which was quickly shut down by government authorities over the course of 1924. The closing episode of the film, in which the hungry masses revolt, burn down the brothel, and assassinate the butcher radically complicates rather than resolves the Melchiorgasse's problems (Coulson 2003, 204–5).

On the other hand, the film casts a highly suspicious light on Frau Greifer's apparently homosexual desires, and it has been charged with letting Egon off the hook for his dalliances, while punishing Lia and Marie for their infidelity (Myers 1993). Certain questions about the film continue to be debated by scholars and critics. For instance, by showing society's double standards and revealing the ways that a patriarchal family structure and economic system destroy women's well-being, does the film inherently endorse and reinforce these conditions? Or does it offer critical exposure that could motivate protest and transformation? Does it advocate violence as a revolutionary means for social change? Is it possible that because of the diversity of its narrative strands the film is able to do all of this at the same time?

Because of its engagement with such historically identifiable issues, themes, and controversies, *The Joyless Street* has often been read as a realistic document of its time. Some film historians coming from a different angle have focused on the important place the film holds in the evolution of film style and genre. It can also be considered as a case study in authorship and the process of collaboration between directors, producers, set designers, screenwriters, and editors in the silent-film era or as an example of the impact of censorship on film distribution and reception. Its production history even tells a great deal about the economic and material conditions behind the development of the studio system and the growth of a national film industry in Germany.

Yet the film's critical stance and aesthetic complexity make it much more than a vessel for socioeconomic information about the inflationary period or a milestone in the evolution of New Objectivity or the social problem film. *The Joyless Street* revealed shocking images and unleashed strong responses from audiences in 1925 because it challenged the status quo in ways other texts did not or could not. Like the other Weimar street films, it served as a space of projection and negotiation for a range of truly modern fantasies and nightmares about life beyond the four walls of home. What distinguishes it from them is how it prompts us to think about the relationship between space, vision, power, and the economy, especially in as far as all four involve gender. Its enduring appeal may be rooted in Pabst's willingness to pose hard questions about the troubled nature of that relationship without always providing definitive answers.

REFERENCES

Cook, David. 1981. *A History of Narrative Film*. New York: Norton.

Coulson, Anthony. 2003. "Entrapment and Escape: Readings of the City in Karl Grune's *The Street* and G. W. Pabst's *The Joyless Street*." In *Expressionist Film: New Perspectives*, ed. Dietrich Scheunemann, 187–209. Rochester, NY: Camden House.

Eichner, Hans. 1994. "City Without Jews: Hugo Bettauer's Vienna." In *Hinter dem schwarzen Vorhang. Festschrift für Anthony W. Riley*, ed. Anthony W. Riley, Friedrich Gaede, Patrick O'Neill, and Ulrich Scheck, 109–27. Tübingen: A. Francke Verlag.

Haas, Willy. 1957. *Die literarische Welt: Erinnerungen*. Munich: Paul List.

Hall, Murray. 1999. "Hugo Bettauer." In *Elektrische Schatten: Beiträge zur Österreichischen Stummfilmgeschichte*, ed. Francesco Bono, Paolo Caneppele, and Günter Krenn, 149–68. Vienna: Film Archiv Austria.

Horak, Jan-Christopher. 1998. "Film History and Film Preservation: Reconstructing the Text of *The Joyless Street* (1925)." *Screening the Past*, no. 5: www.latrobe.edu.au/screeningthepast/firstrelease/fir1298/jhfr5b.html (accessed August 26, 2004).

"Interview with Marc Sorkin." 1955. *Six Talks on G. W. Pabst: The Man, the Director, the Artist. Cinemages* 3:23–40.

Koll, Gerald. 1998. *Pandora's Schätze: Erotikkonzeptionen in den Stummfilmen von G. W. Pabst*. Munich: Schaudig and Ledig.

Kracauer, Siegfried. 1947. *From Caligari to Hitler. A Psychological History of the German Film*. Princeton, NJ: Princeton University Press.

Munby, Jonathan. 1999. "Strassenfilm." In *The BFI Companion to German Cinema*, ed. Thomas Elsaesser and Michael Wedel, 230. London: BFI.

Murray, Bruce. 1990. *Film and the German Left in the Weimar Republic: From Caligari to Kuhle Wampe*. Austin: University of Texas Press.

Myers, Tracy. 1993. "History and Realism: Representations of Women in G. W. Pabst's *The Joyless Street*." In *Gender and German Cinema: Feminist Interventions*. Vol. 2, *German Film History / German History on Film*, ed. Sandra Frieden, Richard W. McCormick, Vibeke R. Petersen, and Laurie Melissa Vogelsang, 43–59. Providence, RI: Berg.

Noveck, Beth Simone. 1995. "Hugo Bettauer's Vienna, 1918–1925." In *Jura Soyfer and His Time*, ed. Donald G. Daviau, 366–87. Riverside, CA: Ariadne Press.

Pabst, Michael. 1997. "Die freudlose Gasse." In *G. W. Pabst*, ed. Wolfgang Jacobsen, 137–50. Berlin: Stiftung Deutsche Kinemathek and Argon Verlag.

Payne, Robert. *The Great Garbo*. New York: Cooper Square Press, 2002.

Petro, Patrice. 1989. *Joyless Streets: Women and Melodramatic Representation in Weimar Germany*. Princeton, NJ: Princeton University Press.

——. 1990. "Film Censorship and the Female Spectator: *The Joyless Street* (1925)." In *The Films of G. W. Pabst: An Extraterritorial Cinema*, ed. Eric Rentschler, 30–40. New Brunswick, NJ: Rutgers University Press.

Rentschler, Eric. 1990. "The Problematic Pabst: An *Auteur* Directed by History." In *The Films of G. W. Pabst: An Extraterritorial Cinema*, ed. Eric Rentschler, 1–23. New Brunswick, NJ: Rutgers University Press.

Widdig, Bernd. 2001. *Culture and Inflation in Weimar Germany*. Berkeley: University of California Press.

EIGHT

TRADITION AS INTELLECTUAL MONTAGE

F.W. MURNAU'S *FAUST* (1926)

MATT ERLIN

"WHO IS THIS FAUST?"

In his study of F. W. Murnau's *Faust*, the French director Eric Rohmer extols the film as a "sort of visual opera" in which Murnau "was able to mobilize all the means at his disposal to ensure a total mastery of [cinematic] space" (Rohmer 1980, 9–10; my translation). His remarks offer just one example of the praise that French commentators in particular have lavished on the film, Murnau's final directorial effort before leaving for the United States in 1926. The film historian Georges Sadoul is similarly rapturous, describing *Faust* as "a great film that equals for the first time the great *Fausts* of literature" (Dabezies 1967, 206; my translation). And in her biography of Murnau, Lotte Eisner speaks admiringly of the "fugues of light" and the "Rembrandtesque tonalities" that characterize the work (Eisner 1973, 165). Eisner's focus on Murnau's visual artistry gives us a sense of what many critics find so impressive in *Faust*. Murnau, often viewed as the most painterly of German directors, in whose films "every centimeter of the screen is active" (Grafe 1974), appears here at the height of his talents. His unique sensitivity to the expressive potential of light and shadow, his meticulous attention to the mise-en-scène, his delight in special effects and innovative camerawork—all these elements combine in *Faust* to create a visual masterpiece in which every shot constitutes a work of art unto itself.

Audiences and critics in Weimar Germany, however, were less impressed. While the film did enjoy some success abroad, in Germany the critical response was largely negative and the public unenthusiastic. Moreover, a year after the film's release, an application from the Prussian Ministry of the Interior led the censorship board to declare the film unsuitable for minors. The "unrestrained sensualism" of the protagonist allegedly posed a threat to the ethical development of young people. By the time of the ruling, however, *Faust* was no longer a presence in German movie theaters anyway—the public had voted with its feet. In the end the film only managed to recoup half of its 2 million Reichsmark production costs (Prodolliet 1978, 51–52).

The film's failure at the box office came at a difficult time for the Ufa studio, which had been plagued by financial difficulties since the currency stabilization in 1924. Having placed its hopes for success on the penetration of the American market, it had recently entered into a controversial joint-venture with Paramount and MGM to raise desperately needed capital. *Faust* was one of a series of big-budget films (along with *The Nibelungen Saga*, *The Last Laugh*, *Tartuffe*, and *Metropolis*) designed to challenge the dominance of Hollywood in Germany and appeal to audiences abroad (Saunders 1994, 69). To this end the studio recruited a cast of international stars—perennial favorite Emil Jannings (*The Last Laugh*, *Tartuffe*) played the role of Mephisto; the golden boy of Swedish cinema, Gösta Ekman, was cast as Faust; and the French singer Yvette Guilbert took the part of Aunt Martha. Lillian Gish was initially considered for the role of Gretchen, but she made her participation contingent on the use of her own cameraman, a condition to which Murnau was unwilling to agree. Ufa eventually accepted his suggestion of the unknown Camilla Horn, who made her screen debut in the film.

On the home front Ufa engaged in an intense and sometimes ingenious marketing effort in the run-up to the film's release. Expectations were already running high as a result of the unprecedented international success of *The Last Laugh*, Murnau's 1924 collaboration with screenwriter Carl Mayer. For *Faust* he had teamed up with Hans Kyser, whose screenplay was published in excerpt form in the trade papers as a way to keep the film in the news. Various articles on the production served the same purpose, and a film-poster contest with substantial cash prizes helped increase the curiosity of the general public. Less successful was the attempt to enhance the film's literary cachet by soliciting intertitles from Gerhard Hauptmann, unofficial poet laureate of the Weimar Republic. Much to Ufa's chagrin, Hauptmann's stilted couplets proved too highbrow and too lengthy to be included without disrupting the flow of the film. After an unsuccessful trial run in an August prescreening for the industry, the complete intertitles were published separately and made available for purchase by moviegoers. Whatever the ultimate significance of this failed collaboration for the quality of the film, it did not seem to cloud the official premiere of *Faust*, held on October 14, 1926, at the opulent Ufa-Palast am Zoo in Berlin. The studio succeeded in transforming the screening into a major cultural event, attended by both Reichschancellor Wilhelm Marx and Foreign Minister Gustav Stresemann. Murnau, who was already in Hollywood, sent along his best wishes by telegram.

The critics began to voice their reservations in the morning newspapers. If more recent evaluations of Murnau's *Faust* have tended to laud the formal excellence of the film, especially the director's attention to the smallest details of composition, contemporary reviews focused at least as much on content. Not surprisingly, discussions often centered on the film's relationship to the Faust tradition, in particular to Goethe's adaptation, as well as on the relationship between the textual and the visual more generally. What bothered many critics was not the audacity of Murnau's attempt to appropriate Germany's national myth for the cinema; after all, the Faust legend had been an extremely popular cinematic subject since the invention of the medium. It was, rather, Murnau's alleged inability to settle on one variant of the legend as his foundation. In its seemingly eclectic combination of elements from Marlowe, the puppet play, the chapbook, and Goethe, Murnau's *Faust* appeared to be less an independent contribution to the Faust tradition than a haphazard citation of it. Kurt Pinthus's review in *Das Tagebuch* is typical in this regard. According to Pinthus, Murnau had two options: either to film the chapbook or to film Goethe's drama. Pinthus would have preferred the former. Murnau's "fanatical undertaking," however, fails not because he decided to film Goethe but because of his attempt at a third possibility, "the compromise of combining the first two possibilities" (Pinthus 1926, 1599). Bernard von Brentano's review in the *Frankfurter Zeitung* was far more vitriolic in its condemnation of the film's slapdash treatment of the sources: "One went to the theater to see *Faust*, a German folk legend. What one saw was an illustration of Goethe's work with a series of changes that had been thoughtlessly undertaken by the director" (Lange-Fuchs 1997, 73). For Brentano the film's identity crisis is mirrored in the unstable (and immoral) character of the protagonist: "But Faust? Who is this Faust? First a doctor who teams up with the devil as a result of his incompetence; then a young man who steals another man's bride, a virgin's honor, and creates unhappiness wherever he goes" (ibid.).

A number of Weimar critics, not only those with a conservative bent, were troubled by the multiple identities of Murnau's protagonist and the seemingly fragmentary character of the film itself. This uneasiness was by no means merely a function of disappointed expectations, as Brentano seems to suggest. To be sure, viewers may have been surprised to find so many references to Goethe in a film that was subtitled "A German Folk Legend," but there is a genuine tension that runs through the film, as the protagonist is associated at various points with diverse elements of the Faust tradition, with medieval and modern, word and image, technology and scholarship, *Zivilisation* and *Kultur*. A careful viewing, however, suggests that Murnau's montage is less arbitrary than it appears. The question raised by Brentano regarding Faust's identity—"Who is this Faust?"—actually constitutes one of the central preoccupations of the film. This chapter will attempt to demonstrate that Murnau's film does have a story to tell, but it is less the story of Faust the cinematic protagonist than of the role of cinema vis-à-vis a particular high-cultural tradition, for which Goethe's *Faust* served in the period as the paradigmatic example. Through its citation of disparate elements of the Faust tradition and its highly self-conscious relation to the cinematic medium, Murnau's *Faust* offers an implicit commentary on contemporary Weimar-era debates concerning the contested status of cinema as art form, as commodity, and as contributor to a sense of national community. In this regard it also provides a unique window on the historical significance of Weimar cinema as a "transitional cinematic practice" characterized by a combination of artistic and popular elements, a cinema in which the production of the "art film" was often part of a strategy of product differentiation for the international market (Elsaesser 1984, 70–73).

AT HOME WITH FAUST

Weimar cinema has often been singled out for its self-conscious obsession with visuality, an obsession that manifests itself in endless depictions of visual pleasure and anxiety, in a foregrounding of specular relations, and in a predilection for self-referential evocations of the cinematic. *Faust* is no exception. Exactly halfway into the film, a fade-in reveals the protagonist sitting alone in a grotto surrounded by mist-covered cliffs. Bearing a conspicuous similarity to the expectant viewer perched in front of a blank movie screen, Faust looks toward a patch of white fog at the top of the frame. Mephisto appears suddenly to his right and tries to shake Faust out of his torpor with a series of temptations (Fig. 8.1). When Faust fails to respond, Mephisto conjures up the image of a crown and promises control of the empire. To no avail. The dejected protagonist, who in the previous sequence had seduced the duchess of Parma on her wedding day, seems to have had his fill of libertinism and material pleasures. As Faust drops his head into his palms, Mephisto jerks away in frustration. Then, as if stirred by an inner voice, Faust looks up again toward the top of the frame, where the fog has dissipated to reveal the feature presentation: an idyllic country scene. Bewitched by the pastoral projection, Faust mouths the word "Heimat!" (homeland) as if in a trance. He then springs to his feet and cries: "Take me home! And at once!"

The concept of *Heimat* was both overdetermined and deeply resonant in the social and political context of Weimar Germany. Faust's enthusiastic invocation of it here calls to mind a wide range of associations, from conservative critiques of modern urban nomadism to the still unsettled status of Germany's postwar borders. Considered within a narrower cultural context, however, the thematization of Faust's *Heimat* in particular, and at this conspicuously self-referential moment, raises more specific questions as to the status of a nationally charged cultural tradition in an era of mass entertainment and to the role of cinema in the

FIGURE 8.1 "Take me home! And at once!" Faust (Gösta Ekman) demands of Mephisto (Emil Jannings) in F. W. Murnau's *Faust* (1926).

conservation and transmission of that tradition. It is possible, in other words, to approach this moment on a metacinematic or metanarrative level, to view Murnau's Faust less as a cinematic protagonist than as a metaphor for the Faust tradition and everything it stands for in Weimar Germany. The film itself seems to suggest such an interpretive strategy, not only through the framing of this particular sequence but also through its idiosyncratic reworking of Faust's initial crisis, and especially in the way it self-consciously presents the opposition between Faust and Mephisto as an opposition between text and image, literature and film. From the beginning Mephisto is cast in the role of visual magician, conjuring objects and seductive images with a wave of the hand or a penetrating gaze. He is, as Russell Berman has insightfully remarked, the embodiment of the cinematic principle in the film, capable of reversing the passage of time, even of raising the dead (Berman 1993, 137). Faust, by contrast, is a man of the book; in fact, he is surrounded by them—at least in his initial incarnations. From this perspective the evolving relationship between Faust and Mephisto in the film can be seen as a reflection on the more general relation between the cinema and the high-literary Faust tradition. By the time of the *Heimat* sequence, however, the straightforward opposition between the two characters set up in the first part of the film has become more complicated. Here as elsewhere a vision drives the plot forward, but in this case the vision has no clear link to Mephisto. He remains motionless, marginalized on the right side of the screen, with his eyes fixed on Faust. The pastoral scene appears to be Faust's own creation, or perhaps that of an extradiegetic authority. This dissociation of Mephisto from the background image, coupled with the evocation of the cinema that occurs through its framing, suggests the existence of a second cinematic principle, one with a higher authority. Mephisto appears as a representative of cinema at its worst—seductive images employed in the pursuit of material gain or sensuous pleasure—but the vision of Faust's *Heimat* suggests the possibility of another type of film. As we will see, this notion of two cinemas figured prominently in Weimar debates over the function and future of the German film. The cultural argument implicit in Faust's desire to return home, however, can only be fully grasped once one recognizes the significance of where he has been. Thus, before turning to these debates and the way in which the film engages them, it is necessary to reconstruct the events that lead up to the cinematic crossroads described above.

Faust begins with a wager—not between the protagonist and Mephisto but between Mephisto and an archangel. At stake, in addition to Faust's soul, is the fate of the entire world, which Mephisto stands to win if he manages to lure Faust away from a life dedicated to the amelioration of the human condition. The stark contrast in this initial confrontation between the blinding radiance of the backlit angel and the dark, shadowy figure of the devil introduces a moral semantics of light and darkness that carries through the entire film. More so than in his other productions, Murnau uses lighting in *Faust* as both a thematic element and a means to organize cinematic space. The clear moral schematic introduced in this initial sequence also gives the first hint of an important modification to the standard variant of the Faust legend. Murnau's protagonist is defined by his social conscience. What drives him is not the thirst for absolute knowledge, as is the case in both the chapbook and Goethe's drama, but the desire to help his fellow human beings. In one of the shots leading up to the celestial wager, the august, silver-haired Faust stands with book in hand and explains to his enraptured students that humankind's greatest gift is the freedom to choose between good and evil (Fig. 8.2). In the subsequent sequence, after Mephisto unleashes a plague on the village, the protagonist struggles day and night to find a cure, and it is his failure in this regard that turns him toward the dark arts. He agrees to the pact with the devil only because the latter promises to help him heal the plague victims.

Although the atmosphere and architecture in these early sequences may evoke the sixteenth-century origins of the historical doctor who first gave rise to the Faust legend, the images speak more directly to the concerns of the Weimar Republic. Even the visions of a historically rooted phenomenon like the plague, which had also figured prominently in Murnau's *Nosferatu* (1922), would have called to mind the mass deaths of the all-too-recent war, as well as those of the subsequent influenza epidemic that ravaged Europe (Elsaesser 2001, 13). And the jostling crowds

FIGURE 8.2   Faust stands with book in hand.

that so often fill the screen, occasionally rendered more threatening by the subtly expressionistic sets of designers Robert Herlth and Walter Röhrig, were both a
staple of Weimar cinema and a feature of everyday life in an increasingly urbanized
Germany. Of particular interest in the context of this chapter, however, is the way
in which the film foregrounds the troubled relationship between these crowds and
the aged Faust. Despite his unflagging efforts and his position of authority in the
village, Faust ultimately proves unable to help them. Even the pact with Mephisto
fails in its aim. As soon as the villagers come to recognize the source of Faust's heal-
ing power, they stone him mercilessly and force him back into isolation.

The film's emphasis on Faust's social conscience can be seen as an aesthetic adaptation made necessary by the nature of the cinematic medium. As both recent
scholarship and some contemporary reviewers of Murnau's film have pointed out,
the purely intellectual nature of Faust's conflict, especially as depicted in Goethe's
drama, is difficult to render visually. The plague motif allows the psychic crisis to be
exteriorized in a way that is more amenable to visual drama (Singer 1989, 366–67).
While this argument provides a plausible explanation for the modification, however, the depiction of Faust as a well-intentioned but ultimately impotent scholar-
philanthropist also needs to be placed within the context of period debates on the
role of the intellectual, whose social relevance was a matter of some controversy in
the mid-1920s. In fact, the staging of these early sequences points to an even more
specific interpretation. As mentioned previously, Faust is associated here with the

written word—he makes his initial appearance with book in hand, piles of books surround him in his study, and ultimately, he articulates his utter desperation at failing to find a cure for the plague by casting his books into the fire. The masses, on the other hand, are clearly in thrall to the visual, as the initial plague sequence makes clear. Prior to the onset of the catastrophe, the villagers are shown enjoying stage performances and shadow plays at a town carnival (Berman 1993, 136). This opposition, which reemerges in another form in the subsequent contrast between Faust and Mephisto, suggests that Faust's impotence and loss of authority in the village can be read as a reflection on the fate of a high-cultural tradition in an era of visual mass entertainment. The highly stylized character of these early representations of Faust would seem to support such a reading. Echoes of Rembrandt and a long tradition of *Faust* illustrations, including those done by Goethe himself, lend Murnau's bearded patriarch a citational quality, making him appear as more of an icon than an actual cinematic protagonist (Gehler and Kasten 1990, 107).

The question of Faust's relevance, moreover, particularly that of Goethe's *Faust* and the entire cultural-educational mission of Weimar classicism, was definitely in the air in the 1920s. Commentators from Reichspresident Friedrich Ebert to Oswald Spengler to Bertolt Brecht all opined on the national significance of the Faust material, often treating it as synonymous with Weimar classicism and sometimes, as in the case of Spengler, viewing it as an allegory of European civilization. Despite Ebert's invocation of both Goethe's *Faust* and "the spirit of Weimar" in his 1919 speech before the National Assembly, many doubted that an elitist, late-eighteenth-century concept of culture could really provide a rallying point for the new Germany. Critics on the left, in particular, questioned whether classical literary texts still had any value for contemporary readers. As Alfred Döblin remarked in a review of Leopold Jessner's 1923 stage production of Goethe's *Faust*: "The entire first part of *Faust* is eighteenth century. It seems to me we're in the twentieth" (Döblin 1976, 174). In a 1929 discussion with Herbert Jhering, Brecht traces the "death" of the classics back to the trauma of the war experience: "If it is true that the soldiers who marched off to war had *Faust* in their knapsacks, those who came back no longer did" (Brecht 1992, 309). Brecht's remark also reminds us that Goethe's drama was understood first and foremost as a work of literature rather than simply the foundation for a stage production, a point that will be important to keep in mind as my argument progresses.

FAUST GOES TO THE MOVIES

Viewed from this angle, Faust's attempt and subsequent failure to help the masses mirrors the perceived sterility of the high-cultural Faust tradition itself. The pact with Mephisto can be seen as a further development of this motif. When one takes into account Mephisto's function as cinematic principle in Murnau's *Faust*, then his partnership with the protagonist appears as a self-referential commentary on the way in which the film itself attempts to transform the Faust legend into cinematic material and thereby infuse it with new life. It is perhaps no coincidence that Faust initially invokes the devil with the help of what appears to be a transitional object, one that blurs the line between print and visual imagery—a book that contains indecipherable signs and symbols rather than words. The irony here is that Faust's alliance with the cinema is staged as a devil's bargain. Although Faust enters into the transaction with Mephisto in order to reach the masses—a gesture that calls to mind arguments in favor of cinema as a means to revivify the classics—he ends up provoking their rage when they discover the source of his power. His decision thus proves to have been misguided, and the film appears to undercut its own legitimacy (Berman 1993, 137).

The subsequent rejuvenation of Faust under Mephisto's influence lends itself to a similar interpretation. In contrast to Goethe's drama, where the author presents Faust's desire for youth as a given, here this desire has to be elicited through an elaborate visual seduction. After the plague fiasco, the protagonist is ready to escape from his alliance with Mephisto through suicide. The latter manages to extract a renewed commitment to their pact, however, by showing him an image—not of a beautiful woman but of his younger self, first reflected in the poison he is about to drink and then captured in a small mirror. Especially in this sequence, then, the alliance with the devil appears as a surrender to the seductive power of the cinema. Moreover, as was the case with the initial agreement, the results would seem to undermine the legitimacy of Murnau's own film. The new and improved "cinematic" Faust, although he has regained his youth and vitality, has also been transformed into a libertine devoid of all interest in societal improvement. In another ironic twist, then, *Faust* as a metacinematic commentary seems to confirm the criticisms of those conservatives who believed that a filmic Faust could only be a profanation. To be sure, a literary model for Faust's hedonistic turn can be found in Goethe's drama, where the protagonist's rejuvenation also marks a rediscovery of the sensual as expressed in the seduction of Gretchen. In the case of Murnau's film, however, the differences prove to be revealing. What follows Faust's rejuvenation is not the Gretchen drama but a lengthy interlude in which the protagonist travels to Italy and seduces the duchess of Parma on her wedding day.

This interlude divides *Faust* into roughly equal halves, and it marks a clear thematic transition in the film narrative. The flight on Mephisto's cloak with which it begins has achieved a kind of legendary status in the commentary on the film, eliciting reflections, for example, on the impact of Murnau's experiences as a World War I fighter pilot on the development of his cinematography (Gehler and Kasten 1990, 27). The sequence also reveals the director's desire to explore the opportunities

FIGURE 8.3   Faust, looking like Rudolph Valentino in *The Sheik* (1921).

created by the mobile camera, which had its big-screen debut in *The Last Laugh*. Although the stationary camera is predominant in *Faust*, a fact that tends to heighten the tableau feel of many of the shots, there are a few notable exceptions. For the flight sequence a miniature roller coaster was constructed, allowing the cameraman, Carl Hoffmann, to move along the entire length of the elaborate model landscape inspired by the painter Albrecht Altdorfer (Kracauer 1947, 148). The lengthy journey makes no substantive contribution to the plot, and it is perhaps best understood as a pure celebration of cinema technology. As such, it reminds us of the degree to which, even in the increasingly commercialized and standardized film industry of the mid-1920s, Weimar filmmakers remained committed to an exploration of the medium for its own sake. In the context of the current argument, however, what is most significant about the long journey is the way it signals Faust's separation from his literary origins, both as protagonist and as embodiment of a textual tradition. If the first half of the film offered a peculiar and indecipherable fusion of Goethe and the chapbook, the Faust who travels to Parma in the second half has no connection to either text. The Parma episode is an obscure motif from the puppet play, one that had recently been reappropriated by the Italian composer Busoni in his 1925 opera *Doktor Faust* (Beaumont 1985, 320). Murnau's film thus appears to have aligned itself entirely with the nontextual at this point, and arguably with the popular as well, since the sequence has nothing in common with

FIGURE 8.4 Mephisto as director.

Busoni beyond the location. The staging of the Parma episode as a superset spectacle, complete with dancing elephants, also calls to mind another visual intertext, namely the big-budget Hollywood productions that were increasingly attracting the ire of Weimar commentators by mid-decade. Faust himself, who has donned a turban and exotic robes for the performance, bears a striking similarity to Rudolph Valentino in *The Sheik* (1921) (Fig. 8.3).

The disappearance of the text holds at the level of plot as well. Gone is the word/image dichotomy that characterized the initial relationship between Faust and Mephisto. Although not a conjurer himself, Faust, by the time of his encounter with the duchess, has become an enthusiastic apostle of the visual. He lures his soon-to-be lover away from her groom with the help of a mechanical flower that emits a hypnotic white light—yet another ambiguous evocation of the cinematic. A final self-referential moment occurs in the last scene of the Parma episode, after Mephisto threatens to reverse Faust's rejuvenation and thereby manages to extort from the protagonist a lifetime commitment to their pact. As Faust and the duchess embrace in the center of a frame within the frame, created by the drapes from the bed canopy, Mephisto appears above and leans over to glare at the lovers (Fig. 8.4). The medium close-up of the lovers' kiss within this second frame makes it clear that this is a cinematic rather than simply a theatrical moment. Mephisto then transforms his cloak into a curtain, hiding the pair from view with a smirk and reminding the viewer of the guilty pleasure of his or her own voyeurism. This final gesture both underscores Mephisto's status as director and brings the entire episode, now clearly demarcated as a film within the film, to an appropriately melodramatic conclusion.

The self-referentiality of these sequences, together with the fragmentary citation of various Faust traditions and genres, might be seen as an indication of a playful irony on the part of Murnau—*Faust* as a precursor to a kind of "postmodern" pastiche. This reading has a certain appeal, especially when one considers the film's conspicuous antinaturalism. To be sure, the expressionistic elements in *Faust* are rather subdued, but it is significant that Murnau, who was known for his interest in using natural landscapes, chose to film *Faust* entirely in the studio (Gehler and Kasten 1990, 44; Koebner 2003, 37). In the Gretchen romance that follows directly on the heels of the Parma episode and provides the narrative foundation for the remainder of the film, Faust interrupts Gretchen as she weaves what are clearly artificial flowers into garlands for a group of children, and then he chases her through a garden landscape that makes little effort to conceal its studio construction. To these examples one could add the previously mentioned appropriations of the traditional Faust iconography, as well as Murnau's references to the iconography of the Renaissance Madonna paintings in his representations of Gretchen (Gehler and Kasten 1990, 107). The extent to which the film foregrounds its own constructedness and citational quality was recognized (or perhaps misrecognized) by contemporary critics. According to Axel Eggebrecht, in the October 16, 1926, edition of *Die Welt am Abend*, "Everything is overplayed, flattened out, and demonstrates the most crass concern with external appearances." More recently, Helmut Schanze (2003) has taken this constructedness as his point of departure and interpreted the film as a "generic *Gesamtkunstwerk*." For Schanze *Faust* brings together disparate art forms and genres and thus reveals an affinity to the idea of the *Gesamtkunstwerk* propagated by Richard Wagner. Inasmuch as the film places these disparate elements in tension with one another, however, it also defies Wagner's concept. Rather than fusing the raw materials into a seamless, organic unity, Murnau grants them a kind of fragmentary autonomy and thereby highlights both the constructedness and historicity of the Faust myth and the dependence of cinema on other art forms (Schanze 2003, 230–32).

GOETHE'S SCREEN TEST

In light of the argument I wish to advance here, however, Schanze's reading would seem to overemphasize the fragmentary quality of Murnau's *Faust*. Although it is true that the film brings together disparate genres and traditions, there appears to be an almost Hegelian logic to their combination. Mephisto's ever tighter hold over

Faust parallels the latter's renunciation of the textual and increasing dependence on the visual, a dependence that ultimately leads to the attack of ennui discussed at the beginning of this chapter. The consequence of this ennui for the protagonist, however, is not a return to the books, at least not at the level of the plot. It leads instead to the appearance of a second visual paradigm in the pastoral projection of his *Heimat*. To the extent that we view this moment as a turning point in the film, moreover, and the subsequent sequences as operating within this second paradigm, they reveal a rootedness in the literary that is absent from Mephisto's cinematic parlor tricks. Faust's return to the village constitutes a homecoming on two levels. The protagonist returns to Germany, and the film realigns itself with the German—and the high-literary—Faust tradition. The second half of *Faust* occupies itself exclusively with the Gretchen story, Goethe's most significant contribution to the legend. At one level this development is certainly an attempt to capitalize on the international appeal of the love story; indeed, some of Murnau's critics viewed it in precisely these terms. Murnau's turn toward Goethe, however, also resolves a dialectical tension set up in the first half of the film, namely, the tension between the traditional and the cinematic Fausts. Once the Gretchen tragedy begins, the Faust who pores over his books in a vain effort to assist the villagers and the Faust who exploits Mephisto's seductive images are synthesized at the level of structure. The books never return to the film's story line, but literature takes on a deeper structural significance as *Faust* evolves from a quirky mixture of multiple sources and directorial invention into an unmistakable adaptation of a single literary work. By the same token, the most conspicuous special effects in the film are no longer linked directly to Mephisto, nor do these visual effects have the same motive force with regard to plot development. Mephisto's gaze still produces the occasional flame, but the more striking visual tricks, such as Gretchen's hallucinations, or the later superimpositions of her anguished countenance onto the landscape, are psychologized and thus woven directly into the film narrative. Significantly then, the film seems to lose its self-consciousness and reflexivity at the point where it most clearly articulates its reliance on Goethe.

The dichotomy set up in *Faust* between two competing modes of visual culture is reminiscent of mid-1920s debates about the unique characteristics of German cinema vis-à-vis the films coming out of Hollywood. The often-voiced opposition between German high culture and Hollywood sensationalism was clearly rather disingenuous, given that only a handful of the hundreds of German films produced annually aspired to anything more than simple entertainment value. Arguments about Germany's unique commitment to high cinematic art and aesthetic education were nonetheless common in the period. They featured prominently in the industry's efforts to protect the domestic market and penetrate foreign markets, especially that of the United States. Fritz Lang sums up the situation well in a 1926 piece entitled "The Future of the Feature Film in Germany": "Germany has never had, and never will have, the gigantic human and financial reserves of the American film industry at its disposal. To its good fortune. For that is exactly what forces us to compensate a purely material imbalance through an intellectual superiority" (Kaes, et al. 1994, 622). This insistence on the "intellectual superiority" of German cinema had become increasingly shrill by mid-decade, at which point Hollywood controlled approximately 40 percent of the German feature-film market and had more or less eliminated the German production of entertainment shorts (Saunders 1994, 54). Articles from trade papers like *Film-Kurier*—which carried titles such as "Ufa Is Armed and Ready" (*Die Ufa ist gerüstet*, September 5, 1925), "German Film Above All" (*Deutscher Film über alles*, September 19, 1925), and "Ranks Closed Against America" (*Geschlossene Front gegen Amerika*, October 8, 1925)—reveal the level of national investment in this cultural competition.

When read as metacinematic commentary, the film's realignment with Goethe immediately following the empty, unsatisfying, "Hollywood" spectacle in Parma appears as a reenactment, at the level of film narrative, of arguments in the film community about the need for a uniquely German cinema grounded in national cultural traditions. It also suggests that the source of this uniqueness is to be found in an affiliation with the project of aesthetic cultivation first inaugurated in Goethe's Weimar. To the extent that we can take him at his word, Murnau's own comments point in this direction. In "Das Murnau-Bankett in New York," an August 14, 1926, *Film-Kurier* article recounting a speech at a banquet held in Murnau's honor in New York, the correspondent paraphrases the filmmaker's rather conventional reservations about American cinema: "In his opinion one cannot call representations of the vulgar and licentious a reflection of life, and label this cheap imitation of life 'art.' It is necessary to select those moments of life that improve and encourage humanity, for already in ancient Greece the term 'art' comprised all that is good, beautiful and true." Murnau's remarkably traditional endorsement of the ennobling character of art lends credence to the claim that his gesture toward Goethe in *Faust* casts the cinema, paradoxically perhaps, as the heir to and refashioner of a high-cultural tradition. The fact that this very realignment was seen by some contemporary critics as a concession to Hollywood only reveals the complexity of the cultural field at the time the film was produced—the contested distinctions between domestic and foreign and between popular and elite cultures. Indeed, one could argue that what makes the Gretchen drama such an appealing way to resolve the dialectic set up in the first part of the film is that Goethe himself originally conceived it as a means to fuse the popular and the cultivated. It thus serves as a particularly appropriate model for the synthesis that Murnau's film seems to advocate.

The ending of the film offers a final example of this search for a synthesis. Here Murnau's *Faust* departs from Goethe, allowing for a last-minute reunion between the two lovers on Gretchen's funeral pyre. Much can be said about this sequence. For some reviewers this "happy" ending represented the worst kind of pandering to the masses. In an otherwise largely propagandistic *Film-Kurier* report following a special screening of the film, the correspondent quotes a "well-known theater critic" as follows: "And then comes the end: Faust and Gretchen floating up toward heaven.—Do you still believe in the aesthetic value of film?" (Herzberg 1926). More recent commentators, however, have wondered whether it makes sense to view this ending as "happy" at all. After all, the lovers do go up in flames. Thomas Koebner describes the film as a love-tragedy without hope and sees this brief reunion before death as a particularly striking example of Murnau's general tendency to portend the instability and ephemerality of any blissful moment (Koebner 2003, 15). In the final seconds the hostile villagers drop to their knees in what appears to be a recognition of their folly, but, as in the case of Faust and Gretchen, the moment of recognition comes too late to do anyone any good. This failed reconciliation may represent Murnau's ultimate denial of the possibility of reconnecting Faust to the masses, but it does pave the way for a different, more successful reconciliation, in this case between two media. As Mephisto attempts to make good his claim on Faust's soul, he is told by the archangel that a single word—*Liebe* [love]—renders his contract null and void. Love conquers all, then, but precisely not as a mere word. Initial appearances to the contrary, the archangel's claim does not constitute a case of Murnau humbly concluding his film with the reestablishment of the priority of the textual. The textual in the traditional sense is represented here by Mephisto's contract, which proves to be without validity. Instead, the penultimate shot of *Faust* features the word *as* dynamic image, a glowing icon expanding against a black backdrop, clearly intended to transcend its merely referential function (Fig. 8.5). The cinema presents itself at this moment as what Hegel would have termed an *Aufhebung* (sublation) of the textual, simultaneously conserving and superseding it. In a sense this word-image encapsulates the harmonization of the literary and the cinematic that Murnau's *Faust* proposes, but perhaps fails to realize successfully, through its particular reworking of the Faust material.

Although *Faust* has received high praise from director-critics like Rohmer, as well as from a number of early historians of German cinema, the film has received very little attention in more recent academic film scholarship. In a sense this is not surprising. The highly stylized, citational character of *Faust*, its distance from the social realism of films like *The Last Laugh*, makes it an unlikely candidate for the historically contextualized approaches that have dominated Anglo-American scholarship on Weimar cinema. It is telling in this context that Siegfried Kracauer, whose much criticized psychohistory *From Caligari to Hitler* has nonetheless served as the starting point for nearly all of the sociohistorical film scholarship on the period, finds himself at a bit of a loss when it comes to *Faust*. He speaks of the "futility of a film which misrepresented, if not ignored, all significant motifs inherent in its

FIGURE 8.5   Liebe (Love): word as dynamic image.

subject matter," and goes on to claim that "*Faust* was not so much a monument as a monumental display of artifices capitalizing on the prestige of national culture. The obsolete theatrical poses to which the actors resorted betrayed the falsity of the whole. While the film had considerable success abroad, it met with indifference in Germany itself. The Germans of the time did not take to Faustian problems, and moreover resented any interference with the traditional notions of the classics" (Kracauer 1947, 148–49).

As I have argued, a close reading of *Faust* does in fact reveal a number of elements that reflect Weimar concerns rather than merely Faustian ones that can be found in many other period films—unruly crowds, mass deaths, and perhaps most important, a sense of the impotence of the individual in the face of anonymous forces. The film's most significant sociohistorical content, however, resides precisely in its logic of stylization and citation, in the very "theatrical poses" that Kracauer found so disturbing. This logic suggests that if Murnau's film ignores "significant motifs" of the Faust legend, it does so in order to address a more pressing issue, namely, whether such motifs still have any relevance in an age of mass entertainment. And in the course of this investigation the film actively engages with debates regarding the role of cinema as a vehicle of cultural education and cultural nationalism in the Weimar Republic. If Weimar cinema is best seen as what Thomas Elsaesser has termed a "transitional cinematic practice," one characterized by the search for a synthesis between mass appeal and artistic self-realization, between aesthetics, technology, and the market, then Murnau's *Faust* proves most interesting for the way in which it exemplifies this search within itself.

REFERENCES

Beaumont, Antony. 1985. *Busoni the Composer*. Bloomington: Indiana University Press.

Berman, Russell. 1993. *Cultural Studies of Modern Germany: History, Representation, and Nationhood*. Madison: University of Wisconsin Press.

Brecht, Bertolt. 1992. *Werke*. Ed. Werner Hecht et al. Vol. 21 (Schriften I). Frankfurt am Main: Suhrkamp.

Dabezies, André. 1967. *Visages de Faust au XX siècle: Littérature, idéologie, et mythes*. Paris: Presses universitaires de France.

"Das Murnau-Bankett in New York." 1926. *Film-Kurier*, August 14.

Döblin, Alfred. 1976. *Ein Kerl muß eine Meinung haben: Berichte und Kritiken, 1921–1924*. Munich: Deutscher Taschenbucher Verlag.

Eisner, Lotte. 1973. *F. W. Murnau*. Berkeley: University of California Press.

Elsaesser, Thomas. 1984. "Film History and Visual Pleasure: Weimar Cinema." In *Cinema Histories, Cinema Practices*, ed. Patricia Mellencamp and Philip Rosen, 47–84. Frederick, MD: University Publications of America.

——. 2001. "Six Degrees of Nosferatu." *Sight and Sound* 11:12–16.

Gehler, Fred, and Ullrich Kasten. 1990. *Friedrich Wilhelm Murnau*. Berlin: Henschelverlag.

Grafe, Frieda. 1974. "Was Fehlt Dem Torso." *Süddeutsche Zeitung*, April 19, 35.

Herzberg, G[eorg]. 1926. "Der Faust-Film vor den Interessenten." Review of *Faust*, dir. F. W. Murnau. *Film-Kurier*, August 26.

Kaes, Anton, Martin Jay, and Edward Dimenberg, eds. 1994. *The Weimar Republic Sourcebook*. Berkeley: University of California Press.

Koebner, Thomas. 2003. "Der Romantische Preuße." In *Friedrich Wilhelm Murnau: Ein Melancholiker des Films*, ed. Hans Helmut Prinzler, 9–52. Berlin: Bertz Verlag.

Kracauer, Siegfried. 1947. *From Caligari to Hitler: A Psychological History of the German Film*. Princeton, NJ: Princeton University Press.

Lange-Fuchs. 1997. *Ja, wäre nur ein Zaubermantel mein! Faust im Film: Eine Dokumentation*. Bonn: Inter Nationes (Orig. pub. 1985)

Pinthus, Kurt. 1926. "Der Faust-Film." Review of *Faust*, dir. F. W. Murnau. *Das Tagebuch*, October 23, 1599–601.

Prodolliet, Ernest. 1978. *Faust in Kino: Die Geschichte des Faustfilms von den Anfängen bis zur Gegenwart*. Freiburg (Switzerland): Universitätsverlag.

Rohmer, Eric. 1980. *Murnaus Faustfilm: Analyse und szenisches Protokoll*. Trans. Frieda Grafe and Enno Patalas. Munich: Carl Hanser. (Orig. pub. 1977.)

Saunders, Thomas J. 1994. *Hollywood in Berlin: American Cinema and Weimar Germany*. Berkeley: University of California Press.

Schanze, Helmut. 2003. "On Murnau's *Faust*: A Generic *Gesamtkunstwerk*?" In *Expressionist Film: New Perspectives*, ed. Dietrich Scheunemann, 223–35. Rochester, NY: Camden House.

Singer, Robert Lewis. 1989. "The Faust Film Adaptation: A Study in the Interrelationship Between Literature and Film." PhD diss., New York University.

[NINE]

METROPOLIS (1927)

CITY, CINEMA, MODERNITY

ANTON KAES

> One of the crucial antinomies of art today is that it wants to be and must be
> squarely utopian, as social reality increasingly impedes utopia, while at the
> same time it should not be utopian so as not to be found guilty of administer-
> ing comfort and illusion. If the utopia of art were actualized, art would come
> to an end.　　　　　　　　　　THEODOR W. ADORNO, *Aesthetic Theory*

OPENING NIGHT

On January 10, 1927, all of Berlin's forty newspapers were abuzz with anticipation
and excitement. *Metropolis*, the monumental new film by Fritz Lang, one and a half
years in the making, was finally to open after an unprecedented advertising campaign that had run for several months. It was widely known that *Metropolis* was the
most expensive and ambitious European film production to date, with an unheard-
of cost of 5.3 million Reichsmark (almost four times its budget); that its shooting
ratio was 1:300 (with more than 1 million meters of film exposed); and that it employed thirty-six thousand extras, including seventy-five hundred children and
one thousand unemployed individuals whose heads had been shaved by one hundred hairdressers for a scene that in the final cut lasted less than a minute. Statisti-
cal hyperbole and such slogans as "a film of titanic dimensions," an "Über-film,"
and "the greatest film ever made, one of the most eternal artworks of all times,"
promised an epic film that could compete with such American spectacles as Raoul
Walsh's three-hour extravaganza, *The Thief of Baghdad* (1924) or Fred Niblo's *Ben
Hur* (1925), which had been shown in Berlin just a year earlier. *Metropolis* was also
eagerly awaited as a sequel to Lang's successful megaproduction of 1924, the two-
part *Die Nibelungen* (*The Nibelungs*), which had established him as the most daring
filmmaker of the 1920s both in visual style and ideological ambition. Dedicated to

the "German Volk," *Die Nibelungen* translated the archetypal German epos into stunning images of gigantic medieval castles and prehistoric forests, built in concrete for Ufa's Neu-Babelsberg studios near Berlin (Hake 1990). Lang, who had studied architecture and painting before he turned to filmmaking, infused all of his films with a rich spatial imagination; he molded his characters and their fictional world to fit his design. Not surprisingly, it was the big-city architecture of New York that struck him first when he visited the United States in the fall of 1924:

> I saw a street lit as if in full daylight by neon lights and, topping them, oversized luminous advertisements moving, turning, flashing, on and off, spiraling ... something that was completely new and nearly fairy-tale-like for a European in those days. ... The buildings seemed to be a vertical veil, shimmering, almost weightless, a luxurious cloth hung from the dark sky to dazzle, distract, and hypnotize. At night the city did not give the impression of being alive; it lived as illusions lived. I knew then that I had to make a film about all of these sensations. (Lang 1924)

Although Lang's wife, the novelist and screenwriter Thea von Harbou, had finished the script for *Metropolis* by the summer of 1924, New York's luminous cityscape left its mark on the film's visual design and electrifying energy. Von Harbou and Lang envisioned a futuristic city as the setting for a plot that dramatized the latent social, sexual, and aesthetic conflicts of Germany in the 1920s. Extending over a broad intellectual terrain, the film drew on discourses ranging from technology, modernity, and dehumanization of labor to class, gender, and generational conflict, and finally to war and revolution. Its convoluted plot was based on von Harbou's story, which had been serialized in the *Berliner Illustrierte Zeitung* (with images from *Metropolis*) before it was published as a book at the time of the film's premiere (von Harbou 1926). Placed in the artistic and social context of the modern era, *Metropolis* is Janus-faced, looking back to the rebellion of a modernist avant-garde and forward to quiet submission under an authoritarian leader. The film displays the modernist dimension in fascism and the fascist dimension in modernity; it creates a site where modernism clashes with modernity.

After its premiere at the Ufa-Palast am Zoo, which was attended by twenty-five hundred guests, including the Reichskanzler and the leaders of finance and industry, *Metropolis* played at the refurbished Ufa Pavillon at the Nollendorfplatz for several months. The theater's exterior walls were covered with a gleaming silver coating. Brilliantly shimmering at night and faintly glistening during the day, the building radiated an eerie otherworldliness. Advertising gimmick as well as technological feat, the silvery walls projected a modernity associated with metal machinery. Futuristic technology was displayed not only in the film's fictional world but also outside, in the public space, which thus became an extension of the movie set. On approaching the theater, Berliners were also confronted with a gigantic steel sculpture that had been taken from the film set and mounted above the entrance. The gonglike sculpture represented a beating heart, offering a humanistic counterpoint to the technical appearance of the exterior walls. The film's central conflict, between the "coldness" of modernity and the sentimentality of the heart, was alluded to even before one entered the theater.

METROPOLIS, THE FILM

Metropolis, the event, clearly overshadowed *Metropolis*, the film. After the intense publicity, expectations were so high that probably no film could have fulfilled them. The papers on the morning following the premiere were almost unanimous in their criticism, pointing out the glaring contradiction between the film's strikingly innovative visual style and its atavistic, if not reactionary, ideology. The utopian solution to the plight of the working class (namely, to be oppressed by a kinder, gentler management) seemed either too facile or too cynical, and the expressionist love story (oedipal son rebels against rich father to win the hand of a working-class girl) seemed incongruous with the film's technological fetishism.

"There is altogether too much of *Metropolis*," the exasperated film critic of *Life* commented when the film opened in New York in March 1927, only two months after its premiere in Berlin, "too much scenery, too many people, too much plot and too many platitudinous ideas" (Sherwood 1927, 24).[1] It is true that intertextual references and resonances abound. The set design, for instance, runs the gamut from cavernous Christian catacombs to abstract cityscapes in the tradition of the futurist architect Antonio Sant'Elia, from the mythical Tower of Babel to art deco interiors, from the abstract moving machine parts at the beginning of the film to the Gothic cathedral at the end. Regarding the film's most iconic images of a future city, the three set designers—Erich Kettelhut, Otto Hunte, and Karl Vollbrecht— may have been inspired by an architectural competition during 1921 and 1922 that looked for the most innovative design of a skyscraper to be built at Berlin's Bahnhof Friedrichstrasse. More than a hundred architects (among them Ludwig Mies van der Rohe, Hans Poelzig, and Hans Scharoun) had presented plans for such a skyscraper, Weimar Germany's ultimate emblem of modernity (Zimmerman 1988). Although a lack of funds precluded actual construction of any entries—a problem further complicated by the fact that Berlin is built on sand, not (like Manhattan) on granite—the set designers' vision for the skyscrapers of *Metropolis* was realized in the form of models and with the help of trick photography that made the tiny set look fantastically large. The film reaches back into the mythical past and forward into the far future; its buildings stretch to the sky, while the inhuman machine halls are underground (Fig. 9.1). This overdrawn vertical structure in the tradition of

FIGURE 9.1 "Vertical veils": buildings stretch to the sky in Fritz Lang's fantasy city (*Metropolis*, 1927).

expressionist architecture is meant to underscore the contrast between the timeless pleasure gardens high above and subterranean darkness deep below, where time is measured in ten-hour shifts.

The bodies of the workers, depersonalized to the point of blending into the film's design, are choreographed in the tradition of the agitprop and *Sprechchor* (chorus) theater of Erwin Piscator. They form what Siegfried Kracauer has called a "mass ornament," in which the individual is radically submerged in highly structured formations (Fig. 9.2). Kracauer saw the same process at work in the marching columns of the military, as in the synchronized dancing style of the popular American girl revues, which mesmerized Berlin in the mid-1920s.[2] These lavish revues often featured more than a hundred dancers, all performing identical movements; they were, in his words, veritable "girl machines."[3] Less than a decade later, Leni Riefenstahl would organize the masses similarly in her documentary of the Nazi Party Congress, *Triumph des Willens* (*Triumph of the Will*, 1935).

"Metropolis, the city of the future," proclaimed the advertising material sent to the press and to movie theaters in 1927, "is the city of eternal social peace—the city of cities in which there is no animosity, no hatred, but only love and understanding" (*Metropolis* publicity brochure 1927). Having gone into production only six years after the failed workers' revolution of 1918–19, *Metropolis* is emphatically

FIGURE 9.2   Workers in formation as "mass ornament."

utopian in its keen desire for social harmony. While it was true that relations be-tween the classes had become relatively stable following the hyperinflation of 1923–24, the reconciliation between labor and management at the conclusion of the film still seemed like a contrived happy ending made in Hollywood. In an inter-view published in the 1960s, Lang recalled: "The main thesis was Mrs. Lang's but I am at least fifty percent responsible because I made the film. You cannot make a social-conscious picture in which you say that the intermediary between the hand and the brain is the heart—I mean that's a fairy tale—definitely. But I was very in-terested in machines" (quoted in Bogdanovich 1967, 124).[4]

MACHINE AESTHETICS

"But I was very interested in machines." Lang's statement reveals precisely his contribution to the novel's predictable love story. In fact, the machine represents the underlying metaphor that places the film within the 1920s discourse on moder-nity and technology. The city, the workers' bodies, and the film itself are all asso-ciated with the machine. The city draws its energy from machines below ground; lights flicker, and flashes of lightning shoot across the sky after the workers de-stroy the gigantic generator that powers the city. The city itself is organized like a

FIGURE 9.3 The machine as central metaphor for modernity.

machine that self-destructs as soon as any part malfunctions. When the workers rebel against their dehumanized status, they are presented as malfunctioning cogs in the city's machinery. Thus management's plan to replace them with robots is only logical: "Machines will be the workers of the future," proclaims Rotwang, the mad scientist.

Metropolis begins with an abstract montage of machinery in motion, set against tall skyscrapers that fill the entire frame. Close-ups of moving pistons and a turbine engine turning in opposite directions build to a crescendo as more gears and movements are incorporated (Fig. 9.3). The sequence is punctuated by the interspliced image of a ten-hour clock, yet another machine, indicating the imminent start of a new shift. The steam whistle blows, releasing the pressure that has built up, and—as a title card announces—a new shift begins. These machines move by themselves; we do not know what they produce or generate, nor do we know who set them in motion.

This fascination with mechanization, which Lang shared with Italian futurists and such avant-gardists as Fernand Léger (whose film *Ballet mécanique* appeared in 1924), also found expression in the work of Ernst Jünger, who hailed the cold elegance and metallic energy of the impersonal machine. "Only our generation begins to reconcile itself to the machine and to see in it not only the useful but the beautiful as well," Jünger wrote in 1925, referring to the front generation of World War I, which experienced the new symbiosis of human being and machine in the first technological war (Jünger 1929, 81; my translation; see also Theweleit 1989). This generation was one that dominated machines as organs of power and energy and one that transformed utilitarianism with primordial passion. The fusion of technology and vitalistic Nietzschean *Lebensphilosophie* corresponds to what Joseph Goebbels would later call "stählerne Romantik" (steely romanticism)—an intoxicating mixture of myth and modernity that Lang also embraces in *Metropolis*.

Wartime mobilization, in which the soldier subordinates his individual freedom to the demands of autocratic planning, also seemed the perfect disciplinary model for industrial production; it was Jünger's contention, expressed in his 1932 book-length treatise *Der Arbeiter* (The Worker), that one day the worker would in fact become a worker-soldier of the type that Lang depicted in *Metropolis*. Jünger's futuristic project blended feudal imagery of service and sacrifice with a modern celebration of efficiency and vitality. It was precisely the war, however, that also showed the destructive potential of modern technology, and the experience of bombing raids, machine-gun fire, and poison gas (invented and first used by Germans in 1915) informed the deep split in the 1920s between technology and humanity. As Jünger put it in his essay "Feuer und Blut" (Fire and Blood):

> The war battle is a terrifying competition of industries, and victory is the success of the competitor that managed to work faster and more ruthlessly. Here the era from which we come shows its cards. The domination of the machine over man, of the servant over the master, becomes apparent, and a deep discord, which in peacetime had already begun to shake the economic and social order, also emerges in the battles in a deadly manner. Here the style of a materialistic generation discloses itself, and technology celebrates a bloody triumph. Here a bill must be paid, one that seemed long forgotten. (Jünger 1978, 450; my translation)

In 1927 the bill was still being paid. The images of large numbers of men in dark uniforms shuffling along in formation in *Metropolis* evoked memories of soldiers marching off to the front. It was the first modern war in which machines (from machine guns to bomber planes) decided the outcome. The consequences of World War I, with nine million dead and many more wounded, were not forgotten by the mid-1920s. Millions of veterans with prostheses and mechanical body parts—half machine, half human—walked the streets, as we know from photographs, as well as paintings and drawings by George Grosz and others. The technological war and its aftermath provided the ultimate context for modernist art in Germany.

Metropolis offers a hallucinatory vision of the relationship between man and machine. The gigantic turbine that dominates the machine room transforms itself before the horrified eyes of Freder into the gaping jaws of a monster, identified in

FIGURE 9.4 The inventor, engineer, and mad scientist Rotwang (Rudolf Klein-Rogge).

a title card as the biblical god Moloch. Taking the visual motif of the man-eating machine from the famous 1914 Italian film *Cabiria*, the film uses superimposition to make the machine take on the features of a fuming god.[5] This sudden metamorphosis reveals *Metropolis*'s underlying ideology, which associates machines with man-eating monsters and the inventor Rotwang with black magic. Reminiscent in both dress and demeanor of Rabbi Löw in Paul Wegener's film *Der Golem: Wie er in die Welt kam* (*The Golem*, 1920), who creates and programs the monstrous golem cyborg, Rotwang's figure equally oscillates between stereotype and occultism (note the five-pointed star on his door, a pentagram identified in von Harbou's novel as "the seal of Solomon"). The film dramatizes Rotwang's categorical outsider status by linking him to a bizarre-looking medieval house surrounded by huge skyscrapers. Inventor of the artificial human machine, as well as sorcerer and magician, Rotwang represents the repressed archaic and nonsynchronous dimension of modernity (Fig. 9.4).

"The more plain and advanced the technology," Ernst Bloch wrote in his perceptive essay "Die Angst des Ingenieurs" (The Fear of the Engineer, 1929), "the more mysteriously it intersected with the old taboo region of vapors, supernatural velocity, Golem-robots, blue thunderbolts. Thus it touched what was once thought of as the realm of magic. An Edison is much closer to Doctor Faustus than to Herbert Spencer. Much of what the old fairy tales of magic promised has been realized by the most modern technology" (Bloch 1965, 353; see also Bloch 1977). Situated between fairy tale and high-tech machinery, the film medium was predestined to represent technical progress and modernization as the intrusion of the horrific and uncanny.

Like most science fiction films, *Metropolis* was highly self-conscious about the representation of technology, because it was technology that produced the special effects and tricks that have characterized the genre ever since Georges Méliès launched his first science fiction film, *Le voyage dans la lune* (*Trip to the Moon*), in 1902. Technology (especially the status of the camera as a machine) had long kept film in Germany from being admitted to the temple of art: how can a machine produce more than a mechanical reproduction of reality? The invention of moving pictures itself was originally seen as a fiction of science, and it may not be simple coincidence that H. G. Wells's classic science fiction novel *The Time Machine* appeared when film was born in 1895.[6]

The most stunning scene in *Metropolis*, Rotwang's transformation of the robot into the likeness of Maria, is mentioned only briefly in von Harbou's novel. In a dazzling display of both scientific and cinematic magic, a replica is created with the help of enormous machines, electricity, and chemistry—the very elements that are also needed to create a lifelike image on photographic film. The new film technology had the ability to conjure up simulacra, machine-made images indistinguishable from reality.[7] When the robot as a machine-come-to-life performs a lascivious dance before a male audience, attracting the spectators' desiring gaze and at the same time tricking them, it becomes an emblem for cinema as such: a product of technical ingenuity, an incarnation of visual pleasure, and a temptress out to deceive those who fall for the illusion of a replica (Fig. 9.5).[8]

The split of Maria into an asexual "good" Maria and an oversexed "bad" Maria, which Andreas Huyssen (1986) has perceptively analyzed, can also be read as a reworking of historical developments that von Harbou and Lang may have regarded as a threat: the emergence of emancipated and sexually liberated women, as well as organized feminist activity in the mid-1920s. The robot Maria, stylized as the "New Woman," rips the social fabric asunder, inciting the workers to rebel and seducing them into self-destructive acts. Her punishment, once she is uncovered as an agent provocateur, is to be burned at the stake. In the machine-woman-as-witch the film collapses the fear of women and machines into one. This nexus of technology, visual pleasure, and fantasy also lay at the core of modern American mass culture, which, according to some cultural critics, had seduced Germany into renouncing its classical canon of high culture. While American modernity conquered the economy, culture, and lifestyle of the entire Western world in the 1920s, German

FIGURE 9.5 The evil Maria (Brigitte Helm) as eroticized dancer.

intellectuals appeared powerless, vacillating between fascination and repulsion. Raoul Hausmann's famous sculpture, which bears a striking resemblance to the robot's head in *Metropolis*, is tellingly entitled "Mechanischer Kopf: Der Geist unserer Zeit" (Mechanical Head: The Spirit of Our Time, 1921).

"The number of people who see films and never read books is in the millions," theater critic Herbert Ihering wrote in despair in 1926. "They are all subordinated to American taste, they are made identical. . . . The American film is the new world militarism, which inexorably marches forward. It is more dangerous than Prussian militarism because it devours not only single individuals but whole countries" (Ihering 1961, 509; my translation). The fear that mass culture might be a secret American weapon, one that would enslave the world by distracting it, found a particular resonance in Germany, where cultural identity had compensated for a lack of national identity for two centuries. Linked to technology, mass consumption, and mass media, American modernity became a powerful agent in the economic and cultural modernization of Germany after the war.

AMERICAN MODERNITY

"How boring Germany is," wrote Bertolt Brecht in a short diary entry dated June 18, 1920. After finding fault with all classes of German society—peasants, middle class, and intellectuals—he concluded, there "remains America" (Brecht 1967, 10). For Brecht, as for other young writers of the early 1920s, America was the only progressive alternative to the still semifeudal lifestyle of Germany. America, more than Russia, was consistently represented as the New World and antithesis to the Old Europe. The relationship between Germany and America was understood as a historically momentous encounter between two radically different cultures, two ways of perceiving and interpreting the world, two divergent cultural languages and systems of signs. The Berlin avant-garde around Brecht and Grosz saw American mass culture as a vehicle for a radical modernization and democratization of German life and culture. America stood for Charlie Chaplin and the movies, for jazz and the Charleston, for boxing and other spectator sports; above all, it represented modernity and the ideal of living in the present.

No other country embraced American modernity more feverishly than Germany after the war. "America was a good idea," a German intellectual remarked, looking back in 1930:

> It was the land of the future. It was at home in its century. We were too young to know it firsthand; nevertheless we loved it. Long enough had the glorious discipline of technology appeared only in the form of tanks, mines, poison gas, for the purpose of annihilating humankind. In America it was at the service of human life. The sympathy expressed for elevators, radio towers, and jazz demonstrated this. It was like a creed. It was the way to beat the sword into a plowshare. It was against cavalry; it was for horsepower. (Joachim 1930, 397–98; my translation)[9]

By the mid-1920s, however, at the beginning of a five-year period of relative political and economic stability, a noticeable shift in the image of America began to take place in Germany. It continued to represent the mass culture of jazz, sports, and cinema, but it increasingly became associated with inhuman technological progress and industrial rationalization as well. Americanism in the economic sphere meant efficiency, discipline, and control, and both the right and the left began criticizing what they considered the encroachment of instrumental rationality and cost effectiveness into all areas—even culture, which in Germany had always been defined as antithetical to the world of commerce.

Adolf Halfeld, a conservative cultural critic, states this unmistakably on the cover of his polemical book *Amerika und der Amerikanismus* (America and Americanism), published in 1927, the year *Metropolis* was released: "Indebted to tradition, the culture of Europe, in particular of Germany, is threatened by America, with its focus on materialism and the mechanization of life. Rationalization in the American example triumphs, even if it kills the human side of humankind" (Halfeld 1927; my translation). And in 1928, when asked by the avant-garde journal *Transition* about the influence of the United States on Europe, the German poet Gottfried Benn answered: "[The American] influence is enormous. There is a group of lyric poets, who think they have composed a poem by writing 'Manhattan.' There is a group of playwrights, who think they reveal the modern drama by having the action take place in an Arizona blockhouse and by having a bottle of whiskey on the table. The entire young German literature since 1918 is working under the slogan of tempo, jazz, cinema, overseas, technical activity by emphasizing the negation of an ensemble of psychic problems." He particularly objected to "the purely utilitarian, the mass article, the collective plan," concluding, not surprisingly, by stating, "Personally I am against Americanism" (Benn 1928, 251; original in English). In Benn's view Americanism had conspired with communism in promoting collectivism and crass materialism at the expense of the German ideals of individualism and idealism, a polemical juxtaposition that structured the cultural debates of the Weimar era and also inscribed itself in *Metropolis*.

By the mid-1920s the term Americanism had come to signify two intricately related phenomena: scientific management of labor and industrial mass production (known as Taylorism and Fordism, respectively), on the one hand, and commercial mass culture, on the other. To speak of America was to evoke an image of a country in which economic productivity, technology, modernity, and democracy went hand in hand with a new urban culture. But to speak of America was also to conjure up a nightmarish picture of a materialistic, mechanized society ruled by exploitation, commercialism, and a lowbrow mass culture cynically catering to the largest possible audience. These contradictory attitudes prevailed throughout the Weimar era, with the critical view gaining dominance after the stock market crash of 1929.

Henry Ford, car manufacturer and popular philosopher, was generally regarded as the official spokesman for American big business. His 1922 autobiography, *My Life and Work*, was translated into German in 1923 and became a bible for all those who wanted to emulate America's economic success. Ford preached the gospel of scientific instrumental rationality couched in humanitarian terms. In a chapter entitled "The Terror of the Machine," he writes: "I have not been able to discover that repetitive labor injures a man in any way. I have been told by parlor experts that repetitive labor is soul- as well as body-destroying, but that has not been the result of our investigations." He goes on to explain:

> There were 7,882 different jobs in the factory. Of these, 949 were classified as heavy work requiring strong, able-bodied, and practically physically perfect men; 3,338 required men of ordinary physical development and strength. The remaining 3,595 jobs were disclosed as requiring no physical exertion and could be performed by the slightest, weakest sort of men. In fact, most of them could be satisfactorily filled by women or older children. The lightest jobs were again classified to discover how many of them required the use of full faculties, and we found that 670 could be filled by legless men, 2,637 by one-legged men, 2 by armless men, 715 by one-armed men, and 10 by blind men. (Ford 1922, 105, 108)

Ford prides himself on the employment of the deaf and mute as well as the tubercular, who, he suggests, should be used mainly outdoors. He concludes, "Yet it is not true that men are mere machines" (ibid., 209). Between 1912 and 1914, following the introduction of the assembly line, the time required to assemble a car was cut from fourteen hours to ninety-three minutes. By 1925, after further refinement and the addition of more conveyor belts, a new car rolled off the assembly line every ten seconds.

Metropolis's highly stylized, almost dancelike, image of rationalized and fully alienated labor visualizes and critiques basic principles of Taylorism and Fordism: repetitive work under the dictates of the clock is bound to create pressure that can be released only in an explosive revolution, which the film represents as a natural catastrophe on the order of an earthquake or flood. The film shows that technology's repressed Other returns with a vengeance.

THE DIALECTICS OF MODERNITY

The much-maligned ending of *Metropolis*—the reconciliation between capital and labor, which has been called simplistic, foolish, reactionary, and worse[10]—is in fact an accurate expression of contradictory German responses to modernity, technological progress, and instrumental rationality. Modernity, in Max Weber's oft-quoted definition, means above all the progressive disenchantment (Entzauberung) of the world, a result of myth and religion being superseded by rational and secular thought. Intertwined with the rise of capitalism, democracy, and mass culture, modernity had a more destabilizing effect in Germany than in France, England, and the United States because Germany lacked an established democratic tradition. Everything capitalist modernity stood for—its challenge to authority, its drive for unbridled economic competition, its disavowal of spiritual and religious values, and its commercialization of culture—collided head-on with still-intact patriarchal and authoritarian structures.

Although the German battle against modernity dates back to the mid-nineteenth century (culminating in World War I), it was the Weimar Republic, Germany's first democratically elected government, that revealed the enduring contradictions within modernity itself. In their magisterial *Dialektik der Aufklärung* (*Dialectic of Enlightenment*) of 1947, Max Horkheimer and Theodor W. Adorno voiced the suspicion that the rationality characteristic of the joint projects of Enlightenment and modernity might rest on a logic of domination and oppression. Writing in the aftermath of two world wars, of Hiroshima and the Holocaust, they argued that the desire to dominate nature entailed the domination of human nature; the quest for human emancipation was thus transmuted and hardened into a system of universal oppression. The legacy of the Enlightenment spirit that informed modernity meant, in short, the triumph of instrumental rationality.[11]

FIGURE 9.6 The much-maligned ending of *Metropolis*: the reconciliation of capital and labor.

Metropolis seeks to counter instrumental rationality with religion, idealism, superstition, irrationalism, sexual abandon, and revolutionary zeal—only to reaffirm in the end a somewhat modified instrumental reason. Both the failed socialist revolution of 1918–19 and the successful fascist takeover in 1933 responded to forces unleashed by modernity in Germany. From today's perspective *Metropolis* incorporates both reactions to modernity, the workers' revolt (in the film cynically masterminded by capital), as well as capital's reclamation of power that stands for what might be called "oppression with a heart." At the end the workers again march in formation and come to a stop only to watch their foreman shake hands with "the ruler" of the city, as the young facilitators of the social peace, Freder and Maria, look on.

Who, then, is excluded from this harmonious ending (Fig. 9.6)? Rotwang falls to his death from the rooftop of the Gothic cathedral while wrestling with Freder, and the sexualized female robot is burned at the stake. What remains is a transformed community that again embraces instrumental rationality, but it is a community that is free from vaguely connoted "Jewish" influence and uncontrolled female sexuality, infused, instead, with German spirituality (see Isenberg 1999). It is the kind of closed community (*Gemeinschaft*, not *Gesellschaft*) that reactionary modernists such as Ernst Jünger, Werner Sombart, and Oswald Spengler had valorized in their writings throughout the 1920s. *Metropolis*'s linkage of modern technology, cultural pessimism, and totalitarian ideology prefigured the National Socialists' resolve to emancipate technology from capitalist exchange and "Jewish material-ism."[12] Hitler, who once defined Aryan culture as a synthesis of "the Greek spirit and Germanic technology" (Jäckel 1972, 28), did not oppose modernity in contrast to völkisch ideologues. Goebbels summed up the official Nazi position on technol-ogy in a speech at the opening of the Berlin Auto Show on February 17, 1939:

> National Socialism never rejected or struggled against technology. Rather, one of its main tasks was to consciously affirm it, to fill it inwardly with soul, to dis-cipline it and to place it in the service of our people and their cultural level. We live in an age that is both romantic and steel-like, that has not lost its depth of feeling. On the contrary, it has discovered a new romanticism in the results of modern inventions and technology. While bourgeois reaction was alien to and filled with incomprehension, if not outright hostility to technology, and while modern skeptics believed the deepest roots of the collapse of European culture lay in it, National Socialism understood how to take the soulless framework of technology and fill it with the rhythm and hot impulses of our time. (quoted in Herf 1984, 196)

This romanticized vision of modernity was meant to obscure the contradictions of a regime that built high-tech weapons systems while insisting on the values of blood and soil.

Metropolis's ideological trajectory is part of a larger debate among German soci-ologists and philosophers about the "intellectual and spiritual revolution," which, as Ernst Troeltsch stated in 1921, was a "revulsion against drill and discipline, against the ideology of success and power … against intellectualism … against the big metropolis and the unnatural … against the rule of money and prestige" (quoted in Ringer 1969, 346). This reaction against capitalist modernity was itself perceived as revolutionary and utopian in the 1920s. Troeltsch put his hopes for a spiritual renewal in the young, as did Lang in Metropolis.

Lang's Metropolis offers one of Germany's most fascinating and complex contri-butions to the vigorous 1920s discourse on modernity. Its message is ambivalent, suggesting that the undoing of modernization and technological progress would bring only self-destruction. This ambivalence is evident in the images that fetishize technology even as they display its cataclysmic power. The machine is the object of fascination and terror, of savagery and myth; its faceless and unlimited power clashes with a narrative that challenges the dehumanization of industrial produc-tion. The violent utopia in the plays of Georg Kaiser's Gas I (1918) and Gas II (1920), as well as Ernst Toller's Die Maschinenstürmer (The Machine Wreckers, 1924), which advocated the destruction of machines to achieve a new humanism, had it-self become dystopian in the advanced technocratic society of 1920s Germany.

After the military defeat and the failed socialist revolution, the Weimar Republic tried hard (especially during the postexpressionist period of "new objectivity") to discard all utopian ideas of German expressionism—in particular its unrealistic and old-fashioned emphasis on the "heart" (and, in a wider sense, on community and humankind) and its rebellion against unrestrained instrumental rationality. These utopian ideals, however, did not vanish. As *Metropolis* illustrates, they could be reactivated as an antidote to unlimited progress and technology. Lang stages the oedipal struggle between an "expressionist" son and his "Americanist" father to make a larger point about the failed project of modernity. The idealism of *Metropolis* should be seen, then, not as a "fault" of the film but as a historically explainable attempt to fight those tendencies of modernity that have undeniably shown themselves to be cruel and dehumanizing. Viewed in its historical context, the film thus dramatizes the protest of German modernism against an overpowering modernity—a modernity that had undermined and negated its emancipatory and utopian potential.

NOTES

1. *Metropolis*, which had an original running time of 153 minutes, was shortened for the American release by Paramount to a "normal" length of 120 minutes. Ufa followed this version after its opening; thus, approximately thirty minutes of the film are lost. Enno Patalas has produced a restored version that seeks to substitute the missing parts by providing explanatory titles from the screenplay and censorship cards. My analysis is based on the restored version (Transit Film) in German from 2003. A "restored authorized edition," with the original 1927 orchestral score and English intertitles, was made available by Kino International in 2002; it runs 124 minutes.

2. "The structure of the mass ornament reflects that of the general contemporary situation. Since the principle of the capitalist production process does not stem purely from nature, it must destroy the natural organisms which it regards either as a means or as a force of resistance. Personality and national community perish when calculability is demanded" (Kracauer 1975, 69).

3. See Kracauer 1931. The workers' automated movements also recall the "mechanical ballet" performed, for instance, by Oskar Schlemmer's Triadic Ballet at the Bauhaus theater in the early and mid-1920s.

4. For the production history of *Metropolis* and interviews with Lang, see also Gehler and Kasten 1990; and Patalas 1986.

5. Chaplin alludes to this motif in a more playful, fairy tale–like way in a scene from *Modern Times* (1936) in which the machine he operates first devours him and then spits him out.

6. On *Metropolis* within the context of science fiction and utopia in Germany see Fisher 1991; and Müller 1989, 212–17.

7. On the importance of the motif of the machine-woman in Auguste de Villiers de L'Isle-Adam's 1886 novel *L'eve future* for cinema see Michelson 1987; and Bellour 1986.

8. For a discussion of the sexual politics of *Metropolis* in general and the nexus between machine and female sexuality in particular see Wollen 1989; Dadoun 1986; Huyssen 1986; Jenkins 1981; and Mellencamp 1981.

9. On the extensive debate over cultural Americanism see Kaes 1983, 265–86; see also Kaes 1988. On Americanism in the economic sphere see Maier 1970.

10. H. G. Wells, for instance, begins his 1927 review as follows: "I have recently seen the silliest film. I do not believe it would be possible to make one sillier. ... It gives in one eddying concentration almost every possible foolishness, cliché, platitude, and muddlement about mechanical progress and progress in general served up with a sauce of sentimentality that is all its own" (quoted in Geduld 1972, 59).

11. See Horkheimer and Adorno (1972); see also Habermas 1987; and Zimmerman 1991.

12. The relationship between Fritz Lang and National Socialism is still under debate. Hitler and Goebbels liked *Die Nibelungen*, as well as *Metropolis*, and wanted to make Lang the head of the entire Nazi film production in 1933. He declined and went to Hollywood instead. His passport shows, however, that he actually returned to Germany on brief sojourns after 1933 (see Werner 2000; and Winkler 1990).

REFERENCES

Adorno, Theodor W. 1984. *Aesthetic Theory*. Trans. C. Lenhardt. Boston: Routledge and Kegan Paul.

Bellour, Raymond. 1986. "Ideal Hadaly." *Camera Obscura* 15 (fall): 111–34.

Benn, Gottfried. 1928. "Inquiry." *Transition* 13 (1928). Repr. in *Gesammelte Werke*, 2218. Wiesbaden: Limes, 1968.

Bloch, Ernst. 1965. "Die Angst des Ingenieurs." In *Gesamtausgabe*. Vol. 9. Frankfurt am Main: Suhrkamp.

——. 1977. "Nonsynchronism and the Obligation to Its Dialectics." *New German Critique* 11 (spring): 23–38.

Bogdanovich, Peter. 1967. *Fritz Lang in America*. New York: Praeger.

Brecht, Bertolt. 1967. *Gesammelte Werke*. Vol. 20. Frankfurt am Main: Suhrkamp.

Dadoun, Roger. 1986. "*Metropolis*: Mother-City—'Mittler'—Hitler." *Camera Obscura* 15 (fall): 137–64.

Fisher, Peter S. 1991. *Fantasy and Politics: Visions of the Future in the Weimar Republic*. Madison: University of Wisconsin Press.

Ford, Henry. 1922. *My Life and Work*. Garden City, NY: Doubleday.

Geduld, Harry M., ed. 1972. *Authors on Film*. Bloomington: Indiana University Press.

Gehler, Fred, and Ullrich Kasten. 1990. *Fritz Lang: Die Stimme von* Metropolis. Berlin: Henschel.

Habermas, Jürgen. 1987. *The Philosophical Discourse of Modernity*. Trans. Frederick Lawrence. Cambridge, MA: MIT Press.

Hake, Sabine. 1990. "Architectural Hi/stories: Fritz Lang and *The Nibelungs*." *Wide Angle* 12 (July): 38–57.

Halfeld, Adolf. 1927. *Amerika und der Amerikanismus*. Jena: Eugen Diederichs.

Herf, Jeffrey. 1984. *Reactionary Modernism: Technology, Culture, and Politics in Weimar and the Third Reich*. Cambridge, UK: Cambridge University Press.

Horkheimer, Max, and Theodor W. Adorno. 1972. *Dialectic of Enlightenment*. Trans. John Cumming. New York: Seabury Press.

Huyssen, Andreas. 1986. "The Vamp and the Machine." In *After the Great Divide: Modernism, Mass Culture, Postmodernism*, 65–81. Bloomington: Indiana University Press.

Ihering, Herbert. 1961. "UFA and Buster Keaton." In *Von Reinhardt bis Brecht*. Vol. 2. Berlin: Aufbau-Verlag.

Isenberg, Noah. 1999. *Between Redemption and Doom: The Strains of German-Jewish Modernism*. Lincoln: University of Nebraska Press.

Jäckel, Eberhard. 1972. *Hitler's World View: A Blueprint for Power*. Trans. Herbert Arnold. Middletown, CT: Wesleyan University Press.

Jenkins, Stephen. 1981. "Lang: Fear and Desire." In *Fritz Lang*. London: British Film Institute.

Joachim, Hans A. 1930. "Romane aus Amerika." *Die neue Rundschau* 41 (September): 397–98.

Jünger, Ernst. 1929. *Feuer und Blut: Ein kleiner Ausschnitt aus einer grossen Schlacht*. 4th ed. Berlin: Frundsberg-Verlag.

——. 1978. *Sämtliche Werke*. Vol. 1. Stuttgart. Klett.

Kaes, Anton, ed. 1983. *Weimarer Republik: Manifeste und Dokumente zur deutschen Literatur, 1918–1933*, 265–86. Stuttgart: Metzler.

——. 1988. "Mass Culture and Modernity: Notes Toward a Social History of Early American and German Cinema." In *America and the Germans: An Assessment of a Three-Hundred-Year History*, ed. Frank Trommler and Joseph McVeigh, 2:317–31. Philadelphia: University of Pennsylvania Press.

Kracauer, Siegfried. 1931. "Girls und Krise." *Frankfurter Zeitung*, April 27.

——. 1975. "The Mass Ornament." *New German Critique* 5 (spring): 67–76.

Lang, Fritz. 1924. "Was ich in Amerika sah." *Film-Kurier*, December 11.

Maier, Charles S. 1970. "Between Taylorism and Technocracy: European Ideologies and the Vision of Industrial Productivity in the 1920s." *Journal of Contemporary History* 5 (April): 27–61.

Mellencamp, Patricia. 1981. "Oedipus and the Robot in *Metropolis*." *Enclitic* 5 (spring): 20–42.

"*Metropolis*: The Fate of Humanity in the Year 2000." 1927. Publicity brochure. Repr. by the Filmmuseum/Stadmuseum Munich, 1988.

Michelson, Annette. 1987. "On the Eve of the Future: The Reasonable Facsimile and the Philosophical Toy." In *October: The First Decade, 1976–1986*, ed. Annette Michelson, Rosalind Krauss, Douglas Crimp, and Joan Copjec, 417–34. Cambridge, MA: MIT Press.

Müller, Götz. 1989. *Gegenwelten: Die Utopie in der deutschen Literatur*. Stuttgart: Metzler.

Patalas, Enno. 1986. "*Metropolis*, Scene 103." *Camera Obscura* 15 (fall): 165–73.

Ringer, Fritz. *The Decline of the German Mandarins: The German Academic Community, 1890–1933*. Cambridge, MA: Harvard University Press, 1969.

Sherwood, R. E. 1927. "The Silent Drama: *Metropolis*." *Life*, March 24.

Sloterdijk, Peter. 1987. *Critique of Cynical Reason*. Trans. Michael Eldred. Minneapolis: University of Minnesota Press.

Theweleit, Klaus. 1989. "The Soldierly Body, the Technological Machine, and the Fascist Aesthetic." In *Male Fantasies*. Vol. 2, *Male Bodies: Psychoanalyzing the White Terror*, trans. Erica Carter and Chris Turner, 197–210. Minneapolis: University of Minnesota Press.

Troeltsch, Ernst. 1921. "Die geistige Revolution." *Kunstwart und Kulturwart* 34 (January): 231.

von Harbou, Thea. 1926. *Metropolis*. Berlin: August Scherl Verlag.

Werner, Gösta. 2000. "Fritz Lang and Goebbels: Myth and Facts." *Film Quarterly* 43 (spring): 24–27.

Winkler, Willi. 1990. "Ein Schlafwandler bei Goebbels." *Spiegel* 48 (November 26): 236–42.

Wollen, Peter. 1989. "Cinema; Americanism; the Robot." *New Formations*, no. 8 (summer): 7–34.

Zimmerman, Florian, ed. 1988. *Der Schrei nach dem Turmhaus: Der Ideenwettbewerb Hochhaus am Bahnhof Friedrichstrasse Berlin, 1921–22*. Berlin: Argon.

Zimmerman, Michael E. 1991. Heidegger's Confrontation with Modernity: Technology, Politics, and Art. Bloomington: Indiana University Press.

BERLIN, SYMPHONY OF A GREAT CITY (1927)

CITY, IMAGE, SOUND

NORA M. ALTER

This morning I saw a fine street whose name slips my mind
New and bright it announced the sun
Executives, workers and sexy stenographers
Walk it four times a day from Monday morning to Saturday
Three times a morning sirens groan there
A choleric bell barks at noon
Billboards, posters, graffitis and
Doorplates twitter like parakeets

GUILLAUME APOLLINAIRE, "Zone"

A close-up of gently rippling water fills the entire screen, and the camera tracks slowly over the expanse—no horizon is in view, only the lapping of small waves that gradually dissolve into a geometric pattern of horizontal lines echoing the motion of the ripples. The abstract form of parallel lines, increasing in intensity and speed, evokes the rhythmic movement of the pistons of a steam engine; then the lines dissolve into the pattern of railroad crossing bars at a train-track juncture. The accompanying sound track parallels the increasing intensity of the image as it builds to a crescendo. We find ourselves on a train that accelerates in sync with the music. The next sequence of shots comprises short takes of a train hurtling down its path; they are intercut with shots of tracks and telegraph lines, and the countryside is soon replaced with images of buildings as the train moves from a rural to an urban setting. A sign, "Berlin 15 Kilometers," visually invites the spectator to participate in a journey into the German metropolis (Fig. 10.1). Advertisements on buildings, track switchings, and the Berlin Anhalter train station flash by just

FIGURE 10.1   In the rapid movement from the provinces to the city, a sign announces the train's final approach to Berlin in Walter Ruttmann's *Berlin, Symphony of a Great City* (1927). Courtesy of the Filmmuseum Berlin, Stiftung Deutsche Kinemathek.

prior to the abrupt halt of the train and the sound track. This remarkable sequence introduces one of the first feature-length films in which a city and not a person is featured as the principal player. The sequence runs the whole spectrum of nonnarrative film techniques to date, from nature sights to abstract shapes and, finally, to images of a large city.

Walter Ruttmann's *Berlin, die Sinfonie der Großstadt* (*Berlin, Symphony of a Great City*, 1927), a quasi-documentary film on the city of Berlin, has secured an important position both within the national canon of Weimar films and within the history of international nonfiction cinema.[1] Ruttmann, born in 1887, initially trained as an architect but very quickly turned to impressionist painting. His career as an artist was interrupted when he was called into military service during World War I, after which he resumed painting under the influence of avant-garde artists such as Cezanne, Matisse, Marc, Kandinsky, Delaunay, and others. Like his contemporary, the filmmaker and visual artist Hans Richter, Ruttmann quickly moved away from abstract painting to experiment with the then relatively new medium of film. At some point between 1913 and 1917 he authored a short proclamation entitled "Kunst und Film" (Art and Film), in which he argued against narrative film, proposing that cinema was an inherently optical art form and therefore should be most closely aligned to painting and dance.[2] A couple of years later, he revised his theory and instead declared that because successive movement was such an integral part of film, the new medium should be situated between painting and music.[3] In 1921 Ruttmann made his first abstract film, *Opus I*, a short work consisting of undulating color-tinted spheres, orbs, and geometric shapes that produced rhythmic patterns. Accompanying the film was a musical score composed by Max Butting. Following the success of *Opus I*, Ruttmann made three other "Opus" films, *II* (1923), *III* (1924), and *IV* (1925).

However important these films are in the history of avant-garde filmmaking—the geometric and abstract sequences inserted into *Berlin, Symphony of a Great City* can be traced back to these earlier works—what brought Ruttmann the greatest acclaim remains *Berlin, Symphony of a Great City*; it is considered to represent the apotheosis of his filmic career. Following *Berlin, Symphony of a Great City*, Ruttmann worked on the film version of Ernst Toller's *Hoppla, Wir Leben!* (1927) and assisted French filmmaker Rene Clair on *Un chapeau de paille d'Italie* (1928). With the advent of sound he began to produce highly experimental and ambitious sound projects including *Deutscher Rundfunk/Toenende Welle* (1928), *Melodie der Welt* (1929), and the remarkable *Wochenende* (1931), which featured a blank image track and only sounds. Although in 1928 Ruttmann was a member of the radical artist/filmmaker group Volks-Film Buehne (Volksverbund fuer Filmkunst), which proclaimed artistic independence from politics, his career took a sharp turn in the 1930s, and he produced films under the Third Reich such as *Blut und Boden* (1933), *Altgermanische Bauernkultur* (1934), *Metall des Himmels* (1935), *Schiff in Not* (1936), *Deutsche Waffenschmieden* (1940), *Deutsche Panzer* (1940), and others.[4] Several of these were classified as "Werbefilm" or "Industriefilm" because they were financed and produced by German industrial complexes such as Mannesmann. However, most damaging for his subsequent reception was his work with Leni Riefenstahl on her infamous party propaganda film, *Triumph of the Will* (1935). There is conflicting information about whether Ruttmann ever joined the Nazi Party, but what is clear is that his ongoing cinematic practice under fascism greatly affected and shaped his reception today.

Berlin, Symphony of a Great City remains a remarkable document not only as a recording of everyday life in the major German metropolis of the 1920s but also as a lasting testament of Ruttmann's extraordinary use of rhythm, cutting, music, and montage to structure film.[5] The initial idea for the film stemmed from Carl Mayer, who was intrigued by the possibility of making a film based on the city of Berlin that would be filmed entirely on location. Mayer and Ruttmann, however, had significantly different views about the final nature of *Berlin, Symphony of a Great City*, and after an initial period of enthusiasm Mayer left the production team.[6] The cinematographer for the project was Karl Freund, who had worked with Fritz Lang, F. W. Murnau, and Paul Wegener. Indeed, it has been argued that, after Mayer, Freund played a large role in the conceptualization and scripting of *Berlin, Symphony of a*

Great City. According to Freund, he and Ruttmann cowrote the storyboard, but he is careful to note that "all of the ideas, including the abstract ideas, came from him [Ruttmann]."[7] To create the audiovisual "symphony" of Berlin, Ruttmann worked closely with the Austrian composer Edmund Meisel, who was known for his atonal and contrapuntal compositions (he was responsible for the score of *Battleship Potemkin*). Meisel conceived of his musical score as an assemblage of noises that characterize a cosmopolitan center. The expectation was that the urban spectator would recognize in the "symphony" sounds that emanated from, and resonated with, the sonic environment of quotidian life in the metropolis. The close collaboration between the composer and the director was unprecedented and resulted in a meticulously choreographed composition of images, music, and rhythms. Whereas Ruttmann's *Opus* films had been structured on the sonata, for *Berlin, Symphony of a Great City* he decided on the larger more encompassing form of a five-movement symphony, which was scored to the five acts of the film.[8] Thus, a slow opening *Andante* composition is played while the city sleeps, followed by a faster *Allegro con fuoco* as it awakes and work begins; a slower, more ponderous *Adagio* guides the mid-day rest, which gives way to an energetic *Allegretto* that accompanies early evening sport and entertainment activities, culminating in a resounding *Finale*.

In retrospect *Berlin, Symphony of a Great City* can be situated within the rise of so-called city films. This international category includes films from the 1920s, such as Paul Strand and Charles Sheeler's *Manhatta* (U.S., 1920), Alberto Cavalcanti's *Rien que les heures* (France, 1926), Dziga Vertov's *Man with a Movie Camera* (Soviet Union, 1929), Jean Vigo's *À propos de Nice* (France, 1929), Robert Florey's *Skyscraper Symphony* (U.S., 1929), Herman Weinberg's *A City Symphony* (U.S., 1930), Kenji Mizoguchi's *Tokai kokyogaku* (Japan, 1929), and Adalberto Kemeny and Rudolf Rex Lustig's *São Paulo, sinfonia da metrópole* (Brazil, 1929). These films, for the most part, were produced before the advent of synchronized sound-and-image recording and were conceived with a separate musical score that was either performed by a live orchestra or set to a distinct sound recording that accompanied the film projection. With the full integration of sound, these "city films" evolved to include interviews with city inhabitants—a characteristic that changed the focus of the work. The technological contribution of handheld sync cameras, and the emergence of cinema verité, generated a new wave of city films, including Jean Rouche's *Chronique d'été* (1961) and Chris Marker's *Le joli Mai* (1961).

More recently there has been an increase of contemplative meditations in city films, such as Godfrey Regio's *Koyaanisqatsi* (1983), with a musical score by Philip Glass, and Daniel Eisenberg's *Something More Than Night* (2003). In these productions the focus returns to the city as the central protagonist.[9] The city as object of contemplation becomes connected with modernity, and representations of cities continue to proliferate in "modernist" media and genres. This same movement affected late-nineteenth-century writers such as Charles Baudelaire and photographers like Eugene Atget, as well as early-twentieth-century poets and novelists from Apollinaire to James Joyce (*Ulysses*' ode to Dublin), John Dos Passos (*Manhattan Trilogy*), and Alfred Döblin (*Berlin Alexanderplatz*). There have also been plenty of painters of the modern metropolis (from Edouard Manet, Gustave Caillbotte, and Georges Seurat to Robert Delaunay, George Grosz, and Otto Dix) and sociologists with similar interests (Georg Simmel, Michel de Certeau, and Henri Lefebvre). It has been argued, however, that a special affinity exists between the urban metropolis and the filmic medium. In part this is attributable to the unique and highly iconic properties of cinema—namely, a close visual resemblance between filmic signs and what they represent. In other words, film as a machine was trusted to accurately record and document real life with an "objectivity," exactitude, and, hence, veracity that neither the writer nor the painter could ever achieve. Still further, because it was designed to capture movement, only cinema was assumed to do justice to the speed and motion that characterized the intense rhythms of the modern metropolis. And finally, in later film, the technical ability to record the soundscape in addition to the visual images secured the bond between cities and cinema.

Arguably, city films can be related to early travelogue films, in which cinema functioned as a means to transport viewers to faraway and exotic locations. It is also important to stress that when Ruttmann shot his film, in the late 1920s, the category of "documentary" cinema did not exist. Indeed the term *documentary* was first used in photography in the late 1920s to refer to a type of photograph that documented or recorded "reality"; only later was it applied to a "truthful," "objective," and nonfictional filmmaking practice. Documentary films as such did not become recognized as a genre until the 1930s, with the work of filmmakers such as John Grierson. In fact, in Germany the term *Dokumentarfilm* was not employed regularly until the second half of the twentieth century. Before, a distinction was made between "feature films" dominated by fictional stories and what we would call today, "nonfiction films."[10] Within the latter group, one agglomerated science films, ethnographic films, colonial films, travel films, newsreels, *Lehrfilme*, or instructional films, culture films (*Kulturfilme*), and "absolute" or abstract art films. Kultur films encompassed a broad degree of subject matter; and absolute or abstract films were for the most part produced by individuals with a background in the visual arts. This last category was illustrated by filmic creations such as Viking Eggeling's *Symphonie diagonale* (1923); Hans Richter's *Rhythmus* series (1921–23), *Filmstudie* (1926), *Inflation* (1928), *Zweigroschenzauber* (1929), and *Rennsymphonie* (1929); Oskar Fischinger's *Münchner Bilderbogen 1* (1924), *Seelischer Konstruktion* (1927), and *Studie Nr. 1* (1929); and László Moholy-Nagy's *Berliner Stilleben* (1926) and *Impressionen vom alten Marseiller Hafen* (1929). This is the type of filmmaking from which Ruttmann emerged, especially with his earlier abstract *Opus* films.

The abstract films were clearly grounded in an aesthetic philosophy. Ruttmann and others considered cinema an art form, with the prevalent narrative cinema representing a continuation of nineteenth-century realism. Their early cinematic experimentation sought to translate avant-garde painting directly into the medium of film. That experimentation influenced undoubtedly the largely abstract nature of many films during the early 1920s. Filmmakers were clearly inspired by the same ideas that prompted the emergence of abstract painting in various European cities in the 1910s. Thus, at an early stage in his filmic career Ruttmann concentrated on how far he could push or adapt the abstract form to celluloid. Hans Richter soon noted, however, that "abstract form in films does not mean the same as in painting where it is the ultimate expression of a long tradition of thousands and thousands of years. Film has to be discovered in its own property" (Richter 1972). In other words, Richter, Ruttmann, and others soon understood that each medium needs to develop within its own tradition and that the advances achieved in one medium cannot be assumed to be relevant in another. Although abstract forms were not a great success in cinema, it was felt that there were other possibilities for development in the filmic medium that did not have to follow the demands of strict realistic narratives meant for mass consumption. Thus, the films from the 1920s show an evolution from the abstract toward more representational, but not necessarily narrative, techniques. It was believed that cinematic verisimilitude offered filmmakers the opportunity to capture the mobile nature of everyday life. In sharp contrast with the trend in narrative film to increase the role of illusion and fantasy through the use of fictional stories and big stars, Ruttmann and others pushed toward further experimentation with photographic realism to see what new territories the form of film could open. Hence, conspicuously absent from *Berlin, Symphony of a Great City* are plot, love story, suspense, happy ending, stars, or even actors—the main role, according to Ruttmann, is assumed by the city playing itself.[11] Ruttmann's film also needs to be contextualized within the broader aesthetic category of *Neue Sachlichkeit* or New Objectivity. *New Objectivity* is difficult to define and "in addition to adjectives such as *pragmatic, realistic, objective*, and *sober* ... [it] was foremost an eminently political and socio-economic phenomenon that reflected the industrialization and urbanization of Germany."[12] One component of New Objectivity includes the concept of *Querschnitt*, or "cross-section," a method of representation that was supposed to show both external and internal parts of the object. *Berlin, Symphony of a Great City*, with its *entfesselte*, or "unleashed," camera that roams throughout the city ostensibly indiscriminately filming whatever comes in its path, has been credited, by Siegfried Kracauer among others, with having "inaugurated the vogue of cross-section, or 'montage,' films" (Kracauer 1947, 188).[13]

It should be stressed that even though Ruttmann moves away from abstract geometrical forms, the structuring principle of *Berlin, Symphony of a Great City* is not based on a narrative but on the rhythm and movements in the cycle of a day. What Ruttmann's camera captures is the modern spectacle of a "world in motion." Not only is the effect of motion achieved through real light and rhythm, but it is also enhanced by a montage technique based on "visual rhyming." The visual rhyming occurs when, for instance, the horizontal geometrical shapes dissolve into concrete crossbars on the railroad track, or when a shot of dogs fighting is followed by one of men fighting. Ruttmann's filmmaking technique is extremely sophisticated in this respect, which is not surprising when one considers that filmmakers like Ruttmann, employed in commercial advertising at the time, were provided with the most advanced equipment. In addition to the obvious importance of the visual dimension of the film, the role that music plays both in organizing and in structuring the cuts and montage cannot be underestimated. *Berlin, Symphony of a Great City* is, to use Béla Balázs's contemporaneous term, a piece of "optical music." It is fully conceived of as a synthesized audiovisual production in which a sound score drives the image track.

Many different themes run through *Berlin, Symphony of a Great City*. I will introduce three of them to assist in ordering the text and opening up lines of interpretation and meaning. First, *Berlin, Symphony of a Great City* takes us to and through the relatively young metropolis of Berlin. As mentioned, the film is structured in five acts (with the appropriate musical movement), each corresponding to a period in the conventional workday: Predawn, Morning, Noon, Afternoon, and Evening. Although only one day is tracked, the filming took over a year and involved three different cameramen: Renmar Kuntze, Robert Baberske, and László Schäffer. The appropriate activities are filmed for each time of day. Initial shots of an awakening city are successively followed by people going to work, taking their lunch break, resuming work, and finally engaging in the leisure and entertainment that accompany the end of the day. Second, *Berlin, Symphony of a Great City* is a self-reflexive film about filmmaking. With acute self-awareness, Ruttmann represents all the major filmic genres prevalent at the time. Finally, *Berlin, Symphony of a Great City* is a film about advertising, at the time a booming development in the business of marketing. To that extent *Berlin, Symphony of a Great City* is a record of the 1920s explosion of advertising and the concomitant transformation of modernity into a society of spectacle. *Berlin, Symphony of a Great City* displays the contemporary world in which exchange value has become ubiquitous.

PART ONE: ONE DAY IN BERLIN

In act 1 the viewer is brought to the sleeping city by train and is positioned like a traveler looking out of the window and watching the landscape rushing by. The familiar trope connecting train travel to the cinematic experience is underscored by Ruttmann's strategic placement of the camera in the sightline of a passenger.[14] The

FIGURE 10.2 In the early morning an empty street awaits the inevitable bustle of the coming day. Courtesy of the Filmmuseum Berlin, Stiftung Deutsche Kinemathek.

spatial movement of the train as it rushes toward Berlin enacts the temporal passage from premodern rural landscape to a modern metropolis: from countryside to *Schrebergärten*, the urban gardening plots popular at the time, to architecture that becomes denser as the train approaches the city. Gradually, factories and modern apartment houses dominate the landscape, replacing the meadows and forests. Berlin is revealed to be a developing city with a vibrant population that pushes for ever-increasing expansion. The journey moves toward the center of the city from the southwest region, racing through Magdeburg and Potsdam, traversing the Berlin suburbs of Steglitz and Friedenau, slowing down through Schoeneberg, until it arrives at its final destination at the Anhalter Bahnhof, near the Potsdamer Platz and the commercial epicenter of the metropolis. The station clock, which reads 5:00 a.m., indicates that the day starts at dawn. Ruttmann's camera tracks the empty streets of the city, reminiscent of the late-nineteenth-century photographs of Charles Marville. Next comes a sustained series of shots of modernist architecture: factories, warehouses, storefronts, and office and apartment buildings designed by such eminent architects as Martin Gropius, Hans Poelzig, and Bruno Taut. All of these combine to produce the image of a young and modern cityscape. By contrast, there are a few aerial shots of the classic eighteenth- and nineteenth-century landmarks of Wilhelmina Berlin, such as the Dome Cathedral and the Imperial Palace.[15] The camera then plunges from its lofty heights into the bowels of the city with shots of the catacombs and sewage tunnels. Ruttmann's emphasis, however, is clearly on the driving beat of the city's surface: the pulse of modernity. Yet at this time of the morning the city appears empty, depopulated, and conspicuously asleep (Fig. 10.2).

The first human depicted is a night watchman, clocking in his beat as he, much like Ruttmann's camera, surveys the silent, sleeping city streets. Gradually people emerge. Some return home after a night of partying; others walk their dogs, clean the sidewalks, and prepare to go to work. Then Ruttmann cuts back to the Anhalter Bahnhof, where large doors swing open to reveal the engine of the regional "S-Bahn" train (marked with its destination: "Potsdam"), which will transport workers to factories on the outskirts of the city. There are multiple shots of factories, and although we see workers inside the gates, Ruttmann's industrial workspace— the inner workings of the city—is surprisingly devoid of human labor. He seems to have forgotten the workers and the social conditions of their labor at the factory gates. Instead the spectator is offered a symphony of mechanized labor: large wheels of machinery are rhythmically set in motion, and their mechanized rotations and movements seem to move in time to a musical score. They have become the parts of an orchestra called modernity. To that end, human labor has become completely invisible in the process of production. Ruttmann's camera aestheticizes the machines, presenting them as kinetic sculptures performing a mechanical ballet. The insinuation is that this is what must happen to humans as well. His shots of machinery testify to his affinity with Italian futurism and its celebration of technology at the expense of the human subject. According to Paul Rotha, it was precisely this focus on technology and machinery instead of on humans that caused Mayer to break with Ruttmann and leave the project.[16] Reviewers at the time were critical of Ruttmann's lack of attention to the human details of everyday life and questioned why, for example, there were no interior shots of the overcrowded dismal living quarters of the workers. Bernhard von Brentano (1927) pronounced that "[i]n Ruttmann's film the human subject is missing." Kracauer is equally troubled by *Berlin, Symphony of a Great City*, and although he admits that it was "the only significant attempt to break away from the common production fare," he finds that ultimately Ruttmann's project is disappointing because "instead of penetrating its enormous object in a way that would betray a true understanding of its social, economic, and political structure, and instead of observing it with human concern," the filmmaker presents a "city of speed and of work," without a "single meaningful relationship" (Kracauer 1995, 318). Perhaps it is through this lens that one can begin to understand Ruttmann's later affiliation with National Socialism and its well-oiled soulless machine.

Act 2 begins with shutters rolling open, at once revealing the windows of the city and evoking the opening of eyelids and the shutters of a camera shooting a film (an image later teased out by Dziga Vertov's 1929 *Man with a Movie Camera*). The city is waking up from a night's slumber. Children make their way to school; citizens purchase fresh bread at the bakery, meat at the butcher's, and milk at the dairy store; garbage is emptied, down comforters aired, and carpets beaten. The clothes indicate that it is summer, and a clock informs us that it is now 8:00 a.m.—three hours after the beginning of the film. Stores open, and horseback riders in the park are juxtaposed to workers sweeping sidewalks, beating out carpets, and cleaning the streets. The body of the city is subject to morning ablutions similar to the morning ritual of washing the human body. In contrast to the vacant streets a few hours earlier, now the camera captures a multitude of busy feet on the sidewalks as people go to work. There is an intensity of human movement; a circulation of goods, people, mass transportation; an accumulation of fashion, commodities, commuters, and more. Even though many people are captured by Ruttmann's camera, they are never individualized and are treated dispassionately, like parts of an enormous machine. Breaking with the atmosphere of act 1, the city has been anthropomorphized and animated, with the camera capturing all the sights of activity of a modern metropolis. The second act closes with shots of the U-Bahn followed by other symbols of modern engineering and technological advances: telephones, telegraph wires, buses, trolleys, and cars (Fig. 10.3). The concept of speed and connectivity is captured with the final image of a spinning rotorelief (with its obvious reference to Marcel Duchamp's *Anémic cinéma*, 1926).

At the beginning of act 3 Ruttmann situates the spectator once again in the space of a railway car—this time a subway as it emerges from an underground tunnel and hurtles into the daybreak of the metropolis. Ruttmann's camera tracks new construction, capturing both human laborers and huge dinosaur-like machines that move earth and matter as they shape the urban landscape. The perspective then shifts dramatically to that of a bird's eye as it looks down on the masses of people and traffic. Indeed, as the camera comes back to earth, its lens is filled with more and more men and women; the streets are densely populated. The crowds are in constant motion, circulating everywhere. Their movement parallels that of the trams, buses, subways, cars, carts, and horse-drawn carriages. All of these movements traverse the screen diagonally and accelerate as the act progresses. Among the individuals that the camera tracks are several women who self-consciously walk the streets. These women have been variously interpreted as female flaneurs or as prostitutes.[17] In either designation they are linked to commerce, trade, and commodities. Flaneur window shoppers gazing at goods and streetwalkers putting goods on display embody a distinct rendition of capitalism in which everything is for sale.[18] These sequences not only show the commodification of women; they

FIGURE 10.3 Bird's-eye view of a busy intersection at midday. Courtesy of the Filmmuseum Berlin, Stiftung Deutsche Kinemathek.

also focus on window displays, mechanical mannequins, and humans who wear advertisements. And there are soapbox preachers, chanting their sermons to those who bother to listen. Finally, as the tempo accelerates, the overdrive of impulses and stimuli multiply their effect, and we see not only men fighting in the streets but animals, too—dogs that go after each other. Then, as if to escape the oppression of the frantic pace of the city, the camera turns to transportation and travel, including signs indicating international destinations such as Zurich, Lucerne, Bonn, culminating in footage of a Lufthansa plane taking off from Berlin's Schönefeld airport. The following shot is taken from the plane and includes clouds, as well as a series of remarkable aerial views of Berlin. Finally, transportation and circulation expand to the realm of ideas and news, and act 3 closes with a series of quick shots that together show the vast volume of daily newspapers in circulation.

   Act 4 begins with the hand of the large clock featured at the start of the film now hitting 12:00 p.m. The machines slow down and come to a stop for the mid-day pause. Workers and laborers put down their tools and cease activities, horses are unharnessed and fed, and businesses close for the afternoon. The camera cuts to different categories of culinary fare, from slop for animals to sausages and soups for the working class to oysters and lobsters for the wealthy. Ruttmann affords the spectator glimpses of the most elegant dining rooms, which cater to the elite and provide refined cuisine, juxtaposed with freestanding street kiosks where sausage and beer are consumed at a counter. Just as at dawn, when Ruttmann provides a take on a broad swathe of social classes preparing for their morning rituals, so, too, at mid-day a whole spectrum of Berlin's population is shown, from the extremely wealthy to the poorest of beggars, men and women alike. This contrast is further emphasized, or perhaps generalized as a law of nature, as even the animals are divided into classes: a small mangy cat rummages through some garbage, a work dog attached to a cart lies down to rest, and exotic lions in the zoo are fed fine cuts of meat while an elephant prepares for a nap. After the people of Berlin have consumed their meals, the cleanup begins with huge industrial mechanical dishwashers processing thousands of plates and cutlery while people prepare for an afternoon rest. The frenzied pace of the previous act has been replaced by a sense of calm—a few scattered children play in the park, and a small barge slowly and silently makes its way through the canals. One sequence stands out: a small girl playing with baby lions followed by an extended tracking shot of another little girl with a toy baby carriage that she valiantly tries to get up some stairs. A few individuals take walks while deep in conversation. A shot of an inner courtyard moves from window to window as women peer out, presumably caught in the act of exchanging daily gossip as they watch the comings and goings in their courtyard.

Abruptly an elephant gets up, and a polar bear lunges out of its pool, shaking itself like a person shrugging off sleep. And with these sudden images the machines slowly start up again, their wheels rotating and pistons pumping as work resumes. The break is over. Ruttmann now focuses on the production of the evening edition of the news—the rush of trying to meet deadlines and make headlines. The typesetters work rapidly, and the papers are packaged as they emerge from the printing machines—sorted, bundled, and ready for distribution. Overblown headlines seem to jump off the screen: "Krise" (crisis), "Mord" (murder), and "Heirat" (marriage), ending with the hammering repetition of "Geld," "Geld," "Geld" (money, money, money) that is repeated frenetically and leads to a journey in which the viewer is hurtled down a roller coaster that threatens to derail at any moment. The camera spins vertiginously, and the image on the screen turns round and round, morphing once again into a dizzying rotorelief. It pauses to rest on a beggar woman, then on a pearl necklace displayed in a shop window. The wind on the street kicks up, and leaves begin to swirl and blow in a motion visually echoing that of the rotorelief. The camera tracks a woman as she crosses a bridge—an unusual close-up of her face reveals her anguished expression as she looks over the railing back and forth and then leaps off into the river to her death. Passersby rush to look in horror as the river swallows up the suicide. This sequence stands out because it is the single obviously staged fictional scene within the entire film. It ruptures the nonfiction convention in a significant way. Following the dark shot of the river, there is a cut to a fashion show where a model struts up and down the runway displaying her body and the clothes she wears. This is followed by a cut to the zoo, where an agitated lion paces back and forth, which rapidly leads in turn to another scene of dogs fighting in the street. The montage of shots accelerates as does the music; the wind intensifies and changes into a storm; trains whiz across the screen; and the frenzied pace overcomes the spectator until an alarm bell rings, and police and firemen mobilize.

Then, as fast as it began to grow, there is a slowing of the tempo as the day comes to an end. The camera depicts workers washing the grime of the day from their bodies. They stream out of the factories—this sequence in particular references cinema's primal scene: the Lumière brothers' *La sortie des usines Lumière* (*Workers Leaving the Lumière Factory*, 1895)—and the gates close. As the hours of the workday run down, people of the leisure world unlock waterways, allowing for a variety of aquatic activities that include rowing, sailing, boating, and swimming. The prescribed leisure and entertainment are not just limited to water sports but include go-karting, cycling, golfing, tennis, horseback riding, footraces, fashion shows, dancing, walking in the park, or relaxing on a park bench with friend or lover. The evening is over.

Act 5 takes us into nighttime, signaled by apartment lights going on in windows circling an inner courtyard. Illuminated signs are everywhere—huge letters fill the screen: KINO (FILM) and FilmPalast. People queue up to purchase tickets for a show—we see them enter a darkened theater; the curtain goes up, and on the screen appear the familiar shoes of the lovable tramp, Charlie Chaplin. The camera cuts to female performers getting ready for a live show, applying makeup and putting on their costumes in preparation for their stage activity in classical theater, ballet, opera, and cabaret. There are shots of trapeze artists, acrobats, magicians, and dancing girls (akin to the infamous Tiller troupe) whose legs in their choreographed mechanized movements evoke the well-oiled motions of industrial machines. Everywhere illuminated signs outline silhouettes of women—the suggestion of erotic play and illicit activities is underscored by the montage of scantily clad female bodies, lingerie shop signs, and one prominent "HOTEL." Then, as if to correct this one-sided vision of nightlife, comes a sequence of shots of winter sports—ice-skating, hockey, snowshoeing, skiing—followed by various equally healthy indoor activities. Gradually, however, these sporting activities take on a competitive edge, and there are shots of velodrome racing, boxing, dance contests and the like, paired with shots of spectators cheering the winners and hoping they have placed their bets on them. Leisure has been transformed into another component of the rat race, and the players have been instrumentalized into either winners or losers, no different from racehorses. This sequence is followed by card playing and gambling, by drinking in pubs. The suggestion is evident: behind every image in the metropolis lurks capital. The shots begin to spin out of control, concluding with a fireworks finale in celebration of the capital city: Berlin.

PART TWO: FILM, THE NEW MEDIUM

Berlin, Symphony of a Great City celebrates a booming metropolis of the early twentieth century, but it also reveres the new technology of film. Within Weimar intellectual circles film's importance was linked to its mass appeal. For example, the cultural critics Walter Benjamin and Siegfried Kracauer both insisted persuasively on the affinity between the medium of film and the modern urban masses (Benjamin 1969; Kracauer 1995). Kracauer, Benjamin, and others saw in film a unique possibility for producing a truly democratic art that would be accessible to all classes of people instead of catering solely to the bourgeois or elite spectator. But this utopian perspective of film also had a negative corollary, of which these critics were aware—namely, that film would be pitched and would appeal to the lowest common denominator among spectators, that it could easily be used for ideological manipulation or for sheer entertainment with little or no cultural, artistic, or intellectual character. This negative critique was championed decades later most vociferously by Max Horkheimer and Theodor W. Adorno, who, in their chapter on the culture industry in *Dialectic of Enlightenment*, characterized film as mass illusion and deception. Kracauer, too, was suspicious of the facility with which film could be manipulated for propagandistic political purposes. Interestingly enough, Kracauer's seminal essay on modernity, industrialization, and cultural production, "The Mass Ornament," was published in two installments in the *Frankfurter Zeitung* the same year that *Berlin, Symphony of a Great City* was released. Both noted the parallel between the mechanized movements of dancing legs and the regulated syncopated movements of gears, shifts, and levers of contemporary industrial production. It is evident, however, that despite all ideological ambivalences, a genuine fascination for film as an extension of modernity, and as the only medium capable of manifesting its many faces, is present in both Ruttmann and Kracauer. Because the image on the screen bears such a close visual resemblance to reality, Kracauer believed that film, more than any other medium, could directly represent a cross section of everyday life (Fig. 10.4). The indiscriminate lens, capturing everything before it and reproducing it with a high degree of verisimilitude, was trusted to create the illusion that what appeared on the screen was real, endowing film with an innate potential as documentary.

Ruttmann experimented with various types of filmmaking in *Berlin, Symphony of a Great City*. Clear references are made to a very broad spectrum of abstract filmmaking: from studies of geometric patterns to forms found in nature and industry, to the spinning rotoreliefs of Marcel Duchamp. Yet the film also features the jarring

FIGURE 10.4 Women leaning out of a window. Courtesy of the Filmmuseum Berlin. Stiftung Deutsche Kinemathek.

suicide sequence, with its touch of fictional melodrama. In particular, the enacted suicide of the young woman is highly emotive as it insists on hyperbolic gestures and facial expression. This sequence includes dramatic shots of madly swirling leaves and an overdetermined metaphor of the wild roller-coaster ride of life. This suicide sequence stands in direct contrast to the montage that directly precedes it: the shot of the downtrodden begging woman followed by an elegant hand removing a pearl necklace from a jewelry display box. By including these documentary shots, Ruttmann suggests that the dominant fictional form of melodrama prevalent in popular cinema is not the only way to show life's brutal inequalities. Real life is presented as a genre as powerful as fiction; the images it provides render the fictional unnecessary. Not coincidentally, the feature film advertised by brightly lit signs in *Berlin, Symphony of a Great City* stars the "little tramp," which underscores how fiction functions to mythologize social conditions. By contrast, *Berlin, Symphony of a Great City* presents itself as based on reality and offers an alternative to the type of popular entertainment packaged by the dominant mode of film production. In the context that *Berlin, Symphony of a Great City* was a "contingency film," whose very existence enabled another import from abroad to be screened, Ruttmann's film may also be read as an insurgent meditation on the possibilities of an "other cinema," a countercinema as it were, substituting "real" filmmaking for the standard fare so readily devoured by the masses.

Ruttmann does not just champion his nonfiction composition against other forms of cinema. He also enters into dialogue with another modern artistic medium, photography. Although its origins date back to the early nineteenth century, photography as an art had reached a high level of sophistication in the 1920s. This medium's innate ability to image the reality passing before the camera, freeze it in time, and even make visible that which the naked human eye could not see was found by artists to be rife with potential. Ruttmann's shots of empty streets resonate strongly with those of Marville half a century earlier. However, many of the images that make up *Berlin, Symphony of a Great City* also evoke the work of more contemporary photographers, such as Eugene Atget's uncanny pictures of empty streets, kiosks, and shop windows. Ruttmann is also clearly in dialogue with László Moholy-Nagy's New Vision photography, with its belief in the superiority of camera vision over conventional forms of perceptual experience. Ruttmann's camera, too, privileges technology over natural vision, the machine over the human eye, deliberately denaturalizing vision and leading straight to the question of whether human vision and technological vision are compatible at all. But the most significant dialogue that *Berlin, Symphony of a Great City* established with photography is with the *Neue Sachlichkeit* (New Objectivity) work of Albert Renger-Patzsch. Renger-Patzsch's detailed prints of machines and modern technology parallel the almost obsessive repetition of Ruttmann's sequences of machinery, factories, and industry. As Renger-Patzsch explained in 1927, "We still don't sufficiently appreciate the opportunity to capture the material of things. The structure of wood, stone, and metal can be shown with a perfection beyond the means of painting. ... To do justice to modern technology's rigid linear structure, to the lofty gridwork of cranes and bridges, to the dynamism of machines operating at one thousand horsepower—only photography is capable of that" (Renger-Patzsch and Kuspit 1993, 48). The fascination, glorification, and aestheticization of inanimate technology, almost to the point of endowing it with subjectivity, betrays a perspective dominated by an overvaluing of pure formal properties.

By setting his images against those of photography, Ruttmann points to the common element of both media: the photographic negative. He also underscores the crucial difference, however: that moving images are inherent to motion picture film. He makes the point that it is precisely its ability to capture movement in time and space through duration, montage, and other editing techniques that makes cinema *the* medium of modernity. Furthermore, Ruttmann's *Berlin, Symphony of a Great City* anticipates sound cinema by evoking a musical symphony through both its title and its structure. This adds yet one more dimension to representation and distances the film even further from the static, singular, and silent photographic image.

PART THREE: SELLING BERLIN

What became increasingly apparent by the late 1920s was that film that focuses on its inherent technological characteristics and on the perceptual modalities that those characteristics can generate is an ideal ally of devices, such as advertising, on which the emerging consumer culture depends (Fig. 10.5). It is not at all accidental that artists who conceived of industrial mass culture as an aesthetic subject came to associate themselves with advertisement culture. In turn, high culture and mass culture, the two spheres that had traditionally been perceived as opposites and mutually exclusive, were now explicitly associated. We see this repeatedly in Ruttmann's *Berlin, Symphony of a Great City*.

Advertising operates on multiple levels in the film. The opening shots feature signs painted on the walls of buildings and store fronts announcing new products. These are followed by a shot of a man pasting posters on a kiosk designed specifically for the purpose of publicity. Later in the film, during the night scenes of the fifth act, the filmscape explodes with illuminated signs advertising multiple varieties of nightlife. Texts, words, and graphic inscriptions proliferate in the city, transforming the urban environment into a complex web of linguistic signifiers whose shared focus is the commodity. Walls are no longer mere architectural support— they are designed to provide surfaces on which to place large advertisements.

The film features advertising not only within the realm of the linguistic but also in the visualization of material goods. Several shots of store windows capture to varying degrees the sophisticated displays featuring jewelry, fashionable clothing, food, children's toys, and other material goods. The particular attention Ruttmann pays to the New Woman is also significant, for the emergence of this social type signals the rise of the new consumer. More than her male counterpart, the New Woman advertises and proclaims the advent of modernity. Wearing fashionable clothes, hats, and jewelry, she is on display in public, window-shopping at leisure and purchasing luxury goods, coupled with another sign of modernity: the car. The totality of *Berlin, Symphony of a Great City* can thus be seen as an advertisement for modernity, with Berlin emerging at the forefront and film as the superior medium through which to showcase the city's spectacular splendor.

But it is not just the dazzling attractions of advertising that are shown. Also highlighted is the radical internalization of modernity. From the bodies of the proletariat (prostitutes who desperately try to sell their bodies, sandwich men whose bodies bear signs for consumer goods, beggars in rags who function as waste removal as they comb the streets) to the uniforms, hats, and coveralls of the working class to the ostentatious fashions of the wealthy, Ruttmann's camera takes it all in. His camera eye does not differentiate between live human bodies in the street and inanimate mannequins and mechanical automatons in store windows. But it is

FIGURE 10.5 A montage encapsulating the big-city excitement, smiling flapper as a central focal
point, was distributed as a publicity still for *Berlin, Symphony of a Great City*. Courtesy of the Filmmuseum Berlin, Stiftung Deutsche Kinemathek.

the high-fashion models on the runway who become the ultimate sign of consumer
society. They represent the fantasy that can never be obtained by the average person. They display another world—inaccessible and remote from the everyday, yet
alluring, sought after, and possible to imitate. High fashion, or, to use the French

term, *mode*, is inextricably linked to modernity. The fashion model represents the flip side of the prostitute—whereas the latter wears clothes to sell her body, the former uses her body to sell clothes.

So, here, in *Berlin, Symphony of a Great City*'s seemingly uninterrupted fusion with advertisement culture, the instrumental potential of *Neue Sachlichkeit* comes into its fullest expression. The cult of the thing, or the object, is integral to Ruttmann's *Berlin, Symphony of a Great City* and to the discussion of the 1920s concern for pure objectivity. The purported aim was to focus on nonmediated perception, on the discovery, description, and perceptual account of things as they were. Of course, such discussions always imply a considerable ideological agenda as well. Here it is important to recall that claims to eradicate the bombast and passion of expressionism—and certainly the staged suicide scene can be read as prototypically expressionistic—were as central to *Neue Sachlichkeit* as were claims to do away with the utopian and euphoric aspirations of the leftist and communist avant-garde of the 1920s. A fundamental element of *Neue Sachlichkeit* ideology was precisely its critical skepticism, and ultimately its rejection, of any model of the dialectical, radical transformation of social conditions.[19] As Walter Benjamin observed (citing Brecht) in his "A Little History of Photography," "less than ever does the mere reflection of reality reveal anything about reality. A photograph of the Krupps work or the AEG tells us next to nothing about these institutions" (Benjamin 1999, 526). Ruttmann's camera, too, is steadfast in its belief in realism and its pursuit of objectivity. It is this insistence on the inherent realism of the filmic medium that associates *Berlin, Symphony of a Great City* with the contemporary campaign for new objectivity. Yet what is ignored in all of these discussions of new objectivity and Ruttmann is the sonic element. For although *Berlin, Symphony of a Great City* is technically a silent film, Ruttmann, through his use of montage, hoped to evoke the acoustic dimensions of big-city life. And it is through his use of visual imagery and editing style that a dynamic acoustic environment is suggested—one that makes *Berlin, Symphony of a Great City* stand out from the silent, objective, rational, and fixed images of photography. To that extent, Ruttmann's work may be seen as prefiguring in significant ways what would decades later be realized as concrete music.

In sum, Ruttmann's symphony of and for Berlin is composed of multiple and diverse movements. The rich visual text is a lush tapestry woven from an overwhelming assemblage of images. Far exceeding the initial expectations for the reception of this "contingency film," *Berlin, Symphony of a Great City* presents not only an invaluable documentation of this dynamic city before it was reduced to a pile of rubble, but it also provides a meditation on the capability of film to offer a counter to mass entertainment and a glimpse of an emergent consumer society that became increasingly spectacular as the century progressed.

NOTES

1. Ruttmann's film was officially made as one of the *Kontingentfilme*, or quota films, for Fox Europe. These films were produced to satisfy the required quota of national films that had to be shot before foreign films could be imported and distributed for screening in Germany. Many such quota films were never released. Attesting to the ongoing fascination and significance that Ruttmann's film holds in German film history is Thomas Schadt's 2002 "remake" tribute entitled *Berlin—Sinfonie einer Großstadt.*

2. The exact date of this short text is not known. "Denn die Kinematographie gehoert unter das Kapitel der *bildenden Kuenste*, und ihre Gesetze sind am naechsten denen der Malerei und des Tanzes verwandt" (Ruttmann 1990a, 73). [Cinema belongs to the discipline of fine arts and its guiding principles are most closely related to those of painting and dance.]

3. "Eine Kunst fuer das Auge, die sich von der Malerei dadurch unterscheidet, dass sie sich zeitlich abspielt (wie Musik), und dass der Schwerpunkt des Kuenstlerischen nicht (wie im Bild) in der Reduktion eines (realen oder Formalen) Vorgangs auf einem Moment liegt, sondern gerade in der zeitlichen Entwicklung des Formalen. Da diese Kunst sich zeitlich abwickelt, ist eines ihrer wichtigsten Elemente der Zeit-Rhythmus des optischen Geschehens" (Ruttmann 1990b, 74). [{Film is} an art form for the eye, that distinguishes itself from painting in that it plays out in time (like music), and the emphasis of the artistic is not (like in a picture) in the reduction of (real or formal) to a singular occurrence in a single moment , but rather in a formal temporal (time-based) medium. Since this art temporally unwinds, one of its most important elements is the rhythmic time of the optical event.]

4. For useful analyses of Ruttmann's films in the 1930s see Fulks 1990; and Uricchio 1990.

5. For a close reading of Ruttmann's editing style and shot analysis in *Berlin, Symphony of a Great City* see Bernstein 1984. Bernstein employs Christian Metz's (1982) theory of the "bracket syntagma" to explain Ruttmann's complex editing technique.

6. For a detailed discussion of the role of Mayer see Goergen 1990, 25–26.

7. "Das Drehbuch habe ich zusammen mit Ruttmann geschrieben. . . . Ich meine das rein technische Schreiben. . . . Ich habe es nachher als Drehbuch akkurat ausgerichtet: die Geduld hatte er nicht. Aber die Ideen, auch die abstrakten Ideen, sind alle von ihm" (Freund, quoted in Goergen 1990, 27). [I wrote the screenplay with Ruttmann. . . . I mean the pure technical act of writing. . . . I helped turn it into a screenplay: he didn't have the patience. But all of the ideas, including the abstract ideas, came from him.]

8. The traditional form of a symphony has four acts; however, there are exceptions, such as Beethoven's Symphony No. 6, Op. 68 "Pastoral."

9. See, for example, Mennel 2008.

10. The actual term *nonfiction films*, or "nichtfiktionale Filme," did not exist during the late 1920s; at the time; however, I am taking my lead from contemporary film critics such as William Uricchio (1990, 58) and others, who refer to *Berlin, Symphony of a Great City* as nonfictional.

11. "Zum ersten Male ist es versucht worden, eine Großstadt zur Trägerin der Hauptrolle eines Films zu machen. Kein Schauspieler, der immer etwas Theater spielt, kein Kind, das zwar and sich filmischer als der Erwachsene ist, kein Tier Star des neuen Fox-Europa-Films: BERLIN. DIE SINFONIE DER GROßSTADT, nur *Berlin* traegt den Film" (Ruttmann in a *Berliner Zeitung* article from September 20, 1927 [repr. in Goergen 1990, 79]). [For the first time an attempt has been made to make a film in which the lead role will be played by a city. Not an actor who plays in the theater, not a child who grows up in a film, not an animal star from the new Fox-Europa Film shall be featured. Instead, in BERLIN. SYMPHONY OF A CITY, only *Berlin* is the star.]

12. See Hermand 1994, 58–59. For a detailed analysis of the complexities of Neue Sachlichkeit see Plumb 2006.

13. For an excellent discussion of how Ruttmann's use of montage and collage in *Berlin, Symphony of a Great City* relates to the theory of *Querschnitt* see Hake 1994.

14. For a detailed discussion connecting Ruttmann's film to the experience of train travel see Kaes 1998. Kaes convincingly argues that the film encodes the experience of migration—with all of its attendant thrills and anxieties—to the Weimar metropolis in the 1920s.

15. Ruttmann's lack of attention to obvious tourist attractions stands in marked contrast to his treatment of Stuttgart, Düsseldorf, and Hamburg during the 1930s. In these locations he focuses his camera extensively on historical markers and buildings advertising the cities as tourist sites. See *Kleiner Film einer grossen der Stadt Düsseldorf am Rhein* (1935), *Stuttgart, die Großstadt zwischen Wald und Reben* (1935), *Stadt Stuttgart, 100: Cannstatter Volksfest* (1935), and *Weltstrasse Seewelthafen Hamburg* (1938).

16. "Carl wollte einen Film ueber die Menschen von Berlin. Das war sein Wunsch. Der Streit zwischen ihm und Ruttmann entstand, weil Ruttmann einen technischen Film drehen wollte, mit Maschinen, Schreibmaschinen—also eine Montage. Carl war damit nicht einverstanden. Er wollte unbedingt einem Film ueber die Menschen drehen" (quoted in Goergen 1990, 26). [Carl wanted to make a film about the people of Berlin. That was his wish. The fight between him and Ruttmann came from the fact that Ruttmann wanted to make a film about technology with machines, typewriters,—a montage film. Carl was not in agreement with that idea. Above all he wanted to make a film about people.]

17. Beginning with Kracauer and other male critics, these women have been viewed as prostitutes; however, Anke Gleber (1999) productively argues against this (male) view and proposes instead that these women represent the female flaneur who is neither necessarily on her way to work nor shopping but is, quite simply, walking in the city.

18. For a detailed analysis of surface culture and the emergence of advertising in Weimar see Ward 2001.

19. As Hermand (1994, 67) notes regarding the outcome of new objectivity, "By yielding everything to market principles of supply and demand, *Neue Sachlichkeit* did reduce the cultural power of the older educated elites, but replaced it with an aesthetic supermarket governed by a culture of homogeneous mass production. . . . After the beginning of the

world economic crisis in 1929, the Nazis found their path laid out for them. With their propagandistic emphasis on culture, idealism, and national values, the Nazis spoke to all those whose thirst for meaning had gone unquenched by the sober, materialist, and contradictory cynicism of *Neue Sachlichkeit*."

REFERENCES

Brentano, Bernhard von. 1927. "*Berlin*." *Kino und Kultur*, September 25.

Benjamin, Walter. 1969. "The Work of Art in the Age of Mechanical Reproduction." 1936. In *Illuminations*. Ed. Hannah Arendt, 217–51. New York: Schocken.

——. 1999. "A Little History of Photography." 1931. In *Walter Benjamin: Selected Writings*. Vol. 2, *1927–1934*, ed. Michael W. Jennings, Howard Eiland, and Gary Smith, 507–30. Cambridge, MA: Harvard University Press.

Bernstein, Matthew. 1984. "Visual Style and Spatial Articulations in *Berlin, Symphony of a City* (1927). *Journal of Film and Video* 36 (fall): 5–12.

Fulks, Barry A. 1990. "Walter Ruttmann, der Avantgardefilm und die Nazi-Moderne." In Goergen 1990, 67–71.

Gleber, Anke. 1999. *The Art of Taking a Walk: Flanerie, Literature, and Film in Weimar Culture*. Princeton, NJ: Princeton University Press.

Goergen, Jeanpaul, ed. 1990. *Walter Ruttmann: Eine Dokumentation*. Berlin: Freunde der Deutschen Kinemathek.

Hake, Sabine. 1994. "Urban Spectacle in Walter Ruttmann's *Berlin: Symphony of the Big City*. In *Dancing on the Volcano: Essays on the Culture of the Weimar Republic*, ed. Thomas W. Kniesche and Stephen Brockmann, 127–37. Columbia, SC: Camden House.

Hermand, Jost. 1994. "Neue-Sachlichkeit: Ideology, Lifestyle, or Artistic Movement?" In *Dancing on the Volcano: Essays on the Culture of the Weimar Republic*, ed. Thomas W. Kniesche and Stephen Brockmann, 57–67. Columbia, SC: Camden House.

Horkheimer, Max, and Theodor W. Adorno. 1988. *Dialectic of Enlightenment*. 1944. New York: Continuum.

Kaes, Anton. 1998. "Leaving Home: Film, Migration, and the Urban Experience." *New German Critique* 74 (spring-summer): 179–92.

Kracauer, Siegfried. 1947. *From Caligari to Hitler: A Psychological History of the German Film*. Princeton, NJ: Princeton University Press.

——. 1995. "Film 1928." In *The Mass Ornament: Weimar Essays*. Trans. and ed. Thomas Y. Levin, 307–20. Cambridge, MA: Harvard University Press.

Mennel, Barbara. 2008. *Cities and Cinema*. London: Routledge.

Plumb, Steve. 2006. *Neue Sachlichkeit, 1918–1933: Unity and Diversity of an Art Movement*. Amsterdam: Rodopi.

Renger-Patzsch, Albert, and Donald B. Kuspit. 1993. *Albert Renger-Patzsch: Joy Before the Object*. New York: Aperture.

"Richter on Film." 1972. Interview by Cecile Starr. *Hans Richter: Early Avant-Garde Films, 1921–1929*. VHS. Arthouse, 1996.

Ruttmann, Walter. 1990a. "Kunst und Kino." 1913–17. In *Walter Ruttmann: Eine Dokumentation*, ed. Jeanpaul Goergen, 73. Berlin: Freunde der Deutschen Kinemathek.

——. 1990b. "Malerei mit Zeit." 1919/1920. In Goergen 1990, 73–74.

Uricchio, William. 1990. "Ruttmann nach 1933." In Goergen 1990, 59–65.

Ward, Janet. 2001. *Weimar Surfaces: Urban Visual Culture in 1920s Germany*. Berkeley: University of California Press.

ELEVEN

SURFACE SHEEN AND CHARGED BODIES

LOUISE BROOKS AS LULU IN *PANDORA'S BOX* (1929)

MARGARET MCCARTHY

From ingénues to femmes fatales, with legions of varyingly androgynous, emancipated "New Women" in between, the Weimar lexicon of femininity encompassed a cast of characters both classic and emergent. Underwritten by male artists and intellectuals, this panoply of female types combined the femme fatale's aggressive sexual proximity with the nonchalance of New Women generally perceived as unsentimental. A heady mix of women, presumably both promiscuous and aloof, bears traces of two historical epochs: Frank Wedekind's notorious Lulu, the subject of his two scandalous plays *Earth-Spirit* and *Pandora's Box*, provides a fin-de-siècle forerunner,[1] while the partly mythic Weimar New Woman, who was free to work, vote, and have sex with men or women, updated Wedekind's femme fatale. Unlike the demands of the femme fatale's rapacious sex drive, the sum total of Weimar women's new freedoms suggested the possibility of self-sustaining females and superfluous males. More important, the incongruity of women both too close and too remote hints at irrational male anxieties, as real and imagined femininity combined to create a double-edged threat to traditional gender roles.

Lulu's most famous filmic counterpart, played by the American actress Louise Brooks in G. W. Pabst's 1929 adaptation of Wedekind's plays,[2] visually embodies both dangers to men: extreme close-ups of her head (Fig. 11.1), gleaming eyes and teeth, which sometimes exceed the filmic frame, blend with shots of Lulu narcissistically immersed in magazines or her own mirror image. While critics have traced the way the film tames and ultimately topples a femme fatale, this chapter will examine what the beleaguered male psyche of the Weimar Republic may have taken from her along the way. If the flip side of angst is fascination, if not envy, Lulu's

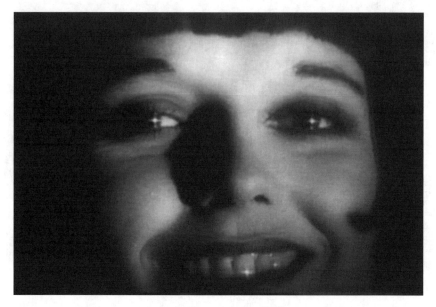

FIGURE 11.1 An extreme close-up of Lulu (Louise Brooks) from G.W. Pabst's *Pandora's Box* (1929).

imperviousness likely provided a powerful antidote to an impaired masculinity as much in thrall to her autonomy as to her sexuality. Likewise, women's presumed solipsism, embodied as well by Weimar women deemed insufficiently detached from cinematic images, could well have signaled a powerfully undivided selfhood to men painfully aware of the split between self and gendered cultural ideals. If one considers all sides of ambiguous gender relations, Lulu's anguished proclamation toward the end of *Pandora's Box*—"they want my blood, they want my life"—suggests not only male retribution but also the need to co-opt femininity for self-sustaining ends. In fact, the original screenplay has Lulu even proclaim the horror of everyone wanting to "suck" her blood and life dry.

Visually, many scenes support this dynamic with pandemonium and orbiting bodies that conjure the possibility of something giving way. Lulu's lavish spectacular excess, particularly in the famous backstage sequence where she embodies Weimar's shimmering surfaces, highlights at the same time Louise Brooks's expressive physicality and compelling persona. Her Lulu evokes an incandescent, sovereign selfhood, with gleaming eyes that appear to animate those orbiting bodies. In the process the film obliquely comments on the ambiguities of audience identification, gaze vs. spectacle, and the way the former closes in on and ultimately takes more than a simple charge from the latter. Energy transferred against a kinetic, chaotic backdrop ultimately gives way, however, to more corporeal means of neutralizing Lulu. Her spilled blood again signals not only just deserts but also the concrete means through which her powers are siphoned off and transplanted into a more acceptable vessel—a male *Lustmörder*, a murderer of passion, in the form of Jack the Ripper.

This process requires a form of identification that differs from Christian Metz's implicitly male spectator, who maintains a voyeuristic distance between object and eye so as not to be overwhelmed. Significantly, Metz argues that being too close would lead him, in fact, to "consume the object" (1982, 60), language that partially resembles a classically female form of identification. As Mary Ann Doane has argued, for women "there is a certain overpresence of the image—she *is* the image" (1982, 78). Metz's voyeurism is replaced with narcissism; the image threatens to overwhelm and consume the female viewer for being so close, recognizable, and present. Siegfried Kracauer understood this process in patronizing terms by describing little shopgirls clandestinely wiping their eyes before the lights come on after Weimar's cinematic melodramas (1995, 303). In turn, Patrice Petro remedied Kracauer's condescension by reading women's highly concentrated gaze as capable of registering the way that melodramatic representations "simultaneously responded to and compensated for women's experiences of everyday life" (Petro 1989, 76). If we return to the basics of identification, namely Freud's notion that fantasy entails multiple points of identification and places of enunciation, is it possible that Weimar men identified across gender not only masochistically but also in a highly intense, if not self-serving, manner that provided its own kinds of compensations?

What film spectators often respond to is the sense, as Lacan scholars Robert Lapsley and Michael Westlake argue, that stars embody their "true" selves: "The dream of an authentic self is, of course, one of the attractions of certain stars. They seem to possess the missing integrity; to retain their authenticity whatever the role. Self-collected, each seems the master of his or her identity, each seems his or her own person" (2006, 266). By not limiting this form of identification to an idealized image gendered as either male or female, Lapsley and Westlake provide a very useful means for understanding Louise Brooks's effect on Weimar men. As I will argue, much of the critical response to both her filmic presence and her overall star persona has underscored her fabled autonomy. As Richard Dyer has argued by way of Max Weber, stars possess a charisma that endows them with "supernatural, superhuman or at least superficially exceptional qualities" (Dyer 1991, 57). Again, this quality provides the logical antidote to Weimar masculinity, which has gone down in history as profoundly compromised and lacking in integrity.

Yet our notions of Weimar's gendered spectatorship often focus on male mastery and animus without acknowledging the psychic service an idealized figure like

Brooks might have provided in the encounter between subject and object. Much has been written, for instance, on the imaginary means that Weimar men employed to tame the New Woman, most notably in the gendered fantasies linked to "New Objectivity," a movement that emerged during Weimar's period of relative stability from 1924 to 1929. Numerous elements ambivalently linked to modernity—mass culture and America's influence on Germany, particularly in the latter's newly emergent "Girlkultur"—combined to conflate the "shock of modernity," as Richard McCormick has argued, with a crisis of "traditional male authority, agency, and identity" (McCormick 2001, 3). New Objectivity consequently called on male artists, intellectuals, and social engineers to remedy this crisis by soberly documenting an excessive modernity partly embodied by the New Woman. Where machines, including the cinematic apparatus, take part in this process, New Objectivity sometimes reveals a partisan project. Andreas Huyssen's (1986) classic essay on Fritz Lang's film *Metropolis*, for example, exposes the lurid manner in which the evil scientist Rotwang renders the film's female lead, Maria, robotic and pliable. By strapping her to a table, a welter of wires emanating from her head, he dramatically subdues femininity via a cold male rationalism. New Objectivity's neat typologies of women—as vamps and ingénues, New Women and struggling proletarian mothers—likewise discursively atomized femininity by pinning it down within manageable categories. Despite such clinical detachment, the overall legacy of the Weimar Republic remains the blurred boundaries of androgynous women and feminized men. Those crisscrossing wires on Maria's head thus provide a particularly apt metaphor, which I would like to link to McCormick's observation about masculinity and femininity as not "fixed, opposite poles of identification" but instead "different endpoints on a spectrum which constantly oscillates" (McCormick 2001, 33).

LOUISE BROOKS'S PERSONA AND PHYSICALITY AS A SOURCE OF LULU'S POWER

Crisscrossing wires and indeterminate gender relations also provide a useful starting point for understanding how Weimar film directors both implanted and extracted their actresses' most famous roles. Film histories of the Weimar Republic invariably compare the Pabst/Brooks pairing with Josef von Sternberg's presumed creation of Marlene Dietrich's film persona. As the swan song of the Weimar femme fatale, Dietrich's Lola Lola in von Sternberg's *The Blue Angel* provides a useful foil and end point to Maria's *Urgestalt*, with Brooks's Lulu as an enigmatic midpoint. Maria's frenetic dance in *Metropolis* winds down considerably in the laconic way that Lola Lola foists and plants her thighs. Dietrich's vaguely disdainful performance of von Sternberg's choreography mocks his adolescent camera angles and reportedly primitive directorial tactics. In the process she exposes the split between actress and role, as if by 1930 the steam has run out of the process, with Dietrich no longer willing to maintain the illusion of oneness with her filmic alter ego. Film lore places Marlene Dietrich in Pabst's office interviewing to play Lulu when Louise Brooks's telegram arrived accepting the role. Rejected by Pabst for being too sexual and obvious, Dietrich had to wait for Lola Lola to restore overt female sexuality to the femme fatale.

Brooks's Lulu, by contrast a childlike androgyne, suggests a presexual being's undivided self rather than Dietrich's alluring, mature sexuality, which was too self-aware to pass for natural. Fittingly, Lulu and Lola Lola relied on different anatomical anchors: gleaming eyes vs. thighs that open and close around the proverbial site of lack. Lulu's eyes as the focus of many overdetermined head shots mobilize sexual energy differently than would a more overtly female body part, resembling instead a surface emanation. "Trieb," or sex drive, finds a modern analog—an electrical charge—itself a transferable medium available to men and women alike. Sustained by Louise Brooks's androgynous allure and fabled autonomy, Lulu became a highly resonant representation of the New Woman's commanding power. Equally important, women's reproductive powers as charged emanations suggest a force capable of sustaining its surroundings. Accordingly, Brooks's work with Pabst reveals in many ways that he took as much from her as the other way round.

Brooks has written that Pabst felt as if he created her, that she was "his Lulu" (Brooks 1974, 102). Lotte Eisner, has argued, however, that Brooks needed no direction, that she prompted Pabst to be better than he was (1973, 296). In fact, Pabst manipulated his actors in ways that prompted a lifelike emotional response rather than corralling them into existing acting conventions. As Brooks put it, Pabst would "saturate me with one clear emotion and turn me loose" (Brooks 1974, 105), which resulted in Brooks's "unmannered plasticity" (Paris 1990, 280), itself as much a product of her years of dance training—in the Kansas dance studios of her youth, with the pioneer modern dance company Denishawn, and on Broadway—than whatever directions Pabst implanted in her.[3] Pabst's ability to provoke Brooks into merely being herself works well with mythologies of both Lulu and Louise Brooks that posit each of them as a free-floating, autonomous phenomenon. In both cases the mythologies cover over the uncertainties of blurry gender relations and of the cinematic apparatus itself.

If film is the "Motor der Moderne," or motor of modernism (Kaes 1993, 100), film history links Weimar women either with cinematic images or with a female audience who presumably mistook such images for their own mirror. Lulu appears to embody this phenomenon again in the scenes where she ponders her mirror reflection or becomes absorbed in fashion magazines. Yet the line between male directors' machinations and manipulated females may, in fact, be superfluous if the spectator's misrecognition of self onscreen sustains the illusion of an autonomous selfhood. For in Lulu's moments with mirrors and magazines she enacts an insular dynamic in which she appears to recharge herself from her visual doubles. In this manner the "box"—here a film projector rather than the female genitalia which the film title otherwise evokes—fuels a different kind of female reproductive power, one that feeds off of its doubles to sustain itself. Again, this process resembles what Patrice Petro has argued about Weimar women at the movies: their intense absorption in melodramatic films worked to mobilize female desires and unconscious fantasies, providing an outlet for a repressed female voice. If this notion of female-to-female empowerment shuts the door on the kind of male identification I sketched out earlier, it may also stoke envy over women's cinematic pleasures and empowerment, especially if one considers the legions of damaged men onscreen with which male moviegoers had to contend.

At the same time, however, the Weimar response to Louise Brooks appeared to inspire more public animus than covert empowerment. As American flapper and Hollywood starlet, conscripted Weimar New Woman, athletic androgyne, and femme fatale, Brooks straddled a troubled cultural divide between Weimar modernity and a form of Americanization often perceived in feminine terms.[4] Not surprisingly, German film critics generally panned her performance, and Pabst himself famously proclaimed that she would end up like her filmic counterpart. The problem with critics conflating Brooks and Lulu, as Sabine Hake has observed, is that they fail to "recognize her contribution to ... [the] negotiation of sexual and cultural differences" (1994, 59) in the Weimar Republic. It took the fawning enamorings of three film historians removed from the Weimar Republic in time and space—Lotte Eisner, Henri Langlois of the Cinémathèque Française, and James Card of the Eastman House—to recognize Brooks's talents and the fascination she inspired as Lulu.[5]

Brooks has gone down in film history as an uncontrolled, uncompromising force of nature who was never fully pressed into the service of commodification, ornamentation, and mass culture. Unwilling to sell out professionally or personally, Brooks cut short her film career, which was effectively over by the time she had reached her early twenties, and entered many lost years of penury and alcoholism. Ultimately, though, she literally wrote herself out of Lulu's demise with highly intelligent, celebrated autobiographical essays, and an afterlife sustained by the support of ardent admirers followed from the 1950s until her death in 1985. Much as dance training underlies Brooks's impressive naturalness onscreen, many years spent practicing the craft of writing account for the seemingly authentic voice that emerges in her autobiographical essays. And just as Pabst manipulated Brooks into "being herself," ardent admiration from Eisner, Langlois, and Card may have helped Brooks to see herself as more than a cross-cultural starlet. Many head shots that both populate *Pandora's Box* and promoted her Hollywood career suggest the extent to which Brooks represented an overdetermined femininity yet exuded enough intelligence and disdain to exceed it.

Some of the most famous photographs of Brooks from the 1920s highlight her famous bob, the haircut of flappers and New Women alike. On the one hand, this "shiny helmet of black hair," as it was often called, makes her head look like a decorative hood ornament, particularly in photos that flatten out her image entirely. In one famous black-and-white shot, Brooks wears a long strand of pearls, her face outlined by undifferentiated black so that it appears to float in space like an ornamental perch. The cover of the expanded edition of *Lulu in Hollywood*, Brooks's collection of autobiographical essays, invokes her famous hair and one eye with what looks like black and white construction paper. The image on the cover of Barry Paris's biography of Brooks, however, adds another dimension that links Brooks's eyes to her lustrous cap of hair. On the one hand, her head looks ornamental as it floats on an upper torso captured in soft focus. But at the same time, piercing eyes staring directly into the camera turn the ornament into an expressive medium that emotes what McCormick calls in *Pandora's Box* a "clever but anxious agency" (2001, 133). The film draws on such contradictory tensions each time it captures Brooks's head in close-up.

PANDORA'S BOX AND LULU'S HEAD

In many such shots her head exceeds the filmic frame, as if Lulu's countenance could only be partially contained. In one particularly eerie shot, Lulu swings on the arm of the acrobat Rodrigo Quast, her smiling face resting on his beefy muscles (Fig. 11.2).[6] Coiled male aggression and Lulu's laughing insouciance structure the scenes that follow, and only much later, in the courtroom scene, where Lulu is charged with murdering her fiancé, the newspaper magnate Dr. Schön, does she begin to understand her vulnerability. When the prosecutor presses for capital punishment, Lulu theatrically clutches her neck. Historically, New Objectivity artists like Otto Dix and George Grosz were strangely fond of depicting decapitated victims of *Lustmörder*, as if the femme fatale's animalistic sex drive could be thus severed.[7] Yet in Pabst's filmic adaptation, this free-floating female visage seems as much an occasion for celebration as a call to castration. His staging of the famous backstage scene renders Brooks's head as an independent planetary body around which all action orbits (Fig. 11.3). It shows Lulu at the height of her powers as spectacle that trumps the gazes that would manipulate her. At the same time, the spectator also glimpses the tensions that will ultimately vanquish her. Lulu's initial incandescent presence suggests a cinematic image both impervious to the audience and undepleted by its demands. Yet by the end of the scene, Lulu must deliver a highly theatrical performance to retain her edge, which presages her loss of power when Jack the Ripper spills her blood.

FIGURE 11.2 Lulu swings on the arm of the acrobat Rodrigo Quast (Krafft Raschig).

Awed by Brooks's "uncommon intelligence" and "dazzling" beauty, Lotte Eisner provides useful metaphors for understanding Brooks's/Lulu's effervescent power in the backstage scene. Eisner describes her as a "pagan idol, tempting, glittery with spangles, feathers, and frills, against a wavering out-of-focus background" (1973, 296, 298). If her comparison invokes Weimar's glittering surfaces, Eisner also describes Lulu's face in the final scenes of the film as a "lunar landscape" (ibid., 299), which suggests something other than Weimar surface culture. More than a distant point on a movie screen, planetary bodies exert their own pull on orbiting bodies. Similarly, Lulu's appeal in the initial moments of the backstage scene rests as much on the autonomy as the allure of spectral bodies. At first glance, Lulu's specular excess in this scene is undeniable, most evident in her outrageous headgear. The first time she exits the stage, Lulu sports a golden cap with an enormous, fringed brim, making her whole head look like the planet Saturn. Later she switches to a cap of illuminated peacock feathers, which vaguely recalls Maria's welter of wires. Mary Ann Doane has described Lulu at this moment as "pure image" (1990, 67), while Thomas Elsaesser has deemed Lulu in general a "forever image" (2000, 281) throughout the film. Yet severed wires help us to understand the fantasy of autonomy the film also plays out in this scene. Janet Ward's work on Weimar surface culture underscores the magnetism of electric, glowing facades sometimes intended to pull spectators through space, like harshly lit posters of the New Woman that beckoned passers-by into movie theaters. The belief that *Licht lockt Leute* ("light

FIGURE 11.3 Lulu, with her outrageous headgear, here shown with the stage manager (Siegfried Arno).

lures people") was also part and parcel of the *Licht-Architektur* of monumental movie theaters and stage sets. Lulu's glowing peacock feathers reference such illuminated monumentalism, invoking as well the beams of light emanating from the projector, as if Lulu were the very motor of her own selfhood.

This fantasy is sustained by a hapless stage manager bandied about by his backstage charges in a way that belies Pabst's careful choreography. Unlike *Metropolis*'s Rotwang, who channels and manipulates electricity and at one point famously chases Maria with the beam of a flashlight, Lulu remains in charge here, causing pandemonium and managing the terms of her own specularity. If the stage manager unwittingly makes a silly spectacle of himself, Lulu's commanding presence creates a stage wherever she stands, and by deftly stepping in and out of costume before us, she exposes her pleasure and control in the whole process. At the same time the backstage setting offsets the precariousness of her situation, since what follows takes on the characteristics of an elemental struggle. Chaotic bodies bumping up against each other, as the incarnation of Weimar's confusing gender roles, give way to a very naked brinkmanship and a return to traditional, if not reactionary, positionings.

Against a backdrop of men running around in open, flowing robes, one sits in his underwear, as Schön's fiancée, and Lulu's rival, enters the scene to survey the spectacle. Earlier Lulu gazed at the fiancée's photograph in Schön's apartment and asked his son, Alwa, "Is she really so beautiful?" Casting women as both spec-

tacle and its consumer, with Lulu's backstage male cohort as bit players, belies
how power is subsequently leveraged in the scene. Lulu's acolytes soon turn into
Schön's minions when she refuses to perform in front of his fiancée, and they close
in on her in a way that briefly eclipses her power as impervious spectacle. Yet to
save her neck, Lulu does, in fact, perform, but melodramatically and for an audience of one. When she and Schön square off against each other in a sequestered
dressing room, she stages a temper tantrum while lying prostrate on a couch, carefully peeking over her shoulder to witness Schön's reaction. The camera isolates
her pumping legs and his attempts to subdue her. Ultimately, of course, he gives in,
proclaiming when Alwa and the fiancée suddenly appear to witness their embrace,
"This will be my execution." As much as one assumes the victory of New Women
over impotent Weimar men here, both Lulu and Schön have, in fact, maneuvered
each other into more traditional camps: Lulu's melodramatic excess represents an
emotional, rather than impervious, femininity, while Schön's tortured psyche and
abusive physicality regresses from New Objectivity detachment to expressionism's
more aggressive masculinity.

Yet the defining frame for *Pandora's Box* has been the former movement, since
film scholars have most often labeled Pabst the premiere director of New Subjectivity given his lifelike mise-en-scène and investment in surface effects.[8] Pabst's
purported manipulation of his actors also fits well with New Objectivity's fantasies
of male control. But when confronted with the physicality and psychology of individual actors, Pabst's vaunted control may have met up with more than it bargained
for. Two oft-recounted anecdotes are pertinent in this regard. Brooks has written
that the actor Fritz Kortner, who played Schön, so disliked her that his rough grasp-
ing in the backstage scene left actual bruises on her arms. Equally significant, when
Pabst asked Brooks to perform an impromptu dance in the film's opening scenes,
she gave him a Denishawn-inspired number that prompted him to exclaim, "But
you are a professional dancer!" (Brooks 1974, 102). Time and again, the film pits
Schön's wooden body language, supplemented here and there with a theatrical
gesture to articulate repressed emotion, against Lulu's natural physicality. Schön's
monocle, in fact, seems a weak alibi for the professed detachment of New Objectivity and barely masks a brimming aggression, rendered in high expressionist,
Max Reinhardt–inspired stage acting. Interestingly, though, both an expressionist
movement vocabulary of contorted gestures and modern dance as an integral part
of Weimar's cult of the body strove to express innermost feelings.[9] Their presence
in the film prompts us to look beyond New Objectivity's cult of surfaces in order to
understand the film's inner dynamics.

For if dance transports the expressiveness of Lulu's face to her entire body,
the power of what seems mere surface ornament increases exponentially. Two
photographs from *The Weimar Sourcebook* illustrate this dynamic, revealing how

the cults of the surface and the body invoke that "too close, too remote" problem with which I began (Figs. 11.4 and 11.5). One photo shows a woman in close-up who puts on lipstick. Her mirror reflection serves as focal point, with her actual face a small, blurry presence off to the side. Her eyes look down toward an open mouth, where fingers wrapped around a tube of lipstick appear both within and in front of the mirror. The fingertips of her other hand graze the mirror, where their numbers are doubled as well. Femininity as surface turns vaguely monstrous in the woman's gaping mouth and bared teeth, plus all those spidery fingers that reproduce them-selves, as pleasurable self-absorption appears to effect what Janet Ward has called "surface-cloning" (2001, 158).[10] To the left a group of women in short skirts and halter tops leap through space in an outdoor setting. With legs splayed in midair, the woman in the middle tilts her head upward, a remote expression of pleasure on her face above flying arms and legs. Splayed legs, of course, carry their own anxious connotations, particularly when lined up next to spidery fingers. The net effect of curled fingers and flying limbs vaguely recalls Medusa's tresses, those snakes that become the grounds for decapitation. If Lulu embodies both specular power and unbound physicality, understanding the mechanics of her own demise requires as much attention to the film's choreography as to its absorption in surfaces. Ulti-mately Lulu's alluring visage must be uncoupled from Brooks's corporeal presence for their joint dynamism to fade.

In the film's opening scenes Lulu handily manages the comings and goings of men in her apartment—the gentlemanly meter man; the boozy Schigolch, as Lulu's ambiguous friend and father-figure; her present lover, Dr. Schön; and the brawny, lowlife acrobat, Rodrigo Quast. Oddly, the way men alight and descend the stairs recalls the tenuous class status, fluctuating identities, and dependencies of women in melodramatic *Treppenfilme*. Altered gender dynamics also become apparent when the meter man's tip falls to the floor, mixed up with money that he himself had extended to the seedy Schigolch. Money moves in the wrong direction here to sustain the illusion of a busy bordello, remaining completely superfluous to Lulu's existence until much later in the film. While clearly a kept woman, Lulu retains her edge by micromanaging her men, providing booze and succor but ultimately leav-ing them all wanting and unfulfilled while she herself remains undepleted by their demands. Camera shots emphasize Lulu's corralling them into the mostly separate and sometimes enclosed spaces of her apartment. Though the apartment's spare, modernist look creates a New Objectivity interior, its various spaces provide a convenient holding pen for barely repressed masculine emotions to which Lulu remains essentially indifferent.

In a nod to Wedekind's play and the stage setting it dictated, the image of a Pierrot hangs on the wall, which both signals New Objectivity's neat typologies of femininity and provides a tasteful prop for Pabst's cool, modernist interior. It

FIGURE 11.4 *Eckstein with Lipstick* (1930). © Ellen Auerbach. Courtesy of The J. Paul Getty Museum, Los Angeles.

also becomes the backdrop to that improvised dance that Pabst obliged Brooks to perform, staged in the film at Schigolch's bidding. While her spontaneous dance suggests an untroubled, carefree relationship between woman and image, the icon itself serves as launchpad to a dynamic dance in a mutually sustaining relationship. Equally important is its effect on Schigolch, who soon drops his harmonica, sputters, and almost throws it at her in anger, as Lulu's insouciance provokes male animus. Significantly, however, Schigolch then proclaims that Lulu should be displayed to the public and signals to Quast, who is waiting on the sidewalk below. Against a modernist backdrop, a burly acrobat from the mass culture sphere of variety shows seems a portentous presence. Quast subsequently inaugurates Lulu's downward trajectory, which commences when she blithely, but ominously, swings from his arm.

In parallel staging Lulu's encounter with Schön also highlights her expressive physicality, which animates the icon, overwhelms Lulu's audience, and ultimately calls for extreme measures. When she and Schön embrace, the scene's staging positions him between the Pierrot and Lulu, or between the fantasy and its concrete offspring. Lulu then lies down before him, a decorative ornament framed by an orchid-shaped lamp to the left and the pillows behind her. When Schön announces his impending marriage, Lulu ratchets up her power by miming an odalisque, stretching her neck seductively and proclaiming he'll have to kill her to be rid of her. Her body language mocks his impotence with the locus of the blood that Jack the Ripper will later spill. If Schön remains incapable of an act that would siphon Lulu's vitality, the camera continually emphasizes the broad expanse of his back, which visually severs Lulu's head and anticipates her final embrace with Jack the Ripper. When Schön later assists her downward trajectory by suggesting that Alwa put Lulu in his variety show, the staging signals their complicity by merging their backs to block a costume sketch that Lulu had fawned over.[11] Taming Lulu requires, on the one hand, the unruly gaze associated with mass culture's chaotic spheres. On the other, it means reducing her image—embodied by the Pierrot as classic icon of femininity and also the more nakedly referential mirror reflections that follow—into the barely referential shadows of Jack the Ripper's foggy mise-en-scène. A return to unmistakably expressionist light and shadow also means more globally that the medium for conducting Lulu's charged incandescence is gone.

FIGURE 11.5 The Hertha Feist dancers, 1923. Courtesy of the Laban Library and Archive, London.

Chaotic masses reach a frenzied pitch in the wedding party that follows the backstage scene. Staged figuratively, and at times literally, like a feeding frenzy, it features a motley crew of servants who serve as audience and combine the raucous pleasures of watching an unfolding spectacle with their own uninhibited gluttony. In this manner, looking presages a bond much more sinister and intense than that of the couples they observe on the dance floor. The range of desires embodied by Alwa, the lesbian Countess Geschwitz, Quast, and Schigolch supplement Schön's tortured agonies. As in the previous scene, the action moves from a confused, open arena—here the party and dance floor—to an enclosed space where something explosive ensues. When a boozed-up Quast and Schigolch enter the bedroom, Quast lingers at the mirror, while Schigolch spills roses on the bridal bed.[12] Their positions set up visual markers for the kinds of autoerotic pleasures that Lulu will subsequently enjoy at the mirror and what remains an empty space of desire at the bed. A sculptural figure of supplication hangs on the wall to magnify Schön's subjective plight and to counter the mirror as badge of Weimar surface culture. When Schön chases Schigolch and Quast from the bedroom with a gun, Lulu gravitates toward the mirror to preen unselfconsciously, her detachment shored up the moment that image and referent find each other. Ominously, Schön appears in the mirror behind her, as if he had intuited the base of her power. (Likewise, in a later scene when Alwa confronts Lulu, he enters her space cinematically via a fade-in, as if speaking her language of image production.) Having removed her acolytes and attacked her specular domain, Schön uses chiaroscuro effects to compete with the film's gleaming surfaces. Long shadows climb the wall behind Lulu, graphically rendering Schön's subjective projections. When he hands her the gun to kill herself, they freeze in a tableau that effectively neutralizes the dynamism of earlier scenes. Lulu is now dwarfed by the supplicating figure, as male subjectivity begins its ascendance. When the gun fires, Alwa cradles his mortally wounded father in pieta tableau, offering the succor previously associated with Lulu.

Lulu's downward spiral continues in the courtroom scene that follows, in which she is both poised and quiescent but also melodramatically theatrical when audience demands assert themselves. Critics invariably point out the defense lawyer's self-conscious nod to cinema when his first line speaks of rendering Lulu's story in a "rapid series of pictures." In what seems an equally self-conscious visual pan, the camera passes before Alwa, Quast, Schigolch, and Geschwitz, sitting together on a bench, who together emote a multilayered response to Lulu's plight. Alwa looks dejected and vaguely embarrassed, Quast and Schigolch smile and laugh, and Geschwitz looks forward earnestly. Audience response runs the gamut here from degenerate to heartfelt desires and culminates when someone pulls the fire alarm to save Lulu, and the entire crowd first swells, then closes in around her. The camera then lingers on the aftermath—shots of overturned chairs, a man transporting a fainted woman, another figure running by hysterically as a man leans against the wall and watches. As I argued earlier, Lulu plays to her audience here in ways that depart from her initial commanding persona: she both flirts with the prosecutor and clutches her neck melodramatically when he demands the death penalty. Ultimately, of course, Lulu elicits an audience response that wants more from her than mere gesture alone. If self-conscious staginess in this scene supplants the power of cinema that Lulu embodies, *Pandora's Box* grants her one last reprieve and moment of specular sovereignty when she returns to Schön's apartment. Here she lingers and preens before the mirror, then peruses some fashion magazines. In fact, several mirrors hang on the walls, which prop up her insular selfhood. Back in her element, Lulu indulges in more surface cloning and then smiles, skips, and dances through the apartment in a return to her previous natural expressiveness.

The agent who engineers Lulu's rapid downfall in the film's final scenes understands the need to separate clone from source if her overall power is to be neutralized. Casti Piani first glimpses Lulu hidden on a train berth, her identity betrayed by a picture in the newspaper. He subsequently blackmails Alwa, maneuvering Lulu and her cohorts into a "discreet" locale, a gambling boat in Egypt, where she will be hidden from view and also captive to Casti Piani's own exploitation. His designation is telling, for the nature of cinema as touchstone for Lulu's power is anything but discreet. The rapid series of pictures slows down with the photographs of Lulu that Casti Piani circulates among his patrons. For the first time Lulu truly is reduced to image. Previously, we saw her gleefully perusing Countess Geschwitz's generic costume sketches or stoically facing the courtroom artists and photographers who captured her image. By hiding the real Lulu and circulating her image, Casti Piani reduces each part to a discrete, exploitable entity, thereby foiling a duo which otherwise worked in autoerotic tandem. Lulu as image paradoxically facilitates the real-life Lulu's commodification as prostitute, as circulated images facilitate the more concrete exchange of sex meant to follow. Significantly, Brooks becomes surprisingly generic in the scenes on the gambling boat, her famous bob altered slightly with her trademark bangs swept to the side. Louise Brooks the actress seems a much less powerful presence when her filmic alter ego becomes an object of exchange. Money finally does matter, becoming the central focus throughout the entire scene. Lulu no longer occupies center stage as she silently witnesses Alwa's downward spiral at the gambling table, then plays Quast and Geschwitz off of each other to generate cash and save herself. Pitting two members of her omnipresent audience against themselves, Lulu briefly deflects the feeding frenzy of earlier scenes. Yet Quast's demise, captured eerily in a shot of a dead eye, anticipates her own fate. If Lulu's cinematic sheen turns lackluster in these scenes, Jack the Ripper will soon claim her vitality in the most egregious manner possible.

The darkened, foggy streets of London where he first appears signal the film's most powerful return to an expressionist aesthetic, buttressed by yet another tortured male in thrall to his drives. In many ways more sympathetic than Schön, Jack exemplifies impotent Weimar males. Lacking Schön's bulky presence and class status, he's shown as a lonely figure wandering the streets of London, swayed by the beneficent, beseeching stare of a woman seeking alms for the Salvation Army. Later he shares the mistletoe she gives him with Lulu in a moment of undisguised sentimentality—a stark foil to the presumed lack of sentimentality characteristic of the New Woman. Jack also suffers from his own visual impairment, which suggests affinities with Weimar male impotence in general: a wanted poster describes his "shifty, unsteady" eyes, which he keeps mostly hidden under a heavy brimmed hat. While providing anonymity, Jack's hat also gives him a much needed shield in his initial confrontation with Lulu. Staged as a confrontation between glittering surfaces, it recalls the way *Metropolis*'s Rotwang drained Maria of her sexuality in a series of light flashes. As Lulu stands above Jack on a stairwell, a series of extreme close-ups captures one final and unmistakable beam of light from her eyes, which literally disarms Jack, who drops the shiny knife behind his back. Fittingly, the screenplay describes Jack's eyes here as "gierige Löcher" (greedy holes), which intensifies an earlier description of them flickering restlessly, with no firm point of focus ("Seine Augen flackern unstet, haben keinen festen Blickpunkt").[13] Their confrontation also occurs against long shadows, creating an overall mise-en-scène in which self and other overlap dramatically. Soon after, Jack follows Lulu up to her impoverished digs, then gives in to his murderous drive when he spots a knife on a table. We never see an actual stabbing, though, just the expanse of his back, Lulu's head on his shoulder, and a demise signaled by the expressionist gesture of her hand falling, as Lulu's incandescent energy is finally sapped.

On the one hand, her "demonism"—whether the sex drive of Wedekind's Lulu or the commanding autonomy of New Women—finds a more socially acceptable vessel when deposited in a man who is again the contemptible but sympathetic, victim of his own drives. Equally important, a transferred charge translates into a kind of rejuvenated physicality, one that benefits the remaining men in Lulu's orbit. Jack leaves Lulu's apartment emoting a resolve missing in his initial aimless wanderings, and the look that passes between him and Alwa at the bottom of the steps seems to prompt a similar response. Previously the camera lingered on a catatonic Alwa, swathed in a blanket as he takes swigs from a bottle of alcohol. *Pandora's Box* ends with his following the passing Salvation Army procession in staging that vaguely recalls the legions of rejuvenated workers who march toward Maria's domain, the cathedral, at the end of *Metropolis*. But as much as Lulu's sapped energies appear to benefit both men, their triumph is at best pyrrhic if one associates the Salvation Army with simply a different female gaze, the beseeching but properly demure stare of the woman who initially approached Jack the Ripper. In other words, *Pandora's Box* culminates with a man still trailing a woman, having reaped a restored physicality from one and hoping for a morally improved universe from the other. In both instances women are the source of what men need to sustain themselves.

Sabine Hake has written that the Weimar Republic is best characterized by the productive tensions that fueled the cinematic medium in myriad form (Hake 2002, 53–54). New Objectivity detachment, which created as much as it observed the New Woman, combined with tormented expressionist thuggery when the creation bit the creator in the ass, provides a dramatic case in point. But the notion that men's animus coexisted with enthrallment helps us to understand "tension" not only in terms of antagonism but also as a cover for mutually dependent relations. Newly ambiguous gender roles opened up space not only for colliding traditions and expectations but also for pleasurable psychic identification—sometimes secret, sometimes overt—with the opposite sex. A reading of *Pandora's Box* that emphasizes what men might have taken from Lulu in the act of subduing her gives new shades of meaning to the concept of feminized men, making it more about repaired selfhood than castration. By emphasizing what was taken from Lulu it also becomes possible to recognize her progeny in the widest sense. And here I speak not only of obvious cinematic reincarnations sporting Brooks's bob, like Melanie Griffith's femme fatale in *Something Wild* or Natalie Portman's prepubescent trained killer in *The Professional*, to name only two examples among many. Rather, Louise Brooks's Lulu perhaps best embodies the democratizing tendencies of Weimar's polymorphous perversity, which Richard McCormick has lauded and linked to today's "emancipatory queerness" (McCormick 2001, 14). Lulu's empowering androgyny, combined with the salutary effects that accrue to feminized men, gives us a crucial contestation of fixed categories that should be Weimar's most beneficial legacy to its onlookers in the early years of our new millennium.

NOTES

1. *Erdgeist (Earth-Spirit)* was written in 1895 and premiered three years later in Leipzig with Wedekind in the lead male role. As Barry Paris observes, Wedekind's play was seen as an attack on German society, and consequently Wedekind landed in jail but became a cause célèbre when he was released in 1900. He wrote his second play about Lulu, *Die Büchse der Pandora (Pandora's Box)* in 1904, and this time Wedekind was denounced as a pornographer. It was not performed in Germany until 1918, the same year that Wedekind died (Paris 1990, 270).

2. Filmed in 1928, *Pandora's Box* premiered on January 30, 1929, in Berlin and on December 1, 1929, in New York. It was preceded by three lesser-known adaptations: *Lulu* (1917),

directed by Alesander von Antalffy; a Hungarian version, also called *Lulu* (1918), by the man who later directed *Casablanca*, Mihaly Kertesz/Michael Curtiz; and *Die Büchse der Pandora* (1919), directed by Arzen von Cserepy and starring Asta Nielson.

3. Brooks famously claimed once in an interview that she had learned to act by watching her fellow Denishawn dancer, Martha Graham, and learned to move by watching Charlie Chaplin (Paris 1990, 107).

4. Paris captures the relevant details of casting Louise Brooks as Lulu: an exhaustive search over months, the near casting of Marlene Dietrich among more than six hundred actresses who tested for the part, and the German press's astonishment that Pabst cast an American actress. Over the course of four weeks Brooks's face appeared on countless publications in Germany, Austria, and even Zagreb. Reaction ran the gamut, from ambivalence to pride that an American star would make a German movie (Paris 1990, 264–65).

5. In 1953 James Card, film curator at the George Eastman House of International Photography in Rochester, went to Paris and requested to see *Pandora's Box* and Brooks's other film with Pabst, *Diary of a Lost Girl*, at the Cinémathèque Française. Both he and the director of the archive, Henri Langlois, were so enthused that they immediately began work to restore the films. In 1955 Langlois curated an exhibit of cinematic artifacts and photos from sixty years of film. Two huge posters were hung on the Musée national d'art moderne—Falconetti from the silent film *Jeanne d'Arc* (1927) and Brooks from *Pandora's Box*. Card subsequently contacted Brooks, living in obscurity in New York, and the two traveled through Europe together in the wake of her resurrected films. Their relationship was both sexual and collaborative, since he encouraged Brooks in the writing of autobiographical essays (Paris 1990, 420–42). Lotte Eisner's discovery of Brooks, however, predated Card's and Langlois'; her glowing praise of Brooks's German film work appeared in *The Haunted Screen*, first published in 1952.

6. Later she swings on a curtain rod in anticipation of joining Quast in an acrobatic act. As much as Brooks's physicality suggests buoyancy and childish delight, her swinging legs also uncannily evoke the gallows.

7. Tatar (1995) documents vast numbers of canvases from the Weimar Republic with the title *Lustmord* and reflects on why male artists should have so strongly identified with sexual killers.

8. Kaes, for instance, links Pabst's style to Roland Barthes' "realism effect" (1993, 60), although Hake argues that his investment in surface effects was supplemented by the psychologically rendered struggles of his protagonists (2002 36). For Doane *Pandora's Box* is "tinged with expressionism in sets and lighting" in a way that complements Pabst's penchant for *Lichtspiel* and obsession with surfaces and atmosphere (1990, 65).

9. Modern dance in the Weimar Republic celebrated pure physicality and creative self-expression in the face of the assembly line of industrial modernity. Rudolf Laban created the "new dance" as an extension of the *Lebensreform* that dated to the turn of the century and fueled Weimar's cult of the body. Laban's student Mary Wigman was one of modern

dance's strongest proponents, as were Valeska Gert and Leni Riefenstahl. Gert wrote that the modern dancer lets go of old theatrical conventions to give "visible expression to his innermost feelings" (1994/1931). Earlier in the United States, Ruth St. Denis and Ted Shawn had pioneered American modern dance with a young Louise Brooks among the ranks of their Denishawn dancers. Brooks's statement, "We dancers reveal your inner selves" (quoted in Paris 1990, 36), points up common ground with modern dance in Germany.

10. Ward uses this term to describe the femme fatale Else from the film *Asphalt*, who is often shown in the film "ruthlessly and destructively reflecting her own 'surfaceness' to herself in a mirror" (2001, 158). Lulu's moments before the mirror, by contrast, seem more pleasurable and salutary.

11. For further analysis of the many male backs in *Pandora's Box* see Coates (1991, 56–57). Coates underscores the desire these backs invoke in the male spectator to insert himself into the frame, but he also considers the way in which they compel more generally the viewer's imagination.

12. Interestingly, Quast and Lulu often seem like kindred spirits. Not only does he anticipate her later positioning at the mirror in this scene, but his demise comes shortly before hers, as if their fates were linked. Historically, dancers and acrobats were both part of Weimar's cult of the body, even if the latter performed a less socially and artistically exalted form. Quast's positioning, one rung down the social ladder from Lulu, not only anticipates Lulu's trajectory, but it also underscores more generally how closely aligned Weimar men and women sometimes were for inhabiting overlapping social spaces.

13. Interestingly, the screenplay also often uses the word *strahlend* (radiant) to describe Lulu's face and eyes and once even the word *elektrisiert* (electrified) to describe her response to Geschwitz's sketches.

REFERENCES

Brooks, Louise. 1974. *Lulu in Hollywood*. Minneapolis: University of Minnesota Press.

Coates, Paul. 1991. *The Gorgon's Gaze: German Cinema, Expressionism, and the Image of Horror*. Cambridge, UK: Cambridge University Press.

Doane, Mary Ann. 1982. "Film and the Masquerade: Theorizing the Female Spectator." *Screen* 23, nos. 3–4 (September-October): 78–87.

——. 1990. "The Erotic Barter: *Pandora's Box* (1929)." In *The Films of G. W. Pabst. An Extra-territorial Cinema*, ed. Eric Rentschler, 62–79. New Brunswick, NJ: Rutgers University Press.

Dyer, Richard. 1991. "Charisma." In *Stardom: Industry of Desire*, ed. Christine Gledhill, 57–59. London: Routledge.

Eisner, Lotte H. 1973. *The Haunted Screen: Expressionism in the German Cinema and the Influence of Max Reinhardt*. Trans. Roger Greaves. Berkeley: University of California Press.

Elsaesser, Thomas. 2000. *Weimar Cinema and After: Germany's Historical Imaginary*. London: Routledge.

Gert, Valeska. 1994/1931. "Dancing." In Kaes, Jay, and Dimendberg 1994, 690. Orig. pub. as "Tanzen." *Schrifttanz* 4, no. 1 (June 1931): 5–7.

Hake, Sabine. 1994. "The Continuous Provocation of Louise Brooks." *German Politics and Society* 32 (summer): 58–75.

_____. 2002. *German National Cinema*. New York: Routledge.

Huyssen, Andreas. 1986. "The Vamp and the Machine: Fritz Lang's *Metropolis*." In *After the Great Divide: Modernism, Mass Culture, Postmodernism*, 65–81. Bloomington: Indiana University Press.

Kaes, Anton. 1993. "Film in der Weimarer Republik: Motor der Moderne." In *Geschichte des deutschen Films*, ed. Wolfgang Jacobsen, Anton Kaes, and Hans Helmut Prinzler, 39–100. Stuttgart: Verlag J. B. Metzler.

Kaes, Anton, Martin Jay, and Edward Dimendberg, eds. 1994. *The Weimar Republic Sourcebook*. Berkeley: University of California Press.

Kracauer, Siegfried. 1995. "The Little Shopgirls Go to the Movies." In *The Mass Ornament: Weimar Essays*. Trans. and ed. Thomas Y. Levin, 291–306. Cambridge, MA: Harvard University Press.

Lapsley, Robert, and Michael Westlake. 2006. *Film Theory: An Introduction*. Manchester, UK: Manchester University Press.

McCormick, Richard W. 2001. *Gender and Sexuality in Weimar Modernity: Film, Literature, and "New Objectivity."* New York: Palgrave.

Metz, Christian. 1982. *The Imaginary Signifier: Psychoanalysis and the Cinema*. Trans. Celia Britton, Annwyl Williams, Ben Brewster, and Alfred Guzzetti. Bloomington: Indiana University Press.

Paris, Barry. 1990. *Louise Brooks*. London: Mandarin.

Petro, Patrice. 1989. *Joyless Streets: Women and Melodramatic Representation in Weimar Germany*. Princeton, NJ: Princeton University Press.

Tatar, Maria. 1995. *Lustmord: Sexual Murder in Weimar Germany*. Princeton, NJ: Princeton University Press.

Ward, Janet. 2001. *Weimar Surfaces: Urban Visual Culture in 1920s Germany*. Berkeley: University of California Press.

TWELVE

THE BEARABLE LIGHTNESS OF BEING

PEOPLE ON SUNDAY (1930)

LUTZ KOEPNICK

I

A motorcycle enters the frame from the right, requiring the camera to pan left to follow the cyclist's path through dense urban traffic. We cut to the image of a crowded sidewalk, seen from what could be the perspective of a passenger located on the upper level of a double-decker bus. First we track along the pedestrians at their own speed, but then the camera will swiftly bypass the walking crowd, its eye invariably directed forward. Next, we see the image of a bridge allowing local trains to cross a busy street. Cars, trains, and pedestrians here flow on various levels from and into different directions; they define a veritable network of urban interchanges and passageways. In the foreground, a huge sign with the letter *U* indicates the invisible presence of yet another layer of traffic: the U-Bahn, or subway, as it plots its way somewhere underneath the asphalt. A sudden low-angle shot moves us much closer to the subway station. We see a man passing by, his body first visible through the spokes of the banister at street level, then obscured by the enormous subway sign. Before long, we cut to a medium shot of a young woman in fashionable attire crossing the street. She walks toward the camera, but her gaze moves unsteadily left and right, in search of something beyond the frame. Repeatedly, her sight is obscured by passing vehicles. The image of this woman is followed by a high-angle long shot of a sidewalk. We see a throng of pedestrians, but—somewhat irritatingly—the camera frustrates our desire to locate the man or the woman we have just seen anywhere onscreen. "Will we ever see them again?" we cannot help but ask ourselves. Did the camera simply show them because they were random members of the crowd—that is, fleeting sights that briefly command the urban dweller's field of vision before disappearing into oblivion again?

The next few shots answer our questions as they return us to the image of the man and the woman and, slowly but surely, map out their precise location in space and topographical relation to each other. First we see the woman, now situated in front of a newspaper stand, her gaze continuously moving from one side to the other. Next, the camera captures the man as he is still standing at the subway station. When, after lighting a cigarette, he suddenly starts to walk, the camera tracks behind him, thus endowing him with a certain authority over the film's production of images. We briefly cut back to her, only to return directly to him as he continues to walk to the right. The shot finally leads up to what any viewer accustomed to classical rules of editing by now will have expected for a while: we will finally see the man and the woman in one and the same frame. As it turns out, however, it is not him that she has been waiting for. He passes her, veers around to look at her looking, but their gaze doesn't meet, nor do they—at least for now—further approach each other. Instead, her eyes keep wandering, in search of something or someone that could finally lift her veil of urban anonymity.

A false start? A mere teaser? The camera cuts back to the image of trains crossing a bridge. Going in either direction, these trains clash in the middle of the frame, as if to allegorize the extent to which the speed of modern urban life in one and the same breath produces and prohibits sudden encounters. But then the camera does return to the two strangers after all: she nervously waiting near the subway station; he starting to circle her ever more closely, trying to catch her attention. A few times we cut back to high-angle shots in which the movements of various vehicles erratically conceal the drama unfolding in front of the subway station. Finally, however, we do see them talk to each other, cross the street, and sit down in a coffee shop, where they will not only engage in a lively conversation but make plans for a trip to a nearby lake for the next day, a Sunday, a day when the pulsating rhythms of the city will come to a brief rest.

Thus begins *Menschen am Sonntag* (*People on Sunday*), a film shot with virtually no budget between July and December 1929 by a new makeshift production company called Filmstudio 1929. Premiering on February 4, 1930, at Ufa's Theater Kurfürstendamm in Berlin, the film elicited enthusiastic responses from critics and audiences alike, not least of all because it did not fit into dominant models of German filmmaking, leisure, and politics circa 1930. At the time of the film's release German society was haunted by ever-increasing financial anxieties and political polarizations in the immediate aftermath of the 1929 New York stock market crash. Film industrialists and theater owners, however, were in the middle of promoting and installing synchronized sound as the new standard of cinema, pleasure, and profit making. Though *People on Sunday*—often celebrated as a neorealist film *avant la lettre*—was dedicated to the plights and pleasures of ordinary people, the street battles and economic worries of late Weimar culture remained extraneous to the film's mise-en-scène. And even though the film's images are full of rhythm, noise, language, and music, Filmstudio 1929 conceived of *People on Sunday* as a silent feature, thereby avoiding the detrimental impact of technical transition problems on the visual quality of German films around 1930. The resulting film struck contemporary viewers not so much because it offered escapist fare but because it focused on the efforts of ordinary people trying to find moments of lightness, bliss, meaning, and playfulness amid the rigid rhythms of their modern existence. The film continues to fascinate audiences to this day because its images, among other things, articulate longings and desires soon to be crushed by the darkening realities of late Weimar life and the rise of National Socialism. Rather than fleeing from history, *People on Sunday* burst into it. Seen from a historical vantage point, the film can be understood as having allowed audiences to take a final breath before being caught in a vortex of violence and mass mobilization.

The film's story is quickly told. A wine merchant named Wolfgang invites Christl, a hopeful film extra, for a jaunt to the countryside on Sunday. Wolfgang's friend, the taxi driver Erwin, after a fight with his girlfriend, Annie, joins the two on Sunday morning, and so does Christl's friend Brigitte, a gramophone saleswoman. Once at the lake, all four engage in a series of playful activities (Fig. 12.1). They bathe, picnic, go for a boat ride, walk, listen to gramophone music, play hide and seek between the trees, and flirt with each other in changing constellations. When they return to the city on Sunday night, their paths go in various directions. When Erwin arrives at his apartment, Annie, whom we saw pouting in bed in the morning after he took off, is still lying in the same position, having slept through the entire Sunday. "The country and the sun and love ... all the beautiful things are a long way off," the film's intertitles comment on the end of the weekend. The final shots ("Monday again") return us to the hectic rhythms of urban speed and industrial labor that denounce—yet, secretly, define the condition of the possibility for—Sunday's spark of playfulness and unbound desire.

Narrative cinema, as we generally know it, rests on characters endowed with principal causal agency. It is driven by psychologically defined individuals who, because of their specific traits and qualities, are eager to solve clear-cut problems and attain specific goals. *People on Sunday* defies this template. The film privileges atmospheric detail over narrative causality, chance and play over goal-oriented action. Here stories do not unfold because certain characters pursue specific agendas or respond to ongoing challenges. Rather, they emerge from the interplay of accidental circumstances and unforeseen encounters. Though in the end we can certainly identify a basic plot, *People on Sunday* never subsumes all its elements to the dictates of narrative progression and character development. Whatever we see

FIGURE 12.1   A happy foursome: playful activities at the lake in *People on Sunday* (1930). Courtesy
of the Filmmuseum Berlin, Stiftung Deutsche Kinemathek.

in this film could have happened differently as well. Whatever we witness our four
protagonists doing could have given cause to yet another story to be told, another
film chronicling the vagaries of modern urban life.

   In the opening sequence of *People on Sunday*, the work of the camera aptly
prefigures the film's loosely knit and anything-but-climactic mode of narration.
Whether positioned on a rooftop, inside a moving bus, or amid pedestrians on a
sidewalk, the eye of the camera gives the impression of scoping the city's visual
field in search of something worth our attention. Though Wolfgang and Christl will
soon command some authority over the camera's movements and points of view,
initially we seem to witness nothing other than the efforts of a camera exploring
the textures of metropolitan life, a camera patiently rummaging around for possible protagonists and appealing narratives. Similar to Christl and Wolfgang's first
encounter, the camera seems to meet its later cast entirely by chance. By emulating
the gaze of a roaming flaneur, an aimless urban stroller, the camera translates typical structures of modern urban experience into a compelling visual style as much
as it displays the very process by which the film comes into being in the first place.
The remainder of the film will consistently follow this formula. A plentitude of unstable handheld camera shots; a rigorously open style, allowing random elements
to invade the limitations of the frame; a host of seemingly unmotivated camera
moves and shot sequences, there solely to produce atmospheric moods rather

FIGURE 12.2 Christl Ehlers and Brigitte Borchert in an atmospheric scene at the lake . Courtesy of the Filmmuseum Berlin. Stiftung Deutsche Kinemathek.

than to propel the course of narrative action (Fig. 12.2); and last but not least, the cinematographer's play with ever-shifting angles and perspectives—all this directs our attention to the role of chance and contingency in modern existence as much as it exhibits the extent to which filmmakers, not ordinary people, cast the arbitrary itineraries of urban life into some kind of entertaining story.

II

Over the course of time, writing on Weimar cinema has mostly been wedded to issues of aesthetic experimentation and individual authorship. Understanding the German cinema of the 1920s as an art cinema par excellence, critical analyses have predominantly focused on the personal styles and distinctive signatures of auteurlike directors, cinematographers, and actors—on their attempts to wrestle with the mandates of commercial expectations and mass cultural distractions. To write about Weimar cinema, until very recently, has first and foremost meant to read certain films as beacons of oppositional meaning amid the barren seas of industrial filmmaking. Often reduced to the body of work considered expressionist, Weimar cinema has thus been canonized as a national cinema whose insistence on autonomous film art and scrupulous authorship warranted cultural diversity and self-critique.

People on Sunday has always occupied, and continues to occupy, an odd place in our thinking about Weimar cinema. Though often—and rightly—praised as an avant-garde feature, the film challenges the categories critics have used in the past to discriminate between art film and popular entertainment. For to think of *People on Sunday* as a film shaped by the creative imagination of one central will or artistic consciousness completely misses the film's curious and highly synthetic production process. *People on Sunday* is everything but an auteur film in the classical sense of the word. Instead, it is a film whose unique formal shapes and narrative energies result from the way in which different and, up to that time, mostly unproven young talents understood how to negotiate conflicting interests and aesthetic visions. *People on Sunday* bears the signature of not one but many authors, and for this reason we may consider it as a film debunking the very aura historically attached to the issue of cinematic authorship and creative self-expression in the first place.

Primarily because of budget constraints, Filmstudio 1929 decided to cast the film's principal roles with lay actors, many of whom would never again appear on German screens after the film's release. A series of short vignettes introduces this cast, as well as the players' social standing, prior to the onset of the film's narrative: the cab driver, Erwin Splettstößer; Brigitte Borchert, a record store employee selling popular music; the former officer, farmer, antiquarian, and gigolo Wolfgang von Waltershausen, currently working as a traveling wine merchant; the extra, Christl Ehlers, eager to find a new film role for herself; and the model, Annie Schreyer. It would clearly go too far to consider these five as a representative cross section of Berlin's population circa 1929. They do, however, represent professions and identities intimately associated with urban modernity—with the dream of social upward mobility, the rise of the culture industries, and the accelerated circulation of bodies and commodities across the city's heterogeneous spaces. And in more or less playing themselves as people oscillating between occupational burdens and leisure-time demands, they are significantly responsible for the film's air of local authenticity, its naturalistic staging of the fortunes, desires, and pleasures of ordinary Berliners in the late 1920s (Fig. 12.3).

But the film owes its unique status in German film history even more to the players who were assembled behind rather than in front of the camera. Conflicting legends abound about who signed for different aspects of the film's making. These legends have often been told with considerable historical hindsight. They have served the purpose of recalling moments of initial fame, as well as struggles over the source of creative inspirations, and should therefore be encountered with a good deal of skepticism. What is clear, however, is—according to the invitation card circulated for the film's Berlin premiere in February 1930[1]—that *People on Sunday* was nominally produced by Moritz Seeler, the head of Filmstudio 1929; written by a young journalist from Vienna named (at that time) Billie Wilder; and directed

FIGURE 12.3   Ordinary People: a close-up of Christl Ehlers. Courtesy of the Filmmuseum Berlin, Stiftung Deutsche Kinemathek.

by the nephew of Nero-Film chiefs Heinrich and Seymour Nebenzahl, Robert Siodmak, with some directorial help from Edgar G. Ulmer. Already known for both his exquisite and technically complex camera work on films such as *Metropolis* (1927), Eugen Schüfftan was in charge of the film's principal photography. What is also known, albeit not indicated on the premiere announcement, is the fact that Kurt Siodmak, Robert's older brother, played some role in the conception of the script and that Fred Zinnemann, a student of law and trained photographer, assisted Schüfftan in photographing the film before—like Ulmer—taking off to Hollywood at some point in the middle of the production process.

This is not the place to sort out the conflicting recollections of Kurt and Robert Siodmak versus Billie Wilder about the crew's individual contributions to the making of *People on Sunday*. At certain moments each of the three was eager to attribute principal authorship of the film to himself, while at other moments nearly everyone involved in the making of the film would credit the collegial atmosphere at the "Romanisches Café," a popular Berlin hangout for writers and intellectuals close to the site of the film's premiere, as the primary source of stimulation. Nor does it seem worthwhile to pursue in further detail here the controversial question of who financed the film and with what amount of money. Let it suffice to

FIGURE 12.4 Portrait of Robert Siodmak, circa 1930. Courtesy of the Filmmuseum Berlin, Stiftung Deutsche Kinemathek.

say that Robert Siodmak—with a gesture of low-budget heroism—spoke of a production sum of five thousand Deutschmarks, granted to him by the Nebenzahls, whereas Seeler and others cited a total amount of twenty thousand Deutschmarks or more as enabling the film's production.[2] What is important to note, however, is that most of the crew involved in *People on Sunday* quickly experienced successful careers within the remaining years of the Weimar studio system, engaged in the making of films whose narrative shapes and cultural stances had very little to do with the avant-gardist sensibilities of their first film. Wilder was to write screenplays for extremely light and popular entertainment flicks; Robert Siodmak (Fig. 12.4) took to directing a wide range of genre films, and his brother Kurt (as Curt) went on to deliver screenplays for polished, albeit quite generic, crime, horror, and science-fiction adventures. The modest marketing of *People on Sunday* presented the film team like precursors to the much later Dogma movement, that is to say, as a group of nonauteur iconoclasts breaking the rules of industrial filmmaking and studio operations. Yet in the last years of the Weimar Republic, the unconventional nature of their first film in no way prevented them from taking on important functions within the commercial studio system and support its stress on genre formulas, high production values, polished scripts, and star personas.

What is equally important to note is that almost all of the team's relatively inexperienced talents—with the exception of Seeler—would wash up over the course of the next decade on the shores of the Hollywood studio system. Moreover, whether they came as émigrés or exiles to the United States, Wilder, the Siodmak brothers, Ulmer, Zinnemann, and Schüfftan not only emerged as major contributors to the American cinema of the war and immediate postwar period, but they all excelled, to varying degrees, at a mode of American filmmaking concerned with images of urban crime and narratives of cynical despair that are radically opposed to the lightness of *People on Sunday*—namely, what came to be known as the film noir cycle that dominated Hollywood screens in the 1940s and 1950s. Given the unruly and disjunctive nature of the final product, who would have been able to predict in 1929 that the crew of *People on Sunday* could advance to principal engineers of Hollywood entertainment? And who would have been able to foresee that Siodmak and his crew would translate their avant-garde sensibilities, of all things, into the visual and narrative inventory of a film genre often associated with the cliché-ridden world of B amusement? How do we get, in other words, from *People on Sunday*'s atmosphere of playfulness and relaxation to Robert Siodmak's dark visions in films such as *Phantom Lady* (1943), *The Killers* (1946), and *Criss Cross* (1949); to Wilder's acerbic cynicism in *Double Indemnity* (1944) and *Sunset Boulevard* (1950); to Ulmer's poverty-row films of angst and paranoia such as *Detour* (1945); to Curt Siodmak's gripping scripts for Universal horror films such as *The Wolf Man* (1941); to Zimmermann's riveting account of postwar troubles in *Act of Violence* (1948) or cold war polarization in *High Noon* (1950); and to Schüfftan's many uncredited contributions as a cinematographer to films of desolation and despair in the 1940s and 1950s?

As I have shown elsewhere (Koepnick 2002), the path of exile for Hitler refugees was one of discontinuity and cultural masquerade, of performative self-refashioning and creative adaptation.[3] Their success in Hollywood relied less on what they represented—or on how they sought to bring Weimar to the Pacific—than on their professional ability to accommodate the studio system's needs for product diversification. And yet, while the production context that led to the rise of film noir in the course of the 1940s differed vastly from what Siodmak and others had encountered in Weimar, it is nevertheless instructive to explore some of the curious echoes and discrepancies between *People on Sunday* and the contributions of its makers to Hollywood cinema in the 1940s—less for the sake of tracing the industrial dynamic of film history than of illuminating the aesthetic composition and formal architecture, the anomaly and idiosyncrasy. Worlds indeed seem to lie between the registers of narrative organization, iconographic stylization, and thematic content of *People on Sunday* and what Siodmak and others were to help produce in the 1940s, yet film noir can serve us as a lens bringing into sharp focus what defines the peculiar aesthetic structure and spectatorial pleasures of *People on Sunday*. While film noir presents urban space as a dystopian enclosure embodying the absurdity,

alienation, and corruption of modern existence, *People on Sunday* offers the possibility of an idyllic other, a rural topography seemingly untouched by the logic of the
city. In contrast to the noir genre and its image of the city as a place of power and
oppression, *People on Sunday* entertains the viewer with a group of urbanites who
temporarily succeed in transforming place into space and, in so doing, institute a
kind of temporality that undoes the city's abstract rhythms. Second, whereas film
noir in the 1940s will bring desire and death into virulent constellations haunted
by repressed pasts, *People on Sunday* encodes desire as play and spontaneity, eman-
cipating the individual from all temporal burdens and opening up the possibility
of uninhibited self-presence. Desire in *People on Sunday* remains literally without
a climax, that is, untainted by a narrative drive that identifies textual closure with
the figure of death. And third, in contradistinction to film noir's future iconography of unrelenting enmity, of urban modernity as a permanent state of exception,
People on Sunday celebrates the modest and anything but spectacular adventures of
the everyday.

   If film noir's narratives will stage a constant need for strategic reason in order
to survive the challenges of modern life, *People on Sunday* indulges in the utopian idea of an absence of strategy and goal-oriented action, a commitment to the
mundane most vividly culminating perhaps in the figure of Annie, whose greatest
pleasure is to spend a whole day in bed, passive and lethargic yet unaffected by the
peculiar modern drive toward spectacle, exceptionality, and confrontation. Amid
Siodmak's, Ulmer's, and Wilder's future world of hard-boiled detectives, ruthless
gangsters, cynical insurance agents, and femmes fatales, the bed as a site of rest
and relaxation will drop literally out of the picture. Of all the heroes directed and
photographed by German émigrés and exiles in Hollywood, the heroes of film noir
sleep the least.

   Given the production crew's talented composition and future fortunes, it is almost unavoidable to approach *People on Sunday* without thinking about what happened to German film culture and the career of talented film practitioners such
as the Siodmak brothers and Wilder after the breakdown of the Weimar Republic.
People on Sunday, in spite of its focus on the textures of the local and everyday, is a
film that gives us pause to reflect on not only the fractured course of German twentieth-century film history but also the trade of images and imaginations between
Hollywood and Germany constitutive of German filmmaking ever since the end of
World War I (Elsaesser 2000, 359–60). *People on Sunday* raises intriguing questions
about the legacy of Weimar cinema in Hollywood; the film urges us to complicate
dominant accounts of how German filmmakers in exile would later recall their
Weimar past to resume their careers and express feelings of despair and dislocation. Yet just as much as we cannot solely assess the history of the Weimar Republic
in light of its catastrophic ending (Peukert 1993, 275), we must also view films such

as *People on Sunday* as having their own history, as films to be judged on their own terms, without judging them against the history of films that followed the destruction of the Weimar Republic, whether these later films where produced by the Nazi film industry or by German exiles in Hollywood trying to negotiate their formal sensibilities with the demands of a Fordist studio system.

As a film defying lofty notions of cinematic authorship as much as dominant templates of narrative integration, *People on Sunday* provides exemplary lessons about how to narrate film history without falling prey to the lures of linear determinism and historical hindsight. The film teaches us to think about the course of time and history, not in terms of a progressive chain of single causes and clear-cut effects but as a vision structured by conflicting temporalities, desires, recollections, and anticipations. And rather than encouraging us to isolate certain signature styles and track their paths through a filmmaker's career trajectory, *People on Sunday*—in its emphasis on the playful and performative—draws our awareness to the fact that filmmakers invent, reinvent, and perform their professional identities and agendas just as much as modern urbanites try out different roles and modes of self-expression under different circumstances. History and film history, as seen in light of *People on Sunday*, is not a history of autonomous individuals authoring their own lives and self-expressions like sculptors mold their clay. Instead, it should be understood as a force field of absent causes and semiautonomous elements whose relationships with one another are principally nontransparent and mediated. *People on Sunday* depicts the present not as a transitory moment allowing goal-oriented individuals to transfer selected aspects of the past to an open-ended future but as a present of simultaneity and contingency, privileging chance, multiplicity, and performativity over classical modernist concepts of linear time, authorship, and historical causality.

III

What *People on Sunday* shares with the work done by its makers during the 1940s in Hollywood is its iconoclastic impulse. Though it does not relish apocalyptic visions and cynical denials of meaning, the film—like the American noir genre of the war and postwar era—expresses fundamental unease about the way in which modern society circulates mass images in order to inundate people's minds, engineer standardized effects, and organize the individual's attention. And similar to the best noir films scripted, directed, or photographed by German émigrés and exiles after 1940, *People on Sunday* translates iconoclastic sentiments into a filmic language eager to examine its own involvement in the modern production and dissemination of images. It is one of the most remarkable qualities of *People on Sunday* that the film does not showcase its self-reflexive iconoclasm like a price tag of avant-garde sophistication but interrogates the politics of modern image construction unobtrusively within its own narrative—as something directly tied to the dreams, desires, obsessions, concerns, and cultural practices of its ordinary characters.

In an early scene, still on the eve of the Sunday outing, we witness a fight between Erwin and Annie, born more out of mutual boredom than anything else. Played out in a domestic setting (the only interior we really get to see in the course of the entire film), the scuffle culminates in Erwin's and Annie's tearing up each other's valuable collection of film-star photographs. Erwin rips up an image of Willy Fritsch, then an up-and-coming matinee idol who in 1929 could be seen in the first German 100-percent-sound production, Hanns Schwarz's *Melodie des Herzen* (*Melody of the Heart*, 1929). Annie, meanwhile, destroys Erwin's revered image of Greta Garbo, one of the principal actors in G. W. Pabst's *Die freudlose Gasse* (*The Joyless Street*, 1925), who in 1929 was already at the threshold of reigning triumphant in Hollywood. Though charged with comical energy, this scene plays an important function in setting up the further course of narrative action, as well as in authenticating the film's own system of presenting its players, defining points of view, and anticipating the viewer's acts of emotional identification. For not only does it, comical nature notwithstanding, prepare the ground for Erwin's passage into the fleeting bliss of spontaneity and gaiety on Sunday, but it also indicates the film's overall status within the growing culture industry of the late Weimar Republic as a film favoring aleatory experiences of joy over the manufactured pleasures of mass cultural entertainment, the thickness of ordinary existence over the auratic extraordinariness of stars as marketed on the cinematic dream screen.

In a later scene we witness a photographer taking a number of snapshots of individual vacationers at the lake. Unconnected to the general narrative, these shots primarily seem to serve the purpose of articulating the filmmakers' commitment to the realism of amateur acting, while also exhibiting the power of the camera to produce images and manipulate the flow of time. The scene starts with images of the crowded beach at the Nikolassee, the lake where the foursome spends the afternoon. We then cut to a long shot of the photographer as he is taking a picture of a group of beachgoers (all, as it has been reported, regulars of the Romanisches Café). Next, we see a series of ten close-ups showing children and adults as they exhibit various facial expressions, communicate with something outside the frame, or simply laugh about their exposed position in front of the camera until the photographer's shutter finally captures their countenance. Whatever they do in front of the camera—whether they giggle, play at being a model, turn extremely serious, or blush out of shyness—is clearly marked as a direct response to the presence of the camera itself, as sudden freeze-frames indicate the decisive moment of photographic exposure.

Photography, it has often been said, brings death to the photographed. It administers shocks to the flow of time and transforms history into a cemetery but in this way also stimulates a curious and often uncanny solidarity between the past and the present. This spectral nature of photography, in the initial part of the photography sequence of *People on Sunday*, seems to haunt the very medium that represents its operation. As it invites us to see the world through a photographer's eye, the film camera here gives up its distinctive purchase on representing movement over time. In resorting to the special effect of the freeze-frame to emulate the photographic medium, motion pictures here seem to lose out to the way in which the medium of photography—precisely by disrupting temporal continuity—connects different instances of presence, refocuses our sense of finitude, and thereby draws our awareness to the many ghosts that populate our own present.

The next series of shots, however, reverses this impression. It liberates the cinematic image from the medusan spell of the photographic image and showcases cinema's unique powers of capturing—of redeeming—the real. First, we see two close-ups whose design turns the temporal logic of the initial ten shots upside down. Instead of freezing motion into stasis, the film now brings still images to life. In the next twenty-four close-ups the camera entirely discards the photographic metaphor: what we see are vignettes of anonymous people looking at or looking away from the camera, captured in and over real time, neither frozen into nor unfrozen from photographic stasis.

At first this series of shots recalls August Sander's contemporaneous, albeit unfinished, visual archive of German society, *Menschen des 20. Jahrhunderts* (*People of the Twentieth Century*), a photographic physiognomy whose most memorable entries captured how Weimar Germans of different rank, status, class, and regional background wanted to be seen in the public eye and how this self-perception informed their individual subject positions.[4] On closer inspection, however, we come to realize that such a comparison is misleading. Rather than understanding the photographic frame as a temporary window on transient realities, Sander's frames indicate the extent to which photographic cameras, as well as our own desired self-perceptions, define the world of the photographed in the first place. Though no less self-reflexive in intent and execution, the final series of moving physiognomies in *People on Sunday*, by contrast, precisely by not converting motion into stasis and by entirely focusing our attention on facial features, seems to release its subjects from the defining frames of both photographic reproduction and social self-perception. In Schüfftan's shots, the technologies of cinematic recording open transitory windows onto the world that reveal rather than reorganize the visual expressions of the real. Though knowing very well that cinematographers must always fail in capturing the unmediated materiality of what is present, Schüfftan's twenty-four vignettes try to reach out through the cinematic frame to touch something that lies beyond it. Cinema here exorcises its historical indebtedness to still photography in the hope of disengaging the individual from the strictures of modern society, including those imposed by modern machines of image production.

At the end of this sequence we cut once again to six still images showing a series of couples in stylized romantic situations. In contrast to what we have seen before, however, we are no longer dealing with freeze-frames but with filmed still photographs. The purpose of these six shots is somewhat ambiguous. Do we see them as stand-ins for the images to be printed later by the beach photographer? Or do we see them because their staged artificiality, *ex negativo*, testifies to the vivid realism and superior expressiveness of Schüfftan's twenty-four earlier vignettes? No matter what our final understanding of these images, the scene ends with shots asking the viewer to look for star images not among the Garbos and Fritschs of the culture industry but among the anonymous visages of ordinary people. Mechanical reproduction here celebrates its own potential to erase traditional boundaries between artists and recipients so as to allow people to portray themselves and see their own reproduction on the screen or photographic paper. As important, it is precisely by incorporating and remediating the logic of still photography that the medium of film here also provides something virtually unseen but often dreamed of in the course of German cinema before and beyond 1929. Inasmuch as it unfetters the photographed and the viewer from the drive of narrative causality and teleological determination, the beach photography scene of *People on Sunday* challenges nothing so much as the figure of death that is so central to both the operations of still photography and conventional storytelling. As if to fulfill the later vision of director Friedrich Munroe in Wim Wenders's *The State of Things* (1982), cinema here presents itself as a tool very capable of doing what the culture industry does not seem to tolerate, namely, to show images not of narrative closure and, hence, of death but of life as it simply and open-endedly goes by.

IV

German film critics, in particular those based in Berlin, mostly welcomed *People on Sunday* passionately. Though there was no dearth of respectable films playing in German theaters in 1929 and 1930, critics applauded what they considered a new tone within the landscapes of German cinema, in spite of the fact that Siodmak and crew had decided not to jump on the bandwagon of synchronized sound film. Herbert Ihering, in his review for the *Berliner Börsen-Courier* (February 5, 1930), praised *People on Sunday* for the "magical ease of its flow of images, more musical than in all sound films." *Film-Kurier* critic Hans Feld emphasized the way in which the film offered universal themes and images as a result of, rather than in spite of, the filmmakers' exploration of local specificity, of contemporary Berlin life (*Film-Kurier*, February 5, 1930). Hanns G. Lustig congratulated the crew of *People on Sunday* for their avant-garde sensibilities, which manifested a refreshing contrast to the literary ambitions of French filmmakers and the aestheticizing visions of German theoreticians of the day (*Tempo*, February 5, 1930). Though left-wing critics such as Alfred Kemeny faulted *People on Sunday* for its "petit-bourgeois tendencies" (Kemeny 1930), they nevertheless endorsed the film because it—like Soviet cinema of the 1920s—allowed real people to play out their own lives onscreen. The only outright disapproval came from the extreme right, articulated by Alfred Rosenberg, one of the chief thinkers of Hitler's future Third Reich, employed in 1930 by Hugenberg's mighty media conglomerate. Significantly, what troubled Rosenberg was not so much the film's subject matter as the filmmakers' attempt to circumnavigate industrial and commercial film practice. Far from being impressed by the film's lack of spectacular shine and its efforts to capture the everyday, Rosenberg criticized *People on Sunday* for upsetting nothing less than the operation of film criticism itself, for challenging the critics' own normative standards and their traditional authority of judgment (Rosenberg 1930).[5]

Rosenberg's critique notwithstanding, the overwhelmingly positive response of Berlin film critics should come as little surprise. For rarely has German cinema offered images of metropolitan life more attuned to the rhythms and atmospheric textures of one particular city. Berlin does not simply provide an accidental backdrop for narrative action. Instead, it figures as one of the film's principal players in and of itself. To be sure, *People on Sunday* might not offer abundant images of Berlin street life, with the exception of the film's opening and a brief interlude transporting the viewer back to the urban center while our four protagonists enjoy the pleasures of the lakeside. Compared to the panoply of impressions in Walter Ruttmann's *Berlin, Symphony of a Great City* (1927), *People on Sunday* was not intended to provide a thrilling panorama of Berlin distractions; it was not meant to take viewers on a tourist ride through the material fabrics of metropolitan modernity. Yet the city of Berlin is secretly present in nearly every shot of the film; the whole narrative hinges on its existence. Berlin is the veil through which we see our four protagonists meet, enjoy themselves, and in the end part again. In contrast to the dystopian mood of the majority of German city films produced in the course of the 1920s (and later),[6] this veil allows us to see Berlin's modernity as a site of both unexpected encounters and sudden attractions, of shock and delight, of catastrophe and exultation. Far from being depicted as an antagonistic element opposed to our protagonists' wills and desires, the Berlin of *People on Sunday* in fact defines the very conditions for modern love and enchantment. Whatever piece of fortune or chance that may bring modern urbanites together here may also cause them to split forever again.

It was not for many years to come that German filmmakers would follow the model of *People on Sunday* and once again embrace Berlin as a peculiar training ground for modern experience and love, that is, embrace the arbitrariness of urban existence without anxiety, gloom, and desperation. In *People on Sunday* Berlin's urban modernity causes people to live and love, not at first but at last sight. Decades of violence, division, and trauma kept German filmmakers and moviegoers alike from realizing that this stigma inflicted on love in a metropolis may open up new paths as much as it closes down old ones. The film's virtual rediscovery and painstaking restoration in the late 1990s is therefore no coincidence.[7] It is symptomatic of the way in which postunification Germany has sought to recall and recuperate visions of time, history, modernization, and change that differ from the ominous models predominant throughout most of Germany's painful twentieth century.

NOTES

1. This information is available in the file on *People on Sunday* at the "Schriftgutabteilung," Filmmuseum Berlin—Stiftung Deutsche Kinemathek.
2. See Alpi 1998, 20; Elbin 1998, 86; Siodmak 1980, 42.
3. For extended analyses of the impact of German exiles on film noir, see Carnelli and Omasta 1997.
4. A selection of this monumental project was published in 1929 under the title *Antlitz der Zeit: Sechzig Aufnahmen deutscher Menschen des 20. Jahrhunderts* (Munich: Transmare Verlag).
5. See also Rosenberg, "Warnung vor dem Experiment," *Kinematograph*, February 14, 1930.
6. For an encyclopedic overview of the city film see Vogt 2001.
7. See Prümm 2000. For details about the restoration process see also Martin Koerber's report in the "Pressekit, Menschen am Sonntag," edited by Nina Golsar, Mathias Knop, and Hans Kohl for the rerelease in 2000 (available in the file on *People on Sunday* at the "Schriftgutabteilung," Filmmuseum Berlin—Stiftung Deutsche Kinemathek).

REFERENCES

Alpi, Deborah Lazaroff. 1998. *Robert Siodmak: A Biography*. Jefferson, NC: McFarland.

Carnelli, Christian, and Michael Omasta, eds. 1997. *Schatten. Exil: Europäische Emigranten im Film Noir*. Vienna: PVS Verleger.

Elbin, Günther. 1998. *Am Sonntag in die Matinee: Moriz Seeler und die Junge Bühne: Eine Spurensuche*. Mannheim: Persona Verlag.

Elsaesser, Thomas. 2000. "To Be or Not to Be: Extra-Territorial in Vienna—Berlin—Hollywood." In *Weimar Cinema and After: Germany's Historical Imaginary*, 361–82. London: Routledge.

Kemeny, Alfred. 1930. "Ein interessanter Filmversuch." *Die rote Fahne*, February 7.

Koepnick, Lutz. 2002. *The Dark Mirror: German Cinema Between Hitler and Hollywood*. Berkeley: University of California Press.

Peukert, Detlev J. K. 1993. *The Weimar Republic: The Crisis of Classical Modernity*. Trans. Richard Deveson. New York: Hill and Wang.

Prümm, Karl. 2000. "Melancholie der Großstadt: Uraufführung in Karlsbad: Der Filmklassiker *Menschen am Sonntag* ist restauriert." *Frankfurter Allgemeine Zeitung*, July 21.

Rosenberg, Alfred. 1930. "Es ist doch nicht so leicht." *Kinematograph*, February 5.

Siodmak, Robert. 1980. *Zwischen Berlin und Hollywood: Erinnerungen eines großen Filmregisseurs*. Ed. Hans C. Blumenberg. Munich: Herbig.

Vogt, Guntram. 2001. *Die Stadt im Film: Deutsche Spielfilme, 1900–2000*. Marburg: Schüren.

THIRTEEN

NATIONAL CINEMAS /
INTERNATIONAL FILM CULTURE

THE BLUE ANGEL (1930) IN
MULTIPLE LANGUAGE VERSIONS

PATRICE PETRO

How do we assess the national and historical status of *The Blue Angel*? This film, together with *The Cabinet of Dr. Caligari* and *M*, is the most widely discussed film of the Weimar period. Because of its highly canonical status, scholars have debated a range of issues related to its production and consumption, notably, its relation to Heinrich Mann's novel and the significance of Josef von Sternberg's changes to it; the novel's implied critique of Wilhelmine Germany (of authority, of patriarchy, and of the belief in outer appearances) versus the film's portrayal of gender relations and the rise of the New Woman in Weimar Germany, as well as across Europe and abroad; the contrasting star personae and acting styles of the film's principal players, Emil Jannings and Marlene Dietrich; and the larger question of German-American competition and collaboration during the 1920s, specifically as these involved Hollywood and Berlin filmmaking industries and personnel at this time.[1]

To frame these issues effectively, however, it is useful to begin by considering this film's canonical status as a national film that circulated within an international film culture. Is *The Blue Angel* a German film prescient about changes taking place in the transition from Weimar to Nazi Germany? Or is it a thoroughly "Americanized" film, reflective of its Hollywood director's professional origins and signature cinematic style? These questions are complicated by the fact that *The Blue Angel* was shot simultaneously in German and English and was always destined to be viewed by multiple national audiences in an international marketplace. Thus, is it more historically accurate to locate this film between (rather than within) national traditions? Did it achieve what its producer, Erich Pommer, hoped for and aspired to with this prestige German sound film, namely, a combination of German and U.S. sensibilities or "synthesis of Hollywood and Neubabelsberg"?[2] Is this synthesis key to understanding its place in film history?

To be sure, *The Blue Angel* remains today perhaps best known as the film that launched Marlene Dietrich's Hollywood career. As many scholars have pointed out, the story of Lola Lola's rise to fame parallels that of Dietrich's own rise to international stardom based precisely on the performance of a hybrid identity or, rather, a synthesis of conventions associated with both Weimar and Hollywood cinema. *The Blue Angel* began production on November 4, 1929, and was completed on January 22, 1930. It premiered in Berlin in April 1930, and was withheld for release in the United States, in its English-language version, until later in the same year, after the successful promotion of Dietrich as a Hollywood star with the release of *Morocco*. The film was made in part at the request of a world-famous actor. Following the success of *The Last Command* and his Oscar for best actor, German film star Emil Jannings had asked Erich Pommer, who himself had just been recalled from Hollywood to Ufa in 1928, to hire Josef von Sternberg for his next, critically important, German film—his first with sound. Jannings had insisted that this production be made in his own country and language but wanted Sternberg to direct. Sternberg welcomed Jannings and Pommer's offer and came to Berlin in the autumn of 1929. Once there, he enlisted the talents of a relatively unknown and untested Dietrich, who surprisingly overshadowed Jannings in her performance and then was signed by Paramount to a two-picture contract in February of 1930. Dietrich attended the premiere of *The Blue Angel* in Berlin on April 1, only to sail for New York later that night. The rest, as they say, is history.

But what *kind* of history exactly? *The Blue Angel* occupies a paradoxical yet significant place in German as well as American film history. It is part of a curious international language landscape and a fascinating example of the complexity and turbulence brought about by the transition to sound. *The Blue Angel* was shot simultaneously in German and English at the Ufa studios in Berlin. Ufa distributed the film in Germany, and Paramount distributed it in the United States. This particular arrangement was the result of long-standing agreements and interchanges between the two companies, notably, the infamous Parufamet Agreement of 1925–26, which enabled Paramount and MGM to enter into an agreement with Ufa to found a joint distribution company.[3] Although this original contract was renegotiated in 1927, with looser terms and restrictions, it served as the basis for this joint venture, which came at a critical time in Ufa's history and in the history of the transition from silent to sound film (Kreimeier 1996, 183).

As many scholars have pointed out, the coming of sound sharpened the issues of cultural identity raised by the international trade in motion pictures and led producers, audiences, and governments alike to reassess their relation to the medium. As Ruth Vasey and Richard Maltby have argued, sound standardized the movies in a very material sense, making them less malleable and restricting their cultural adaptability (Vasey and Maltby 1994). Hollywood's American identity became audible and forced it to confront the cultural and linguistic diversity of its international audience.

To be sure, intertitles had long served as the principal medium for international adaptability. As early as 1927, films were routinely translated into thirty-six languages. Visuals were subject to excision or rearrangement, but titles could be creatively modified to cater to diverse national and cultural groups. Sound technology changed all this, making movies far less adaptable. It was no longer possible, for instance, to rearrange or excise sequences without ruining entire reels. And even recorded music caused problems. Vasey and Maltby point out that Italian and German exhibitors, for example, accustomed to providing their own musical accompaniments, complained that the new sound tracks sounded "too American" for the taste of their audiences.

When sound came to involve "talking," the problem of language specificity and the loss of ambiguity in the treatment of sensitive and especially sexual subjects only compounded these problems. Dubbing was not fully operational, although most major studies experimented with it. The other alternative was more expensive and complex—namely, the production of different talking versions of selected films, each in a different language. Stars could retain their own parts if they were multilingual; otherwise, replacements would be used. By 1930 all major companies were producing foreign-language versions. The most conspicuous action was taken by Paramount, which in 1930 established a studio at Joinville, outside Paris, specifically for the production of multiple-language versions of its films.

The Blue Angel was made just prior to the establishment of operations at Joinville and was always understood to be an Ufa project. As the historian Thomas Saunders explains:

> At the beginning of 1929 Ufa sent a team to the United States to study sound production. On the basis of its findings Ufa decided to proceed at maximum speed to make the switch. The language barrier and patent war notwithstanding, the substantial lag of German development behind Hollywood posed a recognized threat. In addition, American companies began to hire German talent in an attempt to circumvent the language barrier. While the sound revolution brought the repatriation of Conrad Veidt and Emil Jannings, both of whom figured prominently in pioneering German talkies . . . , it also revived suspicions that Hollywood would launch another recruitment drive and plunder the German industry. (Saunders 1994, 228)

As mentioned earlier, Pommer's strategy with *The Blue Angel* was somewhat different from Saunders's scenario of competition and mutual suspicion. In contrast to the general trend of the time, in which German actors and directors were recruited to work in Hollywood, in this case an eminent Hollywood director took up a German producer's request to come to Berlin to direct the world's most popular leading man in his first sound film. Furthermore, like Pommer, Sternberg gambled that he could make a film that was neither German nor American but rather one that would be the synthesis of Hollywood and Neubabelsberg. The German cinema would draw on the talents of an acclaimed Hollywood director, as well as its own internationally famous leading man. Returning to its roots (in German literature, as well as in its far-reaching, sophisticated stage tradition) and reaching out to Hollywood, Ufa would create not one but two language versions that would garner success worldwide.

With this in mind it is interesting to return to the question of how *The Blue Angel* itself represents history—a question of long-standing concern in the vast literature on this film. Some commentators regard any reference to the film's historical realism as utterly misguided. As John Baxter explains, not only was this 1930 film based on a 1905 novella, but from the very "first shot of twisted roofs and crooked smokestacks, one is aware of a nineteenth- rather than twentieth-century ambiance. There are no cars in *The Blue Angel*, no radios or cinemas, and the lamps that hang in almost every shot are gas-burning. Except for a short sequence showing Rath peeling leaves from a calendar that begins at 1923 and ends on 1929, the film is exclusively an image of the Europe in which Sternberg grew up" (Baxter 1971, 70).

In a frequently cited analysis, Siegfried Kracauer takes issue with this kind of assessment. He claims, in his retrospective reading of Weimar cinema in *From Caligari to Hitler*, that *The Blue Angel* remains a document very much reflective of its time: "*The Blue Angel* poses anew the problem of German immaturity," Kracauer famously wrote, "and moreover elaborates its consequences as manifested in the conduct of the boys and of the artists, who like the professor are middle-class offspring. ... It is as if the film implied a warning," Kracauer concludes, "for these screen figures anticipate what will happen in real life a few years later. The boys are born Hitler youths" (Kracauer 1947, 218).[4] Commentators from Andrew Sarris (1980) to Gertrud Koch (1986), even Sternberg himself (1973), have challenged Kracauer's sociological reading of the film, insisting that *The Blue Angel* is best understood as the product of its director's personal history and vivid imagination. Koch puts the matter succinctly. "*The Blue Angel* is probably the first film in which Sternberg produces a merely illusory reality of place, one whose reality originates wholly in his fantasy. ... It is not a German film," writes Koch; it is a von Sternberg film—and one that "foreshadows his later—and more accomplished—artificial and exotic worlds" (1986, 65).

In all the scholarly writing on this film, critics constantly split on this issue of sociology versus auteurism, insisting on either the film's German or Hollywood origins: *The Blue Angel* is either a reflection of its turbulent times or the product of its Hollywood director's vivid imagination. In this regard the most compelling commentary on the film is a 1978 article by the French critic Michel Bouvier entitled "Hollywood on Spree." As Bouvier explains it, "neither the German team nor its famous director's contributions to this film nor the true nationality of the film really matter" (19). Instead, he argues, what matters is the way in which *The Blue Angel* both embraces and extends the Hollywood as well as the German model, and the way it accomplishes this, above all else, by reflecting on the status of cinematic representation and the circulation of images.

This is not to say, of course, that the question of film authorship is unimportant to this film. But rather than pose the issue in psychological or purely individual terms, as most critics tend to do, it is important to recognize the historical significance of Sternberg's status as a U.S. director in Europe at the time of the transition to sound. *The Blue Angel* is in fact among the extremely rare instances of a non-U.S. film produced with the byline of a major Hollywood director, thus reversing the usual trend of the times for European directors to work in Hollywood. It is in this sense that *The Blue Angel* benefits most from a full authorial reading but only within the context of the film's hybrid and transnational status. Indeed, *The Blue Angel* both established and exemplified a procedure distinctly different from Paramount's own Joinville approach to international filmmaking (organized even as *The Blue Angel* was going into release in the mid-spring of 1930). With the presence of its major Hollywood director,[5] not to mention its German producer and international star, *The Blue Angel* was intentionally designed as a "two-originals-no-copy" venture into foreign-language filmmaking.[6] It therefore demanded to be read as an authorial text, and as very different from the typical multiple language versions of the time, which were thought—even at the peak of their production—to be, by definition, debased by their status as copy.

The success of *The Blue Angel*, finally, had as much to do with the director's affinity for Weimar culture and its cultivation of surface effects as it did with the particular casting of Dietrich in the starring role. Reviewers at the time consistently commented on Sternberg's emphasis on surface effects and on the externality of film mechanics.[7] Furthermore, as is well known, Dietrich's own background in cabaret and her reputation for sexual experimentation undeniably enhanced the reception of the film. But the cultivation of surface effects and the exploration of sexuality were as much an American as a German preoccupation at this time. As one historian writes of 1920s New York (although these remarks resonate with 1920s Berlin as well):

> Commentators throughout the 1920s were gripped by the certainty—exhilarat-
> ing to some, troubling to others—that their society had moved headlong into a
> sexualized modernity marked by sophistication and complexity. The 1920s saw
> an increasingly intense public debate over what seemed radically nontraditional
> sexual behavior: a newly aggressive and public middle-class female sexuality,
> exemplified by women who streamlined their bodies into sleek instruments of
> pleasure, embracing styles of dress and expression previously associated only
> with prostitutes; and new forms of specifically sexual identity—male homosexu-
> ality and lesbianism—that blatantly detached sex from procreation, and from
> traditional notions of masculinity and femininity, and made it into a style of life.
> (Hamilton 1997, 118)

Sexuality as a style of life: this statement suggests Dietrich's persona, as well as
Sternberg's aesthetics. Efforts to locate *The Blue Angel* historically, then, must address the multiple locations of which the film is part, and that it explores: its place
in the history of urban entertainment and the loosening of sexual mores; its place
in German history, as well as German and American film history; its impact on the
careers of its director and stars and producer who worked within an international
industry—not to mention the multiple locations of its marketing and distribution.
All of this serves to underscore the film's status as a document of *dislocation*, made
simultaneously in two languages for distribution in an international market.

But even without the existence of two versions in different languages, *The Blue
Angel* would remain a remarkable document about originals and copies and the status of the work of art in an age of mechanical reproduction. An adaptation of a classic
novella by a prominent German writer, the film reflects on the circulation and mul-
tiplication of images, and the very status of cinema as a copy without an original.

Many critics have suggested that the film is itself an extensive quotation of other,
especially German, films. Jannings's role as Professor Rath is an extended quotation of his previous screen roles, from *The Last Laugh* (1924) to *Variety* (1925) to *The
Last Command* (1928). Several images in the film, moreover, are directly drawn from
classical German cinema. The film's opening shot, notes Koch, "consists of an ex-
pressionistically chaotic landscape of rooftops and chimneys: a stylistic quotation,
placing the film firmly in a film-historical context" (1986, 69). More than this, the
film quotes as much from the other arts as it does from film culture.[8] George Grosz,
for example, was a regular visitor to the film set; his *Lustmord* paintings would appear to have inspired the blackboard image of Professor Rath carrying off Lola's leg,
although within the fiction, this is ostensibly the work of Rath's students.

Beyond direct quotation, the film explores throughout the status of pictures
and postcards and posters that circulate among students, professor, cabaret audiences, and locales. We in fact first see Lola as a poster image (Fig. 13.1), which a

FIGURE 13.1   Lola Lola as poster image in Josef von Sternberg's *The Blue Angel* (1930).

washerwoman cleans and then poses next to, in an attempt to emulate the posture of the small town's theatrical star. In the course of the film, moreover, theatricality gives way to distinctly cinematic representation: in our first encounter with Lola, the performer, for instance, both she and the set are dressed in the iconography of cheap vaudeville. She interacts with cabaret performers onstage as well as with members of the audience. In her final performance, by contrast, she is the main performer framed by a group of synchronized, Tiller Girl–type, female dancers (Fig. 13.2). She sings, now in close-up, for a cinematic rather than a theatrical audience and is thereby transformed from theatrical to cinematic icon.

Most important, the postcards and posters that appear throughout this film are laden with symbolism, objects reminiscent of Dada and collage and urban art, with a narrative force of their own. They offer the students, and then the professor, a chance to personally engage with Lola's image, in that each gets his very own erotic dance by just blowing on the paper skirt on the postcard (Fig. 13.3). Just as Walter Benjamin (1999) argued that availability and easy access to the art image through mass production destroys the aura, so do the replicated picture postcards lack presence in space and time. They lack the ability to lay claim to the significance of the real thing. The illustrations and poster art that cover the windows and cabaret walls arouse and entice the boys and the professor to attend Lola's performances in search of authenticity. In fact, the professor becomes obsessed with positioning himself closer to the original form of the reproduced Lola. But no matter how

FIGURE 13.2 Lola (Marlene Dietrich) in her final number, framed by a group of female dancers.

close he gets, even in marriage, he can never truly possess Lola; the original that he imagined her to be never existed to begin with. Once Rath is transformed from professor to pusher of erotic commodities to vaudeville clown, it becomes clear that Lola, the seductress, lives in a public rather than a private realm.

Most interesting in this regard is the fact that Lola is constantly confronted by her own images, whether via the posters that plaster the walls backstage or in the form of the postcards she always carries with her. As I suggested earlier, the French critic Michel Bouvier (1978, 29) points out that Lola's relationship to her own image does not "generate a narcissism that would demand an ascetic manipulation of the body." Instead, claims Bouvier, "it makes the relation between model and image problematic," raising the issue of "which really determines the other?" These remarks recall the washerwoman who emulates the poster image and encourage us to consider a more thoughtful investigation of the status of original and copy.

Without a doubt, the existence of multiple language versions of this film complicates the notion of a copy even further. At least four versions of *The Blue Angel* are still in circulation: the shorter German version, about 90 minutes long, which dates from a 1947 U.S. release; the longer German version, now known as "the director's cut," which is 106 minutes long, and which claims to represent the film in its initial German release; and, finally, two English-language versions, the first released in 1930 and then reissued on VHS in the 1990s, which is about 90 minutes long, and a second release of this 1930s version in 2001 on DVD, which is 100

FIGURE 13.3 The postcard images of Lola which feature the erotic thrill of the paper skirt.

minutes long.[9] While the existence of multiple versions of this film raises all kinds of questions for rethinking the place of *The Blue Angel* in film history, I would like to underscore here how these changes profoundly affect our perceptions of Weimar and Hollywood cinema, especially our perceptions of Lola and Rath.

Even a cursory analysis of the film's most important song, "Ich bin von Kopf bis Fuß"/"Falling in Love Again," reveals how the English-language versions transform Lola from a creature of sexual instinct to a helpless romantic. The English-language versions, moreover, minimize the explicitly sexual, direct, and often surprising instances of what might be considered rude or vulgar or obscene. (Lola can spit into her makeup box and adjust her panties in all language versions, but she can sing with her legs apart, hips in the air, and with direct erotic intent only in German.)

The changes to Rath's character in the English-language versions are equally significant, although they ultimately serve to diminish our sympathy for him. For example, in one of the English versions (the VHS version from the 1990s) we never see the professor's gaze at the provocative postcard of Lola and thus are not given a window onto his erotic fantasy. With the scene entirely cut from this version, we can only assume that he goes to the Blue Angel in search of his students, whom he intends to reprimand, which merely reinforces his melodramatic and one-dimensional portrayal of the tyrannical German pedant. This English version also omits many seemingly peripheral, symbolic, or narratively unessential sequences—

notably, the opening sequence with the maid's discovery of Rath's dead bird, which serves as a key motif in the film, linking Rath to Lola (and her very much alive, singing bird), as well as to their marriage and to his cock-crowing and final humiliation onstage.

More than this, however, even when sexually provocative sequences are not omitted, they are often played very differently in different language versions. In the 1990s English-language version, for instance, the professor is ashamed and uncomfortable about returning Lola's underwear (he can't bring himself to tell her what is in the package), whereas in both of the German versions, he admits to taking the garment and to mistaking it for something that was his. Other examples can be cited: the German versions show us a racially mixed cabaret audience, with prominent black members in the crowd. There are no such racially mixed audiences in the VHS English-language version, again, no doubt, a result of the Production Code and the fear of offending white U.S. audiences in the South. This English-language version, in fact, deletes several key sequences that establish a milieu as well as the characters' relationship to it and to one another. For instance, Lola's relationship with the strongman, Mazeppa (Hans Albers), is cut short. And after Rath's jealous attack on Lola, when Kiepert (Kurt Gerron) comes to the storeroom to release him from his straightjacket, neither man says anything, which is in marked contrast to the German versions, where Kiepert sadly and compassionately asks Rath if all of this were really worth it for a woman. The German versions make it clear that Rath's crisis and humiliation are as much economic as psychological and sexual. Near the end of the film, Rath burns pages from the calendar that begins in 1923 and ends in 1929. Although both versions mark the passage of time through this device, only the German versions comment directly on the economic situation, which affects Mazeppa and Lola and the entire cabaret company, as well as the peculiar fate of a once-prominent professor.

In addition to the cutting of certain scenes and the revision of others, much erotic content is eliminated or underplayed in the English-language versions. My favorite example is when Rosa Valetti, who plays the magician's wife, sees Rath in Lola's dressing room holding Lola's underwear. In the English-language versions she merely shakes her finger and remains silent; she thereby functions as a moral observer (waving a tsk-tsk finger at Rath). In the German versions, by contrast, she spies the underwear, looks at him directly with a wry sense of humor and says, "I don't want to hear any complaints out of you!"

The question of language, of course, is fundamental to all films that are made available in multiple language formats. In *The Blue Angel*, especially, but not only in the English-language versions, it becomes clear that the film's narrative and dramatic weight is shifted to an English-speaking axis. When Rath first speaks to Lola in German, she responds quizzically, "Sorry, you'll have to talk my language," as if she doesn't understand him. American vernacular is also added to the English-language versions, most always in connection with Lola, who is made to speak such lines as: "Hold your horses!" "Fold up Your Tent" (for shut up), "Patriotic Hokum" (in response to the words of a German song), and "Shake a leg." In the English-language versions, moreover, she is an English actress, and he is a German high school teacher. In the German versions she is a bohemian "artiste" (with all its attendant associations), whereas he teaches Shakespeare (a change instituted by Sternberg, since the author Rath quotes in the Mann novel is Homer). In the English-language versions Rath remains a one-dimensional tyrant: he forces his students to write the English word *the* two hundred times. In the German versions, by contrast, he assigns them an essay topic on Mark Antony, asking them to consider, "What would have happened if Mark Antony hadn't held his oration"—in other words, if he hadn't spoken on his own behalf.

Rath's choice of assignment has a particular resonance with his own condition, as he progressively loses his command of language and the authority of his position in the course of the film. For it is not merely the addition of dialogue or American slang but the painful silences that distinguish the English- from the German-language versions. Without a doubt this is a vestige of early sound cinema and underscores the hybridity, as well as the practical problems, of multiple language versions. As is well documented, Jannings had his own fears of and hesitations with the English language (Sternberg 1973, 123–51). And Dietrich, who spoke very little English at this time—even though her contract specified that the film be shot in two versions—ostensibly required the talents of Berlin's best vocal coach to improve her voice. Friedrich Hollander created songs that would disguise Dietrich's linguistic deficiencies; most of them are based on two notes, with many words half-spoken rather than sung.

But the cumulative effect of these changes is to diminish our sympathy for Rath and to downplay Lola's eroticism, as well as the sexual and emotional complexity of their relationship. One key sequence illuminates these differences most forcefully. The sequence involves the public revelation of Rath's infatuation with Lola and takes place in his classroom. In the German versions the headmaster overhears the rioting in Rath's classroom, runs down the hall, enters the room, and admonishes the students to sit down. He looks at the students' drawings of Rath and Lola on the blackboard. His first comment is, "Not bad." He sides with the students and then vilifies Lola, to which Rath responds with gallantry and strong words; this is no loose woman but a woman who will become his wife. The action in this sequence revolves solely around Rath's words: his sudden decision to marry Lola, which seems to surprise even him, establishes him as courageous and principled; he is not just a tyrant or humiliated victim. The headmaster, by contrast, emerges from this encounter as a petty bureaucrat who has no problem with Rath's relationship with

Lola, only with his decision to marry her. He then passes the decision about Rath's fate on to higher authorities.

In the English versions the action proceeds differently. In a clear attempt to cut down on English dialogue, the scene is played almost in silence; the headmaster makes no mention of the art work or Lola but merely says, "I'm sorry my friend. You leave me no choice. I must request your resignation." Rath has no words to defend Lola or himself; in fact, he doesn't speak at all. The change undoubtedly has to do with the inability of the supporting cast to speak English and perhaps also with the demands of the Hayes Code. Of course, Rath is dismissed in both versions because he has had sex outside marriage. The German versions, however, attack the phenomenal hypocrisy of a situation in which he can sleep with Lola but cannot, as upstanding member of the bourgeoisie and *Gymnasiallehrer*, actually marry "a woman like that" and retain his position.

Significantly, Jannings is linked with death from the beginning of the film. Whether he is associated with his dead canary or the fate of the silent clown, whom we only later realize was once Lola's lover, Rath's gradual progress toward the vaudeville stage and loss of language are symbols that point to his inevitable degradation and destruction. To be sure, Jannings's star persona was built on such degradation and humiliation, yet with *The Blue Angel* Rath's—or rather, Jannings's—humiliation seems much more poignant and profound. As many critics have noted, the film was supposed to launch Jannings from the silent screen to the sound film and solidify his reputation as international cinema's premiere performer, but instead it inaugurated Dietrich's career. In this recounting Jannings becomes emblematic of German silent cinema more generally: trained in the expressionistic, theatrical tradition, Jannings could not compete with Dietrich's cooler, surface-oriented, cinematic style. As one critic puts it, "As Rath, Jannings gives a tour de force of mannerist acting, easily superior to that of *The Last Laugh* and *Variety*, the themes of which *The Blue Angel* recalls. His style was a dying one ... but as Lola, Marlene Dietrich began a collaboration with the director that was to result in one of the most original creations in the history of cinema" (Baxter 1971, 70).

This is, of course, a standard interpretation and one not without merit. But it misses what was also lost, or at least what was muted and ultimately transformed, in international film culture at this time. To be sure, Lola Lola, the cabaret singer, returns in *Morocco* (1930) as Amy Jolly, the exotic and unknown woman with the mysterious past, fully the product of Paramount's public-relations machine. This unknowability, however, was adapted to a new and profoundly Hollywood cinematic style: *Morocco* is suggestive whereas *The Blue Angel* is erotic, although in the case of the English-language version, the sexuality remains understated if nonetheless understood. As John Baxter points out, the mixture was very much to American tastes, and "Paramount signed director and star to contracts for a further three films, at a much higher salary" (Baxter 1971, 81).

The Blue Angel obviously reflects on the tensions—cultural, aesthetic, economic, social—that so define the hybridity of this period: the tensions between theater and cinema, Europe and America, the Old World and the New, youth and age, high culture and low. In *The Blue Angel*, of course, just as in *The Last Command* or even *The Jazz Singer*, these tensions are given embodiment in the central characters and, in the case of this particular film, in the themes of German versus English, the cabaret versus Shakespeare. I nevertheless submit that *The Blue Angel* is not simply a film about Jannings or the loss of the Old World to the New. In fact, what remains distinctive about *The Blue Angel* is the peculiarity of an international urban culture, defined as much by New York as by Berlin in the 1920s, which Dietrich has since come to embody and personify. In an essay on "Marlene Dietrich and German Nationalism," Gertrud Koch discusses this distinctiveness by describing Dietrich's Lola as "the image iconic of both memory and leaving; the image of a woman as openly sexual and lascivious as she is motherly; an image that died, along with the Weimar Republic, in National Socialism."[10]

This returns us to where we began—to the question of how we might best understand this film's national and historical status. We must be attentive to the history of the film's multiple productions and the histories of its multiple receptions in the period of time spanning the late 1920s until today. A recently released Kino DVD of the film, for example, boasts the inclusion of a new, more complete English-language version of *The Blue Angel*. This latest version is promoted as "definitive"—superior to the English-language version that circulated for almost two decades on VHS (and earlier in the United States, I assume, on film). To be sure, the new Kino DVD reveals many surprises. For example, in this English-language version, Jannings's name remains above the opening title—unlike the VHS version, which features Dietrich's name first. The maid still discovers and incinerates the dead bird. Rath still is seen gazing at the postcard of Lola, and the shot of the postcard marks the transition to the cabaret, as in the German version. Rath also shyly admits that the underwear is in the parcel he brings to Lola on the second night. Even more significant, the pan over the racially mixed audience during Rath's introduction from the side balcony is the same as in the German-language version.

Rather than the definitive or original or uncontested version, it would therefore appear that some of the English-language version scenes were shot in more than one way—for different English-language audiences. Indeed, several of the English-language passages in the Kino DVD clearly are dubbed, and the production notes indicate that some dubbing and reshooting of the English version was undertaken in May 1930, under the direction of Carl Winston, after Sternberg and Dietrich were gone. So what are we to make of this most-recent version of *The Blue Angel*? Some scholars have suggested that it is critical to establish and reconstruct the original version of this film—and, indeed, of other notable German films (such as G. W. Pabst's *The Joyless Street*). Indeed, some have gone so far as to claim that film historians such as myself have "only seen mutilated versions that in no way represent the original, leading them to false conclusions, based on the evidence that only existed in such false versions" (Horak 1998).

Given the very status of *The Blue Angel* as copy, it would seem pointless to establish which version of the film—in either English or German—stands as the "original." This is not to say, of course, that analysis of the multiple versions of this multiple-language film might not shed significant light on different historical contexts of the film's reception. The 1947 German version, for instance, which closes with Dietrich onstage rather than closing with Rath in his classroom, would seem to respond directly to Dietrich's new status and visibility as radio star and American patriot following World War II. Furthermore, as I suggested earlier, the 1990s English-language version, with its elision of significant scenes, especially the scene of the racially mixed cabaret audience, would appear to be the U.S. release of the film in the 1930s, given what we know about the Production Code at this time and its overriding concern (in the case of this film, as well as many others) not to offend white audiences in the South. Needless to say, the instability of *The Blue Angel* and its multiple language versions makes it impossible to pretend that the Kino DVD restores the work in its supposedly timeless originality. It exists only as another copy, yet another compelling remnant of an international film and urban culture without an original, which was endlessly copied but never equaled in the United States and lost entirely to Germany in the 1930s. This is the historical legacy of *The Blue Angel* in all of its versions and why it remains so compelling for rethinking the history of national cinemas within international film culture today.

NOTES

This chapter was adapted from a longer piece on *The Blue Angel*, both versions written in close collaboration with Nataša Ďurovičová, who has written extensively on multiple-language versions. Her research and arguments have inspired my thinking here, as elsewhere.

1. For an excellent discussion of these issues see Kosta, forthcoming.
2. See Pommer 1932. This article, among many others written by Pommer at the time, is included in English translation in Higson and Maltby 1999, 325–96.
3. On Parufamet see Kreimeier 1996; and Saunders 1994.
4. Interestingly, in his 1930 review of the film in *Die Neue Rundschau* (Berlin), Kracauer expresses an alternative view of the film: "This film," he writes, "avoids with an assiduity which must have been exhausting, any reference which could move us to include present social conditions. It suppresses the social environment which would force itself upon the naïve spectator of Unrat's catastrophe, it tears the performers out of any social context in which they have gained contemporary significance and places them in a vacuum. Neither Lola nor Unrat has enough air to breathe, which confirms the claim that it is less

the reality of their existence that is to be demonstrated, than the existence of reality that is to be veiled" (translated and reprinted in Baxter 1980, 22).

5. As Sarris puts it, "The film was produced simultaneously in German and English language versions for the maximum benefit of the Paramount-UFA combine in world markets, and thus with this one excursion to Europe all the ambiguity of Sternberg's origins reappeared as the 'von' in his name was finally vindicated. After *The Blue Angel*, Sternberg would once more be treated in retrospect as a European legend corrupted by Hollywood lucre" (1980, 697).

6. I owe this insight to Nataša Ďurovičová.

7. B. G. Bravermann wrote in a 1934 issue of *Experimental Cinema*: "In Sternberg we have a director who concentrates on surface effects, who emphasizes the externals of film mechanics in a most inarticulate manner and represents his own delirious fancies as real life" (repr. in Baxter 1980, 29).

8. As Sternberg (1973) relates: "Every notable in Berlin was on my stage at one time or another. Not only representatives of the press, writers, actors, directors, and even Max Reinhardt were present (his main concern was how a sibilant could be recorded), but sculptors and painters, among them George Grosz, who gave me a book on his work" (143).

9. The DVD box lists the running times as 106 minutes (German), 94 (English), but the films actually clock in at 102 (German) and 100 (English).

10. Koch quotes a previously unpublished text by Franz Hessel from the 1920s: "Those dangerous women incarnated by Marlene Dietrich do not give one the feeling that they mean too much harm. As cheery Lola from the Blue Angel, she takes the schoolteacher's ruffled, bearded head in her kind and maternal hands, pats the cheeks of this man so tenderly enchanted by her as though he were a child, looks up at her poor victim with a bridal smile when he makes this supremely unworthy woman his wife, and smiles him his dream of pure happiness" (1993, 13).

REFERENCES

Baxter, John. 1971. *The Cinema of Josef von Sternberg*. London: A. S. Barnes.

Baxter, Peter, ed. 1980. *Sternberg*. London: BFI.

Benjamin, Walter. 1999. "The Work of Art in the Age of Mechanical Reproduction." Repr. in translation in *Film Theory and Criticism: Introductory Readings*, ed. Leo Braudy and Marshall Cohen, 731–51. 5th ed. New York: Oxford University Press.

Bouvier, Michel. 1978. "Hollywood on Spree." *Ça cinéma* 18:19–35.

Hamilton, Mary Beth. 1997. *When I'm Bad I'm Better: Mae West, Sex, and American Entertainment*. Berkeley: University of California Press.

Higson, Andrew, and Richard Maltby, eds. 1999. *"Film Europe" and "Film America": Cinema, Commerce, and Cultural Exchange, 1920–1939*. Devon: University of Exeter Press.

Horak, Jan-Christopher. 1998. "Film History and Film Preservation: Reconstructing the Text of *The Joyless Street* (1925)." *Screening the Past*, no. 5: www.latrobe.edu.au/screeningthepast/firstrelease/fir1298/jhfr5b.html (accessed April 30, 2008).

Koch, Gertrud. 1986. "Between Two Worlds: Von Sternberg's *The Blue Angel* (1930)." In *German Film and Literature: Adaptations and Transformations*, ed. Eric Rentschler, 60–72. New York: Methuen.

——. 1993. "Exorcised: Marlene Dietrich and German Nationalism." In *Women and Film: A Sight and Sound Reader*, ed. Pam Cook and Philip Dodd, 10–15. Philadelphia: Temple University Press.

Kosta, Barbara. Forthcoming. *Willing Seduction:* The Blue Angel, *Marlene Dietrich, and Mass Culture*. New York: Palgrave.

Kracauer, Siegfried. 1947. *From Caligari to Hitler: A Psychological History of the German Film*. Princeton, NJ: Princeton University Press.

Kreimeier, Klaus. 1996. *The Ufa Story: A History of Germany's Greatest Film Company, 1918–1945*. New York: Hill and Wang.

Pommer, Erich. 1932. "The International Talking Film." In *Universal Filmlexikon*, ed. Frank Arnau, 4–15. Berlin: Universal Filmlexikon.

Sarris, Andrew. 1980. "'The Blue Angel' and 'Morocco.'" In *Great Film Directors: A Critical Anthology*, ed. Leo Braudy and Morris Dickstein, 697–702. New York: Oxford University Press.

Saunders, Thomas J. 1994. *Hollywood in Berlin: American Cinema and Weimar Germany*. Berkeley: University of California Press.

Sternberg, Josef von. 1973. *Fun in a Chinese Laundry*. New York: Collier.

Vasey, Ruth, and Richard Maltby. 1994. "The International Language Problem: European Reactions to Hollywood's Conversion to Sound." In *Hollywood in Europe: Experiences of a Cultural Hegemony* (Amsterdam: VU University Press, 1994), 68–93.

FOURTEEN

COMING OUT OF THE UNIFORM

POLITICAL AND SEXUAL EMANCIPATION IN
LEONTINE SAGAN'S *MÄDCHEN IN UNIFORM* (1931)

RICHARD W. MCCORMICK

At home, you know, they are always talking about the time that is coming when we shall need soldiers again, and mothers of soldiers.

CHRISTA WINSLOE, *Girls in Uniform* (1930)

We sat together at the movies, it was a film about girls in uniform. They were high-class girls, but it was the same for them as for me. You care for someone, and what you get sometimes is tears and a red nose. You care for someone—it can't be understood at all, it makes no lousy difference whether it's a man or a woman or dear God almighty.

IRMGARD KEUN, *The Artificial Silk Girl* (1932)

The most well-known German woman to direct films remains Leni Riefenstahl. But before her famous propaganda film for the Nazis, *Triumph of the Will* (1935), and before her directorial debut with the "mountain film" *The Blue Light* (1932), there was another film made by a woman, one that was not only a national but an international success, and one with very different politics. This antiauthoritarian film was the most famous film made during the Weimar Republic by a woman, and, given how often male writers and intellectuals have demonized new models of gender and sexual behavior in Weimar—e.g., Erich Kästner (1931); Siegfried Kracauer (1947); and Peter Gay (1968)—it is important to discuss this film because it celebrated an almost unspoken form of sexuality that threatened the status quo.

This 1931 film is *Mädchen in Uniform* (*Girls in Uniform*), and it was not only directed by a woman, Leontine Sagan, but it was also adapted from a popular stage drama written by a woman (Christa Winsloe) and acted by an all-female cast. It was a popular and entertaining film that nonetheless took a clear position in favor of Weimar's most democratic and emancipatory tendencies and in opposition to the authoritarian and repressive forces mobilizing to destroy the republic in the crisis years of the early 1930s. Hitler's ascension to power in 1933 would put an end to the relative tolerance for the blurring and transgressing of traditional gender and sexual boundaries that had characterized popular culture in Germany's first democracy.

Mädchen in Uniform is a film that is implicated within a number of progressive and emancipatory discourses of the late Weimar Republic: the movement for homosexual rights and the flourishing of urban, queer subcultures; "New Objectivity" and other avant-garde tendencies in the arts and popular culture; and the intersection of modernity, the movies, and democratic egalitarianism. It is with regard to such discourses about gender and sexuality, as well as about aesthetics and politics, that I will attempt to contextualize this film.

The film can be considered an early antifascist film; certainly its representation of authoritarian, militaristic "Prussianism" is clearly negative. Although women in the film are by no means portrayed as innocent of Prussianism—the film's "villain" is after all the boarding school's headmistress—the film nonetheless depicts the school's values as both antidemocratic and patriarchal. And the greatest threat to such a value system turns out to be women's emotional attachments, which are portrayed as disruptive of the school's rules and hierarchy. The school's authoritarian values are shown in turn to be deadly.

As B. Ruby Rich (1984) asserted in her famous essay on the film, over the course of the film's reception its antiauthoritarian stance was almost always emphasized, while its sexual politics were mostly ignored until the 1970s. This is evident in two of the most canonical verdicts on the film, written by German critics who first saw the film in 1931 but at the time of their writing, years after its initial release, were in exile: writing in 1947, Siegfried Kracauer discussed the film exclusively in terms of its antiauthoritarianism, which he found too meek, including it in a chapter titled "Timid Heresies" (1947, 226–29). In *The Haunted Screen* (which originally appeared in French in 1952), Lotte Eisner was much more positive, calling *Mädchen in Uniform* the "last word" on the repressive practices of the Prussian aristocracy (Eisner 1969, 325–26). Eisner's main interest in this film (and all films) was aesthetic, but by implying that its stylistic beauty can be ascribed to Sagan's "feminine reading" of German film traditions, she anticipated some potential for a feminist interpretation. To the extent she dealt with the film's sexual politics, however, her reading was problematic.

Sexuality has complicated the film's reception from the very beginning. Central to its narrative is a fairly overt homoeroticism. Critics for years tended to downplay the erotic aspect of the schoolgirl Manuela's infatuation for her teacher Fräulein von Bernburg. Kracauer, for instance, in disagreeing with the critical consensus about the extent (and the "boldness") of the film's antiauthoritarianism, nonetheless manages to repress almost any allusion to the film's homoeroticism, leading one to suspect that for him Manuela's love for Bernburg was a distasteful "trivialization" of any political message in the film.[1]

When the film was rediscovered in the 1970s, it became a cult film in the United States, England, and France among feminists. Many lesbians had a special appreciation for the film, considering it an early "coming-out" film that affirmed love between women. The reaction of many German feminists to this reception of the film was that it was too simple, that it ignored the film's politics and its original historical context (Gramann and Schlüpmann 1981; Lenssen, Fehervary, and Mayne 1981–82). In the early 1980s Rich wrote a long and persuasive discussion of the film, with extensive research into its political and historical context; she maintained that the film is indeed a lesbian "coming-out" film (Rich 1993, 64) and that there is no contradiction between the film's sexual politics and its antifascism: in fact they are integrally related. Richard Dyer has done a thorough analysis of the film's place within gay and lesbian debates on homosexuality in the 1920s (Dyer 1990, 31–60).

There are, however, critics and scholars who question reading the film as either a coming-out film or as an antifascist film. Lisa Ohm (1993) has argued that *Mädchen in Uniform* is not at all about coming out, and she offers a much more negative reading of the film's politics with regard to fascism (more or less agreeing with Kracauer 1947). She stresses the dominant influence of the film's producer, Carl Froelich, hardly an antifascist, as it would turn out. Froelich had great control over the look of the film and the shape of the narrative, and he created the happy ending of the film, which reversed the ending in Winsloe's original play. Christa Reinig (1983) sees this changed ending as completely contradicting Winsloe's intentions. Other objections have to do with the issue of motherhood as it is depicted in the film: does Fräulein von Bernburg represent a substitute mother to Manuela or an object of erotic desire for her—or both? Jeanne Ellen Freiburg (1994) connects the discourse on motherhood in the film to reactionary social ideologies and forces in the early 1930s. Is the film about lesbianism, mothering, or both, and what difference does this make for the evaluation of the film's politics? Does the film attempt to subvert, or is it too "timid" or even in some sense complicit with the rise of fascism? In attempting to answer these questions, I maintain that it is useful to contextualize the film in terms of its relation to the cultural sensibility known as "New Objectivity" in the middle and later years of the Weimar Republic.

FROM STAGE TO SCREEN

The screenplay for *Mädchen in Uniform* was adapted from a play by Christa Winsloe that had gone through two versions. It was produced first in Leipzig as *Ritter Nérestan* (*The Knight Nerestan*) in 1930, directed by Otto Werther and starring

FIGURE 14.1   Just before the
kiss: soon after this encounter in
the dormitory between Fräulein
von Bernburg (Dorothea Wieck)
and Manuela (Hertha Thiele)
in Leontine Sagan's *Mädchen in
Uniform* (1931), Bernburg kisses
Manuela on the lips. Courtesy of
the Filmmuseum Berlin, Stiftung
Deutsche Kinemathek.

Hertha Thiele as Manuela; then it was produced in Berlin as *Gestern und Heute*
(*Yesterday and Today*) in 1931, directed by Leontine Sagan, first with Gina Falkenberg as Manuela, and then with Hertha Thiele in the lead role. Both versions were
great popular successes, so much so that plans were made to film it. The film was
completed later in 1931, and it was produced by Carl Froelich, who was listed in the
credits as responsible for "artistic supervision" ("künstlerische Oberleitung"); he
also chose the film's title, *Mädchen in Uniform*. With some supervision by Froelich,
then, Sagan directed the film. Winsloe cowrote the screenplay with F. S. Andam,
and Thiele played Manuela. The film became a big hit, both within Germany and
internationally, and the critics generally praised it as well: "One spoke of the best
film of the year. In the USA, too, the critics were enthusiastic" (Wendtland 1990,
223). Like the original play, the film is the story of fourteen-and-a-half-year-old
Manuela, whose mother has been dead for some time and whose father is an officer.
Manuela is brought by her aunt to a boarding school for the daughters of Prussian
officers and nobility. The school is characterized by the rigid, authoritarian discipline demanded by its headmistress, who is determined to raise obedient "mothers of soldiers." The school also seems to be in rather bad financial straits, feeding

and clothing its charges in an extremely stingy manner; the headmistress tries to portray this as a virtue, saying, "We Prussians have starved ourselves to greatness!" ("Wir Preußen haben uns groß gehungert!").

The only sympathetic teacher is Fräulein von Bernburg, who modifies her strictness with a fair amount of open kindness and affection, symbolized best perhaps by her ritual of giving a good-night kiss on the forehead to each one of the girls in her dormitory (Fig. 14.1). Learning that Manuela has lost her mother, Bernburg shows her some special attention, and Manuela responds to this unaccustomed kindness by breaking the unspoken rules of the ritualized good-night kiss on the first night she experiences it. She throws her arms around Bernburg, and Bernburg then kisses her on the lips in one of the most famous close-ups of the film. Manuela becomes so infatuated with Bernburg that she cannot perform well in her class. Bernburg, learning from the staff that Manuela's underclothes are in woeful shape, gives the pupil a chemise to wear from her own underwear drawer.

Manuela gives an outstanding performance in the school play, dressed as a man in the leading role of Schiller's *Don Carlos* (Fig. 14.2). Getting drunk on spiked punch at the party after the play, she tells the other girls of the chemise from Bernburg that she is wearing, and she proclaims her love for the teacher. The headmistress witnesses this proclamation and declares a scandal; she has Manuela isolated from all contact with the other girls, and she forbids Bernburg to see her again. Bernburg does talk to Manuela but only to explain why it is best that they do not see each other anymore. The headmistress berates Bernburg for doing even that much, and this leads to a showdown between the two women. Bernburg defends Manuela's feelings as love, not sin, and she declares that she will resign rather than continue to watch the headmistress turn the girls into scared and timid creatures. Meanwhile those very girls, concerned about Manuela, break the rules and begin to search for her. Bernburg, too, has a premonition that something is wrong, and she joins them just as they have found Manuela—just as they succeed in stopping her at the last minute from jumping to her death from the top of the school's central stairwell. Bernburg confronts the headmistress with the tragedy that has been only barely averted. Stunned and for the first time silenced, the headmistress walks away down the corridor, seemingly defeated; meanwhile, the military bugles of Potsdam sound outside the school.

Kracauer mentions the bugles at the end of the film to make his point that the revolt was merely a "timid heresy": the authority structure outside the school remains unchanged by anything that has gone on inside it. The only thing that happens inside the school is the victory of Bernburg, who has only attempted to humanize its authoritarian system, something that Kracauer sees as "in the interest of its preservation" (1947, 228–29). This interpretation, however, overlooks the transformation of Bernburg at the end of the film: as Rich argues, up to this point

FIGURE 14.2   Manuela in drag: Manuela as Don Carlos, who confronts his "forbidden love," his stepmother, the queen. Courtesy of the Filmmuseum Berlin. Stiftung Deutsche Kinemathek.

she has indeed played "good cop" to the headmistress's "bad cop" (1993, 68–69), but in her final debate with the headmistress she decides to quit the "system" altogether, now fully aware of the toll it takes on the girls. On learning that her complicity with the system has nearly killed Manuela, she only becomes more defiant, not less (Rich 1993, 76–78). As for Kracauer's charge that the "happy" ending of the film ignores larger political forces, the fact is that his point about outside forces is made by the film itself. It relativizes the headmistress's defeat with those very bugles, reminding us of the powerful patriarchal militarism beyond the walls of the school. The ending is more open than he would have it: Manuela survives, but what happens next is unclear.

The political warning in the film about the situation in Germany is actually fairly explicit. Edelgard, the schoolgirl whose pedigree is the most aristocratic of all her classmates, states: "At home, you know, they are always talking about the time that is coming when we shall need soldiers again, and mothers of soldiers" (cf. Winsloe 1933, 61). This makes the implications of the headmistress's views about the purpose of educating her charges very clear in the context of Germany in the early 1930s— and the accuracy of the prediction is uncanny. For earlier in the film, the headmistress stressed the goal of creating "mothers of soldiers"—and the film's opposition to all that the headmistress stands for is unmistakable. Also relevant is the fact that most of the important figures who made the film—Winsloe, Sagan, Thiele—went into exile soon after the Nazi seizure of power (*Machtergreifung*) in 1933.

One person who did not go into exile and who played a very important role in making the film was Carl Froelich, who continued his filmmaking career successfully through the Third Reich. After his production of the anti-Prussian *Mädchen in Uniform*, Froelich would go on to direct *The Hymn of Leuthen* (*Der Choral von Leuthen*, 1933), one of the many films (from the 1920s into the 1940s) that catered to nationalist tastes by glorifying Prussian history. According to Hertha Thiele in a 1981 interview, Froelich was involved in the decision that banned her from film acting in the Third Reich. She also stated that in making *Mädchen in Uniform*, it had been Froelich who tried to mute the play's homoeroticism for commercial reasons (Thiele 1981, 34).

Among the people who made the film, the only women definitely known to be lesbian were Winsloe, who was actually "coming out" during the very years that the various versions of the story were written (Dyer 1990, 35), and Erika Mann, who played the teacher who directs the play in the film, Fräulein von Attems. But the argument for a lesbian reading of *Mädchen in Uniform* is based on much more than these biographical facts. Thiele explained that in the first production of the play, the Leipzig production, its lesbian aspect had been more or less avoided but that Leontine Sagan's Berlin production of the play was different: "Sagan had directed the play back then in the theater as purely lesbian." Margarete Melzer played Bernburg in the Berlin play, and Thiele characterized Melzer as "a completely masculine type" ("ein absolut männlicher Typ"; Thiele 1981, 32). One of Froelich's attempts to mute the lesbianism of the Berlin production was thus to replace Melzer with the much more stereotypically "feminine" Dorothea Wieck. As first noted by Gramann and Schlüpmann (1981, 30), who interviewed Thiele, one gets the impression from Thiele's comments that there was a split between the makers of the film, Sagan and Winsloe being on one side and Froelich on the other, with Froelich having the advantage of technical knowledge of film production and control of the film crew on his side.

MÄDCHEN AND NEW OBJECTIVITY?

Lotte Eisner's only reference to questions of sexual identity in *Mädchen in Uniform* "contrives to make the film sound somewhat anti-lesbian" (Dyer 1990, 32). She asserts that the film touches on a mere adolescent "phase," implying that the school is to blame for misreading an otherwise normal adolescent phase of confusion (Eisner 1969, 326; see also Krusche 1993, 339–40). Eisner ascribes the film's high aesthetic quality to Sagan's "feminine reading of the *Kammerspielfilm* [chamber-play film]," which "led her to turn her back on the 'new objectivity'" (Eisner 1969, 325). There can be no doubt that New Objectivity was in many ways perceived as a very "masculine" sensibility and that *Mädchen in Uniform* can be read as a very "feminine" film (Dyer 1990, 38–41). The *Kammerspielfilm* tradition that Eisner mentions, however, was arguably much more naturalistic than expressionistic. Whereas in the early 1920s, in a *Kammerspielfilm* like Leopold Jessner's *Hintertreppe* (1921), there was undoubtedly expressionistic exaggeration in acting style and set design, little of that can be found in *Mädchen in Uniform*.

Beyond such quibbles about genre and style, however, the film can be related to New Objectivity and various discourses associated with it in a number of ways. For a start, of course, one only needs to mention the film's emancipatory sexual politics that Eisner manages to distort. In addition, the film manifests a number of specific, positive attitudes toward phenomena commonly associated with modernity in Weimar: jazz, the adulation of film stars, "trashy" popular novels, and "sex appeal." It is important to remember that the Americanism and the modern mass culture so celebrated in New Objectivity meant above all three things: "sports, the movies, and jazz" (Lindner 1994, 171).

The film sets up a number of clear oppositions both on the narrative and the stylistic level, all of which work to portray the aristocratic "old order" negatively and a new, emerging "modern" order in positive terms. The hierarchical, militaristic, and antidemocratic order that the school upholds is obviously embodied by the headmistress, whose bearing, medallion, gait, and cane are obvious allusions to Frederick the Great of Prussia, as commentators since Eggebrecht (1931, 11) have noted (cf. Kracauer 1947, 226). Next in the hierarchy comes the headmistress's toady, Fräulein von Kesten, and then the intimidated, insecure, competitive staff of teachers. The obvious exception is Bernburg, whose reformist humanism leads her eventually to revolt and to side with the pupils, the young girls who best embody an emerging modern, democratic, egalitarian order. It is the world of the girls that provides the strongest contrast to the stifling military discipline, the archaic pomp, and the hypocrisy of the school and all it represents. The girls are characterized by their pranks, their love of modern mass culture, their insouciant rebelliousness (exemplified best by the character Ilse), their enthusiasm and emotion, their crushes on each other, and ultimately their insurrectionary solidarity, which saves Manuela from suicide.

The association of the girls with modernity and mass culture is clear: in the locker room Ilse proudly shows off her hidden collage of photos of the film star Hans Albers, arguing that he has more "sex appeal"—she uses the English term—than the actress Henny Porten, who is apparently the favorite film star of some of the other girls. Meanwhile there is an amusing visual reference to Weimar's obsession with sports and body culture, as two other girls giggle at pin-ups of scantily clad

FIGURE 14.3 Jazzing it up: after the play the schoolgirls dance to popular tunes at the party.
Courtesy of the Filmmuseum Berlin, Stiftung Deutsche Kinemathek.

male athletes. Finding the romantic novel Manuela is reading, Ilse grabs it, opens
it, and reads a "racy" passage aloud to the girls. The girls are obviously attracted to
"trivial" romance novels and other mass cultural pleasures, all of which are forbidden. At the party after Manuela's bravura performance of Schiller (high culture but
in drag), the girls quickly tire of waltzes and demand jazz from their fellow pupil at
the piano (Fig. 14.3). The headmistress and the school are tied to an older high culture, and even that culture appears to be a censored, very narrow, rather uncom-
prehending version of German classicism. As the headmistress has tea with the
aristocratic alumnae, they worry about Schiller writing too "freely."

    In stylistic terms the film—like most German films of the era—is indebted to
the chiaroscuro effects created by lighting techniques first developed during the
early expressionist cinema of the 1920s. Some of the ways in which the film uses
lighting correspond to a dualistic scheme opposing innocence to evil, as exemplified most obviously by the bright close-ups of blond Manuela in contrast to the
dark costumes of the headmistress and the staff and the shadowy, confining spaces
of the school or the looming abyss of the staircase so central to the structure of
both the school and the narrative. But even with regard to the filming of the staircase there is ambiguity in the use of shadows, for it is here that Bernburg first sees
Manuela, before the latter notices her. As Bernburg looks over the pupil approv-
ingly (indeed, with a mixture of voyeurism and desire), the shadows over the stair-

well seem to convey both danger and erotic tension. Even more ambiguous, and not at all chiaroscuro, is the muted lighting of the dormitory after Bernburg dims the lights to begin the nightly ritual of the good-night kiss: here there is little that is ominous, only the creation of an aura that has something of religious ritual yet also romantic and erotic undertones.

As in most early German sound films, there is some music and some singing. There is martial music over the opening montage, and it will continue to be associated with the visual images of Prussian power with which the film opens, so that when the bugles are heard at the end of the film, those images will be evoked without being shown. The martial music is undermined from the very beginning of the film, however, by undertones in the music expressing a fanciful lightness that can be associated with the girls who are such unwilling initiates into this militaristic order. This levity is also emphasized when the girls are shown singing—the beauty of their voices reminds us of the song heard outside the classroom window in Josef von Sternberg's *The Blue Angel* (1930), but here we see the girls singing. The patriotism of the lyrics of this song glorifying Prussia is undermined by the close-up of Ilse and the amplification of her voice as she turns praise for Prussia into a complaint about the meager diet at the school. And of course there is jazz, associated with the party when "innocent Manuela" makes her rebellious declaration of love.

It is the style of montage that opens the film, however, that best illustrates how distinct it is from expressionist style—and how much it, like so many other German films since the mid-1920s, betrays the influence of Soviet filmmaking, which since the success of Eisenstein's *Potemkin* had been as great as the influence of Chaplin and the American cinema. As Rich (1993, 63, 83) notes, the documentary montage that depicts the authoritarian Prussian grandeur of Potsdam not only provides a dynamic contrast to the more theatrical interior scenes of the film, with its moving camera and quick cutting; it also performs an important narrative function. At the very beginning of the film it establishes the oppressive social context of which the school is an integral part, and it is to an economically brief reprise of similar shots of that outside world to which the film returns at two crucial moments: just after the close-up of Bernburg's kissing Manuela on the lips, and again after she gives her the chemise. Thus after two of the most important events in the narrative of the love developing between Bernburg and Manuela, the film reminds the viewer of the dominant authoritarian (and patriarchal) order violated by these erotic infractions.

Also significant is the contrast between the visual content of the opening montage and the style with which it is filmed. The neoclassical palaces and statues of Potsdam, with their obvious attempt to claim a timeless authority for a relatively young aristocratic order, are filmed with a constructivist tension that in effect deconstructs their symmetrical harmony and their pompous veneer of high culture.

These architectural structures could not be more distinct from favored constructivist (and social realist) subjects: cranes, factories, modern buildings, construction sites (there is such a sequence in Brecht and Dudow's *Kuhle Wampe* of 1932, which also featured Hertha Thiele). But while the content of the opening images is neoclassical, the manner in which they are filmed accentuates angles and diagonals in tension. Structures designed to emanate classical harmony are framed so as to make them seem grotesque and asymmetrical, and this technique can also be noted in the shots of the famous stairwell in the school. The building used in the film was Potsdam's Kaiserin-Augusta Stift, the very boarding school Winsloe herself had attended as a child (Thiele 1981, 34). The school's stairwell, like the building itself, was built in a style that emphasized neoclassical grace and harmony, but the stairwell is shot from high above and from such oblique angles that it appears quite ominous and almost abstract.

There is thus an obvious polarization in the film on both stylistic and narrative levels: between an authoritarian regime garbed in neoclassical grace and a modern dissonant style of camerawork and editing; between that repressive order on the outside of the school and the antiauthoritarian—and sexual—revolt breaking out on the inside of the school; between the Prussian rigidity of the headmistress and the spirited, democratic anarchy of the girls over whom she presides. To this polarization might be added the stylistic contrast between, on the one hand, the film's use of originally expressionist lighting techniques and, on the other hand, its use of montage and "documentary" footage of Potsdam and the school. In addition one could mention the use of so many nonactresses to portray the pupils: twenty-five girls from secondary schools all over Germany were selected to portray the pupils in the film (other than the important speaking roles such as Manuela, Ilse, and Edelgard; see "Von der höheren Tochterschule zum Film" 1931). Such details provide evidence of its connection to trends in New Objective/"realist" filmmaking in Germany in the late 1920s and early 1930s.

Some aspects of all this tension and conflict in the film may reflect the political polarization in the aftermath of the economic depression that began in late 1929: the tension between the right and the left, between authoritarian and democratic forces. In looking at the politics specifically depicted in the film, one might perhaps concur with Kracauer (1947) that the film is too timid with regard to the depiction of class in the film: the focus here is on a school for upper-class girls, after all. But the critique of the hierarchical values of the school is fairly clear in the film: the servants in the school are depicted positively and, like the girls, are shown to be irreverent about the attitudes of the people who run the school. The cross-cutting after the play, which juxtaposes the celebration of the girls with that of the servants, aligns those two groups against the staid tea party held by the headmistress with the aristocratic patronesses of the school.

And this tension between the authoritarian values of the school and the more democratic values of the students and the servants is clearly related to the deep political polarization that had characterized the Weimar Republic from the beginning. It may have eased a bit during the "stabilized" prosperity after 1924, but it had never disappeared, as the crisis after 1929 made quite clear. On the narrative level, at any rate, this is clearly what the film is "about," whether or not one agrees with Kracauer that it is too timid in its attack on reactionary forces. This is also why (pace Freiburg 1994) it is not merely due to hindsight that it is persuasive to read the film as antifascist. The tensions within the film articulate political tensions between the right and the left that were quite real at the time. These were not new tensions, and they had very much to do with the struggle for power soon to be won by the fascists in Germany.

It is also true, however, that the polarization between reactionary evil and emancipated modernity as established in the film may be a bit too simple, indeed suspect, as Kracauer maintained. I would also assert that the polarization in the film can be related to other contentious debates about the film, not just with regard to whether it is truly antifascist but whether its politics on female identity and sexual identity are as progressive as we might like to think.

FEMALE IDENTITY: LESBIANISM AND/OR MOTHERHOOD?

As I have noted, some have asserted that the film is neither antifascist nor emancipatory in its sexual politics, in contradiction to Rich (1993) and Dyer (1990), who assert that it is both. Again: to what extent, if at all, is the film "lesbian"? As we have seen, the people most responsible for the film were working to some extent at cross-purposes: Winsloe and Sagan seem to have been committed to an openly lesbian film, at least from Thiele's characterization of the Berlin production of the play (Thiele 1981, 32), whereas Froelich wanted to make the thematization of lesbian love less overt (ibid., 34). Perhaps this topic is not completely explicit in the resulting film, yet many early critics acknowledged it, even though they often tried to dismiss it as something harmless, an adolescent phase. Most critics praised the film; in a more negative review there is perhaps more forthrightness: the conservative *Kinematograph* objected mostly to the satirizing of Potsdam (and national values), which it found unnecessary and in bad taste. But its review also contains the somewhat acid remark that viewers who have not been initiated into all "erotic specialties" might not understand what the film is about. Herbert Ihering, however, who was very positive about the film ("One of the best, cleanest, clearest films of the year"), was even more forthright, calling it a tragedy with a "slightly lesbian emphasis"(quoted in Wendtland 1990, 223).

Why was this lesbian aspect to the narrative only *slightly* emphasized? This may have been more the result of the fact that the filmmakers were working at cross-purposes than of anything specific that Froelich did. For some of the changes we know him to have made, in spite of his reputed intention to tone down any overt homoeroticism in the interest of commercial success, do not necessarily have the effect of lessening the lesbian component to the film, as Dyer demonstrates, at least within the context of lesbian and gay debates about homosexuality in the Weimar period. In that context the replacement of Melzer with Wieck in the role of Bernburg can be seen to signify the replacement of an androgynous "butch" or *Bubi*-style of lesbianism with a "female-identified" type of lesbianism.

According to Dyer's characterization of that specific historical context in Weimar, there were within both the male and female homosexual communities two main philosophies or discourses of homosexuality, as it were, each opposing the other but both part of the broader community. One was the androgynous, "in-betweenist" model, the "third sex" in Magnus Hirschfeld's famous formulation, including "masculinized" (or "butch") women and "feminized" men; the other was the same-sex identified model, that is, of male-identified ("butch") gay men and female-identified ("femme") lesbians. The advantage of the latter model for lesbians in a homophobic society was greater invisibility, and homophobia was increasing in late Weimar. Beyond this pragmatic consideration, however, the fact that in a film like *Mädchen in Uniform* the central relationship "can be seen as simultaneously a pupil-teacher, mother-daughter, and a lesbian one" is, as Dyer writes, an ambiguity that is "a source of delight" (1990, 39). Thus the film appeals both to a general female solidarity and to lesbian sensitivities in such a way as to make it difficult to separate the two—a pleasurable ambiguity that today would be considered queer.[2]

Furthermore, Dyer argues that one cannot avoid the lesbianism of the narrative by stressing motherless Manuela's search for a replacement mother figure. This stress on motherhood was the strategy behind the attempts Thiele describes for muting the film's lesbianism in the Leipzig production, and it remains the interpretive emphasis of a critic such as Ohm, who disputes that the film thematizes lesbianism in an emancipatory way. But Dyer asserts that the "mother-daughter quality" of the relationship between Manuela and Bernburg only makes the film "*more* lesbian, not less"—especially since it is a typical feature of early-twentieth-century lesbian novels (Dyer 1990, 55).

Nonetheless, the "female-identified" strategy could have negative political consequences for the film. Dyer clearly associates the "male-identified" tendency with reactionary tendencies in Weimar, namely a homosocial "masculinism" clearly aligned with the right and specifically with the Nazis (see Hewitt 1996). But Dyer admits no such problem with regard to the glorification of essential femininity within the "female-identified" tendency. In an era in which a very traditional cult of German womanhood, in combination with the cult of German motherhood, was about to triumph, however, this glorification seems more problematic. Indeed, in the early 1930s a return to traditional femininity was already triumphing over the fashionable trends a few years earlier associated with the "masculinized" New Woman.

On the simplest level: to the extent the lesbianism of the film remains camouflaged, it can be denied. This is what Lotte Eisner does: she compliments the film's "feminine" qualities while making it appear that Manuela's infatuation is merely a "phase" exacerbated in an "unhealthy" way by the school. And to the extent that the lesbianism is denied, the film becomes less radical. This is a dynamic, of course, that is still at work in much more recent films: "The unconscious deployment . . . of a cinematic lesbian continuum organized around the figure of the femme is politically and erotically ambiguous, both presenting and erasing lesbian identities and sexualities" (Holmlund 1991; quoted in Doty 1993, 44).

In the context of Germany in the early 1930s there is an even more troubling possibility: a much more conservative concept, that of a "separate sphere" for women, might be relevant to the film in a way that undermines its reputed antifascism. The concept of a "separate sphere" is what Claudia Koonz (1987) found so fundamental to explaining the willingness of women to cooperate with fascists. The attraction to the idea of a "separate sphere" for women was characteristic of many middle-class women, especially those involved in church groups and opposed to (or threatened by) any "emancipation," but also those in the bourgeois women's movement, especially its conservative wing. This attraction was connected to a number of elements: a distaste for the more "masculine" New Woman of the 1920s who worked in the "man's world"; a fear of the loss of middle-class privilege, which having to work often connoted for middle-class women; but also, as Koonz asserts, a somewhat realistic appraisal of how little equality with men had actually been won compared to what the Weimar Constitution had promised (Koonz 1987, 1–17). Competing with men seemed undesirable and/or futile, and the idea of a return to some mythic past wherein women could achieve some autonomy in their "traditional" sphere of influence seemed positive to some. Koonz maintains that this attitude helps to explain why so many women put up so little resistance to the victory of such an obviously misogynous movement as Nazism—and indeed why some women enthusiastically joined the National Socialist movement.

If this sort of "separate sphere" were indeed glorified in *Mädchen in Uniform*, it would indeed be troubling, but this is not the case. Such a sphere is thematized in the film, but it is criticized, not valorized. For the boarding school itself serves as—and to some extent represents—such a traditional "female sphere," and it is this aspect against which Manuela and Bernburg rebel: a school that keeps girls separate in order to train them to be obedient wives who will give birth to soldiers—precisely the role for women that National Socialism would soon gloriously proclaim. Here the erotic love of Manuela for Bernburg makes the rebellion all the more radical, for what could be a greater threat to the traditional female role than lesbianism, especially when that traditional role was defined so explicitly (both within the film and in the Weimar Republic in general, at least in its later years) in terms of motherhood, pronatalism, and militarism—giving birth to soldiers?

Lesbianism would certainly be a threat to a worldview whose goal for women above all is that they increase the birthrate. Lesbians, like other women, are usually able to give birth, and many are mothers, but this fact would probably not comfort the pronatalists, if it in fact occurred to them at all. Nonetheless, it can be argued that the discourse of motherhood pervades *Mädchen in Uniform*: certainly Bernburg describes her more nurturing teaching philosophy as explicitly "maternal," and her decision to stand up for Manuela is not only a courageous "coming out" but also a stand on behalf of all the young women whose spirits are being crushed by the school. Freiburg (1994) and Reisdorfer (1993, 192–203) both see maternalism as central to the film. Reisdorfer, however, reads the film's handling of maternity positively, in the tradition of German feminism, whereas Freiburg reads it negatively, connected ultimately to the reactionary gender politics of the Nazis.

The bourgeois ideology of motherhood had been used by feminists since the nineteenth century in Germany and elsewhere as strategy for increasing women's sphere of activity—the concept of "social motherhood," for instance, which justified women's move into professions like teaching, nursing, and social work. This strategy was pragmatic in the nineteenth century and not necessarily reactionary, but it was also related to reactionary tendencies, which would indeed lead to the cult of motherhood in fascism. It seems to me, however, that moving from a strict biological/reproductive understanding of motherhood obviously loosens the concept from biologically determinist/essentialist notions of femininity. Arguably, even "social motherhood" already establishes some distance from such notions. Lesbianism, however, when combined with a "maternal" concern for the welfare of younger women, certainly does it much more clearly—and in a way that the fascist cult of motherhood most definitely does *not*. Is not the "mothering" in *Mädchen in Uniform* actually a form of female solidarity that includes a defense of homoerotic love—and a defense that is mounted not only by lesbians?

It is true that—as Rich (1993) asserts—so long as Bernburg plays "good cop" by directing all the homoerotic impulses of the girls toward herself, thus making them both harmless and beneficial to the institution with which she is identified, Bernburg is complicit in shoring up the school as a traditionalist "separate sphere." But as soon as Manuela's love transgresses the bounds of what is allowed, Bernburg, after a somewhat craven period of hesitation, defiantly chooses to quit the school and openly side with Manuela.

Thus we must return to the question of how much the film mutes the explicitly lesbian nature of Manuela's love for Bernburg. Why does the headmistress scream "Skandal!" when she hears Manuela's speech about the chemise from Bernburg—

and about her love for Bernburg? Why does she demand Manuela be isolated and worry about "contagion"? Why does her chief flunky, Fräulein von Kesten, tell Edelgard that she is too young to understand exactly why Manuela must be isolated? Why does the headmistress tell Bernburg that Manuela's attitude is a "sin," and why does Bernburg defiantly reply that what the headmistress calls "sin" is "the great spirit of love which has a thousand forms"? While the film may allow some viewers to ignore or downplay its lesbianism (in harmony with Froelich's commercial motivations and intentions), the narrative really does not make sense without it.

There has nonetheless been some disagreement about whether the film actually depicts Bernburg's coming out (as opposed to Manuela's). Rich (1993) asserts that it does, but Gramann and Schlüpmann (1981) are not so sure. The logic of the two famous superimpositions of Manuela's face over Bernburg's, however, is that they are from Bernburg's perspective, thus indicating that she, too, is haunted by Manuela and, therefore, that she, too, is in love. The first of the two superimpositions, it should be added, happens as Manuela begins to recite a psalm from the Song of Solomon; the passionate words of this song can easily be taken for the expression of secular love, as well as of religious devotion. Manuela begins reciting the words as Bernburg watches her from the front of the classroom. It is from a reaction shot of Bernburg that the superimposition of Manuela's image begins.

Another point of controversy has been the film's "happy ending," another mostly commercial choice by Froelich, who thought a suicide at the end of the film would be "grotesque" (Thiele 1981, 35). Does this affirmative ending undermine either the film's lesbianism or its antiauthoritarianism? Whatever Froelich's intentions, the fact that Manuela does not commit suicide is a great improvement on the conventional ending of traditional lesbian novels: "deviance" punished with the suicide of the "deviant" (see Rich 1993, 112–13; Dyer 1990, 36–38).[3]

That the film was both accessible and extremely popular is proof that popular culture at the end of the Weimar Republic was not invariably reactionary, as so many critics have assumed (cf. Barndt 1999, 44–45). The fact that the suicide is averted at the end of the film by the open rebellion and solidarity of the other schoolgirls and Bernburg underscores the antiauthoritarian reading; the revolt against authority is all the more radical when the lesbianism is taken into account (Zimnik 2000, 178). The two discourses—antiauthoritarianism and lesbian rights—are intertwined and not only within the text of the film. To separate issues of sexual freedom from other political struggles is a mistake, as feminists above all have so long emphasized. Homophobia was a crucial aspect of fascism, and it remains one of the most important weapons of some of the most patriarchal, reactionary, oppressive, and ultimately antidemocratic forces at work today. Its defeat in this film, however momentary, is one that should cheer us all.

NOTES

1. In fairness to Kracauer it must be stated that his initial reaction to the film (see Kracauer 1931) was much more positive. He found it a refreshing alternative to all the military films being made; he also did not ignore the sexual issues in the film, referring to Manuela's infatuation with Bernburg as a "passion of puberty." Given Miriam Hansen's (1996) reference to Kracauer's "own gay sensibility" (173), his public reaction to the subject of homoeroticism in the film is probably complicated.

2. See Kuzniar (2000) on the definition of *queer*, especially her first chapter on Weimar cinema (21–56).

3. Sometimes students today find the implied erotic attraction between Bernburg and her pupil inappropriate. Here it is necessary to stress the connection to the traditional lesbian novel and its basis in *fantasy*, which is also relevant to this fiction film. The film's main character, although supposedly fourteen and a half, was portrayed by Hertha Thiele, who was actually twenty-three (and in fact only four months younger than Dorothea Wieck, who played Bernburg). Furthermore, the fact that Bernburg faces up to the erotic aspect of her affection for Manuela does not mean that she "rides off into the sunset" with her or that she would in any way act on the erotic attraction "after the film ends." The ending of the film is, again, open.

REFERENCES

Barndt, Kerstin. 1999. "Sentiment und Sachlichkeit: Schreib—und Lesewesen der Neuen Frau am Ende der Weimarer Republik." PhD diss., Free University of Berlin. A revised version of this dissertation has been published as a book: *Sentiment und Sachlichkeit: Der Roman der Neuen Frau in der Weimarer Republik*. Cologne, Germany: Böhlau, 2003.

Doty, Alexander. 1993. *Making Things Perfectly Queer: Interpreting Mass Culture*. Minneapolis: University of Minnesota Press.

Dyer, Richard. 1990. "Lesbian and Gay Cinema in Weimar Germany." *New German Critique* 51 (fall): 5–60.

Eggebrecht, Axel. 1931. Review of *Mädchen in Uniform*. *Die Weltbühne* (Berlin), December 26.

Eisner, Lotte. 1969. *The Haunted Screen: Expressionism in the German Cinema and the Influence of Max Reinhardt*. Trans. Roger Greaves. Berkeley: University of California Press. (Orig. pub. 1952 as *L'Ecran démonique*).

Freiburg, Jeanne Ellen. 1994. "Regulatory Bodies: Gendered Visions of the State in German and Swedish Cinema." PhD diss., University of Minnesota.

Frieden, Sandra, Richard McCormick, Vibeke Petersen, and Melissa Vogelsang, eds. 1993. *Gender and German Cinema: Feminist Interventions*. 2 vols. Providence, RI: Berg.

Gay, Peter. 1968. *Weimar Culture: The Outsider as Insider*. New York: Harper & Row.

Gramann, Karola, and Heide Schlüpmann. 1981. Vorbemerkung [Introduction] to "Momente erotischer Utopie—ästhetisierte Verdrängung: Zu *Mädchen in Uniform* und *Anna und Elisabeth.*" *Frauen & Film* 28 (June): 28–31.

Hansen, Miriam. 1996. "America, Paris, the Alps: Kracauer and Benjamin on Cinema and Modernity." In *Amerikanisierung: Traum und Alptraum im Deutschland des. 20. Jahrhunderts*, ed. Alf Lüdtke, Inge Marſsolek, and Adelheid von Saldern, 161–98. Stuttgart: Franz Steiner.

Hewitt, Andrew. 1996. *Political Inversions: Homosexuality, Fascism, and the Modernist Imaginary*. Stanford, CA: Stanford University Press.

Holmlund, Christine. 1991. "When Is a Lesbian Not a Lesbian? The Lesbian Continuum and the Mainstream Femme Film." *Camera Obscura* 25/26 (January–May): 145–78.

Kästner, Erich. 1931. *Fabian: Die Geschichte eines Moralisten*. Zürich: Atrium Verlag.

Keun, Irmgard. 1991. *The Artificial Silk Girl*. Munich: Deutscher Taschenbuch Verlag. (Orig. pub. 1932 as *Das Kunstseidene Mädchen*.)

Kinematograph (Berlin). 1931. Review of *Mädchen in Uniform*. November 28.

Koonz, Claudia. 1987. *Mothers in the Fatherland: Women, the Family, and Nazi Politics*. New York: St. Martin's.

Kracauer, Siegfried. 1931. "Revolte im Mädchenstift: Ein guter deutscher Film!" *Frankfurter Zeitung*, December 1. Repr. in Kracauer, *Werke*, ed. Inka Mülder Bach with Mirjam Wenzel and Sabine Biebl. Vol. 6.2, *Kleine Schriften zum Film*, 562–65. Frankfurt am Main: Suhrkamp, 2004.

——. 1947. *From Caligari to Hitler: A Psychological History of the German Film*. Princeton, NJ: Princeton University Press.

Krusche, Dieter, with Jürgen Labenski. 1993. *Reclams Film—Führer*. 9th ed. Rev. and exp. Stuttgart: Reclam.

Kuzniar, Alice A. 2000. *The Queer German Cinema*. Stanford, CA: Stanford University Press.

Lenssen, Claudia, Helen Fehervary, and Judith Mayne. 1981–82. "From Hitler to Hepburn: A Discussion of Women's Film Production and Reception." *New German Critique* 24/25: 172–85.

Lindner, Martin. 1994. *Leben in der Krise: Zeitromane der neuen Sachlichkeit und die intellektuelle Mentalität der klassischen Moderne*. Stuttgart: Metzler.

Ohm, Lisa. 1993. "The Filmic Adaptation of the Novel *The Child Manuela*: Christa Winsloe's Child Heroine Becomes a *Girl in Uniform*." In Frieden et al. 1993, 2:97–104.

Reinig, Christa. 1983. "Christa Reinig über Christa Winsloe." In Christa Winsloe, *Mädchen in Uniform: Roman*, 241–48. Munich: Frauenoffensive.

Reisdorfer, Kathryn. 1993. "Seeing Through the Screen: An Examination of Women in Soviet and German Popular Cinema in the Inter-War Years." PhD diss., University of Minnesota.

Rich, B. Ruby. 1993. "From Repressive Tolerance to Erotic Liberation: *Girls in Uniform*." In Frieden et al., 2:61–96. (Orig. pub. 1984.)

Thiele, Hertha. 1981. "Gestern und Heute: Gespräch mit Hertha Thiele." Interview by Heide Schlüpmann and Karola Gramann. *Frauen & Film* 28:32–41.

"Von der höheren Tochterschule zum Film: Ein Querschnitt durch fünfundzwanzig junge Mädchen von heute." 1931. *Uhu* 12:34–42.

Wendtland, Karlheinz. 1990. *Geliebter Kientopp: Sämtliche deutsche Spielfilme von 1929–1945 mit zahlreichen Künstlerbiographien. Jahrgang 1929/30* and *Jahrgang 1931*. Berlin: Medium Film.

Winsloe, Christa. 1933. *Girls in Uniform: A Play in Three Acts*. Trans. Barbara Burnham. Boston: Little, Brown. (Orig. pub. 1930 as *Gestern und Heute [Ritter Nérestan]: Schauspiel in Drei Akten*. Vienna: Georg Marton.)

Zimnik, Nina. 2000. "No Man, No Cry? The Film *Girls in Uniform* and Its Discourses of Political Regime." *Women in German Yearbook* 15:161–83.

FRITZ LANG'S *M* (1931)

AN OPEN CASE

TODD HERZOG

Fritz Lang's 1931 film *M* is perhaps the most critically acclaimed German film ever made. A 1995 survey of more than three hundred film historians, film journalists, and film professionals conducted by the *Deutscher Kinematheksverbund* ranked *M* at the top of its list of the one hundred most important German films made during cinema's first century. The first edition of the standard history of German cinema chooses a still from *M* as the only image to adorn its front cover (Jacobsen, Kaes, and Prinzler 1993). It has been quoted in countless subsequent films from Fritz Hippert's *The Eternal Jew* (1940) to Woody Allen's *Shadows and Fog* (1992) and Jean-Luc Godard's *Histoire(s) du cinéma* (1988–98), and it was remade in an American version by Joseph Losey in 1951. It has attracted considerable critical attention from the most important scholars of German cinema, from Siegfried Kracauer and Lotte Eisner to Anton Kaes and Tom Gunning. This chapter builds on that same critical tradition to provide an introduction to the film that Lang considered his one enduring masterpiece (Labarthe 1967). I will in turn examine its technical achievements, the place it occupies within Lang's oeuvre, and its relationship to the late Weimar era in which it was made. I hope to demonstrate why *M* continues to exert such an influence on filmmakers, critics, and audiences. The enduring power of this film, I believe, lies not only in its dazzling display of cinematic artistry but in the difficult questions that it poses and in its refusal to give definite answers.

SOUND AND IMAGE

M was Lang's first sound film, and, as Eisner has noted, he uses this new cinematic technique with "astonishing mastery and maturity" (Eisner 1976, 117). Many critics have highlighted Lang's innovative use of sound in *M*. Kracauer notes, for example, that sound is employed to intensify the sense of horror and dread in a manner "unparalleled in the history of the talkies" (Kracauer 1947, 220); Kaes argues that Lang makes sound technology "a structural feature of the narrative itself" (Kaes 2000a, 18); Gunning points to the way in which "a sound can open up an off screen space, imprinting a space we see on screen with the voice or sound coming from an unseen space" (Gunning 2000, 165). These analyses of *M*'s use of sound technology all revolve around the sound track's ability to work with the visual track, serving to expand the field of vision and complement onscreen images with offscreen sounds. This is undoubtedly one of Lang's great achievements in *M*. Sound and image combine effectively to tell a compelling story. The relationship between the two tracks is, however, not always a conciliatory one in this film: sound and image are not only in dialogue but often in direct competition with one another for the audience's attention and sympathies.

The film's famous opening scene immediately establishes this competition between sound and image that Lang develops throughout the course of the film. Following the credits, which are delivered in silence, punctuated only by a single, jarring gong, *M* opens with a dark screen—no image, only the sound of a little girl reciting a familiar tune:

> Wait, wait just a little while
> Then the black man will come after you
> With his little chopper
> He will make mince meat out of you.

Contemporary audiences would have immediately recognized this as a variation on the "Haarmann Song," a popular nursery rhyme about the notorious serial killer Fritz Haarmann, who was convicted of multiple murders and executed in 1925. Lang's inclusion of the "Haarmann Song" serves to locate *M* in a specific historical context, the world of the Weimar Republic at the time of the film's release, and to place it in dialogue with that world. Lang's use of the black screen during the girl's recitation of the first line of this song serves to draw the audience's attention immediately to a disconnect between sound and image—a split between aural evidence and visual evidence. We hear before we see.

The scene continues to develop this opposition between sound and image. A woman appears to reproach the children for singing "that awful song" and shouts, almost self-reflexively, "Can't you hear me!" After a brief silence, the child's voice resumes chanting the "Haarmann Song," which we again hear without the camera being fixed on an image of the children. This effect of hearing a sound before its source is revealed visually will be repeated throughout the film: we hear a woman's heavy breathing before she comes into view carrying a basket of laundry; we

FIGURE 15.1   Innocence at play: children in a courtyard in Fritz Lang's *M* (1931).

hear a car's horn before it passes by; and, most significant, we hear the murderer whistling his theme song, Grieg's "In the Hall of the Mountain King," from Henrik Ibsen's *Peer Gynt*, before we see his image.

But *M* is certainly not a film without images. Indeed, it has produced some of the most memorable and most imitated shots of any German film. Just as the sound track establishes its presence in the opening scene, so, too, does the camera. The first image we see is a group of children in the courtyard of a working-class district in Berlin (Fig. 15.1). The camera tilts up to a balcony, awaiting the arrival of the woman who will scold the children. Kaes describes the camera in this scene as "all-knowing . . . omniscient, assuming" (Kaes 2000a, 12–13), while Gunning notes that "it has a will of its own" and is "an observing presence outside the consciousness of any character" (Gunning 2000, 166). Surely it is both, but it is also a remarkably awkward observer. It is immediately evident that the camera has assumed a rather clumsy position that does not afford a clear view of either the children or the mother, just as it will continually be unable to fix the murderer adequately within its gaze. Throughout the film, sound is continually revealed as a more rapid and more reliable conveyer of information than is sight. In fact, Beckert (Peter Lorre) is ultimately betrayed by his whistle, not his image. It is, indeed, a wonderful irony that the much-sought criminal is ultimately "spotted" by a blind man. But it is more than an ironic joke made by a director in his first sound film; it points to a central concern of the film, which expands the competition between the technologies of sound and image to a competition between methods of criminal investigation.

"A CITY TRACKS A MURDERER": METHODS OF CRIMINAL INVESTIGATION

Nearly every commentator on *M* has mentioned its connection to Peter Kürten, the notorious serial killer known as the "Vampire of Düsseldorf." Kürten was convicted on nine counts of murder and seven counts of attempted murder shortly before *M* premiered, and he was executed while the film was still in distribution (see Tatar 1995; Herzog 2000; and Kaes 2000a, 2000b). Lang himself, however, repeatedly denied that Kürten was the inspiration for his film. In an interview conducted more than three decades after the premiere of *M*, film historian Gero Gandert asked Lang how he came on his film's theme and whether the notorious Weimar German serial killers Kürten, Haarmann, or Großmann served as "contemporary models" for the fictional child-murderer Beckert. "Who can truly say how he comes upon a theme? What influences him?" was Lang's evasive response (Lang 1963, 123–24). Though Gandert does not press him on the question, Lang for some reason feels compelled to return—unprompted—to his denial of Kürten's influence later in the interview. Gandert asks about the well-known anecdote, reported by Siegfried Kracauer, that Lang changed the title of the film from *Murderers Among Us* to *M* under pressure from a member of the Nazi Party. Lang, however, answers another (unposed) question: "For once Siegfried Kracauer was not incorrect, except for his assertion that *M* was a film about the Düsseldorf child-murderer Kürten. First, Kürten was not a child murderer, and second the manuscript for *M* was completed before Kürten was arrested" (Lang 1963, 127).

At this point in the interview, one gets the feeling that Lang protests too much, somewhat like a suspect being interviewed by the police and continually denying his "guilt" in response to the charge of having modeled his film on the Kürten case. And, interestingly, he seems to betray himself here, getting his chronology confused. According to contemporary reports in both *Lichtbild-Bühne* and *Der Kinematograph*, the script for *M* was completed at the end of November 1930, and production on the film began in mid-December of the same year. Kürten had been arrested on May 24, 1930 and was undergoing psychiatric evaluation during the period in which the script was being completed and the film was being shot.

Despite Lang's repeated disclaimers and regardless of the chronology of the filming, the fact that *M* premiered on May 11, 1931, slightly more than two weeks after Kürten was convicted on nine counts of murder and seven counts of attempted murder, and was still in distribution when Kürten was executed two months later, led nearly every contemporary reviewer to associate Lang's film with the Düsseldorf events. Herbert Ihering, for example, labeled the film "an intellectual analysis of the problem of the Kürten case" and, like most critics, condemned Lang for the tastelessness of his timing: "The case of Peter Kürten as the plot of a novel, no, that is not possible" (Ihering 1931). Gabriele Tergit, a pioneer in the field of trial reportage in the 1920s and well acquainted with recent criminal events, recognized M as a thinly veiled version of the Kürten case: "The murderer film M is the hastiest attempt to capitalize on events. Just after the beast is in court, he is already on the screen" (Tergit 1931, 844). Tergit's attack on M reminds us that this now classic film was, at the time of its release, disparaged as something akin to the modern "movie-of-the-week," whose plot has been "ripped from today's headlines."

Lang's film does not, of course, follow the Kürten case in detail: Beckert is exclusively a child-murderer, whereas Kürten indiscriminately killed women, men, children, and even animals; Lang sets his film in Berlin, rather than Düsseldorf; and, most important, Kürten was ultimately captured by the police, not the underworld, as Beckert is in Lang's film. Lang's "fatty Lohmann," however, is clearly a stand-in for "fatty Gennat," the famous homicide detective assigned to the Kürten case, and even such details as the importance of the color of the murderer's pencil are lifted directly from the case. The program issued to accompany the film's premiere even stressed the link between the Düsseldorf murders and Lang's film, incorporating statements by key figures from the Düsseldorf investigation and reproducing the letters that Kürten had written to the press.

Most post–World War II critics mention the connection between Lang's film and the Kürten case, but the implications of these links are worth pursuing in greater detail. By stressing the connection—as well as Lang's later uneasiness about it—we might recover some of the initial shock value of the film. For Lang's classic film must be read as an urgent and controversial intervention in the ongoing debates surrounding the Kürten case—about the process of police investigation, the role of the public, and, crucially, the link between visuality and criminality. M traces the breakdown of systems of investigation that are based on the tracking of visual clues (as in classic detective work) and beliefs about criminal physiognomy (as in the pervasive theories of Cesare Lombroso), as well as the emergence of a new institution that will take the place of these outdated systems. Read in light of the crisis produced by the Kürten case, Lang's film can be seen as an attempt to develop a new system of social defense based not on outdated notions of scientific or police investigation but rather on the development of a modern, mobilized populace evident in numerous popular and professional discussions of criminal investigation in the later Weimar Republic (see Herzog 2000).

There are, of course, two investigations in M: the police search and the gangsters' search. Critics since Kracauer have made much of the scene in which the two are connected through cross-cutting between the police discussion and the gang-sters' discussion of how to capture the killer: "At times," as Noël Carroll observes, "the editing almost elides the two meetings; a criminal could be seen as addressing an official and vice versa" (Carroll 1998, 94). This use of montage, Carroll further notes, "is grounded by a thematic point—namely, the identification of the two groups" (ibid.). Maria Tatar argues that in this scene "it begins to dawn on the spec-tator that there is no real difference between the two factions" (Tatar 1995, 166). These are perceptive points; however, I would like to emphasize the ways in which the investigations of the two groups are contrasted in this scene and throughout the film. Though both the gangsters and the police share a common purpose—the capture of the child-murderer—Lang stages in this scene and throughout the film a competition between the opposing methodologies of the two groups.

The police are consistently shown to be following the time-honored method of searching for clues. They examine fingerprints, dig up scraps of paper and cigarette butts, and quite literally seek out the traces that the killer leaves behind in the form of imprints on his writing surface or bits of red pencil lead on the windowsill. The police investigation depends on *visual* clues—the method of tracking a criminal through the traces he leaves behind. Inspector Lohmann (Otto Wernicke) is every bit as punctilious as his real-life model, the director of the Berlin Homicide Divi-sion, Inspector Gennat, carefully following up "more than 1,500 detailed clues" that are collected in "sixty thick volumes."

In a remarkable scene in which the police chief explains his investigation to a government minister who is pushing for results, the two visual regimes that had long dominated discussions of criminality are both shown to be ineffective through Lang's ingenious use of oppositions between the visual track and the sound track. As the police chief explains the difficulty of tracing fingerprints and the need to gather clues and submit them to the archive, the film launches into a documen-tary-like sequence, in which the tedious process of evidence collection is detailed through amplified close-ups of fingerprints intercut with scenes of detectives col-lecting scraps of paper from crime scenes. Even as the president admits that it is "almost impossible to recover a useful fingerprint from a piece of paper that has passed through so many hands" (Lang 1963, 24), we are shown an enormous pro-jection of a fingerprint, an "unreadable clue" (Bergstrom 1990, 171), being carefully studied by the police. Later in the sequence, we follow a crumpled piece of paper found at a crime scene on an unsuccessful journey in search of the store it came from. Visual evidence, whether a fingerprint or a scrap of paper, does not lead to the individual who left such evidence behind, but the police seem to lack alterna-tives to such established investigative protocol. The overall tone underscores the hopelessness and inadequacy of the process.

During one part of this long sequence, Lang cuts away to an archive, where a po-lice expert paces in front of an entire wall of files, dictating a description of the still-

FIGURE 15.2   At the archives: a graphologist constructs a profile of the unknown serial killer.

unknown criminal. There follows an additional cut to a shot of the child-murderer, Beckert, standing in front of a mirror in his apartment as the expert in the archive is heard in a voice-over describing the pronounced psychological defects of the murderer. The expert is a graphologist, who is constructing a profile of the unknown murderer based on his handwriting in a letter to a local paper. According to the graphologist, whose thick glasses, restless pacing on and off camera, and theatrical intonations seem to be a parody of such experts, the murderer shows traces of insanity: "In the whole form of his writing there is an elusive, but intensely palpable trace of madness" (Fig. 15.2). Meanwhile, the visual image shows Beckert pulling the corners of his mouth down, grotesquely distorting his face and constructing himself temporarily as the obviously subhuman beast that he is described to be (Fig. 15.3). The sound and the visuals come from two different scenes, and they are employed to comment on each other. According to the criminalist, whose description we hear on the sound track, the criminal is different—pathological—and it follows that he should be readily apparent as different. And, for a moment, Beckert's body betrays his deviant nature, just as criminal anthropologists such as Lombroso had suggested and just as the police expert seems to be arguing.

The normal trajectory of the process of investigation, however, is shown to be reversed in this scene: whereas the criminalist seems to be using a clue to gather information about the criminal, construct a profile of him, and thereby distinguish the criminal from the innocents, in actuality the process moves as much in the opposite direction—the criminalist's description actually seems to impact Beckert's appearance, as if Beckert were following "instructions" about what his

FIGURE 15.3   Is his guilt written on his face? Triptych of Beckert (Peter Lorre) inspecting himself in the mirror.

profile should look like (though, of course, unlike the audience, he cannot hear the expert's description). We see here a sort of looping effect, in which the criminal adapts to and adopts notions of what he is supposed to be like—he begins to conform to a type. The archives (which are powerfully represented in this scene as the wall of files before which the handwriting expert paces, dictating yet another report to be placed in the files) not only gather information to construct composite profiles; they play a role in forming individuals as types. Serial killers, in particular, frequently take an enormous interest in researching the literature, both popular and clinical, on serial murder. Peter Kürten, for example, confessed to learning the "trade" of serial killing by reading not only stories of Jack the Ripper but also Lombroso's criminological treatises.

Criminological discourse and the law seem in this scene not so much to be reading signs in the criminal as writing their signs onto the face of the criminal. But, of course, nothing is written onto Beckert's body; his mouth quickly returns to its normal position, and with it he returns to invisibility within society—he is no longer a "type" that can be spotted. His body is as unreadable a clue as the fingerprint and the crumpled scrap of paper depicted elsewhere in the sequence. Indeed, as both Kaes and Gunning note in their discussions of this scene, the camera cuts to

FIGURE 15.4 The gangster method of investigation: preemptive strike.

Beckert looking in the mirror precisely at the point the police expert comments on his writing style's "expression of play-acting" and cuts back to the archive on the word "madness" (See Kaes 2000b, 166–68; and Gunning 2000, 178–79). Which, finally, is it? Acting or madness? The film never answers this question, pursuing instead the seemingly more urgent question of how to identify and distinguish the killer.

The disjuncture between the sound and image tracks in this scene between the pathogen being described and the man-next-door being seen is one of Lang's many masterful uses of the new medium of sound in his first talkie. It is also the central problem that the film works through: the breakdown of stable, visible boundaries between criminal and noncriminal and the ineffectiveness of tracking the individual body through evidence. As an elderly detective later addresses the police gathered to discuss the case: "This is perhaps a man who, outside of the state in which he kills, is a harmless-looking, upstanding citizen. . . . Without this . . . I want to say . . . private harmlessness in murderers it is not conceivable that a man such as Großmann, Haarmann, can live for years in the same building with many other residents, without attracting any trace of suspicion." At this point the only mention in the film of the real-life serial killers Großmann and Haarmann, this crisis of visibility leads to a call for the police to solicit the help of the public in capturing the murderer. When an officer recommends asking for the public's help, however, Lohmann vehemently opposes the suggestion: "Enough with the cooperation of the public!" he snaps. "When I even think about it, it makes me want to vomit."

FIGURE 15.5 The police method of investigation: painstaking detective work.

Lohmann then launches into a tirade against the same public "psychoses" that Gennat had seen as impeding his investigation of the Kürten case.

The police, with their clues, archives, and criminological experts, are unable to apprehend the killer. It is the gangsters, by following a very different method, who get to him first. Shortly after Lohmann's tirade against the enlistment of the public's help, Schränker (Gustaf Gründgers), the leader of the gangsters, slaps his hand down over a map of Berlin and insists that the entire city must be put under surveillance by enlisting the help of the organization of beggars: "We must cover the city with a net of spies. Every square meter must be under constant surveillance. No child in this city will be allowed to take a step without us knowing about it." Schränker's map, covered by his black-gloved hand, contrasts with Lohmann's map, on which circles are slowly drawn as clues are sifted and categorized (Figs. 15.4 and 15.5). Unlike the police, the gangsters do not have archives, do not follow traces, and, in general, do not rely on visual clues. Indeed, they do not rely on clues at all; they do not attempt to proceed from the crime scene to the criminal. Instead, they enlist the aid of the public (the organization of beggars) and construct a new system of total surveillance that, interestingly, concentrates not on sight, but rather on *aural* clues. It is indeed a wonderful conceit, as Tatar points out, that it is ultimately a blind man who "spots" the criminal (Tatar 1995, 169). But it is much more than an ironic joke; it is also the central argument of the film. Relying neither on the hermeneutics of crime nor on a scientific system of measuring criminal difference, the gangsters turn instead to a system of surveillance and of marking. In

FIGURE 15.6   The criminal is made visible. Beckert, marked with the M.

the film's most famous scene, Beckert stands again in front of a mirror, as he had in the earlier scene in which he distorted his face and thereby questioned whether his criminality was as visible as the police profile indicated. This time, however, he looks with horror at a chalk letter M on his back that marks him as the murderer. The body of the criminal finally betrays his criminality—he has been *made visible* in order to be tracked (Fig. 15.6).

During the Weimar Republic a protracted debate took place over how to modernize the process of criminal investigation. In cases such as that of Peter Kürten, traditional methods of visual investigation seemed to go into crisis. As the serial killer continued to elude capture, it became clear that the "Vampire of Düsseldorf" bore no resemblance to a creature such as F. W. Murnau's Nosferatu but instead blended imperceptibly into the population. It also became clear that the investigation conducted by the police, employing Gennat's famously careful and punctilious methods, was ineffective. Journals like *Kriminal-Magazin*, criminologists such as Robert Heindl, and popular crime writers such as Curt Elwenspoek began to call for a new method of investigation: a vigilant populace united against a common criminal.[1] Critics of *M*—including Lang himself in post–World War II interviews—have long identified this emergence of a mobilized populace over the course of the film, and most critics have seen it as the real object of the film's narrative thrust, while Beckert assumes the improbable role of victim. I would now like to turn to the question of who is depicted as a victim and who might be said to be the film's protagonist. For a consideration of these questions is essential to determining the complex ways in which this film anticipates National Socialist practices.

M'S OPEN QUESTIONS

Critics have long debated who the real protagonist of *M* is. Beckert would be the obvious choice, but, as Noël Burch has pointed out, he appears more as an absence than a presence, especially in the first half of the film (Burch 1991, 21–22). It is clear that in *M* Lang is primarily interested not in the personality of the murderer, nor in his crimes, but rather in the public investigation of the murder. This might lead one to posit Lohmann as the film's protagonist, but, as Gunning notes, he does not enter until twenty minutes into the film and is absent from many key scenes (Gunning 2000, 164). Lang's atypical crime film places neither the detective nor the criminal at the undisputed center of the narrative. Indeed, no single character can be said to be the key figure around which the film is structured or one whose point of view is adopted by the camera or the narrative. Kaes argues that the camera adopts "a relentlessly panoptic resolve and detached 'cold gaze'" (Kaes 2000a, 46). Gunning also adopts this perspective, advancing the compelling argument that the city itself could be seen as the true protagonist of the film (Gunning 2000, 164). This perspective of the city as protagonist would align *M* with other contemporary modernist narratives, such as Alfred Döblin's *Berlin Alexanderplatz* (1929), a novel with which Lang's film shares many affinities. I agree with Kaes and Gunning that neither Beckert nor Lohmann can be seen as a proper protagonist in this film. The notion of the city as protagonist is convincing, but I would argue that the story that *M* tells is actually of the development of a central organizing figure. Over the course of the film, *M*'s true protagonist emerges, and again as in Döblin's urban crime story this protagonist is not an individual, nor an entirely abstract entity, but rather the populace. *M* imagines the development of a paradoxical entity: a mass *community* united in a shared trauma and against a common enemy.

   This story is told in striking visual terms. The first half of the film is largely preoccupied with detailing empty spaces: vacant basements, open fields, empty streets. As the film proceeds, these empty spaces give way—beginning with the reports of the murder of Elsie and culminating in the gangster-courtroom scene—to spaces filled with people. Walter Benjamin once remarked of Atget's photographs of empty Parisian streets that "he photographed them like a crime scene. The crime scene is also empty of people" (Benjamin 1977, 148). The empty public spaces of the early part of *M* are all, essentially, crime scenes or potential crime scenes; the occupied spaces at the end, however, cannot be crime scenes. The killer is unable to continue his murders. But the prevention of crime and the ultimate capture of the killer are only part of the story that *M* tells. It also relates how disengaged private

FIGURE 15.7 A gangster family portrait.

life gives way to engaged public life over the course of the film. Gradually a community forms around—and against—the child-murderer, as the empty spaces that characterize the opening sequences give way to crowded public spaces. The broken families from the beginning of the film ultimately gather for what looks like a mass family portrait at the gangster's "kangaroo court" trial of Beckert (Fig. 15.7). This is a paranoid community, to be sure, but Lang's world here, as in most of his films, is a paranoid world, in which danger is ever present and usually invisible.

I do not wish to argue that Lang intended to endorse mass hysteria as an effective means of crime prevention. Nor would I argue that he intended to dismiss it. The enduring effect of *M* lies precisely in the film's refusal to deliver a clear moral or to propose a specific course of action. This is why the final scene, in which the three mothers admonish the parents in the audience to pay attention to their children, so often disappoints viewers as hollow and disproportionate to the complexity of matters as they had been presented in the film. Read in light of the crisis of criminal investigation during the Weimar Republic, as I believe it must be, *M* can indeed be seen as an attempt to wrestle with the problems presented by cases such as that of Peter Kürten, problems for which there were and are no simple answers. At the time of his film's premiere Lang referred to it as "a documentary report" and announced his intention "to correspond to the objectivity of the period in which we are living and to produce a film solely from documentary reports" (Lang 1931, 267–69).

Among the signs of the time that Lang expresses a desire to examine is "the horrifying psychotic fear of the populace" (Lang 1931, 267–69). The standard line of criticism on *M* since the end of World War II has repeatedly taken up this statement and read Lang's serial killer as a sort of victim and the psychosis of the populace as the real target of Lang's attack. No critic has pursued this reading as brilliantly as Maria Tatar, who argues that "Lang succeeds in turning a man who commits 'the most heinous crime' [Lang's phrase] into a sympathetic, if also pathetic, character.... By the end of the film, Beckert's pathology begins to take a back seat to the hysteria of the mothers, who are prepared to rush him and to tear him limb from limb" (Tatar 1995, 164). In light of the Düsseldorf murders, however, the notion of the killer as sympathetic victim is difficult to sustain. Contemporary reviews frequently mention the aggressive reactions of the audience to the film. Describing the scene in which Beckert confesses his inability to control his murderous impulses to an unsympathetic underworld tribunal, Hans Fell notes: "The women, in contrast—and not only those on the screen—advocate rendering him harmless through extermination" (Fell 1931). Tergit reported enthusiastic applause throughout the audience at the film's gala premiere during the scene in which a gangster argues against sending Beckert to a legitimate court, where he would surely be found mentally incompetent and thus avoid execution. "Man is so conditioned," writes Tergit, "that he wants a victim right away. Scratch a bit at the surface and a Tartar will always come into view. There were many Tartars in the Ufa-Theater am Zoo at the premiere" (Tergit 1931, 895). A reviewer for the Nazi publication *Der Angriff* found *M* well in accordance with his own political tendencies, lauding the film as "the best argument against those who oppose the death penalty" (Anon. 1931). And Joseph Goebbels recorded in his diary after seeing *M*: "Fantastic! Against humanitarian soppiness. For the death penalty. Well made. Lang will be our director one day" (Gunning 2000, 192).

The subsequent crimes of the National Socialists clearly affect the way in which we view the film. Beckert as the outsider pursued by an angry mass and ultimately forced to wear a mark identifying him conjures up images of the victims of the Nazis. It is not difficult to see a connection between the chalk *M* that brands Beckert at the end of Lang's film and the yellow Star of David that Jews were forced to wear so that they would not be able to "disguise" themselves as "Germans." Felix Nußbaum's famous *Self-Portrait with a Jewish Passport* (1943) recalls the famous scene from *M* in which Beckert sees himself in the mirror and notices the *M* on his shoulder. Nußbaum's painting highlights the Nazi's mania for identification and the shock of the self-experience of the identified. Surely one component of *M* leads fairly directly from Beckert as victim of an angry mob to the Jews as victims of National Socialism.

But, as Gunning rightly warns, it is not only unconvincing but also dangerous to view the film as either proto-Nazi or anti-Nazi (Gunning 2000, 197–98). The latter view sees Beckert as a victim and the film as voicing opposition to the angry lynch mob that ruthlessly pursues him. In this view the film warns against the dangers of the criminal policies that would be implemented under National Socialism. Alternatively, the former view sees Beckert as a dangerous pathogen that must be eliminated for society to return to proper functioning and the mobilized mass as the heroic citizens who accomplish this task. In this view the film advocates the criminal policies that would be implemented under National Socialism. In complicated ways the film seeks to explore both views of Beckert. The film is thus at once both proto-Nazi and anti-Nazi. *M* presents a complex view of a complex society in a state of crisis over the dangers of the modern world and the competing methods to confront these dangers. "It is," as Gunning argues, "precisely the manner in which the film is pre-Nazi that makes it so complex" (Gunning 2000, 198). It depicts the hopelessness of traditional methods of criminal investigation in dealing with modern criminals and modern society and presents the enticement, as well as the danger, of the mass community as an alternative to these methods of controlling the world that no longer seem valid.

THE AFTERLIFE OF M

Lang would make one more film, *The Testament of Dr. Mabuse* (1933), before fleeing Germany in 1933 for France and then the United States. Lang's own version of his flight from his homeland involves a sudden, fearful, and treacherous escape from Hitler's Germany. Though the decision was likely much more considered and the facts much less romantic, it remains true that Lang did not accept the powerful position in the Nazi regime offered to him, choosing instead to go into exile and develop a clearly anti-Nazi stance. He divorced his wife, Thea von Harbou, the screenwriter for *M* and collaborator on numerous other films, who remained in Germany and became a supporter of Hitler's regime. Lang's final German film before his leaving the country, *The Testament of Dr. Mabuse*, plays off of his earlier crime films, most notably his two-part 1922 epic *Dr. Mabuse, the Gambler* and *M*. In his 1933 *Mabuse* film Lang resurrects not only his famous criminal from 1922 but also the police commissioner Lohmann from *M*. But this Lohmann (again portrayed by Otto Wernicke, reprising his role from *M*) operates in a very different world from that of the detective in *M*. Lohmann may be the same Gennat-like detective whose methods are resolutely archival and systematic, but the system he embodies is no longer an outdated system that fails to contain criminal chaos. The archive (which is again strikingly represented in a key scene) is now a successful alternative to crime and disorder. By 1933 Lang could clearly see the threat of Hitler and National Socialism that had seemed more obscure and questionable two years earlier. *The Testament of Dr. Mabuse* was immediately banned by the Nazis, and Lang fled Germany.

Lang's career flourished in Hollywood, as he directed more than two dozen films before returning to Germany in the 1950s to direct his final films. He frequently drew on the crime theme that he had pursued in *M*, but he never recaptured the power and complexity that he showed in his early German films. One of his early Hollywood films, *Fury* (1936), addresses the issue of mobs and justice that he had explored in *M*. Filmed three years after Hitler had come to power and in a very different context, *Fury* can be seen as an attempt to reinterpret *M* as a parable about the dangers of mass hysteria, just as were Lang's post-1933 statements about *M*. Indeed, many of Lang's Hollywood crime films seem on some level to be responses to *M*, continually revisiting what Kaes calls "the nexus of crime, mass culture and urban modernity" (Kaes 2000a, 79), and treating this interplay with a significantly less ambiguous and more critical view than he had in his 1931 film.

Peter Lorre also fled Germany when Hitler came to power, first for France, then England, and finally the United States. He appeared in numerous Hollywood B movies, typically typecast as the odd psychopathic character, before returning to Germany to direct his only film, *The Lost One*, which premiered in 1951. In this remarkable and sadly forgotten film, Lorre casts himself as a doctor, employed by the Nazis, who murders his wife and discovers the depths of his homicidal tendencies. Lorre's film owes a clear debt to *M* and is one of the rare post–World War II attempts to look unflinchingly at the world of everyday crime and its relationship to the great crimes of the National Socialist regime. *The Lost One* was a commercial failure. Lorre never directed another film, and his acting career declined noticeably from that point until his death in 1964.

All in all, *M* has stayed in circulation, in one way or another, since its initial release in 1931. Just two years after Goebbels praised it in his diary, it was banned by the Nazis and removed from distribution. The Nazis did make use of the film's famous kangaroo court scene in which Beckert pleads for understanding that he is unable to control his murderous impulses. This scene is incorporated into the anti-Semitic propaganda film *The Eternal Jew* (1940), to which a voice-over narration is added that equates it as a confession of "the Jew Lorre" that he and other Jews are driven by an uncontrollable impulse to murder. The ambivalence of Goebbels and the Nazis about precisely where *M* fits into National Socialist ideology (from "Lang will be our director one day" to "the Jew Lorre" who portrays murderous Jews as helpless victims) has its origins within the film itself, which wavers constantly between endorsing and criticizing precisely the practices the Nazis would begin to put into effect two years after the film's premiere.

Joseph Losey's American remake of *M* premiered in 1951, updating Lang's narrative and setting it in contemporary Los Angeles. Seymour Nebenzal, the producer of both the 1931 and 1951 versions of *M*, originally offered the job of directing the remake to Lang, who declined, arguing that his classic film should not be remade. But, as Kaes has pointed out, Lang's entire post-*M* career "could be called, with only slight exaggeration, one grand reworking of *M*" (Kaes 2000a, 78). Just as *M*'s ubiquitous images continue to haunt German and international cinema, its ambivalent answers to open questions continued to haunt Lang to the end of his long and productive career. And this powerful and problematic film continues to challenge, intrigue, and provoke audiences and critics to this day.

NOTE

1. In 1930 *Kriminal-Magazin* published the article "Das Geheimnis von Düsseldorf: Wer ist der Mörder?" (The Mystery of Düsseldorf: Who Is the Murderer?) (repr. in Lenk and Kaever 1974). For more on Robert Heindl and Curt Elwenspoek see Heindl (1926) and Elwenspoek (1931).

REFERENCES

Anon. 1931. " 'M.' " *Der Angriff*, May 30.

Benjamin, Walter. 1977. "Das Kunstwerk im Zeitalter seiner technischen Reproduzierbarkeit." In *Illuminationen*. Frankfurt am Main: Suhrkamp.

Bergstrom, Janet. 1990. "Psychological Explanation in the Films of Lang and Pabst." In *Psychoanalysis & Cinema*, ed. E. Ann Kaplan, 163–80. New York: Routledge, 1990.

Burch, Noël. 1991. "Fritz Lang: German Period." In *In and Out of Synch: The Awakening of a Cine-Dreamer*. Trans. Ben Brewster. Aldershot: Scolar Press.

Carroll, Noël. 1998. "Lang, Pabst, and Sound." In *Interpreting the Moving Image*, 92–104. Cambridge, UK: Cambridge University Press.

"Das Geheimnis von Düsseldorf: Wer ist der Mörder?" 1930. *Kriminal-Magazin*, Sonderausgabe. Repr. in Lenk and Kaever 1974, 13–37.

Eisner, Lotte. 1976. *Fritz Lang*. New York: Da Capo Press.

Elwenspoek, Curt. 1931. *Mord und Totschlag: Polizei greift ein!* Stuttgart: Dieck.

Fell, Hans. 1931. "Fritz Lang's Tonfilm: 'M.' " *Film-Kurier*, May 12.

Gunning, Tom. 2000. *The Films of Fritz Lang: Allegories of Vision and Modernity*. London: BFI.

Heindl, Robert. 1926. *Der Berufsverbrecher: Ein Beitrag zur Strafrechtsreform*. Berlin: Pan-Verlag Rolf Heise.

Herzog, Todd. 2000. " 'Den Verbrecher erkennen': Zur Geschichte der Kriminalistik." In *Gesichter der Weimarer Republik*, ed. Claudia Schmölers and Sander L. Gilman, 51–75. Köln: DuMont Buchverlag.

Ihering, Herbert. 1931. " 'M.' " *Berliner Börsen-Kurrier*, May 12.

Jacobsen, Wolfgang, Anton Kaes, Heinz Helmut Prinzler, eds. 1993. *Geschichte des deutschen Films*. Stuttgart: Metzler.

Kaes, Anton. 2000a. *M*. London: BFI.

——. 2000b. "Das bewegte Gesicht: Zur Grofsaufnahme im Film." In *Gesichter der Weimarer Republik*, ed. Claudia Schmölers and Sander L. Gilman, 156–64. Köln: DuMont Buchverlag.

Kracauer, Siegfried. 1947. *From Caligari to Hitler: A Psychological History of the German Film*. Princeton, NJ: Princeton University Press.

Labarthe, André S., dir. 1967. "Le dinosaure et le bébé, dialogue en huit parties entre Fritz Lang et Jean-Luc Godard." *Cinéastes de notre temps* [Télévision séries].

Lang, Fritz. 1931. "Mein Film 'M'—ein Tatsachenbericht." *Die Filmwoche*, May 20. Repr. in *Fritz Lang: Die Stimme von Metropolis*, ed. Fred Gehler and Ullrich Kasten, 267–70. Berlin: Henschel Verlag.

——. 1963. *M: Protokoll*. Hamburg: Marion von Schröder.

Lenk, Elisabeth, and Roswitha Kaever, eds. 1974. *Leben und Wirken des Peter Kürten, genannt der Vampir von Düsseldorf*. München: Rogner und Bernhard.

Tatar, Maria. 1995. *Lustmord: Sexual Murder in Weimar Germany*. Princeton, NJ: Princeton University Press.

Tergit, Gabriele. 1931. "Der Fritz-Lang Film: Der Film des Sadismus." *Die Weltbühne* 27, no. 23:844–45.

SIXTEEN

WHOSE REVOLUTION?

THE SUBJECT OF *KUHLE WAMPE* (1932)

MARC SILBERMAN

While early Weimar cinema developed specific visual, narrative, and technological effects to depict the volatile social relations of the period, *Kuhle Wampe oder Wem gehört die Welt?* (*Kuhle Wampe*, 1932) marks a more radical, overtly politicized appeal to the spectator in the context of social polarization toward the end of the Weimar Republic.[1] Indebted to the example of Soviet montage, this noncommercial, independent production demonstrates how a politicized cinema that goes beyond issues of radical content tries to mobilize its audience. In this model the spectator's imaginary activity engages an empowering cognitive process of seeing context and recognizing connections rather than the voyeurism and spectacle of the commercial Weimar cinema. Addressed to a fractured and even indifferent working-class audience buffeted by the consequences of social and economic crisis, the film suggests why and how only a collective subject can sustain the emancipatory claims of revolutionary change. Produced collectively by Slatan Dudow, Bertolt Brecht, Ernst Ottwalt, and Hanns Eisler under the protection of the Communist Party and with the participation of many prominent leftist artists, *Kuhle Wampe* was released less than a year before the Nazi takeover in 1933. In this respect the project reveals symptomatic hopes and illusions on the part of the left at this time of social crisis, but it also marks a turning point in discussions concerning the nature of cinematic representation, as well as the abrupt end point in a decade-long development of leftist filmmaking in Germany. With the onset of the Third Reich, it was at the top of Joseph Goebbels's list of films to be withdrawn from distribution. Only in 1955 would a copy of *Kuhle Wampe* resurface in East Germany (Herlinghaus 1965) to become part of the revitalized leftist film culture in West Germany in the late 1960s (Witte 1972).

For the film industry, the latter half of the 1920s was characterized by increasing centralization and monopolization in all sectors, including technological development, production, distribution, exhibition, even marketing and press coverage. The period of economic stabilization introduced in 1924 and 1925, with the guarantee of American financial support, created a situation in which the German market suddenly became highly vulnerable to the export intentions of other countries, especially in the cinema branch (Murray 1990, 57–64). By 1926 all the major production companies that had not yet fused or gone bankrupt entered into capitalization arrangements with American film companies, thereby formalizing their financial dependency and effectively neutralizing Germany as America's most important competitor in the international market. One year later, in 1927, Alfred Hugenberg reorganized the largest German film company, Ufa, with the support of politically conservative and nationalistic interests. As a result it became part of one of the world's largest media conglomerates, whose principal holdings included newspapers, a major publishing house, and a news agency (Kreimeier 1996, 158–72). The competition for investment capital to underwrite film production began to influence film content and form more obviously than ever before. The commercial cinema increasingly standardized its offerings for what it considered a homogeneous urban public, abandoning the commitment to differentiated audiences as had been the case, for instance, with the expressionist "art cinema" or the melodramatic chamber-play film (*Kammerspielfilm*) appealing to female spectators. Moreover, it sought to gentrify production values and material by imitating Hollywood standards. Although there was still a place for isolated examples of experimental filmmaking (e.g., Walter Ruttmann's *Berlin, Symphony of a Great City*, 1927, or the collaborative film *People on Sunday*, 1930) and even for sophisticated, socially critical films like G. W. Pabst's *The Joyless Street* (1925), the studios directed their energies primarily toward the few expensive, international prestige films like Fritz Lang's *Metropolis* (1927) or toward the many low-cost, lowbrow films that avoided controversy in favor of the obvious and the formulaic.

Kuhle Wampe fell outside the boundaries of commercial film production and stands as an example of ambitious efforts during the 1920s to develop in Germany an independent, noncommercial cinema for the political and entertainment needs of the organized working class. Even before the war working-class organizations and industrial unions had supported a network of social and cultural agencies. With the split of the working-class movement into a social-democratic and a communist wing after the war, these efforts expanded further and led at times to a competitive, sometimes politically counterproductive, rivalry. As far as the cinema was concerned, both working-class parties were late to recognize its revolutionary technological and aesthetic implications, thus misjudging the political potential inherent in the medium. Basically, the left positioned itself defensively in a critical posture defined by conservative and traditional cultural values (Silberman 2002).

The Social Democratic Party (SPD) focused its attention on creating new distribution outlets under its own control and raising the taste of the working-class public through film journalism. By the mid-1920s the party had established a central distributor for cultural, informational, and high-quality studio films. In addition, it organized and trained mobile projection teams for screenings among union groups and at educational meetings in order to circumvent the increasing impact of state censorship or the boycotts organized by commercial distributors. Direct investment in film production was minimal and had ceased entirely by 1929. The German Communist Party (KPD) adopted a somewhat different, more defensive, policy. Despite Lenin's stress on the cinema as the most important of the arts, the party rejected popular films as a tool in the hands of the capitalist class to divert the attention of the workers from the class struggle—meaning more plainly the cinema as it existed in the form of commercial entertainment films. Nonetheless, this suspicious attitude toward the mass media as a manipulatory instrument continued to define the party's policy throughout the 1920s. The cinema, with its suggestive images, was seen as a means of influencing public opinion, and the KPD's goal was to harness this power in conventional forms of critical realism in order to manage the purported emotional and identificatory effect for its own ideological ends (Heller 1985, 145–56).

By focusing attention on the medium's content rather than its signifying and representational systems, leftist critics remained blind to the emancipatory, cognitive possibilities of the cinema. Not until the new Soviet films by Sergei Eisenstein, Vsevolod Pudovkin, and Dziga Vertov, which were distributed in Germany beginning in 1926, did a different kind of visual and agitational model for the cinematic medium prove that there was a viable leftist alternative to the commercial industry. With the founding of the Prometheus-Film Corporation in 1926 as a distribution outlet for Soviet films and, more important, as a company with sufficient capital to underwrite worker-oriented films produced in Germany, the KPD had established a means of producing its own features aimed at mobilizing the working class (Murray 1990, 65–74). *Kuhle Wampe*, the last production planned by Prometheus before it went bankrupt in 1932, reveals the contradictions in the notion of a proletarian alternative public sphere under the conditions of economic collapse prior to the Nazis' appropriation of power in 1933.

The Prometheus initiative appeared to challenge the commercial film industry, but the actual results were not impressive. The examples of Soviet innovation in film narration had less effect on the German cinema than on other visual, literary, and dramatic arts, where discussions concerning realism and montage techniques dominated leftist circles (Willett 1978). Both documentary and feature-length entertainment films produced by Prometheus stressed the proletarian content as a contrast to the commercial industry at the expense of formal innovation. As a result, many productions celebrated their status as "class-conscious" alternatives to the dominant cinema although they imitated already popular successes of the major studios.

Piel Jutzi's *Mutter Krausens Fahrt ins Glück* (*Mother Krause's Journey into Happiness*, 1929) is a case in point. Banking on the established taste for "Zille films," a subgenre of the naturalistic social drama drawing on anecdotes and characters from Berlin's slums, which the graphic artist Heinrich Zille had memorialized, Jutzi tells the heartrending tale of a family in which the mother commits suicide out of financial desperation, while her daughter finds a new meaning in life by sharing her lover's political commitment to the working-class movement. The film highlights images of working-class misery aimed, on the one hand, against the idealizing illusions of the "dream factory" and, on the other, at awakening empathy in the spectator through the pathos and victimization of the young heroine. These images of urban misery are set against beautiful images of nature, where the workers spend their free time. The everyday working world, in other words, is not depicted as a site of contradiction and struggle, as the left's political program proclaimed, but rather as an oppressive world to be tolerated. The final sequence, with its optimistic images of the heroine being swept away in a street demonstration, is an unmotivated resolution to the tangled love affair and its tragic consequences for the mother. At the time, however, it signaled a milestone, since this was the first fictional feature film from Germany that pointed directly to class struggle as an alternative to political resignation among the proletariat (Pettifer 1975–76). Yet the declamatory conclusion reveals in the portrayal of the heroine's spontaneous "coming to class consciousness" under the authority of her male companion a voluntarism characteristic of Communist Party cultural policy in general.

Mother Krause's Journey into Happiness marked the high point of Prometheus's success, for 1929 witnessed two crucial developments that exacerbated the weaknesses of an independent leftist cinema: the introduction of the sound film and the onset of the international market crash. For the commercial film industry the coming of sound was a blessing in disguise, a new technology that, despite its high investment costs, promised to increase flagging audience attendance owing to its novelty. An undercapitalized firm like Prometheus, however, found it impossible to compete. The worldwide Depression only complicated these tendencies. The major studios produced more and more escapist fare for an audience that had less and less discretionary income to buy admission tickets, and Prometheus, which had released as many as fifteen productions a year between 1927 and 1930, had cut back to only four shorts in 1931 and two shorts and *Kuhle Wampe* in 1932. Other leftist support foundered as well. The growing polarization of German society affected working-class cultural agencies, which were devoting reduced resources to battle ever harsher state censorship. By 1929 the SPD had ceased investment in film production, and the KPD abandoned its support of feature-length entertainment films in favor of agitational and informational shorts. This latter move underscored the party's political commitment to an authoritarian discourse in which it assumed the role of the vanguard, a position figured in the *Mother Krause* film in the final images of the political demonstration. *Kuhle Wampe* is an anomaly, then, in more than one sense. Whereas the left's strategy in both politics and culture had evolved a hierarchical model in which an elite represents, informs, and acts for the interests of the masses, this collaborative film production argues for a dialectic of political form and social content that engages the spectator in a process of imagining a revolutionary collective subject.

As Prometheus's financial situation became more precarious, it came up with the idea of making a feature-length film on the youth movement and its sports organizations as a means of cashing in on and supporting the idealism among leftist youth (Hoellering 1974–75). Early in 1931 Slatan Dudow—a Bulgarian who, after studying theater in Berlin, had become involved with Erwin Piscator's political stage and Brecht in 1929 (Gersch 1975, 104)—approached the company with a film sketch about unemployment and resignation in a working-class family (Brecht 1997a). Despite its financial difficulties, Prometheus accepted the project with an eye to integrating the sports theme into what would become its first sound film. Before the film was finished, the firm went bankrupt, and only with financial support from the Swiss Praesens-Film company was *Kuhle Wampe* completed, with the shoot lasting, intermittently, almost three quarters of a year from August 1931 until February 1932 (Lindner and Gerz 2002, 438).

For Brecht these were the years during which he was formulating his "materialist aesthetics" through the study of Marxist texts. Seeking new answers to the question "what is political art?" he was experimenting with models for linking cultural production to social change in his *Lehrstücke* (didactic plays), in film scenarios, and in theoretical essays such as those that accompanied his court case against the producers of the filmed version of *Die Dreigroschenoper* (*The Threepenny Opera*). The Brecht/Weill musical, the most successful play of the Weimar years, had thrust the author into the international limelight, and G. W. Pabst's film version of the play had opened in February 1931 to rave reviews. Brecht, who was concerned with the implications of his play's success in a thoroughly bourgeois theater institution, had written a new film scenario in order to radicalize both the formal means of distanciation and the anticapitalist message. The producer and Pabst refused, however, to recognize Brecht's rights as author to revise the play, so he and Weill sued in a widely publicized trial immediately preceding the shoot of *Kuhle Wampe*. In the 1932 book-length essay *Der Dreigroschenprozeß* (*The Threepenny Lawsuit*), Brecht presents his most extended and coherent analysis of the film medium's impact on the way art represents reality and the way the reader or spectator sees (Brecht 2000a). The trial, and Brecht's presentation of it, was a brilliant example of applied dialectics that counterposed two ideological institutions: the state justice system, with its norms of contract law and copyright protection, against the film industry's media practice, with its economic exigencies and forms of cultural legitimation. In fact, the lawsuit against the film production company was the point of departure, but the text of the essay neither documents the trial nor raises the issues of cinematic adaptation surrounding his scenario or, for that matter, Pabst's film. Rather, Brecht assumed the persona of the naive artist for the purposes of his "sociological experiment," demonstrating how new technologies and capitalist market mechanisms had removed the means of production from the hands of the artist and in the process destroyed the idealistic and metaphysical ideology of cultural production. The modern artist, like the laborer in industrial society, had no choice but to organize collectively. Here Brecht sought to unmask the contradiction between bourgeois ideologies of autonomous art and the demands of capitalist production in the culture sphere (Giles 1997).

If *The Threepenny Lawsuit* represents Brecht's most sophisticated contribution to media theory, then the 1932 film *Kuhle Wampe* can be considered his most important legacy in film history, the only example of his practical work that came close to realizing the idea of deindividualizing (aesthetic) production in the cinema. Not only the film's planning and shooting but also its image of the industrial metropolis and the polarized working class integrate the collective experience with new ways of representing reality (Vogt 2001, 282–86). The collective that came together around Brecht and Dudow was in part dictated by difficult and impoverished production conditions but also reflected the attempt to counteract the hierarchical studio arrangements in the commercial industry. Dudow brought in novelist Ernst Ottwalt, to whom the film scenario is attributed along with Brecht, because of his intimate knowledge of the working-class environment. Hanns Eisler, who was working with Brecht and Dudow on the stage production of Brecht's *Die Mutter* (*The Mother*), also joined the team. He had experience writing modernist film music (e.g., for a revised version of Walter Ruttmann's 1927 experimental film *Opus 3* and for Viktor Trivas's *Niemandsland* [*Hell on Earth*], 1931) and enjoyed a reputation for his popular workers' songs (Adank 1977). Brecht's wife, Helene Weigel, who sings one of Eisler's ballads, and Ernst Busch, who plays the lead role, Fritz, were also well-known actors in the workers' theater movement. Finally, the appearance of the leading German agitprop theater group, "Das rote Sprachrohr" (The Red Megaphone), as well as the participation of thousands of enthusiasts organized in workers' sports clubs for the final section of the film, brought an unusual degree of visibility and public interest to the collective project. Brecht himself emphasized the collective nature of the project as part of its political commitment to an alternative to the capitalist mode of production (Brecht 2000b). Although the film's credits, as well as the original poster, list Dudow as director, Brecht and Ottwald (*sic*) as scriptwriters, and Eisler as music composer, the Berlin censor's commentary lists Brecht as director, assisted by Dudow (Brecht 1969, 122).[2] The film should run at least under both Dudow's and Brecht's names, but especially in its post-1960s reception it is frequently attributed to Brecht alone, erroneously (Fig. 16.1).

Kuhle Wampe's theme is a departure from the "traditional" proletarian film productions supported by Prometheus and the Communist Party. In what seems to have been a conscious effort to respond to the hierarchical discourse of authority in *Mother Krause's Journey into Happiness*, it takes up similar plot elements from the social drama, including a suicide, a love affair, leisure activities, and the emancipation of the daughter through her political work. *Kuhle Wampe*, however, thematizes apolitical behavior as a reality of the working class, contrary to the denunciatory position more typical of official leftist party views. Hence, the film problematizes precisely the issue that in the early 1930s was proving to be a fertile basis for the other, fascist discourse of authority as well. In the period of crisis characterizing the last years of the Weimar Republic, the structural instability of the working class caused by unemployment and impoverishment made it particularly susceptible to middlebrow ideologies of social harmony and classless statism proposed by the National Socialists. *Kuhle Wampe* addresses various aspects of this issue not so much to clarify its causes but to show the powerlessness resulting from the desire to escape from politics altogether. In this respect the film differs radically from Jutzi's melodrama and other socially critical portrayals of working-class family life, such as Leo Mittler's 1929 *Jenseits der Straße* (*Harbor Drift*) or Hans Tintner's 1930 *Cyankali* (*Cyanide*), as well as from the industry's attempts to capitalize on the effects of the depression with escapist comedies such as Wilhelm Thiele's 1930 musical *Die Drei von der Tankstelle* (*The Three from the Filling Station*).

Beyond its thematic and political distinction *Kuhle Wampe* introduces a different structural approach. Brecht was familiar with the montage principles of Soviet cinema, and they revealed an experimental energy parallel to his own explorations in the Epic Theater. What he found congenial was the constructivist principle of cinematic montage, premised on the idea of interruption and collision. This type of montage editing brings together images or shots that do not "fit" but insist on being "read" by the spectator, eliciting cognitive activity such as observing, evaluating, and deciding (Webber 1999). Interruptive montage editing becomes the basis of a pedagogical model of spectator activity. *Kuhle Wampe* was, in fact, an important opportunity for Brecht to test his Epic Theater principles in the film medium, which he thought used the most advanced artistic means of representation and therefore promised the greatest political impact. The cinema confirmed his notion that technological changes have a massive stake in constituting and interpreting reality, yet just as Brecht's dramaturgical practice was directed against the "culinary" theater, so he rejected the idea of transforming film into a "high" art form

Nach mehrmaligem Verbot freigegeben!

Kuhle Wampe
oder: WEM GEHÖRT DIE WELT

U-R-F

Manuskript: Brecht und Ottwald / Musik: Hanns Eisler

REGIE: S. TH. DUDOW

Kamera: Günther Krampf

Produktionsleitung: Georg M. Höllering,   Robert Scharfenberg

Darsteller:

Hertha Thiele, Ernst Busch, Martha Wolter, Adolf Fischer,
Lili Schönborn, Max Sablotzki, Alfred Schaefer, Gerhard
Bienert, Martha Burchardi, Karl-Heinz Carell, Carl Dahmen,
Fritz Erpenbeck, Josef Hanoczek, Richard Hilgert, Hugo
Werner-Kahle, Hermann Krehan, Paul Kretzburg, Anna
Müller-Linke, Rudolf Nehls, Erich Peters, Olly Rummel,
Willi Schur, Martha Seemann, Hans Stern, Carl Wagner

**4000 Arbeitersportler / Eine Arbeiterspieltruppe
Uthmann-Chor / Sängervereinigung Norden
Arbeitersänger Groß-Berlin / Chor der Berliner Staatsoper**

Architekten: Robert Scharfenberg, Carl P. Haacker / Auf-
nahmeleiter: Karl Ehrlich / Tonaufnahmen: Tobis Melofilm
System: Tobis-Klangfilm / Musikalische Leitung: Josef Schmid
Orchester: Lewis Ruth / Balladen: Helene Weigel und Ernst
Busch / Tonschnitt: Peter Meyrowitz

Uraufführung: Heute im Atrium

Weltvertrieb und Verleih für Deutschland:

PRAESENS-FILM G.M.B.H.

Berlin SW 68, Friedrichstraße 23 — Fernsprecher: A 7 Dönhoff 3803

FIGURE 16.1 Original *Kuhle Wampe* poster for the opening at the Berlin Atrium cinema (1932), advertising the film's release after multiple prohibitions by the censor. Courtesy of the Bertolt Brecht Archive, Stiftung Akademie der Künste, Berlin.

as an alternative to the trivial products of the entertainment industry. Rather he saw the cinema as a mass art with revolutionary potential. In addition, his interest in realism, in how images produce knowledge about "reality" under specific and changing historical conditions, dominated his theoretical and practical work from 1928 to 1933. Finally, Brecht's interest in Marxism made him increasingly critical of bourgeois cultural institutions so that he welcomed the opportunity to address what he perceived as the mass audience, not as an amorphous monolith but rather as a dynamic amalgam (Rippey 2007).

Brecht considered the cinema closer to visual arts, like painting or photography, than to the dramatic or narrative arts. For that reason his attention focused on the organization of the images within the cinematic frame, as well as between frames, privileging the disjointed quality of montage. Dudow, Brecht, and Ottwalt also shared an interest in the documentary nature of the cinema and its promise of referentiality and authenticity. Hence, they avoided the mimetic notion of realism that relies on the reproduction of an illusion of reality and instead invested their energy in the conscious selection and composition of reality. This explains why the camera work in *Kuhle Wampe* is relatively restrained, even uninteresting, when compared to the virtuosity and expressiveness of the earlier Weimar cinema. On the other hand, Dudow and Brecht integrated from the Soviet cinema an awareness of cinematic punctuation, which they exploited to the full. *Kuhle Wampe* resembles, then, *The Last Laugh* insofar as the image dominates the word and composition draws attention to its construction, but it constructs images not as spectacle but rather as part of a rhetorical argument; that is, the film relates images to the context in order to reveal social processes.

To shift spectator interest from the story to dramatized acts of cognition, the plot contains a minimum of story elements presented as a loose sequence of episodes divided into three sections. Section 1 introduces the Bönike family and its disintegration under the pressure of unemployment. Section 2 pursues the family problems through the complications in the daughter's relationship to her lover. Section 3 suggests a resolution in the young couple's tension and an alternative to the parents' resignation in the face of impoverishment when the lovers reunite at the Workers' Sports Festival (Brecht 2000c). Counterbalancing this narrative continuity and its temporal unfolding, however, are the rhetorical effects that establish the relationship between seeing and persuasion. The first section, for example, opens not with an establishing shot but with a prologue or overture: a collage of quick takes from dynamically contrasting camera angles, localizing the action geographically in Berlin (image of the Brandenburg Gate), in a working-class quarter of the city (shots of a factory and tenements), and temporally during the depression (sequence of newspaper headlines indicating the steep rise in unemployment figures). The printed title ("One Unemployed Worker Less") and the overture-like

FIGURE 16.2 The montage sequence of bicycles in *Kuhle Wampe* (1932) condenses into striking images the desperation of the job search by the unemployed workers. Frame enlargement by Kristin Thompson, Madison, WI.

opening music—highly theatrical markings of this and each subsequent section, reminiscent of Brecht's stage productions—cue the spectator to the film's structural pattern: a self-conscious narration unfolds to solicit the spectator's active role in a cognitive process. The montage of static, discontinuous images suggests, in other words, not the reproduction of reality but its construction; and the stress on the documentary aspect of each shot has an almost fine-arts, photographic quality rather than a dramatic or narrative quality. Moreover, the sequence reveals a striking economy of images indicating location, urban space, and economic crisis.

The next sequence continues to develop strategies that stress the way of looking. Introduced by the printed title "The Job Hunt," the editing rhythm retards with a long take of a group of job seekers gathering at a corner and waiting for the daily classified ads to be distributed. When the delivery boy arrives, they grab the leaflets, scan them with eyes of experienced job seekers, and jump on their bicycles. The pace quickens with rapidly cut shots, often from extreme angles. The sequence of images describes a pattern of circularity as a metaphor for the hopelessness of the job search: the wheels turning, the feet pumping bike pedals, the ever quicker turnaround at closed factory gates (Fig. 16.2). Accompanying these introductory segments is Eisler's pulsating music—fast, staccato, and dissonant—underlining the abrupt montage editing and structuring the viewer's relation to the bicycle race and its message of desperation through speed and repetition (Alter 2004, 81).

These first sequences introduce several crucial aspects that are central for the film's understanding of the cinema's political potential. Brecht's theory of Epic Theater, which in many respects was tested in this film, stresses the social *Gestus* as a central performance and representational principle for structuring meaning (Silberman 2006). Understood both as mental attitude and physical bearing, *gestus* for Brecht informs all aspects of performance, including acting, music, dialogue, and set. It concentrates and amplifies details in order to emphasize the context and conditions of what is shown or done. In contrast to the Epic Theater, *gestus* in *Kuhle Wampe* shifts to the camera and editing, in particular to their functions of interrupting and citing reality. Breaking the illusion of total visibility, montage becomes a means of deconstructing everyday actions and expressions into their social determinants and inscribing in them the conditions of their construction. The bikeride sequence offers a good example of this focus on external action. The "gestic camera" interrupts the representation of reality in order to cite and repeat discrete elements. In fact, one could summarize the mounting frustration conveyed by the biking sequence in the *gestus* (gesture) of the young man who crumples up the leaflet and throws it away in the final shot. For Brecht such a *gestus* articulates the moment when we spectators may recognize ourselves in the film's reality and at the same time see ourselves being confronted with reality as a construct. If it functions properly, this is the moment when we cease to be in agreement with ourselves, the moment when we become able to agree (or disagree) with the reality around us and then begin to consider how to change it.

If the bike race is constructed around the dynamics of movement, this movement leads inexorably to the suicide of the young man in the next sequence. Returning home from the unsuccessful job search, Franz must listen to the criticism of his equally unemployed father and worried mother (Fig. 16.3). Having finished lunch, even his sympathetic sister Anni leaves him sitting at the table, while the camera cuts to a homily hanging on the kitchen wall: "Don't blame the morn that brings hardship and work. It's wonderful to care for those one loves." The family's impoverishment, exacerbated by the parents' platitudes, leads him to jump out the window, showing how isolation, indifference, and anonymity bring self-destruction to this family. The detail shot showing Franz removing his watch and placing it on a table before jumping to his death becomes especially significant in this context: we do not see the expression of an inner emotion but the conscious performance of that inner emotion *as* affect. The camera's deliberate movement toward and focus on the gesture of removing the watch produces that inner emotion for us to see. Furthermore, the sequence does not propose an answer to this young man's

FIGURE 16.3 The impoverished family reproduces lowbrow behavior that will drive the despondent young Bönicke (Alfred Schäfer), at left, to commit suicide. Courtesy of the Filmmuseum Berlin, Stiftung deutsche Kinemathek, Berlin.

desperation but rather appeals to the spectator to recognize the conditions that produce this suicide.

The film's first section closes, finally, with a woman looking directly at the camera and commenting: "He had his best years still to come." The direct address brings into play the rhetoric of cinematic subject-object relations by suggesting that the spectator is not only looking but is also being seen. The dialectic of looking and seeing is expanded to include the spectator, who is implicated directly in a self-conscious process by being caught up in the network of social looks. The persistent montage in *Kuhle Wampe* is, then, a rhetorical structure, consisting of interruptions (expository titles, inserts, songs, choruses), contrasts of sound and image (commentary, voice-off, autonomous music), documentary-like quotes (Berlin streets and architecture, newspaper headlines), and disruptive editing (unusual camera angles spliced together, sudden extreme close-ups, direct address to the camera). The montage grasps images and action in the context of their political and institutional conditions, signaling the spectator that this film is to be watched and evaluated. For Brecht reality is not what the spectator sees but what the spectator re-cognizes, that which is behind the visible. The "epic cinema," then, asks the viewer to take control of vision and seeing in response to the montage.

After the son's suicide the narrative's second section focuses on the daughter as a counterpoint to the son's pointless death. Once again a collage sequence opens the section but this time with a more lyrical overture consisting of nature images and accompanied by symphonic music. The following episodes alternately portray Anni's dilemmas and the useless hypocrisy and resignation of her parents. In a sequence parallel in structure and message to Franz's job hunt, for example, Anni appears in a series of elliptical shots at various government agencies trying to prevent her family's eviction from their apartment owing to their failure to pay the rent. Characteristic for the rhetorical construction is the eviction "scene" itself, reduced to a synecdoche, a part standing for the entire action. One shot only frames the mother, who stands on a ladder and unfastens a lamp from the ceiling while an offscreen voice (a judge) reads the eviction notice in a bored monotone. Anni's lover, Fritz, invites the family to join him at Kuhle Wampe; the titular tent city was in fact a summer campsite on the eastern periphery of Berlin that by 1932 had become a popular refuge for working-class families evicted from their homes. Here, as a voice-over commentary and the quick sequence of images suggest, middlebrow patterns of behavior are reproduced in the settlement's pedantic cleanliness and in the inhabitants' efforts to escape the reality of impoverishment through the illusion of normalcy.

The "Mata Hari" sequence is a paradigmatic example of this behavior modeled after Sergei Eisenstein's notion of the polyphonic montage that produces an abstract idea from the collision of the parts. While Anni's father reads with fascination a passage from the newspaper about the adventures of the vamp Mata Hari, tripping over foreign words and deliciously enjoying the suggestive sensuality in the description of the dancer's nude body, the mother calculates the weekly food expenses, oblivious to the father's voice, which continues throughout the sequence (Fig. 16.4). The montage juxtaposes their two very different facial expressions with close-ups of price tags for food items, setting in relation through speech, written signs, and contrasting images the boredom and emptiness fed by the pulp press, on the one hand, and the family's everyday distress, on the other.

The following sequence contextualizes the relation of fantasized sexuality and poverty by contrasting the consequences of Anni and Fritz's love affair, for she has become pregnant and considers an abortion. A lyrically composed montage renders in a kind of stream of consciousness her apprehensions about bearing a child. Images of children, toys, store windows with infant clothing, and baby products dissolve into shots of her work termination notice, a midwife's office sign, burial caskets, and her brother's lifeless body, accompanied throughout by musical themes from the film and from children's songs. This sequence is striking, even anomalous, because it is the film's sole concession to realist conventions of psychological motivation. Apparently the film originally addressed the abortion issue

FIGURE 16.4 While the elder Bönicke (Max Sablotzki) reads about the sexual exploits of Mata Hari, mother Bönicke (Lilli Schönborn) struggles with her accounts for the next week. Frame enlargement by Kristin Thompson, Madison, WI.

more directly, but the titles and dialogue concerning state laws controlling the woman's body and the relationship between money and access to abortion were censored (Klaus 1990, 127). The last sequence in the second section, the family's celebration of Anni's engagement to the reluctant Fritz, brings full circle the exposition of alienation and regression in the apolitical working-class family that began in the first section. Through slapstick and hyperbole the scene shows in a few grotesque strokes the family's collapse into a drunken brawl. Anni, confronted with this model of family life and Fritz's own regret at losing his freedom through marriage, breaks off the engagement.

The third section opens with the printed title "Who Owns the World?" and opposes to the destructive individualism displayed in the film's first two sections the collective spirit invested in the Workers' Sports Festival. Consistent with the stress on collective action, the family's story is subordinated now to the larger framework of class solidarity as an alternative to family disintegration. By far the most didactically structured section, it, too, opens with a collage, composed of industrial motifs coupled with musical themes from Eisler's signature "Solidarity Song," which, through repetition, becomes a veritable refrain of the section. Four scenes present different aspects of the workers' organizational and educational work that contrast and respond to the family dilemmas in the narrative's first two parts: cooperative

FIGURE 16.5   The cramped space of a subway car encompasses a cross section of the city's inhabitants, who engage in a polemical debate about changing the world. Frame enlargement by Kristin Thompson, Madison, WI.

planning, group activities, noncompetitive races, and an agitprop skit showing how neighbors' solidarity can prevent a family's eviction from their apartment. The final scene or coda transfers the lesson of solidarity from the sports festival to a political discussion, from image to word. Pressed into a subway car is a sociopolitical cross section of the city's inhabitants returning from their weekend recreation, each of whom comments on a newspaper article reporting that 24 million pounds of coffee were burned by the Brazilian government to protect the falling commodity price (Fig. 16.5). The quick, polemical argument, mirrored by a camera cutting rapidly within the cramped space from one face to another, climaxes in the question: "Who will change the world?" Anni's friend Gerda, speaking directly to the camera in a challenge to the spectator, responds: "Those who don't like it."

Kuhle Wampe is an early and exceptional example of how to link questions of representation, social change, and the subject who will effect that change. It presents a visually rhetorical argument that intends to persuade the spectator. Corresponding to the foregrounding of rhetorical means is the subordination of character and causality. Characters lack psychological depth, and causality is extraindividual, suggested by the collage sequences and brief references to macropolitical conditions. A realistic motivation for events arises only from the "verisimilitude" of the images' documentary quality, whose referentiality "quotes" the real like a case study rather than projecting the illusion of a seamless reality as totality. The narrative relies, then, on a complex web of fragments in which the autonomy of the scenes draws attention to the spectator's cognitive process of connecting them.

Dudow, Brecht, Ottwalt, and Eisler produced the film with a historical spectator in mind, the class-conscious workers who in the early 1930s were familiar with and sympathetic to the political demand for solidarity projected in the last section. Although its rhetorical structure reveals a consistent logic drawn from that assumption, the collaborative team plays on a tension between the expected and expectable message of political practice and the complication of that synthetic message through the narrational rhetoric. In contrast to leftist films of the 1920s, which typically bind the spectator to the spectacle through conventional narrative patterns of identification and catharsis, *Kuhle Wampe* constructs a dynamic relation of contradiction between continuity and discontinuity. It does not aim at providing an answer for the spectator, but it does aim at awakening the spectator's recognition of the possibility for change. This emphasis on the spectator as producer of meaning is inscribed in the disjointed representation and in the different set of relations to "reality" that it implies. Hence, an imaginary relation is constituted through a collective subject whose position is only provisional, projected in the space between the film's final question (who will change the world?) and answer (those who don't like it!).

Kuhle Wampe was finally released for distribution on April 25, 1932, after several cuts demanded by the censorship board were made in the original version, and it opened in Berlin on May 30. The ambivalence that characterized the film's contemporaneous reception indicates the consequences of its open structure (Korte 1998, 245–65). As Brecht himself recognized, the politically sympathetic critics of the left and even those in the Communist Party understood *Kuhle Wampe* less well than the censors who initially forbade its distribution. The censors, like the filmmakers themselves, were most concerned with the film's overall impact and identified the power of the critique in the rhetorical structure, whereas progressive and leftist critics missed a clear, partisan message (Brecht 1969, 143–67; Kühn, Tümmler, and Wimmer 1978, 2:130–85). Although the film's successful but short-lived run throughout Germany in 1932–33 seems to indicate that there did exist historically a class-conscious spectator who could respond to the challenge elicited by such a "constructivist film," the total elimination of the left-wing public sphere with the onset of National Socialism in March 1933 raised questions about the viability of the provisional collective subject projected in the film narration.

Kuhle Wampe's impact as a model for politically motivated revolutionary cinema and as an alternative to studio conventions was in fact negligible. The conditions under which the film was conceived and produced—always with an eye to the eventuality of censorship problems and to its precarious financial backing—necessitat-

ed compromises at every level of its realization. This meant that the already complicated filmic structure, drawing on avant-garde Soviet practices, had to camouflage
further its agitational thrust behind the relatively harmless allegory of sports races
and the appeal of the youthful participants. In fact, the original screenplay, which
became accessible only in 1997 (Brecht 1997b), indicates plans for a much more
complex structure that was to include the political discussion in the subway car
as an independent fourth section with additional music, contrasting songs, and
images of demonstrations around the world (Lindner and Gerz 2002, 454). Moreover, the National Socialists' victory shortly after the film's release meant both an
interruption in its distribution and, more significant, in the working-class struggle
which was its subject. This may explain the later ambivalence of the filmmakers'
contemporaries. Retrospectively, the film historian Lotte Eisner was struck by the
images of the mass sports rally in the final section of *Kuhle Wampe* as an unwitting
anticipation of Nazi parades (Eisner 1969, 335), while Siegfried Kracauer, looking
back in 1947 at his 1932 defense of the film against the initial censor's ban, noted the
generational optimism reflected in the glorification of youth, a tendency that he
saw in early Nazi films as well (Kracauer 2004, 247). Indeed, some of the first films
produced in the Third Reich—for example, Hans Steinhoff's *Hitlerjunge Quex* (*Hitler Youth Quex*), Franz Seitz's *SA-Mann Brand*, and Franz Wenzler's *Hans Westmar*
(all 1933)—echo situations, techniques, and images from *Kuhle Wampe*.

   A younger generation of filmmakers, cinemagoers, and critics raised new questions about the film's historical contradictions. *Kuhle Wampe* reasserted itself in
the post-1968 politicization of the public sphere within a tradition of political cinema through Brecht's ideas on the nature of cinematic representation and more
generally his reflections on political art. In West Germany, New German Cinema
directors like Alexander Kluge, Jean-Marie Straub and Danièle Huillet, Rainer
Werner Fassbinder, Harun Farocki, and Helke Sander owed much to the Brechtian
model. The most radical and consistent student of Brecht's aesthetics, however,
was Jean-Luc Godard, and through his films, especially *Tout va bien* (*All's Well*,
1972), he mediated much of the theoretical tradition for which Brecht stands in the
French, Anglo-American, and Latin American cinemas (Byg 1997). Furthermore,
in the mid-1970s Brecht's modernist aesthetics and *Kuhle Wampe* became important touchstones for discussions about the possibilities and limitations of political
filmmaking among English and French critics and scholars (Walsh 1981; Mueller
1989). The end of the cold war, Germany's reunification, the new thirty-volume
critical edition of Brecht's works in German (1988–2000), and the historicization
of his contributions in the context of the centennial commemorating his birth in
1998 have not diminished the interest in *Kuhle Wampe*, not least in response to my
own reading (Silberman 1995, 34–48). Contrary to the dominant left interpretation of the film's optimistic closure, Lindner and Gerz suggest a Derridian read-

ing of the discussion in the subway car and the final chorus of the Solidarity Song ("Forward and Don't Forget") as a melancholic reminder of Marx's specter haunting Europe (Lindner and Gerz 2002, 455). Gal Kirn insists on the need to account not only for the spectator's cognitive activity but for the work of the unconscious as well in the film's construction of the political subject (Kirn 2007, 38). Theodore Rippey focuses on the film's revolutionary corporality, showing that the filmmakers' attempt to engage the physical and emotional losses of young working people in their treatment of romantic and erotic life had less to do with party politics and industrial labor than with the desires and frustrations of young Germans in the crumbling Weimar Republic (Rippey 2007). *Kuhle Wampe*, in other words, maintains its status as an exemplary work, negotiating the dialectical relation between aesthetic innovation and political commitment in the cinema, demonstrating that any discourse about the real and the cognitive relations that govern it cannot escape an examination of how we represent "reality" and how those representations constitute that very reality.

NOTES

1. This is an extensively revised and updated version of "The Rhetoric of the Image: Slatan Dudov and Bertolt Brecht's *Kuhle Wampe or Who Owns the World*" (Silberman 1995, 34–48). The film's original, German title was *Kuhle Wampe oder Wem gehört die Welt?* (which translates literally as "Kuhle Wampe or Who Owns the World?"). The British distribution title was *Kuhle Wampe or Whither Germany?*
2. Interested readers can see the censorship documents at www.deutsches-filminstitut. de/filme/f001509.htm#zensur (accessed March 19, 2008).

REFERENCES

Adank, Thomas. 1977. "Hanns Eisler und die Musik in *Kuhle Wampe*." In *Erobert den Film!* ed. Neue Gesellschaft für bildende Kunst, 65–67. Berlin: NGBK.

Alter, Nora M. 2004. "The Politics and Sounds of Everyday Life in *Kuhle Wampe*." In *Sound Matters: Essays on the Acoustics of Modern German Culture*, ed. Nora M. Alter and Lutz Koepnick, 80–90. New York: Berghahn.

Brecht, Bertolt. 1969. *Kuhle Wampe: Protokoll des Films und Materialien.* Ed. Wolfgang Gersch and Werner Hecht. Frankfurt am Main: Suhrkamp.

——. 1997a. Exposé *Kuhle Wampe*. 1931. In Bertolt Brecht, *Werke*. Ed. Werner Hecht, Jan Knopf, Werner Mittenzwei, and Klaus-Detlef Müller. Vol. 19:719–23. Frankfurt am Main: Suhrkamp.

——. 1997b. "Weekend—Kuhle Wampe: Ein Tonfilm" [original screenplay]. In Bertolt Brecht, *Werke*. Ed. Werner Hecht, Jan Knopf, Werner Mittenzwei, and Klaus-Detlef Müller. Vol. 19:441–571. Frankfurt am Main: Suhrkamp.

——. 2000a. "The Threepenny Lawsuit: A Sociological Experiment." 1932. In Silberman 2000, 147–99.

——. 2000b. "The Sound Film *Kuhle Wampe* or *Who Owns the World*." 1932. In Silberman 2000, 204–6.

——. 2000c. "*Kuhle Wampe* or *Who Owns the World?*" [scene segmentation]. In Silberman 2000, 209–58.

Byg, Barton. 1997. "Brecht, New Waves, and Political Modernism in Cinema." In *A Bertolt Brecht Reference Companion*, ed. Siegfried Mews, 220–37. Westport, CT: Greenwood Press.

Eisner, Lotte. 1969. *The Haunted Screen: Expressionism in the German Cinema and the Influence of Max Reinhardt*. Trans. Roger Greaves. Berkeley: University of California Press.

Gersch, Wolfgang. 1975. *Film bei Brecht: Bertolt Brechts praktische und theoretische Auseinandersetzung mit dem Film*. Munich: Hanser.

Giles, Steve. 1997. *Bertolt Brecht and Critical Theory: Marxism, Modernity, and the Threepenny Lawsuit*. Bern: Peter Lang.

Heller, Heinz B. 1985. *Literarische Intelligenz und Film: Zu Veränderungen der ästhetischen Theorie und Praxis unter dem Eindruck des Films 1910–1930 in Deutschland*. Tübingen: Niemeyer.

Herlinghaus, Hermann. 1965. *Slatan Dudow*. Berlin, GDR: Henschelverlag.

Hoellering, George. 1974–75. "Making *Kuhle Wampe*: An Interview with George Hoellering." Interview by Ben Brewster and Colin MacCabe. *Screen* 15, no. 4:71–79.

Kirn, Gal. 2007. "*Kuhle Wampe*: Politics of Montage, De-montage of Politics?" In *Film-Philosophy* 11, no. 1:33–48. www.film-philosophy.com/2007v11n1/kirn.pdf (accessed March 20, 2008).

Klaus, Ulrich J. 1990. *Deutsche Tonfilme: Filmlexikon der abendfüllenden deutschen und deutschsprachigen Tonfilme nach ihren deutschen Uraufführungen*. Vol. 3: Jahrgang 1932. Berlin: Klaus.

Korte, Helmut. 1998. *Der Spielfilm und das Ende der Weimarer Republik*. Göttingen: Vandenhoeck & Ruprecht.

Kracauer, Siegfried. 2004. *From Caligari to Hitler: A Psychological History of the German Film*. Ed. Leonardo Quaresima. Rev. and exp. ed. Princeton, NJ: Princeton University Press.

Kreimeier, Klaus. 1996. *The Ufa Story: A History of Germany's Greatest Film Company, 1918–1945*. Trans. Robert Kimber and Rita Kimber. New York: Hill and Wang.

Kühn, Gertraude, Karl Tümmler, and Walter Wimmer, eds. 1978. *Film und revolutionäre Arbeiterbewegung in Deutschland, 1918–1932: Dokumente und Materialien*. 2 vols. Berlin, GDR: Henschelverlag.

Lindner, Burkhard, and Raimund Gerz. 2002. "*Kuhle Wampe oder Wem gehört die Welt?*" In *Brecht-Handbuch*, ed. Jan Knopf, 3:432–57. Stuttgart: Metzler.

Mueller, Roswitha. 1989. *Bertolt Brecht and the Theory of Media*. Lincoln: University of Nebraska Press.

Murray, Bruce A. 1990. *Film and the German Left in the Weimar Republic: From* Caligari *to* Kuhle Wampe. Austin: University of Texas Press.

Pettifer, James. 1975–76. "The Limits of Naturalism." *Screen* 16, no. 4:5–11.

Rippey, Theodore. 2007. "*Kuhle Wampe* and the Problem of Corporal Culture." *Cinema Journal* 47, no. 1 (fall): 3–25.

Silberman, Marc. 1995. *German Cinema: Texts in Context*. Detroit: Wayne State University Press.

——, ed. and trans. 2000. *Bertolt Brecht on Film and Radio*. London: Methuen.

——. 2002. "The Political Cinema as Oppositional Practice: Weimar and Beyond." In *The German Cinema Book*, ed. Tim Bergfelder, Erica Carter, and Deniz Göktürk, 165–72. London: BFI.

——. 2006. "Brecht's Gestus: Staging Contradictions." In *The Brecht Yearbook*. Vol. 31. Ed. Jürgen Hillesheim, 318–35. Pittsburgh: International Brecht Society.

Vogt, Guntram. 2001. "Slatan Dudow—*Kuhle Wampe oder Wem gehört die Welt* (1932)." In *Die Stadt im Film: Deutsche Spielfilme, 1900–2000*, 277–86. Marburg: Schüren.

Walsh, Martin. 1981. *The Brechtian Aspect of Radical Cinema*. London: BFI.

Webber, Andrew. 1999. "*Kuhle Wampe*, or How to Read a Film." In *From Classical Shades to Vickers Victorious: Shifting Perspectives in British German Studies*, ed. Steve Giles and Peter Graves, 171–82. Bern: Peter Lang.

Willett, John. 1978. *Art and Politics in the Weimar Period: The New Sobriety, 1917–1933*. New York: Pantheon.

Witte, Karsten. 1972. "Brecht und der Film." In *Bertolt Brecht I*, ed. Heinz Ludwig Arnold, 81–99. Sonderband aus der Reihe Text + Kritik. Munich: Richard Boorberg Verlag.

FILMOGRAPHY

Das Cabinet des Dr. Caligari / The Cabinet of Dr. Caligari

Decla-Bioscop, premiere on February 27, 1920
Director: Robert Wiene
Producers: Erich Pommer and Rudolph Meinert
Script: Carl Mayer and Hans Janowitz
Based on a story by Hans Janowitz
Cinematography: Willy Hameister
Art Direction: Walter Reimann, Hermann Warm, and Walter Röhrig
Assistant Director: Rochus Gliese
Original Music: Giuseppe Becce
CAST:
Werner Krauss: Dr. Caligari
Conrad Veidt: Cesare
Lil Dagover: Jane
Friedrich Fehér: Francis
Hans Heinz von Twardowski: Alan
Rudolf Letinger: Dr. Olson
Rudolf Klein-Rogge: Captured murderer

Der Golem, wie er in die Welt kam / The Golem: How He Came into the World

PAGU-Ufa, premiere on October 29, 1920
Director: Paul Wegener
Producer: Paul Davidson

Script: Paul Wegener and Henrik Galeen, based on the novel by Gustav Meyrink
Cinematography: Karl Freund and Guido Seebar
Art Direction: Hans Poelzig
Costume Design: Rochus Gliese
Original Music: Hans Landsberger
CAST:
Paul Wegener: The Golem
Albert Steinrück: Rabbi Löw
Lydia Salmonova: Miriam Löw
Ernest Deutsch: Famulus
Otto Gebühr: Emperor Rudolf II
Lothar Müthel: Knight Florian

Das indische Grabmal / *The Indian Tomb*

Part 1: Die Sendung des Joghi / *The Mission of the Yogi*
Part 2: Der Tiger von Eschnapur / *The Tiger of Bengal*
May-Film, premiere on October 22, 1921 (Part 1); November 19, 1921 (Part 2)
Director: Joe May
Producer: Joe May
Script: Thea von Harbou and Fritz Lang, based on a story by Thea von Harbou
Cinematography: Werner Brandes
Camera Assistant: Karl Puth
Art Direction: Martin Jacoby-Boy and Otto Hunte
Assistant Art Directors: Erich Kettelhut and Karl Vollbrecht
Costume Design: Martin Jacoby-Boy and Otto Hunte
Music: Wilhelm Löwitt
CAST:
Mia May: Irene Amundsen
Olaf Fønss: Herbert Rowland
Conrad Veidt: Ayan III, the Maharajah of Bengal
Erna Morena: Savitri, the Maharajah's wife
Bernhard Goetzke: Ramigani "Rami," a yogi
Lya De Putti: Mirrjha
Paul Richter: MacAllen
Georg John: A penitent
Louis Brody: The Maharajah's servant

Nosferatu, eine Symphonie des Grauens / Nosferatu, a Symphony of Horror

Prana-Film, premiere on March 4, 1922
Director: F. W. Murnau
Producers: Albin Grau and Enrico Dieckmann
Script: Henrik Galeen, from the novel *Dracula*, by Bram Stoker
Cinematography: Fritz Arno Wagner
Art Direction: Albin Grau
Costume Design: Albin Grau
Music: Hans Erdmann
CAST:
Max Schreck: Count Orlok
Alexander Granach: Knock/Renfield
Gustav von Wanerheim: Waldemar Hutter/Jonathan Harker
Greta Schröder/Schroeder: Ellen/Mina
G. H. Schnell: Harding
Ruth Landshoff: Annie
John Gottow: Professor Bulwer
Max Nemetz: Ship captain
Gustav Botz: Professor Sievers

Dr. Mabuse, der Spieler / Dr. Mabuse, the Gambler

Part I: Dr. Mabuse, der Spieler—Ein Bild der Zeit (Dr. Mabuse, the Gambler—A Picture of the Time)
Part II: Inferno—Menschen der Zeit (Inferno—Men of the Time)
Uco-Film/Decla-Bioscop, premiere on April 27, 1922
Director: Fritz Lang
Producer: Erich Pommer
Script: Thea von Harbou, from the novel by Norbert Jacques
Cinematography: Carl Hoffmann
Art Direction: Otto Hunte and Karl Stahl-Urrach
Assistant Art Director: Erich Kettelhut and Karl Vollbrecht
Costume Design: Vally Reinecke
Music: Konrad Elfers
CAST:
Rudolf Klein-Rogge: Dr. Mabuse
Bernhard Goetzke: State Attorney von Wenk
Alfred Abel: Count Told
Aud Egede Nissen: Cara Carozza

Gertrud Welcker: Countess Told
Paul Richter: Edgar Hull
Robert Forster-Larringa: Spoerri
Julius E. Hermann: Schramm

Der letzte Mann / The Last Laugh

Ufa, premier December 23, 1924
Director: F. W. Murnau
Producer: Erich Pommer
Script: Carl Mayer
Art Designers: Robert Herlth and Walter Röhrig
Cinematography: Karl Freund
Music: Giuseppe Becce
CAST:
Emil Jannings: Hotel porter
Maly Delschaft: The porter's daughter
Max Hiller: The niece's fiancé
Emilie Kurtz: The fiancé's aunt
Hans Unterkircher: Hotel manager

Die freudlose Gasse / The Joyless Street

Sofar-Film, premiere on May 18, 1925
Director: G. W. Pabst
Producers: Michael Salkind and Romain Pinès
Script: Willi Haas, from the novel by Hugo Bettauer
Cinematography: Guido Seeber, Walter Robert Lach
Lighting: Curt Oertel
Editing: Marc Sorkin, Anatole Litvak, and G. W. Pabst
Art Directors: Otto Erdmann and Hans Söhnle
CAST:
Greta Garbo: Grete Rumfort
Asta Nielsen: Maria Lechner
Henry Stuart: Egon Stirner
Einar Hanson: Lieutenant Davy
Werner Krauss: Geiringer, the Butcher of Melchior Street
Valeska Gert: Frau Greifer
Jaro Fürth: Councilor Rumfort
Loni Nest: Mariandl Rumfort
Max Kohlhase: Maria's father

Sylvia Torff: Maria's mother
Alexander Murski: Dr. Leid, the lawyer
Tamara Tolstoi: Lia Leid
Countess Agnes Esterhazy: Regina Rosenow
Robert Garrison: Don Alfonso Cañez
Karl Etlinger: Bank director Rosenow
Ilka Grüning: Frau Rosenow
Hertha von Walther: Else

Faust (or Faust—Eine deutsche Volkssage) / Faust—A German Folk Legend

Ufa, October 14, 1926
Director: F. W. Murnau
Producer: Erich Pommer
Script: Hans Kyser, from a story by Johann Wolfgang Goethe
Cinematography: Carl Hoffmann
Art Direction: Walter Röhrig and Rudolf Hertl
Assistant Art Director: Arno Richter
Assistant Cameraman: Erich Grohmann
Costumes: Walter Röhrig and Rudolf Hertl
Original Music by: Werner Richard Heymann
CAST:
Gösta Ekman: Faust
Emil Jannings: Mephisto
Camilla Horn: Gretchen
Frieda Richard: Gretchen's mother
William Dieterle: Valentin
Yvette Guilbert: Marthe Schwerdtlein
Eric Barclay: Duke of Parma
Hanna Ralph: Duchess of Parma
Werner Fuetterer: Archangel Gabriel

Metropolis

Ufa, premiere on January 10, 1927
Director: Fritz Lang
Producer: Erich Pommer
Script: Fritz Lang and Thea von Harbou, based on a story by Thea von Harbou
Cinematography: Karl Freund and Günther Rittau
Art Direction: Otto Hunte, Erich Kettelhut, and Karl Vollbrecht
Music: Gottfried Huppertz

CAST:
Brigitte Helm: Maria and False Maria
Alfred Abel: Joh Fredersen
Gustav Fröhlich: Freder
Rudolf Klein-Rogge: Rotwang
Fritz Rasp: Slim
Theodor Loos: Josaphat
Erwin Biswanger: No. 11811
Heinrich George: Groth

Berlin, die Sinfonie der Großstadt / Berlin, Symphony of a Great City

Fox-Europa, premiere on September 23, 1927
Director: Walter Ruttmann
Script: Walter Ruttmann, Karl Freund, from an idea by Carl Mayer
Art Designer: Erich Kettelhut
Editor: Walter Ruttmann
Cinematography: Reimar Kuntze, Robert Baberske, László Schäffer, Karl Freund
Original Music: Edmund Miesel

Die Büchse der Pandora / Pandora's Box

Nero-Film, premiere on February 9, 1929
Director: G. W. Pabst
Producer: Seymour Nebenzahl
Script: Ladislaus Vajda, from the plays of Frank Wedekind
Cinematography: Günther Krampf
Set Design: Andrei Andreiev
Costumes: Gottlieb Hesch
Assistant Directors: Paul Falkenberg and Marc Sorkin
CAST:
Louise Brooks: Lulu
Fritz Kortner: Dr. Peter Schön
Franz Lederer: Alva Schön
Carl Goetz: Schigolch
Krafft Raschig: Rodrigo Quast
Alice Roberts: Countess Anna Geschwitz
Daisy d'Ora: Dr. Schön's fiancée
Gustav Diessl: Jack the Ripper
Siegfried Arno: Stage manager

Menschen am Sonntag / People on Sunday

Filmstudio 1929, premiere on February 4, 1930
Directors: Robert Siodmak and Edgar G. Ulmer
Cinematography: Eugen Schüfftan
Camera Assistant: Fred Zinnemann
Screenplay: Billy Wilder, Robert Siodmak, based on an idea by Curt Siodmak
Original Music: Otto Stenzeel
CAST:
Erwin Splettstößer: Taxi driver
Brigitte Borchert: Record shop sales girl
Wolfgang von Waltershausen: Wine salesman
Christl Ehlers: Film extra
Annie Schreyer: Model

Der blaue Engel / The Blue Angel

Ufa, premiere on April 1, 1930
Director: Josef von Sternberg
Producer: Erich Pommer
Screenplay: Robert Liebmann
Script: Carl Zuckmayer, Karl Vollmöller, from the book *Professor Unrat*, by Heinrich Mann
Cinematography: Günther Rittau and Hans Schneeberger
Set Design: Otto Hunte and Emil Hasler
Art Direction: Otto Hunte
Costumes: Tihamer Várady and Karl-Ludwig Holub
Music: Friedrich Hollaender, with orchestrations by Franz Wachsmann
Lyrics: Friedrich Hollaender and Robert Liebmann
CAST:
Emil Jannings: Professor Immanuel Rath
Marlene Dietrich: Lola Lola
Kurt Gerron: Magician Kiepert
Rosa Veltti: Guste Kiepert
Hans Albers: Mazeppa
Reinhold Bernt: A clown
Eduard von Winterstein: Headmaster
Rolf Müller: Angst
Rolant Varno: Lohmann
Karl Balhaus: Ertzum

Robert Klein-Lörk: Goldstaub
Ilse Fürstenberg: Rath's housekeeper
Friedrich Hollaender: Pianist
Weintraubs-Syncopators: Musicians

M

Nero-Film, premiere on May 11, 1931
Director: Fritz Lang
Producer: Seymour Nebenzahl
Script: Fritz Lang, Thea von Harbou
Cinematography: Fritz Arno Wagner
Art Director: Emil Hasler
Editor: Paul Falkenberg
CAST:
Peter Lorre: Hans Beckert
Ellen Widmann: Frau Beckmann
Inge Landgut: Elsie Beckmann
Otto Wernicke: Inspector Karl Lohmann
Theodor Loos: Inspector Groeber
Gustaf Gründgens: Schränker
Friedrich Gnaß: Franz, the burglar
Fritz Odemar: The cheater
Paul Kemp: Pickpocket
Theo Lingen: Bauernfänger
Rudolf Blümner: Beckert's defender
Georg John: Blind panhandler
Franz Stein: Minister
Ernst Stahl-Nachbaur: Police chief
Gerhard Bienert: Criminal secretary
Karl Platen: Damowitz, night watchman
Rosa Valetti: Elisabeth Winkler, Beckert's landlady

Mädchen in Uniform / *Girls in Uniform*

Deutsche Film-Gemeinschaft, premiere November 27, 1931
Director: Leontine Sagan
Artistic Supervision: Carl Froelich
Producer: Frank Wysbar
Script: Christa Winsloe and F. D. Andam, based on a play by Christa Winsloe

Cinematography: Reimar Kuntze and Franz Weihmayr
Art Design: Fritz Maurischat
Editor: Oswald Hafenrichter
Sound: Karl Brodmerker
Music: Hansom Milde-Meissner
CAST:
Dorthea Wieck: Fräulein von Bernburg
Hertha Thiele: Manuela von Meinhardis
Ellen Schwanneke: Ilse von Westhagen
Annemarie von Rochhausen: Edelgard, Countess von Mengsberg
Emilie Unda: Headmistress
Hedwig Schlichter: Fräulein von Kesten
Gertrud de Lalsky: Manuela's aunt
Marte Hein: Duchess
Lene Berdolt: Fräulein von Gärschner
Lisi Scheerbach: "Mlle" Oeuillet
Margory Bodker: Miss Evans
Erika Mann: Fräulein von Attems

Kuhle Wampe oder Wem gehört die Welt? / *Kuhle Wampe or Who Owns the World?*

Prometheus, premiere on May 30, 1932
Director: Slatan Theodor Dudow
Producers: Georg M. Höllering, Robert Scharfenberg
Script: Bertolt Brecht, Ernst Ottwald
Cinematography: Günther Krampf
Set design: Robert Scharfenberg, Carl P. Haacker
Sound: Carl Erich Kroschke, Fritz Michaelis
Music: Hanns Eisler
CAST:
Hertha Thiele: Anni Bönike
Martha Wolter: Gerda
Lilli Schönborn: Mrs. Bönike
Ernst Busch: Fritz
Adolf Fischer: Kurt
Max Sablotzki: Mr. Bönike
Alfred Schäfer: Franz Bönike
Willi Schur: Otto

CONTRIBUTORS

Nora M. Alter is Professor of German, Film, and Media Studies at the University of Florida. She is author of *Vietnam Protest Theatre: The Television War on Stage* (1996); *Projecting History: Non-Fiction German Film* (2002); *Chris Marker* (2006); and co-editor, with Lutz Koepnick, of *Sound Matters: Essays on the Acoustics of Modern German Culture* (2004). She is currently completing a new book on the international essay film.

Stefan Andriopoulos is Associate Professor of German Literature at Columbia University. He has published several monographs and anthologies on media history, literary history, and the history of science, including, most recently, *Possessed: Hypnotic Crimes, Corporate Fiction, and the Invention of Cinema* (2008). He is currently finishing a new book project, "Ghostly Visions: German Idealism, the Gothic Novel, and Optical Media."

Thomas Elsaesser is Professor in the Department of Media and Culture and Director of Research Film and Television at the University of Amsterdam. His most recent books, as author and editor, include *Weimar Cinema and After* (2000); *Metropolis* (2000); *Studying Contemporary American Film* (2002); *Filmgeschichte und Frühes Kino* (2002); *The Last Great American Picture Show* (2004); *Harun Farocki: Working on the Sightlines* (2004); *European Cinema: Face to Face with Hollywood* (2005); *Terror und Trauma* (2007); and *Filmtheorie zur Einführung* (2007).

Matt Erlin is Associate Professor of German at Washington University in St. Louis. He is the author of *Berlin's Forgotten Future: City, History, and Enlightenment in Eighteenth-Century Germany* (2004); and coeditor, with Lynne Tatlock, of *German Cul-*

ture in Nineteenth-Century America: Reception, Adaptation, Transformation (2005). His current research examines the discourse of luxury in the Enlightenment and its relevance for the emergence of new conceptions of literature and aesthetic experience in the period.

Tom Gunning is the Edwin A. and Betty L. Bergman Distinguished Service Professor and Chair of the Committee on Cinema and Media Studies at the University of Chicago. He is the author of *D. W. Griffith and the Origins of American Narrative Film: The Early Years at Biograph* (1991); and *The Films of Fritz Lang: Allegories of Vision and Modernity* (2000); and is editor of the Cinema and Modernity series at the University of Chicago Press.

Sabine Hake is the Texas Chair of German Literature and Culture in the Department of Germanic Studies at the University of Texas at Austin. She has published several books and articles on German film and Weimar culture, including *German National Cinema* (2001; 2nd edition 2008); and *Topographies of Class: Modern Architecture and Mass Society in Weimar Berlin* (2008). Her current research focuses on fascist imagery in world cinema.

Sara F. Hall is Assistant Professor of Germanic Studies at the University of Illinois, Chicago. Her work on German film culture has appeared in such journals as *German Quarterly* and *Historical Journal of Film, Radio, and Television*. She has recently completed a book-length manuscript titled "Police Presence: Cinema and the Production of Law and Order in Weimar Germany." Her current research focuses on the political and institutional uses of film technologies, the contributions of women filmmakers to the early German and Austrian film industries, and the impact of censorship on silent-film texts and audiences.

Todd Herzog is Associate Professor of German Studies at the University of Cincinnati. He is the coeditor, with Sander Gilman, of *A New Germany in a New Europe* (2001); and author of *Crime Stories: Criminalistic Fantasy and the Culture of Crisis in Weimar Germany* (2009). He has written articles on the image of America in recent German-Jewish literature, theories of biological and cultural hybridity, the role of film in criminal investigation, and the modernist case history.

Noah Isenberg is Associate Professor of University Humanities at the New School, where he teaches literature, film, and intellectual history. His books include *Between Redemption and Doom: The Strains of German-Jewish Modernism* (1999; 2nd edition 2008); an English translation and edition of Arnold Zweig's *The Face of East European Jewry* (2004); and a monograph on Edgar G. Ulmer's *Detour* (2008). He is currently finishing a full-scale critical study of Ulmer's film career.

Anton Kaes is Class of 1939 Chair and Professor of German and Film Studies at the University of California at Berkeley. Among his books, as author and editor, are *From "Hitler" to "Heimat": The Return of History as Film* (1989); *The Weimar Republic Sourcebook* (1994); *M* (2000); and *Germany in Transit: Nation and Migration, 1955–2005* (2007). His latest book, *Shell Shock Cinema: Weimar Germany and the Wounds of War*, is forthcoming from Princeton University Press in 2009.

Lutz Koepnick is Professor of German, Film, and Media Studies at Washington University in St. Louis and Curator of New Media at the university's Mildred Lane Kemper Art Museum. He is the author of *Nothungs Modernität: Wagners "Ring" und die Poesie der Politik im neunzehnten Jahrhundert* (1994); *Walter Benjamin and the Aesthetics of Power* (1999); *The Dark Mirror: German Cinema Between Hitler and Hollywood* (2002); and *Framing Attention: Windows on Modern German Culture* (2007).

Margaret McCarthy is Associate Professor of German at Davidson College, where she teaches twentieth-century German literature and film. She coedited, with Randall Halle, *Light Motives: German Popular Film in Perspective* (2003); and has published essays on Ingeborg Bachmann, Wim Wenders, Louise Brooks, and G. W. Pabst, Doris Dörrie, Luc Besson, and Anne Duden. At present she is coeditor of the *Women in German Yearbook*.

Richard W. McCormick is Professor of German at the University of Minnesota, where he teaches German film, literature, and culture. His books, as author and editor, include *Politics of the Self: Feminism and the Postmodern in West German Literature & Film* (1991); *Gender and German Cinema: Feminist Interventions* (1993); *Gender and Sexuality in Weimar Modernity: Film, Literature, and "New Objectivity"* (2001); *German Essays on Film* (2004); and *Legacies of Modernism: Art and Politics in Northern Europe, 1890–1950* (2006).

Patrice Petro is Professor of English and Film Studies at the University of Wisconsin, Milwaukee, where she is also Director of the Center for International Education. She is the author and editor of nine books, including *Joyless Streets: Women and Melodramatic Representation in Weimar Germany* (1989); *Aftershocks of the New: Feminism and Film History* (2002); and *Rethinking Global Security: Media, Popular Culture, and the "War on Terror"* (2006). She is currently president of the Society for Cinema and Media Studies.

Christian Rogowski is Professor of German at Amherst College. He is the author of two books and several articles on the Austrian author Robert Musil, as well as a multimedia CD-ROM for teaching German Cultural Studies. His current research interests include German film history, the legacy of German colonialism, and issues of racial difference in the culture of the Weimar Republic.

Marc Silberman teaches in the German Department at the University of Wisconsin, Madison, where he specializes in twentieth-century culture, literature, theater, and film studies. His publications include *German Cinema: Texts in Context* (1995); an edited and translated volume, *Brecht on Film and Radio* (2000); and the special issue of *Film History* on cold war German Cinema (2006).

INDEX

Initial articles in all languages are ignored in alphabetization. Major discussions of films are under the German title, with cross-references from English titles. Figures are indicated by f following the page number.

185–87, 186f; homosexuality in, 88; ideological trajectory of, 187–88; intertextual
references, 175; machine aesthetics in,
177–82; machine metaphor in, 177–78, 178f;
male suppression of femininity in, 220;
man-eating machine motif, 179–80, 188n5;
New York architecture and, 174; opening
of, 173–75; robot Maria in, 181–82, 182f;
Rotwanger as outsider, 180, 180f; self-consciousness about technology, 181; as sequel
to *Die Nibelungen,* 173; set design, 175–76,
176f; shortened versions of, 188n1; utopian
vision of social harmony, 176–77; visual
style vs. ideology, 175
Metz, Christian, 219
Meyrink, Gustav, 36
Minnelli, Liza, 3
Mistress of the World / Die Herrin der Welt (May,
1919), 60, 62, 66
Mittler, Leo, 317
mobile camera, 163–64
modernity: advertising and, 209–211; of Berlin
in *People on Sunday,* 251–52; connection
between empty abstraction and gambling,
105; destabilizing effect in Germany,
185–86; dialectics of, 185–88; ending of
Metropolis as contradictory response to,
185–86, 186f; identity and, 100–101; interlocking technology in *Dr. Mabuse,* 95–99;
Nazi position on, 187; positive attitudes
in *Mädchen in Uniform,* 278; shock of, 220;
space and time of, 98–99. *See also* American
modernity
Modern Times (Chaplin, 1936), 188n5
Moll, Albert, 15
Möller, Kai, 52n8
montage: cross-section films, 198; in *Kuhle
Wampe,* 317, 319–21, 320f, 322; in Lang's *M,*
295–96, 300f, 301f; in *Mädchen in Uniform,*
280
Morena, Erna, 69
motherhood: discourse in *Mädchen in Uniform,*
273, 283, 285

*Mother Krause's Journey into Happiness / Mutter
Krausens Fahrt ins Glück* (Jutzi, 1929), 314
Münsterberg, Hugo: on cinematic flashbacks,
25; on conflict between viewer's perception and knowledge in film, 24; on hypnotic
power of films, 16–17, 26; rejecting hypnotic crime simulations, 20
Murnau, F. W.: death of, 79; domination and
submission in films of, 119–20; fictional
biography of, 88–89; homosexuality of,
87–89; influences on, 84–85; international
projects for Ufa, 85; as painterly director,
155; *Tabu, a Story of the South Seas* (1931),
79–80; use of mobile camera, 163–64; war
experiences and film career, 85, 163–64. See
also *Faust—Eine deutsche Volkssage* (Murnau, 1926); *Der letzte Mann* (Murnau, 1924);
Nosferatu, eine Symphonie des Grauens
(Murnau, 1922)
musical scores: for city films, 196; for *Der
Golem,* 40; for *The Indian Tomb,* 67–68,
75; for *The Last Laugh,* 122; for *Mädchen in
Uniform,* 280
*Mutter Krausens Fahrt ins Glück / Mother
Krause's Journey into Happiness* (Jutzi,
1929), 314
My Life and Work (Ford), 184

National Socialism (Nazi Party): end of tolerance for blurred sexual boundaries, 272;
homosocial masculinism of, 283; *Kuhle
Wampe* and, 311, 327; Lang's relationship
with, 189n12; *M* as proto-Nazi vs. anti-
Nazi, 305–306; modernity and, 187; New
Objectivity and, 213n19; pressure on Lang
to change title of *M,* 294; propaganda films
of, 307
Nebenzal, Seymour, 291, 307
Negri, Pola, 60
New Objectivity (*Neue Sachlichkeit*): in *Berlin,
Symphony of a Great City,* 198; components
of, 198; expressionism and, 211; gendered
fantasies and, 220; in *The Joyless Street,* 139–

FILM + CULTURE

A SERIES OF COLUMBIA UNIVERSITY PRESS

EDITED BY JOHN BELTON